THE ALL BLACKS

THE ALL BLACKS

T. P. McLEAN

Sidgwick & Jackson
Limited
London

First published in Great Britain in 1991
by Sidgwick & Jackson Limited

ISBN 0-283-06078-6

Typeset by Florencetype Ltd, Kewstoke, Avon
Printed by Mackays of Chatham, Kent

for Sidgwick & Jackson Limited
Cavaye Place
London SW10 9PG

Picture Acknowledgements

The author and publishers would like to thank Roy Williams for undertaking the picture
research and the *New Zealand Herald* and Peter Bush for all their help.

Colour: All colour pictures are reproduced by permission of Peter Bush.

Black and white: Front page of the *London Illustrated News*, picture of George Nepia, the
1924 All Blacks v Wales match reproduced by permission of *London Illustrated News*. Team
picture of the 1924 All Blacks reproduced by permission of the Hulton Picture Library.
Line-out in the Wales v New Zealand Centenary Match, Graham Mourie in the match
against Monmouthshire, Bryan Williams scoring against Scotland, Colin Meads and Benoit
Dauga contesting the ball reproduced by permission of Peter Bush. Billy Wallace, the 1905
All Blacks, George Nicholson, the 1914 All Blacks, the Brownlie brothers, the All Black
luncheon menu, Colin Meads passing to Chris Laidlaw, F.R. Allen, Tom Morrison, Kevin
Briscoe with the ball, third test against the Springboks in 1956, Keith Arnold, Peter
Johnstone and Bleddyn Williams, Vince Bevan diving for the ball, Ron Elvidge heading for
a try, Pat Caughey and Dai Williams, the 1937 Springboks, Nelson Mitchell, Bill Meates
and Malcolm Thomas supplied by T.P. McLean. All other pictures reproduced by permission of the *New Zealand Herald*.

The author and publishers have used their best endeavours to trace the copyright owners
of all the pictures used. They would be happy to hear from anyone who recognises any of the
pictures as belonging to them.

CONTENTS

INTRODUCTION

*L*uck, you could call it: a fluke. Had not Sir David Monro, Speaker of the New Zealand House of Representatives in the 1860s, decided to complete the education of his son, Charles John, in England, it is possible that the country's winter team-sport would have been either the developing game of Australian Rules, then played in the city of Christchurch, or Association Football, favoured by most British migrants.

As it was, young Monro, having experienced in London the excitement of the game which took its name from the public school where it had been accidentally discovered in 1823, returned home to Nelson with a passion for Rugby Union Football. After staging the first game of rugby there in 1870, he took his Nelson team, 'The Lunatics', to Wellington, where they beat the newly formed local football club; and from then on, rugby took hold everywhere.

Foremost among enthusiasts of the game were the Maoris, whose warrior spirit had fostered the strength, stamina, courage and guile which were the indispensable attributes of rugby football. In due course, twenty-one Maoris and four Whites (*pakehas*, the Maoris called them), were formed into a team which in the course of more than one year's travelling played 107 matches in New Zealand, Australia and the Old Country – the British Isles.

In 1903 New Zealand and Australia met at international level. The following year a British touring team was defeated in a lone representativ . match. The victory gripped New Zealand. One year later the most famous rugby tour of all time was made by the All Blacks (as they now came to be known), captained by Ulster-born David Gallaher. At the end of a long, fatiguing tour of the British Isles, this team of all the talents had lost only one match (and that was controversial), to Wales, by one try to nil.

From 1903 until the end of 1990, the All Blacks have won more than 70 per cent of their international matches, with an aggregate of 4252 points against 2379 conceded. Only one nation, South Africa, has regularly beaten them; and New Zealanders have their own explanation for that.

The purpose of this book is to discuss players, personalities, matches, tours and great occasions. Two New Zealand historians, Neville McMillan and Rod Chester, who since 1978 have collaborated on monumental books about Kiwi rugby – *Men in Black*, *Centenary* and *The Visitors* – have provided invaluable data. Their Auckland publishers, Moa Publications, has a whole string of other works devoted to the game. In 1987, Terry Godwin published *The Complete Who's Who of International Rugby* (Blandford Press), and this, too, has been greatly helpful. Lastly, there is *Rothman*'s *Rugby Union Year Book*, which annually takes a cosmic view of the game.

The astonishing and edifying features of New Zealand's achievements in international rugby have been the consistency of performance, the wealth of talented players and the special skills of a few who in popular esteem qualify for the pantheon reserved for heroes of the sport. As a loyal member of the British Empire and its successor, the Commonwealth, New Zealand has been gratified that many of its leading men and women, young and old, have received honours and awards. Yet there can be no prouder title than the recognition: 'He is an All Black'. Colin Meads, one of the greatest, was accustomed, every time he changed into his All Black strip before a match, to place his hand on the Silver Fern emblem on the left breast. The touch assured him that he was, indeed, one of the elect, a representative of a small, isolated, distant country which, despite many limitations, not least of population, established itself, from the very first, as the greatest rugby nation on earth.

T.P. McLean

CHAPTER ONE

ALL HAIL 'THE LUNATICS' 1870-1905

*T*oward the end of the summer of 1869–70, Charles John Monro, 19 years old, returned to the home of his parents in the cathedral city of Nelson, at the northern tip of the South Island of New Zealand. His father, Sir Charles Monro, owner of one of the largest runs, or farms, of that area and also Speaker of the House of Representatives in the New Zealand Parliament, had sent him to finish his schooling at Christ College, in the London suburb of Finchley. Nothing is known of his academic attainments there or of his future career ambitions. But it was soon apparent that he had cultivated an enthusiasm, even passion, for the game of Rugby Union football which had been sweeping through England's Public Schools since, at Rugby School in 1823, a praepostor, or prefect, named William Webb Ellis, in defiance of the rules of the time, had 'first picked up the ball and run with it, thus originating the distinctive feature of the rugby game'.

Monro talked to the young bloods of Nelson, including senior pupils at the local college, about the joys and glories of this manly sport. He was a good missionary. Within a few weeks, he had organized teams from the Town and the College. On 14 May 1870, the teams met. Town won, by 2 goals to nil. The players were wholly taken with the sport. Everything was virile in this new country which had become a Colony of the British Empire no more than 30 years previously. Rugby, even at first acquaintance, seemed an ideal way to express that virility.

Monro decided to spread the gospel, to Wellington, the seat of Government. He visited the city and talked to the young men, who likewise reacted with keen interest. A group called the Wellington Football Club was formed. Monro was a hardy chap. Because the only suitable playing field within walking distance of the city, the Basin Reserve, was partly under water, he prospected as far as Petone, a settlement on the shores of Wellington's harbour and at the head of the Hutt Valley which stretched many miles westward to the Tararua Ranges. Monro's was a goodly hike –

1

at least seven miles by today's smooth highways, longer and rougher at that time. A stony patch of ground on which the Petone railway station was later built seemed suitable for a match. Officers of the Wellington Club accepted Monro's proposal to bring a Nelson team to the city for a challenge.

Politicians, especially those in high places, have their values. When young Monro told Julius Vogel, later knighted for services to the Crown, that the Government steamer *Luna* was soon to call at Nelson and that a number of local lads would appreciate passage on it 'for a particular purpose', Vogel waved a Ministerial hand. The match was arranged for 12 September 1870. Boarding the *Luna* in glee, the Nelsonians immediately christened themselves 'The Lunatics'. Stony the pitch might be – but Nelson men were strong. They won the match by 3 goals to nil.

It is no exaggeration to say that the match, the Wellington club and the 'Lunatics' combined to make rugby the foremost sport, indeed the national game, of this distant, isolated country – an isolation that prompted Rudyard Kipling subsequently to describe Auckland, the largest city, as 'last, lone-liest, loveliest, exquisite, apart'.

Monro, a man of substance throughout his life, later moved north, buying 50 acres close to the burgeoning settlement of Palmerston North, in the heart of North Island. After he died, in his eighties, steps were taken to expand the famous agricultural college there into a university of many faculties. Massey University grew up on the Monro land; and in a rare gesture of noble sentiment, the New Zealand Rugby Union eventually caused to be built, on a hillside overlooking the campus, a plain, planked seat. The inscription notes that the seat is a memorial to Charles John Monro, founder of rugby in New Zealand. The view from the spot extends over plains, mountains, cities and townships. And everywhere there are fields, dotted with tiny figures: men and boys, pitting their strength and skill against each other in the game which the 'Lunatics' inspired. From then on, rugby was truly on the way.

On the way! The phrase cannot convey the enthusiasm and passion which swept through the Colony, bringing together, in town, hamlet and isolated settlement (and there were many of these at the time), young men eager to play. By 1870, wars, skirmishes and bloody raids between the White settlers, stiffened by regiments of the British Army, and the indigenous Maori were only just petering out. The Maoris felt betrayed when one White government after another declined to ratify the Treaty of Waitangi which had been signed by many of their chiefs on 6 February 1840. Land rights, land forfeitures to the Crown, stirred the passions of a brave and hardy people. They fought with skill and valour; and, inevitably, they were beaten down by superior numbers.

Sufficient cause, one could surmise, for the Maori to feel that the last place they might ever want to confront *pakehas* ('white' men) would be on the rugby field. Yet, astonishingly, the game seemed to have been invented expressly for them. For centuries before the introduction of the musket to New Zealand, Maoris had pursued tribal conflicts with surprising cunning and courage. Now, discovering that these qualities were ideally suited to this fast, attacking game, the Maoris promptly fell for the sport. One of their greatest men, Frederick Bennett, had in youth been consecrated as a priest in the Anglican Church, where his service in one parish after another endowed him with unrivalled understanding of his people. He earned lasting respect, too, from *pakehas*, and was the first to be offered the ultimate tribute – the see of Waiapu, the Maoris' own bishopric. He was deeply learned and profoundly wise; and his observation that rugby had 'sublimated the warlike passions of the Maori people' was shrewd, sensible and, best of all, true.

Eighteen years after Charles Monro founded the game, in 1888, a British team, captained by that great Corinthian A.E. Stoddart, who also represented England at cricket, paid two visits to the Colony. From late April until the end of May, the team played nine matches. It then went off to Australia for three months, returning to New Zealand for ten more games played between 8 September and 3 October.

The tour was epochal on two counts. As far as the actual game was concerned, the British revealed to Colonial players the possibilities and opportunities of attacking through the backs – hitherto New Zealanders had believed this to be prohibited by the laws of the game because it meant ball-carriers were being screened by team-mates (the forwards), who must be operating from offside positions.

In a wider context, the first phase of the tour brought together two men of extraordinarily dissimilar backgrounds. Joe Warbrick, of a famous Maori family, had played the game in several parts of the country. In 1884, he was a threequarter in the first New Zealand team to tour abroad. It was unbeaten in eight matches in New South Wales. Thus he was both a gifted player and a well-trained observer of the finer talents and leading teams in the land. The other man, a wealthy English expatriate, Thomas Eyton, had lived much of lis life within the sound of the thud of boot on ball and body at the Rectory Field, home of Blackheath, the first rugby club ever to be formed.

The encounter between representatives of two such widely disparate cultures must have been fascinating, and one can only conjecture as to how it was conducted. It should be remembered that the Maori had no written language. Its history was handed down, generation after generation, by speakers skilled in oratory. Not seen so often nowadays, except on especially important occasions, is the Maori elder in full cry. He may carry a mat made of the feathers of the kiwi or of the sacred bird, the huia, draped across a shoulder, and if he is one of the old brigade, he will be clutching a walking-stick. He will begin speaking quietly, but soon enough he will be invoking the gods, the greater moments of Maori life, in phrases of such extraordinary velocity that the voice rises to a sustained scream.

It is just possible that Warbrick used the eloquent methods of his ancestors in conveying to Eyton his opinion, based on a sight of the touring British players, that Maoris could be formed into a team of comparable quality. He may have talked of the 'new blossoming orchards' of Maori playing skill and of a 'spring as sweet as the garden of God' – reflecting the fact that within only a few years, the gifted Maori had already mastered the game.

No matter how they conversed, both men were clearly agreed that a team representing the best of New Zealand could more than hold its own against opposition from abroad. Warbrick undertook to find the men – it was jointly decided to include four *pakehas* in the playing group of twenty-six – and Eyton promised to rustle up engagements, especially in Britain, which would keep the team on the move and sufficiently occupied to pay their way.

The tour which followed was unprecedented and has hardly been rivalled since, in any sport. Little more than a month after Stoddart's side had concluded their first visit to the country, the 'New Zealand Native Team' was in being. It played nine matches at home between 23 June and 31 July 1888. Then, with Eyton acting as forerunner, drumming up trade, the group headed for Australia, basing itself in Melbourne.

Two months later the team arrived in London. Nor could the supposedly conservative Rugby Football Union of England be accused of dragging the chain. By the time the Natives took the field for their first match at Richmond on 3 October 1888, no fewer than 50 matches had already been arranged; and the match-list was eventually extended to the enormous total of 74, the last being played on 27 March 1889. The team's skill was much admired, even if some of the Press, taken aback by the preliminary *haka*, or war dance, criticized it for playing with excessive exuberance.

Sights were then set for New Zealand where, between 23 June (anniversary of the team's first match) and 24 August, 17 more matches were played. Although one of the greater Maori players, Tom Ellison, who became the first member of his race to be admitted to the New Zealand Bar, wrote that the tour comprised 108 matches, it is now generally accepted that 107 was the correct total.

As, over the years, members of the team died, each was buried, in accordance with Maori tradition, with his most precious possessions. Consequently, few relics remain of the team's blazers, caps and playing-gear. Of existing tour fragments, none is more touching than the letter from Ihimaira ('The Smiler') to his grandfather, Te Muera Rangitauhama:

'Great is my affection towards you all. . . . My inmost heart is full of love and I cannot help keeping you constantly in remembrance. O, sirs! Salutations to you all. May God be gracious and keep you all in health. . . . And now, about our travels. After Melbourne, we sailed across the great water to England, which we reached in a month and two weeks. I suffered most of all from sea-sickness, as did Nehua. We could eat no food for over a week but recovered when crossing the Line, which divides that world from this. . . . We entered the Red Sea and saw the place where Moses crossed over with the children of Israel when they were pursued by Pharaoh and his hosts, who were overwhelmed and drowned in the returning waters. . . . Four days after arrival in England, we met a team picked from ten clubs and beat them by 4 points to 1, in the presence of a vast multitude of people. . . . I like the travelling about greatly. I have been presented with a valuable ring by a lady of great rank. It cost at least £6 and contains diamonds set in gold. . . . May God preserve you, and the tribe. From your loving grandchild.'

The 1888 tour had been a triumph on several counts. A game of artifice and speed, bravery and cool skill, had rapidly become the working man's sport in a country where work was considered a sacred right. Moreover, rugby had been totally embraced by the Maori people. And perhaps the most significant triumph was that a harmoniously integrated team, consisting of individuals totally indifferent to the colour of one another's skin, had treated crowds in the Old Country to a sporting spectacle of high drama and entertainment.

Except in the imagination, one cannot see much of New Zealand from the Monro Memorial Seat. Beyond Palmerston North lie the Manawatu Plains, which march to the densely forested ranges of the Wanganui River region and thence onward to the great massif of Ruahepu (9000 ft) which, hundreds of years ago, was shorn of a third of its bulk in an explosion that, according to vulcanologists, would have made the gigantic eruption of Krakatoa in 1883 sound like a popgun. There is rugby here in plenty; at Massey University, in the city proper, at Marton, Feilding and Hunterville, Mangaweka, Taihape, Ohakune and Waiouru, and in countless places on the road to Ruahepu. But then, as you travel the 109,000 square miles of New Zealand's territory, there are few areas without rugby, except, naturally, in the great spine of the Southern Alps on South Island, and the ranges of the North Island which extend all the way to East Cape and which are crowned by Hikurangi, the lovely mountain whose summit is first place in the world to receive the rays of the morning sun.

The Monro Seat, nevertheless, is a good spot in which to ruminate on the great characters who helped to build that solid fortress which was to be New Zealand rugby. Bob Whiteside, big, fast, indomitable, illuminated Auckland rugby in the 1880s. Some seventy years later, one of his teammates, Albert Braund, a scrumhalf known as 'The Little Jewel', during an Old-Timers' Day at Auckland's famous field of Eden Park, was invited to nominate the greatest player he had ever seen. 'There was only one,' the little old man softly said. 'Bob Whiteside.'

Paddy Keogh, a transplanted Englishman, was sometimes accused of playing to the gallery. No such criticism attached to Tom Ellison, inventor of the New Zealand scrummage formation in which two men packed in the first row, three in the second and two in the back, while the eighth man, named wing-forward or rover, stood out to put the ball into the scrummage, reinforcing his side's attack close to the mass of players or harrying opponents close in. Because neither side could be certain of winning the ball at the scrummage, each backline was forced to adopt attacking formation; and for almost forty years, New Zealand rugby was permeated with this positive attitude and invigorated by the boldness which such play encouraged. Came the night, in 1930, at a formal dinner, when James Baxter, of the Rugby Football Union, alleged that the New Zealand wing-forward was a cheat because he operated from offside positions. While a nation fumed and grieved, the International Board, within a year, proscribed the New Zealand scrummage and ruled that the front line must contain three men.

That calamity, however, lay many years ahead. Meantime, the New Zealanders celebrated their famous men – almost invariably rugby players. Such a one was Will McKenzie, the oldest of five brothers who all attained extraordinary distinction in the game; big, burly, bald-headed Ted, the only man ever to be appointed sole selector of New Zealand international teams; Jack, a fine player who deliberately curtailed his career; Bert, likewise big and bald, an international referee who after one celebrated misruling put off reporters by remarking, 'I do not recall the incident'; and Norman, of similar physique and appearance, whose Hawkes Bay provincial team of the 1920s, with its profusion of great players, produced some of the finest attacking rugby the game has ever witnessed.

Will McKenzie, who with good reason was known as 'Offside Mac', spent hours of convalescence from bouts of quinsy diagramming the possibilities of attacking ploys. In 1897, he played for Wellington against Otago at Dunedin in a game of such vigour that the crowd bayed for his team's blood and the fixture entered history as 'The Butchers' Match'. McKenzie, a swell who boasted a top hat and frock coat, paraded the main streets of Dunedin that night, exciting the crowds to frenzied abuse and dismissing their jeers with the careless wave of a French Revolutionary signalling the descent of the guillotine. In that year, McKenzie, playing for New Zealand at the Sydney Cricket Ground, was ordered from the field for an infringement and limped off painfully, feigning injury. The crowd cheered him to the echo for his courage in trying to continue; and nobody seemed to question why he was not replaced.

Along came George Smith, so small in youth as a jockey that he rode the winner of the New Zealand Cup, and so fast and energetic, a year or two later, that he was virtually unbeatable in the national championships at the 120- and 140-yards hurdles – 3 ft 6 in high. In his one visit to England, Smith set an Amateur Athletic Association record over the sticks which stood for many years. He played in the New Zealand rugby team in Australia in 1897, dropped out of the game and returned later to score one of the greatest of international tries.

By now Otago, which had stolidly resisted the formation of the New Zealand Rugby Union until, in 1892, it was satisfied that the game would not be entirely governed by the moguls of Wellington, was a hothouse of talented players and original thinkers. It was because of his Otago background that Ellison offered the 2–3–2 scrummage. The five-eighths formation, in which the two backs next to the scrumhalf were called first and second, on the understanding that either might attack on whatever side of the scrum he chose, was born in Dunedin. James Duncan, a five-eighths with a bald head (which he concealed with a cap), a drooping moustache and a massive opinion of his own talents, was all but anointed for his powers as a tactical Napoleon. From farther south came a boot-clicker, Billy Stead, whose Maori blood was indiscernible in his faintly tanned, freckled face. He was a five-eighths *sans peur et sans reproche*, esteemed by his colleagues as a back in a million.

A Taranaki threequarter of substantial means, Alfred Bayly was so admired as a player and leader that he twice captained New Zealand teams and within two years of his retirement in 1899 was made a selector – an utter impossibility, these days. He was only 41 when elected President of the New Zealand Rugby Union in 1907 – equally unthinkable today – and, sadly, died in office that year. Bayly had toured with an Otago threequarter, 'Barney' Armit. When, in a match of 1899, Taranaki versus Otago, Armit came at him, hotfoot for a try and making a gigantic leap to ensure it, Bayly, reacting instinctively, reached up and clipped on his heels. Armit crashed head-first to the ground. His neck was broken and he died a few days later. Bayly chose to retire, ensuring that Armit's mother for the rest of her life would receive £1 a week either from himself or, later, his estate.

By now a new star – arguably the greatest – was emerging from the younger generation. Billy Wallace's finest feats were to come after the completion of Fortress New Zealand. Yet at the age of 19 he was involved in 'The Butchers' Match' and thereafter, until at the close of his career Wellington's citizens presented him with a purse containing 400 sovereigns – enough, in those days, to set up his own foundry – he was the nonpareil of the game. He suffered all sorts of injury. After being kicked in one game, his left hand remained misshapen for the rest of his life. Yet, match in, match out, whether playing in the midfield, on the wing or at fullback, he utilized his speed, swerve and sidestep to dynamic effect.

Wallace is best remembered, and rightly, as the first of New Zealand's great fullbacks; yet it was as an Admirable Crichton of the backline, rather than as a fullback, that he best served his province and his country. And the nation paid him the ultimate tribute when they nicknamed him 'Carbine', after New Zealand's greatest racehorse, winner of the Melbourne Cup in 1890.

By the turn of the century, New Zealand rugby, a mere thirty years old, had become a remarkable force. More was to follow. The 1903 team, captained by Jimmy Duncan, which toured New South Wales and Queensland and played the first true international in the history of the New Zealand game, was for years considered to be the finest ever fielded. In the last but one of the ten matches played – and won – Australia was defeated by 22 points to 3. Play began evenly, with a penalty goal to each side. Wallace, with the first of his two goals from a fair catch – such kicks were worth 4 points in those days – put New Zealand into a 7–3 lead at the half-time break. Then the New Zealanders dazzled the crowd of 30,000 with tries by Opai Asher and Dick McGregor, of the threequarters, and one by George Tyler, of the front row. Wallace placed a penalty goal, a goal to a try and those two goals from a mark to set off what became a record-scoring career with 12 points.

By the end of the tour of France in 1990, New Zealand had played 249 internationals and a vast number of lesser fixtures. As is evident from Chapter Twelve, recording the achievements, the success rate was consistently high. In fact, only South Africa has bettered this record over the years; and there is hardly a New Zealander who, when discussing this imbalance, does not somehow allude to two unfortunate reasons for this state of affairs – the difficulties of breathing up on the high veldt and the low quality of refereeing in South Africa.

These international matches have understandably engendered high drama, strong passion and bitter dispute. Yet, notwithstanding key matches during later, and greater, tours, none of these surpassed in importance the second international played at Athletic Park in Wellington, on 13 August 1904, against Great Britain, captained by David Revell Bedell-Sivright, who was capped twenty-two times for Scotland.

The British had so far been unbeaten in thirteen matches in Australia. The team contained many excellent players. Among the backs, Rhys Gabe, Willie Llewellyn, Teddy Morgan and Percy Bush belonged to the Welsh side which, eighty-seven years on, is still immortalized. A.B. O'Brien and P.F. McEvedy, of the threequarters, were New Zealanders completing post-graduate medical degrees at London's Guy's Hospital. Tommy Vile, a champion little halfback who became an international referee, affixed a New Zealand name to the gate of his Newport house; and Arthur Harding, a great Welsh forward, was so impressed by the New Zealand quality of life that he later migrated and spent the rest of his life Down Under.

The British may have suffered from over-confidence and the fact that the strangely surly captain, aptly nicknamed 'Darkie', was not available for the international; he was held to be a fine player and his presence might have changed the character of the game – and the scoreline. Yet, from the start of the visit to New Zealand, Bedell-Sivright was patronizing in attitude. By word and manner, he conveyed disparagement of the Colonials. They were, after all, newcomers to the game and had no rugby schools to compare with his own, Fettes, in Edinburgh, or universities of the standing of Cambridge, where he had studied for the first part of his medical degree before returning to Edinburgh.

New Zealand fielded a fine team: a backline of Dick McGregor (fullback), Duncan McGregor, Eric Harper and Billy Wallace in the threequarters, Morrie Wood and Billy Stead (captain) at five-eighths, and Peter Harvey at scrumhalf, has seldom been surpassed in quality. The forwards, too, were strong, eager and industrious, gifted in ball-handling and running. David Gallaher, at wing-forward, had served in the South African War. Billy Glenn, of the back-row, was later more famous as a Member of Parliament, and could really run; his partner, Charles Seeling, remains among the greatest forwards ever to play for New Zealand. Tom Cross, who, with reason, was known as 'Angry', Bernie Fanning, an exceptionally tall lock-forward, and George Nicholson, formed the second row. The hookers were 'Paddy' McMinn, never again to win a cap, and George Tyler, a strong, tough, humorous chap who once shook hands with King George V and thereafter wore a glove which he refused to remove for some considerable time.

Public interest in the 'test' match was enormous, with special trains being run to Wellington. Twenty-five thousand spectators packed the ground. Conditions were fine on a firm pitch. New Zealand began fierily. For half an hour they attacked and were foiled, sometimes narrowly. Then, from a penalty awarded by Canterbury referee F.T. Evans, wing threequarter Wallace placed a goal. On the call of half-time, Harding goaled for Britain to level the score. The second half began with a spurt of tactical punting by the British. The New Zealand forwards pressed for possession, offering ample ball to backs who, had they not been opposed by a line of the finest quality, might have run away with the game. It took a move cunningly engineered by Stead to break up the defence at last with a run from first five-eighths. Rapid passing gave the ball to McGregor on the wing, who ran around fullback O'Brien for a try. As play surged up and down field, New Zealand scrumhalf Harvey set off a back movement and, once again, McGregor, showing his pace and determination, headed for the corner-flag and the decisive try. At no-side, therefore, the score read: New Zealand 9, Great Britain 3. Hundreds rushed on to the field to hoist McGregor shoulder-high and carry him in triumph to the locker-room.

It was, without doubt, the most significant result in New Zealand rugby history. The kids from the waybacks had beaten their masters, fairly and squarely. Nevertheless, Bedell-Sivright tried to diminish it, declaring, in typically sour terms, that if New Zealand were to visit the Old Country, its players might succeed against underdog teams but would stand no chance of defeating the four national sides.

New Zealand rugby had grown up in isolation – virtually in a vacuum. Difficulties of travel, of communication, of even mustering a club team at the right place at the appointed time, had been formidable, at times heart-breaking. The contribution of the dairy-farmers, working long hours and milking by hand under lamplight, was crucial. Often enough these hardy men were the backbone of the team, not least in the forward play. But the appeal of the game spread through the community at large. J.P. Firth, headmaster of Wellington College, preceded, by a few years, two Victoria University men, H.H. Oestler and A.H. Johnstone, both judges of the New Zealand Supreme Court. Billy Hardham, a member of the Petone club in Wellington, won the Victoria Cross in the South African War. Square-jawed George Forbes farmed at Hurunui in North Canterbury, playing quality rugby the while, and went on to become Prime Minister.

The first thirty-three years was the apprenticeship period. Gradually the fortress of New Zealand rugby was put together, and the beating of the team representing the four countries which had played the game longest and, therefore, best, completed the process triumphantly. With this turning point, the time had arrived for the New Zealand game and players to take a cast at the outside world. The sport of rugby had instilled New Zealanders with pride in their country. Such fervour was to be of vital consequence as the nation marched into the twentieth century.

CHAPTER TWO

'WE ARE ALL BLACK'
1905

*T*om Ellison, who sadly died in 1904, at the early age of 36, was the first true genius of New Zealand rugby. As a player, he captained his country; as a planner, he originated the 2–3–2 scrummage formation which was paramount to two tours from which one team emerged as 'The Incomparables', the other as 'The Invincibles'; and his book, *The Art of Rugby Football*, published in the year of his death, made a profound impact on the game.

Most importantly, not least in the light of modern developments which have tended seriously to diminish the standing of rugby as an amateur sport, it was Ellison who, writing in 1898, proposed that players chosen for long tours should be financially reimbursed by a weekly sum equal to, but not more than, their working salary or wage. Players not in bona fide employment at the time of selection should be paid up to £2 per week; and no allowance should exceed £4 a week.

Five years previously, the Rugby Football Union of England had been shattered by a breakaway movement which demanded that players be paid for time lost from work. This developed into the Northern Union, which had a catastrophic impact on the game. Had Ellison's ideas ever been communicated to the rugby unions of the British Isles, they would have been scorned as Colonial claptrap. Yet, about ninety years later, the Governor of the Reserve Bank of New Zealand, Sir Spencer Russell, pointed out that the £2 of 1898 would now be worth precisely $NZ178.52. By curious chance, the equivalent of £4 – roughly $NZ357 – was about the same as that currently being paid, by decision of the International Rugby Football Board, to players both on tour and engaged in home internationals against visiting teams. It is likely, in fact, that if Ellison's proposals had been generally accepted within a year or two of their publication, they would have prevented those infractions of the International Board's

Regulations Relating to Amateurism, which were subsequently to plague the game.

Although Ellison's financial ideas passed into limbo, another of his suggestions met with a happier outcome. In 1893, at the first annual meeting of the New Zealand Rugby Football Union, Ellison proposed that the uniform for the New Zealand Representative Team should be 'Black Jersey with Silver Fernleaf, Black Cap with Silver Monogram, White Knickerbockers, Black Stockings'. Until the 1920s, when two narrow white rings were substituted, a broad white band ran around the turnover of the stockings.

Dr Samuel Johnson's definition of genius as 'a mind of large general powers accidentally determined in some particular direction' precisely applied to Ellison. His choice of black as the staple colour of the uniform was inspired. In heraldry, black is sable; and sable signifies 'prudence, wisdom, constancy'.

New Zealand rugby had been represented in Australia by teams which had toured in 1884, 1893 (Ellison was captain), 1897, 1903 (including the first official international) and, very briefly, for three matches, 1905. Meanwhile, in 1882, 1886, 1894 and 1901, New Zealand had hosted teams from New South Wales. In 1896, the Queensland team were visitors. Most significantly, in 1888 and 1904, as already mentioned, teams from the British Isles, led respectively by A.E. Stoddart and 'Darkie' Bedell-Sivright, had toured New Zealand. Stoddart's team won 13 of its 19 matches. The 1904 team did less well, winning only two of five official games, losing an unofficial match at Rotorua against the first Maori side to play a touring team, and finally being defeated in the memorable Wellington international.

In 41 matches played by the various New Zealand teams in Australia between 1884 and 1905, two were lost. In 68 matches played in New Zealand from 1882 to 1904, the tourists won 26 and lost 37. These were powerful statements of the strength of New Zealand rugby, culminating in the famous victory on 13 August 1904 at Athletic Park.

Despite 'Darkie' Bedell-Sivright's predictions, the auguries were good, therefore, for the first official New Zealand tour of Great Britain. On 30 July 1905, in weather so foul that only a few well-wishers stood dockside to utter a lingering cheer, the liner *Rimutaka*, bound for Plymouth, backed out into Wellington harbour, turned and headed for the huge, empty Pacific. Forty-two days later the 29 players of the team descended to a waiting tender, where they were greeted by Rowland Hill, honorary secretary of the Rugby Football Union. Also aboard the tender was C. Wray Palliser, an expatriate who represented the New Zealand Rugby Union in England. He had argued unsuccessfully for a New Zealand tour in the 1890s, but not until 1903 was the proposal accepted by both countries. Palliser expressed his sentiments in the *Daily Mail*. 'I shall never forget that bleak and gloomy morning when I turned out at 3:20 with an expectant heart to board the tender and welcome to Old England the rugger players from the "Land of the Long White Cloud", who had come on so audacious an errand. "What!

New Zealand coming to play against the clubs and counties of England? Well, was there ever such cheek?" The remark was addressed to me by a football acquaintance and what was I to expect, after that? It had never occurred to me to look upon the venture in that light. I dread to consider what this candid friend's remark would have been, had I further enlightened him that not only were these daring Colonials to play clubs and counties, they were also prepared to tackle such bodies as united England, Ireland, Scotland and Wales!'

Two newspapermen were also on the tender. No one now remembers who they were. But one of the reporters seems to have bearded a player, questioning him as to the colour of the team's jersey; its knickers; its stockings. To each question, the player answered with one word – 'Black.'

The conversation ended when the player, in a burst of eloquence, remarked, 'We are all black.'

Old-timers of the craft can call up an image of that reporter. He is trying to look nonchalant; but there is a cunning gleam to his expression. By good luck rather than expert management, he has landed a scoop. Back in Plymouth, he heads for his office and his desk. His movements are furtive, secretive; until the triumphant moment when he lays before his Sports Editor the item which leads off by proclaiming that 'the All Blacks have arrived'!

Hamish Stuart, a former Scottish international and now one of the leading British critics of the game, watched the All Blacks open their tour by defeating Devon at Exeter on Saturday 16 September. His appraisal appeared in the *Athletic News*, then regarded as the finest of sporting papers, with a standing and reputation comparable to that of the modern French daily *L'Équipe*.

'. . . Judged by Saturday,' wrote Stuart, 'the New Zealanders do not play a distinctive game. The five-eighths are simply extra centres. Indeed, the combination was somewhat ragged, and the back play as a whole utterly failed to suggest that the system has the slightest claim to be considered superior to the Welsh system.'

Stuart's was not the only disparaging note. The *Daily Telegraph* observed: 'Much of the New Zealand passing was slow and faulty, the ball often being parted with in a somewhat reckless manner; and though at times their general combination was admirable, it unquestionably fell short of the Welsh standard.'

It is old hat that the All Blacks won by 55 points to 4 (twelve tries, eight converted by Wallace, and a penalty goal against a drop goal), and that the chief sub-editor of an unnamed London daily, refusing to believe it, awarded New Zealand 5 points and Devon 4. This massive victory became something of a burden – Sinbad's Old Man of the Sea – for succeeding All Black touring teams. In 1924, for example, C.G. Porter's side slid in and out of pother before they managed to win their first match by 11 points to nil. When, almost 40 years later, the Fourth All Blacks whipped up 21 points in the first half of their opening match, visions of 1905 floated before discerning eyes. In 40 further minutes of valiant effort, the team scored just 3 points. Hamish Stuart might have said harsh things about such a display.

Durham, the county champions and sixth on the itinerary, proved harder going. This was Geordie country where life was traditionally rough and tough. The team played with commensurate pride, and the All Blacks, 16–3 at the finish, were glad to hear the final whistle. Warm appreciations of the all-round abilities of the All Blacks were tempered by constant criticisms of David Gallaher's role at wing-forward. It was asserted, by old internationals and cub reporters alike, that the rover's role was fundamentally obstructionist. Gallaher's invariable habit of wearing heavy shin-guards outside his stockings, held in place by buckles at the heel and just below the knee, added fuel to the flames. The pads not only looked menacing but seemed out of character in an amateur sport.

By the 14th match, against Surrey and played at Richmond on 1 November, for much of the time in drenching rain, the animus against Gallaher (who was not, in fact, playing) appeared to have affected the referee, William Williams, who gave the impression of finding nothing good in the New Zealanders' game. J.A. Buttery, a strong and faithful supporter of the All Blacks, memorably headlined the match in the *Daily Mail* as 'A Whistling Fantasia'. The paper telegraphed three prominent referees who had been in the crowd to invite their comments on Williams's reported statement that he had pulled up the All Blacks for 'not playing the game'. C.W.T. Finch, from Devon, replied: 'Nothing flagrant; no breaches of the rules; and absolutely no "dirty trickery".' Adam Turnbull responded from Durham, 'I saw nothing to justify reprimand or appellation "dirty trickery". I never penalized once for such.' A.J. Davies of Glamorgan simply answered: 'No.' 'Old Marlburian', writing to the *Daily Mail* from Claygate, noted: 'It may interest you to know that in the match the whistle blew 33 times from the restart of the game after the first goal to half-time (15 minutes). This averages, over the 80 minutes, say, 180 times! Could any game be popular under such conditions'.

On the night following the match, Arthur Davenport, a well known comedian, sang a song with a lusty chorus which ran:

> 'But we won't give in yet,
> For we must not forget
> That we still have some whistles to spare;
> Surrey ought to have won,
> And, in fact, would have done.
> But the referee ran short of air.'

The next match of the tour, the 15th, was played on 4 November against the oldest of all rugby clubs, Blackheath. It was won by 32 points to nil. Blackheath's threequarters included S.F. Cooper, who was to be secretary of the Rugby Football Union from 1924 to 1927, and an Irishman serving in the British Army, Basil Maclear, big, aggressive, imaginative and widely talented; though criticized for being slow on the break, the New Zealanders considered him to be the finest opposition back of the tour.

Many years later, Billy Wallace contended that the All Blacks reached their peak at Blackheath's Rectory Field and that the rest of the tour was, however imperceptibly, downhill going.

Cambridge, too, although beaten 14–0 with a goal and three tries, was a shock to the New Zealand system, partly explained by the fact that the match was played only two days after the 47–0 victory against Oxford on 7 November, and various players had to be rested. Hence the choice of Billy Wallace at five-eighths. He tackled fiercely and punted judiciously, but as to breaking the defensive line in the style of the specialists, Stead, Mynott and Hunter, he seemed not to have the ghost of an idea. George Smith, too, disappointed. Once, in front of goal, he needed only to pass to 'General' Booth, who could have walked to a try. Smith froze – with such conspicuous skill that no fewer than three Cambridge men were able, in the one movement, to dash him down. The New Zealand performance, too, was seriously affected when both wings, Thomson and McGregor, were reduced in speed and swerve by injuries, Thomson with a strained thigh sinew, McGregor hobbled after a severe crack on the ankle.

Cambridge, nevertheless, expressed the best of University rugby. A boy not yet 18, Kenneth Macleod, who two days before the match had won the 100 yards at the freshmen's sports in the nippy time of 10.6 seconds, would, on the strength of his play, follow his elder brother Lewis, the Cambridge captain who had already won four caps, into the Scottish team to take on the All Blacks. The Scottish back, John Scoular, also went straight from the match into the Scotland side. One of the Cambridge forwards, Hugh Monteith, later won eight caps for Scotland. And yet to win the first of his three caps for England was a forward with the resounding name of Frederick van der Byl Hopley, born in Salisbury, Rhodesia. Previously heavyweight boxing champion of England's public schools, he was twice to be a reserve for South Africa.

The New Zealand performance over the entire tour was all the more praiseworthy after the storms, both literal and figurative, of the recent sea-voyage. Eight days out of Wellington, David Gallaher told a team-meeting that he was resigning the captaincy, immediately, having been given to understand that the players wanted a captain of their own choice. Billy Stead stood up. 'Where David goes, I go,' he said, in effect. Other members of the selection committee, George Dixon, coach Jimmy Duncan and the players' representative, Billy Wallace, promptly announced that they too would resign.

What, or who, caused the rumpus? Gallaher was a natural choice, on every count, perhaps, save one; he was not, apparently, ideally gifted as a player. The famous Hawkes Bay coach and selector of the 1920s, Norman McKenzie, who in 1905 was heading for provincial representative status, mildly observed that Gallaher was 'perhaps' not the greatest of wing forwards, but at once qualified the indictment, adding that he was 'acutely skilled' as a judge of men and tactical moves. These qualities, McKenzie contended, were vitally important factors for the success of the tour. Several of the chosen forwards were not of the first class, let alone topnotch international standards. Gallaher's skills, not least in team selection, clearly outweighed the weaknesses.

David Gallaher's qualities of leadership had already been proved in another field. In 1901, he enlisted for service in the South African War and was posted to the Sixth Contingent of the New Zealand Mounted Rifles. An excellent horseman, he was made a scout of the advance guard, and shortly after New Year 1902 was involved in an engagement against a large force of Boers at Spitskoop. During their service the contingent lost 20 men dead from combat or disease, and 17 wounded. Gallaher then stayed on to join the Tenth Contingent and was promoted to the rank of squadron sergeant-major. It hardly needs saying that war in the open veldt was a supreme test of character. The Boers were superlative horsemen and marksmen. They were fighting for their land. Any man who went through battle against them had to be made of stern stuff. And Gallaher's bravery was unchallenged, right up to his death on 4 October 1917 at Passchendaele.

So why the sneaky whispering among the All Blacks against their appointed captain? The fact that his fellow-selectors immediately and unqualifiedly supported Gallaher was the finest of testimonials. George Dixon declared that the appointments of Gallaher and Stead must stand, because they had been made by the Rugby Union; whereupon Frank Glasgow, one of the finest of forwards, proposed a resolution which stated that 'this meeting heartily endorses the appointments made by the management committee'. Dixon, who later noted in his diary that 'the situation was awkward', accepted Glasgow's suggestion. Wonder of wonders, no more than 17 votes were case for Gallaher by the party of 29. Might it have been something to do with the fact that Gallaher was not native-born – even though he was only five years old when, with his parents, seven brothers and two sisters, he migrated from Ramelton, in County Donegal, to Katikati, in the Bay of Plenty?

Despite all the controversy and upset, the team's performances in the British Isles, especially taking into account injuries which often reduced the side to about 20 players, were remarkable. The figures speak for themselves: 109 tries scored against 5 conceded; 96 goals from tries against 2 conceded; one goal from a mark, or fair catch; 2 drop goals against 2; and 4 penalty points against 2. It added up to a grand total of 830 points by the All Blacks against 39 by all opponents.

Results against the club, university and county teams were mostly one-sided and the big test was obviously the four internationals. It is interesting to note that only 18 members of the squad were played in these matches. The 11 who appeared in all four were Gillett, Wallace, Beans, Hunter, Roberts, Seeling, Glasgow, Tyler, Casey, O'Sullivan and McDonald. The two key men of the team each missed one, due to indisposition, Gallaher the Irish match, Stead the Welsh. Indeed, the injury list was stupefyingly long for such a small group, including strains, sprains and fever.

The match against Scotland remains one of the greatest achievements in All Black history. It was marred only by the fact that the attitude of the Scottish Rugby Union, before and after the match, was unforgivably insulting. The All Blacks were not met on their arrival in Edinburgh; and following the match, they dined with the Australasian Society, having received no invitation to take food and wine with their opponents. This disconcerting behaviour, so at variance with normal Caledonian hospitality, was ascribable principally to the secretary of the union, J. Aikman Smith. Noting that the All Blacks were receiving a chit worth 3 shillings as a daily out-of-pocket allowance, he persuaded his committee that the New Zealanders were professionals, and refused to recognize the match as an international. As a despot, he did as he pleased. His union did not provide a ball for the match. He made no provision, although the match was played in mid-November, to have the field of Inverleith covered against the possibility of frost. He bluntly refused George Dixon's request that Scotland pay £200 to the New Zealanders for their appearance; and, because he refused to guarantee the gate, Scotland did themselves out of their fair share, whereas the All Blacks' share of the takings was £1000 clear.

It turned out to be a most wonderful game of rugby. The pity was that the two teams had no chance to celebrate together, in traditional Scottish style, and to establish the warmth and harmony that should have crowned such a memorable encounter.

CHAPTER THREE

THE
BIG FOUR
1905

O n the day of the Scotland match, the 20th in the All Blacks tour, the field, predictably, was rock-hard from frost, and dangerous. It ought not to have been used; and the match, in fact, only went ahead because Dixon and his senior players, believing from the size of the crowd that a riot could occur were it to be cancelled or postponed, agreed to play. Yet in spite of the pre-match provocations, the game fulfilled its promise and proved to be of the highest character, played at a furious pace. In the early stages, elementary blunders by the New Zealanders, probably due to the unfamiliar and daunting conditions of the field, resulted in missed scoring chances. Wallace went in at the right-hand corner and was called back for a forward pass. (Kennedy, the Irish referee, wore boots without sprigs or bars and was frequently too far from the play.) Scotland, relieved, set up a fierce rush – from an offside position, Dixon tersely noted in his account of the match – which ended just short of the New Zealand goal-line, with the spectators ecstatically screaming, 'Feet, Scotland, Fe-e-e-e-e-et!' From a 5-yard scrummage, Greig nipped the ball to Simson, whose dropkick at goal was unerring. First blood to Scotland.

Seeling broke away, dribbling, and nabbed Scoular as the latter caught and tried to clear the ball. Glasgow, close at hand, dribbled the loose ball onward and, over the goal-line, fell upon it for a try. Minutes later, the New Zealanders scored again. Roberts cut out Stead with a skip pass (no modern invention, this) to Hunter. On to Deans, thence to Smith and the try was a demonstration of perfect rugby. Less than perfect, however, was the pass into space by an All Black forward Dixon chose not to identify. Away went the Scottish forwards, bundling all over Gillett as he tried to stem the rush and carrying on to the goal for a try by J.C. M'Callum.

The fierce encounter continued, with Scotland seeking to dominate possession and New Zealand trying every trick they had developed during their tour. As the minutes ticked by, with Scotland ahead 7–6, the likelihood of a home victory stirred the crowd to near-hysterics. No more than

17

four minutes remained when the All Blacks turned the tide. Roberts's pass was so long that neither Stead nor Hunter in the five-eighths could get a hand to the ball. Deans did; and immediately – this was the beauty of the movement – passed to Smith, who found himself in the clear, with only Scoular barring the door. Smith had the space and the speed; rounding his man, he hurtled to the corner for the try that put New Zealand two points ahead.

The crowd was stilled. The Scots were stunned. Stead punted deep, so far that the ball, in its last lazy bounce, trickled across the goal-line. Of all people, burly Bill Cunningham, the Maori lock who had been the last man chosen for the tour, was the only one cool enough to seize the ball and fall on it for the try.

So to victory, by 12 points to 7. When Kennedy blew for no-side, the stadium was hushed. In silence, the spectators, many openly in tears, trudged disbelievingly into the darkening November gloom.

R.J. Phillips, author of *The Story of Scottish Rugby*, published in 1925, started his account of the match in generous fashion: 'No team,' he wrote, 'left a more permanent impression than the New Zealand All Black side of 1905–06. Their football was of high quality and their physique and the personal ability of the players rendered them a formidable combination. In the match at Inverleith, the Scottish team all but scored a success and were leading by a point until five minutes of the close of play when, by something approaching hurricane play, the New Zealanders ran in a couple of tries before time had expired.

'In response to the New Zealand five-eighths position, Scotland played an extra man, Louis Greig, behind the scrummage. K.G. Macleod, making his first appearance in an international, saved a score by the exercise of his speed when the ball was kicked over the Scottish fullback's head. The game was played on a treacherous ground recovering from frost.'

So much for the praise. Now came the sting in the tail. 'As a general impression,' Phillips continued, 'the play did not reveal anything necessary or desirable to the Scottish style of game.'

Dear, stubborn Caledonia. The prejudice against the New Zealanders surfaced again two decades later when in 1924–5, the season in which Scotland won the Triple Crown and the Five Nations Championship, the Scottish Rugby Union declined to face Cliff Porter's All Black Invincibles. It would have been a marvellous game.

In the event, Scotland has never defeated the All Blacks at international level, although there was a scoreless draw in 1963–4, and a Scottish team did beat the New Zealand Army team in 1945–6. The gesture by Charles Saxton, the New Zealand captain, of marching across the Murrayfield turf to congratulate his Scottish counterpart, Keith Geddes, perhaps banked the fires of resentment which had flickered or blazed at times between the two countries ever since the Bedell-Sivright and Aikman Smith days.

The international against Ireland, the 22nd match of the All Blacks' tour, was, at any rate for the first half, a splendid encounter. The half-time score of 5–0 was improved to 15–0 by the end, Deans scoring two tries and

McDonald one, while Wallace, playing at fullback for the only time in an international on the tour, placed all three goals. The Irish backline included Maclear, a centre, J.C. Parke, who was also a first-class lawn tennis player, and, on the wing, Harry Thrift. If Maclear was fast, Thrift was even faster. Many years later he became honorary secretary of the International Rugby Board.

'It was,' wrote Dixon, 'a most exciting and exhilarating exhibition of football. Ireland relied entirely on her forwards for attack; and what a brilliant set they were! Fast, fearless and dashing, their headlong dashes down the field were of a character to stir the most phlegmatic. Little wonder, then, that the excitable Irishmen around the field were worked up to a state of almost delirious enthusiasm as rush succeeded rush. Headlong as were these rushes, there was nothing haphazard about them. There were always four or five, or more, participants, and the ball was kept so close and foot-passes so cleverly made that only an exceptionally clever and fearless defence could have hoped to cope with it. I, personally, have seen nothing quite so good of its kind since the 'eighties', when a similar class of forward play was evident in New Zealand.'

So then, to England, and the 24th tour game. From the beginning, the English Press had been more generous with their praise and shown less complacency in their comparisons than the Scots. J.E. Raphael, who played for England against Gallaher's men, wrote in the *Athletic News*: 'The difference between English and New Zealand rugby is the difference between a team which apparently has nothing more to learn and a team which by slavish adherence to cobwebbed tradition has much to unlearn. People keep saying, "Wait till they meet a nation!", forgetting that all New Zealand is not much more than a county. The success of the New Zealanders is the best thing for English rugby, since it will compel divorce from tradition and encourage the free indulgence of intelligent thought.'

Another English critic wrote: 'Nothing quite so brilliant as the intuitive combination of New Zealand back-play has ever been seen.' And the correspondent of the *Daily Mirror*, using more picturesque phraseology, could scarcely be restrained: 'They move like blood-horses, while the gait of the Middlesex men is more suggestive of a Shire stallion. . . . They play as if their hopes of eternal welfare depended upon success, every nerve and sinew braced all up to snapping point. They are as persistent as a lot of wasps, as clever and alert as a crowd of monkeys. . . . They work together like the parts of a well-constructed watch. . . . The New Zealanders are here, equipped for victory, and they have gained their equipment by recognizing that nothing but hard work and thorough drill can win success.'

Like Ireland, England also yielded 15 points. 'We would not have minded the points,' remarked Raphael, 'except that they were all from tries!' Poor England! Their team lacked the fire of the Scots, the tigerish rushes of the Irish, the genuine quality of the Welsh. The match was played at Crystal Palace, an edifice which astounded the New Zealanders; and, according to report, if the paid attendance was 40,000 – some said 45,000 – the actual crowd might have been 30,000 larger. Touts cleaned up as tickets priced at half-a-crown (two shillings and six pence) were bartered at the gates for a guinea (one pound, one shilling). The presence of many women, not a few most elegantly attired, was noted; it would not be so, one newspaper reported, at an Association Football international. Truth to tell, however, the loudest roar for England came when the team posed for photographs against a goalpost.

Next day's newspaper headlines told the story of the match. 'Our Colonial Conquerors' and 'England's Crushing Defeat by the Invincible New Zealanders' were typical. The *Weekly Dispatch*, then in its 105th year of publication and since vanished without trace, set the scene: 'Punctually at the advertised time, the two teams entered the field. The band struck up – the little Union Jacks on the touchline fluttered bravely – the sun shone with winter brightness and, after one hearty cheer, the vast crowd settled down to watch. The contrast between the two fifteens was noticeable as soon as they appeared – the New Zealanders being uniformly big and broad, while the Englishmen, though some were veritable sons of Arak, lacked that homogeneous symmetry which must have an effect on combination. The two halves, Gent and Braithwaite, looked like little boys; and a man from the North was heard to exclaim in his broad tongue, "Why, them little laaads will be chawed oop. They ought to be 'ome in bed." Nevertheless, the "little lads" gave a very good account of themselves.

'Grouping themselves together, the New Zealanders sang their weird Maori war-song, which convulsed many of the Englishmen with laughter, and then scattered across the field to their positions. V.H. Cartwright placed the ball in the centre, the referee blew his whistle and with a long, high kick, the English captain opened the game. With a dash, the English forwards followed up. But the kick was too long and not high enough, and before they were able to reach it, it was safely in the hands of Deans.

'It soars from his foot high in the air, and before Hind, the centre threequarter, can catch it, seven New Zealanders thunder down upon him, and he disappears, for a moment, from view. . . .'

And that, really, summed up the game in which England were quite outmatched. Cartwright, first capped in 1903, led a team which included no more than six other internationals, and was thus demonstrably inexperienced at the highest level. Gent, the 'little boy' at scrumhalf, was qualified for both Wales and England, choosing the latter before embarking on a career as schoolmaster and rugby critic. (In the latter capacity, he represented the *Sunday Times* of London with Karl Mullen's Lions of 1950 who, at least on the social side, were the most popular of all teams to tour New Zealand. Poor Dai, desperately pining for his wife and his school, abandoned the tour about midway with the ringing declaration that 'no man over 50 should ever cover a rugby tour' – a recommendation which few professional critics, Kiwi, English, Welsh or French, have supported.)

The hero of New Zealand was Duncan McGregor, the fast, elusive wing threequarter, who scored four tries. Sadly, his reputation with his teammates was smirched when word got about, after the subsequent game with Wales, that he had 'sold' the All Blacks' plan of attack for some pieces of silver, and had been a 'sleeper' during that vital match. McGregor was one of the few members of the 1905 team to tour England with the All Golds in 1907–08 and remained in Wales to play for Merthyr until an ankle injury ended his career. Back in New Zealand, he later became a rugby league selector and referee.

The climax of the tour was the international against Wales. From the beginning of the All Blacks' tour, the Welsh had been watching their progress with steely, calculating eyes, studying and evaluating the success-ful New Zealand methods, and working out effective counters. They were profound students of the game, their supporters passionately patriotic. And what a golden era it was for them! Between 1900 and 1911, the Red Dragons were masters of British rugby. Only once, in all those years, did they lose at home, 11–0 to the original Springboks of 1906, at Swansea. The record was otherwise staggering: 35 victories in 43 matches, one drawn and seven lost, with a points record of 534 scored against 228 conceded.

The quality of the team which defeated the All Blacks 3–0 at Cardiff Arms Park may be measured by two plays of special significance. The first was the try itself, scored in the left-hand corner by the left wing, Teddy Morgan. Dicky Owen, at scrumhalf, feinted to pass to the flyhalf, Percy Bush, at a scrummage moving right, then flashed the ball across the pack into the hands of Cliff Pritchard, playing at rover in the New Zealand fashion. As Wallace went in for the tackle, Pritchard passed to Rhys Gabe; on to Morgan, who rounded Gillett at fullback and scorched to a memorable try.

The second was the resistance, by the Welsh, after an apparently fair try by Deans, made from a superb midfield break by Wallace, had been overruled by John Dallas, the Scottish referee, who judged that Deans had been grounded by Morgan. At the ruling of a scrum 5 yards from the Welsh goal-line, the All Blacks might have been expected, with all their experi-ence, to produce so powerful a thrust as to deny the Welsh the ball and create a ruck, or loose scrummage, from which possession could have been won. This was a moment demanding the most intense concentration by the Welsh; and they responded faithfully, clearing the line and forming again that defensive pattern which held, as it had for most of the second half, against the most determined attempts of the All Blacks to score.

In attack and in defence, the Welsh had established true qualities of greatness. A reporter of the *South Wales Daily News*, soon after no-side, made his way to the dressing-rooms. 'When I found Gallaher,' he wrote, 'he was shaking Gwyn Nicholls [captain of Wales] by the hand and telling him with sincerity that the best team had won. . . . Then the few of us who were present witnessed the interesting spectacle of the rival captains exchanging jerseys. Gallaher was wearing the red dragon-ornamented raiment of the Welsh when I asked for his opinion. "It was," he said, "a rattling good game, played out to the bitter end, with the result that the best team won." "Is there any point about the match," I asked, "which you regard as unsatisfactory?" "No," Gallaher replied. "As I said before, the better team won; and I am content." '

It may be argued, with hindsight, that for the All Blacks, the strain of playing such concentrated rugby – this was their 28th match in 88 days – was beginning to show. Their weariness was evident in the remaining part of the tour. Although they scraped home against Glamorgan, Swansea, Cardiff and Newport, there were uncharacteristic blunders in both attack and defence, and other signs of falling off from the high standards of the earlier games.

Gallaher's reaction to the result of the international ought to have abated the wrath and stilled the controversy which, even a few minutes after the end of play, was beginning to stir and which has persisted, off and on, to the present day. What has to be said, unequivocally, is that if referee John Dallas ruled that a try had not been scored, that was final. By the Laws of Rugby, he, as sole judge of fact, was the only competent authority.

Nevertheless, with the passing of years, the hubbub over the 'try that never was' refused to die down. After the 1924 All Blacks had licked the Welsh 19–0 at Swansea, Teddy Morgan jotted on Cliff Porter's dining-card the words, 'Deans did score!', which prompted Billy Wallace, a mild-mannered man, to explode furiously at the memory of the injustice visited on his team.

During the 1930s, referee John Dallas sparked off the controversy anew by writing, for the Welsh Rugby Union, his observations on the incident based on the notes he had made after the game. Deans, wrote Dallas, had been tackled by Morgan. The ball was grounded 6–12 inches from the Welsh goal-line. He himself had been on the line, between the uprights, and well sited to see what happened. As soon as the tackle occurred, he whistled to signal a scrummage. Approaching Deans, he noticed that the All Black was now across the goal-line, the ball in his hands. Moreover, he observed that some Welshmen were dragging Deans back into the field of play. Dallas now wrote that he had no reason to alter his original ruling. He caused a scrummage to be formed on or near the spot where he had seen Deans brought to ground in a tackle.

Not all were satisfied. Others, after the match, voiced their opinions, not so much about the try as concerning Dallas's capabilities as a referee. On the following Monday the *Manchester Guardian* said, bluntly: 'The referee was uncommonly sharp on Gallaher. He watched the New Zealander with an untiring eye, gave several penalties against him and harassed him mercilessly with the whistle. Dallas seemed once or twice to be almost too ready to pull up the New Zealand players. Once, he stopped a movement of the backs for a knock-on that was not a knock-on; and no pass that was not pronouncedly backward escaped without a shrill "Halt" from the referee.'

The correspondent of the *Otago Daily Times* weighed in: 'The referee was most unaccountable in many of his decisions. He seemed to be under the impression that Gallaher always put in the ball unfairly, and whistled eight free kicks for Wales. New Zealand got three, the whole game. Deans scored a try without a doubt, the Welsh themselves stating so, but being pulled back over the line again, a scrum was ordered. Mr Dallas did not run about the play as much as New Zealand referees do.'

In his book, *The Triumphant Tour of the New Zealand Footballers*, George Dixon was circumspect. 'The referee,' he wrote, 'was somewhat slow, judged by a New Zealand standard – not with the whistle – but in the matter of keeping up with the play when any specially fast bit of work occurred. As is customary with many referees in the Old Country, he went out, on a greasy ground, with ordinary walking boots, no buttons or bars, and clad in ordinary clothing, including the orthodox high collar. Another extraordinary thing is the fact that when a scrum was formed, he insisted upon the ball being put in on the opposite side of the scrum to that upon which he was standing, so it was thus impossible for him to see what was going on at the edge of the scrum.'

In the diary that he kept so meticulously throughout the tour, Dixon spoke more freely. 'The refereeing,' he noted, 'was not what would be called first class according to New Zealand standards. No referee who is commonly 30 or 40 yards behind the play when a fast bit of work occurs can be classed A1.' And he reiterated the observations about Mr Dallas's strange choice of apparel.

At the appearance of Bob Stuart's All Blacks of 1953–4 in Wales, the BBC went to considerable trouble and expense to resuscitate the story. They could not produce Dallas, who had died in 1942; but they did offer a most convincing witness in Rhys Gabe, the great centre who had toured New Zealand with Bedell-Sivright's team in 1904 and who won 24 caps between 1901 and 1908. The programme suggested that Teddy Morgan had been mistaken in claiming to have tackled Deans, his grasp of facts being somewhat uncertain in later life. Indeed, Gabe now stated that it was *he* who had gone for Deans and prevented him from thrusting his body, with the ball in outstretched arms, toward the goal-line. This appeared to support, conclusively, the general Welsh account (challenged by the All Blacks to a man) that Deans, in fact, had failed to reach the try-line.

The BBC version of events might not have stood up had the unfortunate John Dallas been alive at the time. In 1935 a member of the current All Blacks team was entertained in Dallas's home in Aberdeen. It was bitterly cold. The two men were sitting in front of a fire. Out of the blue, Dallas, by then a Sheriff of the High Court, remarked, without prompting: 'I have something to tell you. I was – you may not have known this – the referee of the Welsh game of 1905 which the All Blacks lost. At the time of the Deans incident, I was behind the play. I did not really see the situation – I did not see what happened.'

'I had the impression,' the All Black said, many years later, 'that the old boy was making a sort of confession, that he was glad to get off his chest something which, presumably, had been troubling him for a long time. He left no doubt in my mind that he was unable to decide whether Deans had scored, or not. It was a remarkable experience for me.'

It is common knowledge that Deans telegraphed the *Daily Mail* to say he had grounded the ball in the Welsh in-goal; common knowledge that the *Mail* did not publish an item which could have stirred strong resentment among its Welsh readers; common knowledge, too, that Bob Deans, on his death-bed, three years after the match, declared, 'I did score the try.'

The scoreline of the 1905 match still reads: Wales 3, New Zealand 0. When Maoris sing hymns, they end with a lovely cadence, 'Amine' ('Ar-mee-nay'). So be it.

CHAPTER FOUR

DISSENT AND DIVISION
1906-19

*A*fter the glories and triumphs of 1905, the years leading up to the First World War saw New Zealand rugby assailed by internal disputes. True, there were further successes. Yet these threatened to be outweighed by controversy and crisis.

Shortly after the All Blacks returned from their British tour, the New Zealand sporting public was astounded to hear that four members of that side had 'deserted' to a team which called itself the 'All Golds'. Other famous All Blacks followed the example, some settling permanently in England. This issue divided families and destroyed friendships. The All Golds rebel movement resulted in an even more extraordinary development. According to the New Zealand Rugby League Annual a crisis arose in 1912 when a meeting of delegates to the Canterbury Rugby Union 'decided to recommend to the New Zealand Rugby Union that it consider the adoption of the Northern Union game.' The annual said that the recommendation was defeated by 34 votes to 28 at a general meeting of the New Zealand union in November 1912. Canterbury's remit was supported by Auckland, Bush Districts, Hawkes Bay, Canterbury, South Canterbury, Otago and Southland.

The statement in the annual was tendentious. In December 1990, the chief executive officer of the New Zealand Rugby Union, George Verry, said that on 14 November 1912 a special general meeting of the New Zealand union, requisitioned by Canterbury, had discussed Canterbury's proposal 'That the New Zealand union be requested to instruct the Secretary to make an immediate application to the English Rugby Union for authority to make such alterations and amendments to the Laws of the Game as may, from time to time, be found necessary to, or advisable in, the interests of the game in this Dominion.'

Mr Verry noted from the Minutes that 'after discussion, a division was taken, the motion being lost – ayes 28, noes 34.' Canterbury, Mr Verry noted, 'had submitted proposals regarding individual Laws but when the basic motion was defeated, declined to go ahead with them. However, a delegate from another union moved various proposed alterations. They referred to knock-on and thrown-forward, scrummage, lineout, points for a goal from a mark and points for "a goal potted from the field". Hence,' Mr Verry concluded, 'although the voting at 28 for and 34 against was quoted correctly, the subject of the motion bore no relationship to embracing the Northern Union game.'

Outwardly, the quality of New Zealand rugby remained high and the results looked impressive. For example, during the 1907, 1910 and 1914 tours of Australia, out of 24 matches played, only one was lost and another drawn. And against four touring parties to New Zealand – Australia in 1905 and 1913, an Anglo-Welsh team in 1908, and an American Universities' side in 1910, the All Blacks and local teams won 20, lost 16 and drew two games.

During those years, the All Blacks played 13 matches of international status. They won nine, drew two and lost two, being unbeaten in any individual series. One game lost to Australia, 11–0, was the second test of 1910, played at the Sydney Cricket Ground. The other defeat, 16–5, was in the third and last test of the tour by the Australians in 1913, played at Lancaster Park in Christchurch, a field which has not been unkind to them over the years.

One of the drawn matches, 5–5, was the third test of the tour of Australia in 1907, at the Sydney Cricket Ground. The other, 3–3, was the second of three tests against Arthur Harding's Anglo-Welsh team of 1908 at Athletic Park, Wellington. The visitors scored a try, while the All Blacks only managed a penalty goal, and the game was played in deep slush – conditions hardly fit either for man or beast.

The immortal *Sydney Bulletin*, a tabloid with its outer pages coloured in red, used to note the passing of the famous and the notorious under the headline, 'Into the Silence'. The term could well have applied to the period of New Zealand rugby which succeeded the tour of 1905. Despite the statistics, this era was, and is, little discussed, for little pride was taken in the achievements. A particularly hollow win was the international against All-America, played at Berkeley, California, in November 1913, even though the All Blacks scored a record number of 11 tries in the runaway 51 points to 3 victory.

Three years previously, an American Universities' team had toured both in Australia and New Zealand, where it lost, though not overwhelmingly, to Wellington, Otago, Canterbury and Wanganui, finally coming up against David Gallaher's Auckland side. Auckland at the time held the Ranfurly Shield, a challenge contest among all the provincial teams affiliated to the New Zealand Rugby Union, and was one of the strongest ever fielded by this powerful province. The scoreline, 13–13, reflected well on both sides, and suggested that American rugby had considerable potential.

In 1912 Australia had reciprocated by sending a fully representative national team to the Pacific coast. It was beaten 13–12 by Stanford

University, 6–5 by the University of California, and struggled to defeat All-California, a euphemism for All-America. When the Americans, justifiably confident, decided to go one better by visiting New Zealand, the local rugby greybeards stroked their chins thoughtfully. They had a duty to sustain the high standing of the strongest rugby nation in the world. So they could not afford to send to California a team – New Zealand Universities, Junior All Blacks or whatever – which might be clobbered as the Australians had been. Damage to the country's prestige would be irreparable.

The New Zealand Rugby Union thus instructed its selectors, David Gallaher and Simon Mynott of the 1905 team, S.F. Wilson of Canterbury and V.G. Cavanagh Sen. ('Old Vic') of Otago, to choose a full-scale representative side. Alex McDonald, also of 1905 fame, was appointed captain. By the standards of the time, McDonald was a veteran – 30 years old – yet still scored 11 of the team's 156 tries. He commanded such backs as Teddy Roberts, at scrumhalf, possibly the strongest and sharpest halfback ever bred by New Zealand; Frank Mitchinson, one of the true greats, whether at five-eighths or, as now, in the threequarters; and 'Doddy' Gray, who played in the 1908 and 1913 All Black teams, a five-eighths of a class above Mynott. The threequarters also included Tom Lynch, who scored 37 tries in 23 matches in All Black uniform; 'Dick' Roberts of Taranaki, a brilliant player who scored 102 points in 22 matches, including five tests; and Leonard ('Jack') Stohr, first New Zealand player to place three penalty goals in a match, who in a match against Transvaal in the tour of South Africa in 1919 placed a goal from inside his own half – a flight of at least 70 yards to the crossbar.

Among other members of the side were 'Mick' Cain, a hard man from Taranaki who, not entering the game until he was 21, and then as a replacement for an injured player in a club match, went on to play 102 matches at first-class level; Jim Wylie, a tall Aucklander, who returned to California and later gave a lavish welcome to the 1953 All Blacks on their way home through San Francisco; and George Maurice Victor Sellars – an Auckland hooker who played in no fewer than 12 Ranfurly Shield challenges. Popularly known as H.M.G., Sellars confessed in his autobiography, written with the author of this book, that actually he was plain 'George'; the initials were a wheeze invented by Bill Irvine in 1924 to counter the many English players who carried a great number of 'handles'.

On the face of it, the 1913 tour was the most successful of all time – 16 matches played and won, 610 points scored and only 6 conceded. In fact, it was an unmitigated sadness. The hammerings inflicted by the All Blacks killed the budding rugby movement in the United States.

The prospects of rugby complementing traditional American football had been encouraging. In the course of the All Blacks' 1905 tour, the critic of *The Sporting Life*, Captain the Hon. Southwell Fitzgerald (writing as 'Judex'), observed: 'The fact that President [Theodore] Roosevelt has urged upon Yale, Harvard and Princeton Universities to modify their inter-University football in such a way as to do away with the brutality of the game which marks it as it is now played in the United States, and also the additional fact that the powers-that-be in these Universities have promised the President that the rules prohibiting roughness shall be obeyed in every way is, to my mind, a grand opportunity for establishing the Rugby Union game in the United States.'

The Auckland historians Neville McMillan and Rod Chester, in their book *Centenary*, published in 1984, remarked of the 1913 tour: 'In 1904, there were more deaths from injuries in American football than there were among sailors in the biggest naval engagement of the Spanish-American War of 1898. The popularity of the game began to wane, especially in California, where the State Governor banned it. High Schools and universities began to adopt rugby, which became the major football game played in the State.'

Between 1914 and 1918, six important universities, including Southern California and Stanford, reverted to the American game. Had the New Zealand Rugby Union despatched a Universities' team or a representative side on the lines of the modern Barbarians, as missionaries of true amateur rugby at its best, things might have been otherwise. The union's decision, and the tour, were a disaster.

It has to be said, nevertheless, that between 1905 and 1914 many of the Incomparables enhanced their reputations at home and abroad while new players displayed similar qualities. Jimmy Hunter, captain in 1907, was supplanted by Billy Stead for two of the three tests against the Anglo-Welshmen. Then Freddie Roberts took a turn until McDonald came along. Meanwhile, backs of the calibre of Frank Mitchinson, 'Jack' Stohr, Jimmy Ryan, Dick Roberts, Tom Lynch and Teddy Roberts were making their mark on the game. Frank Fryer, a Hawkes Bay man who played most of his rugby for Canterbury, twice used his extreme speed to score five tries in matches below international class; and another speedster, Victor Macky, of Auckland, though capped only once, scored all four tries in a 12–0 defeat of Wellington in a Ranfurly Shield match.

Fine forwards from all over the country battled for places in the All Blacks. 'Ned' Hughes, a Southland hooker, played in all three tests in Australia in 1907, and at the age of 40 appeared in the first test against the 1921 Springboks. Also from Southland were the brothers Purdue, vigorous, inexhaustible competitors, and Jimmy Ridland, who was excluded from the 1913 team, despite his fine play against the Australians. 'Bolla' Francis, a 6 ft 3 in Auckland flanker, whose sister married David Gallaher, was accounted unlucky not to have made the 1905 side. Harry Avery, a wing-forward, was to have a distinguished record with the New Zealand Expeditionary Force, remained in the Regular Army and served through the Second World War as a brigadier. And an Otago lock, Henry Paton, was a durable powerhouse, who gripped his hookers so firmly that they were forced to thrust directly ahead instead of wavering and upsetting the balance of the scrum.

Perhaps the most remarkable forward of all was a Wellingtonian who was christened Nathaniel Arthur Wilson but who was always known as 'Ranji'.

He was a dark-complexioned half-caste, English and West Indian, who played flanker with true devilry, fixing opposing inside backs with so menacing an eye that many, after a taste or two of his tackles, seemed to lose balance and stumble before they reached the ball. The Laws then permitted a forward to jump into a lineout, and 'Ranji' did this with positive glee; and because he was as hard as nails, the opposing line tended to bend the moment he made contact. 'Ranji' should later have been a first choice for the New Zealand Army team which toured South Africa in 1919; but although thirty years were to pass before apartheid was officially introduced, South African Whites, whether of English or Afrikaner origin, already operated a Colour bar, so that non-White membership of sporting and social clubs was unthinkable. It was made plain to the selectors that Wilson's presence in the Army side would be unacceptable. 'Ranji' did not seem to mind. His playing career was over before the 1921 Springboks made their inaugural tour. In 1922 he became a Wellington selector and in 1924–5 was one of seven national selectors to pick the All Black team which travelled undefeated through England, Wales, Ireland and France.

Significantly, several Maori teams were formed in these years. Two of them toured Australia, in 1910 and 1913. In 1911, Alex Takarangi, a Wanganui player of outstanding skills, led a team through New Zealand. In 1912, the stalwart lock of 1905, Bill Cunningham, captained a Maori team which lost to Auckland, 27–0. And in 1914, Harry Jacob, a legendary figure from the Horowhenua district, dominated a team which lost 15–13 to Wellington.

★ ★ ★

In 1908, Arthur Harding, who had toured with Bedell-Sivright, led his Anglo-Welsh team on a tour of New Zealand. The side contained, among its ten international caps, E.J. Jackett, who had played fullback for England against Gallaher's team; Freddy Chapman, a wing of exceptional speed; Johnny Williams, another wing, whose 17 caps for Wales included matches against the 1906 Springboks and 1908 Wallabies; H.H. ('Jumbo') Vassall, a centre of extraordinary brilliance who, despite glowing prospects, unaccountably gave up the game; P.F. McEvedy, a Wellingtonian who was completing his post-graduate medical studies in London; and Jack Williams, of the 1905 Welsh team which had beaten the All Blacks.

Harding's men won nine, drew one and lost seven of 17 games played in New Zealand and went on to Australia to win five out of seven games there. To his amazement, since he had not played at superior level since 1905, Billy Stead was recalled to captain the All Blacks for the first test, which was comfortably won 32–3. He was then replaced by Jimmy Hunter for the 3–3 draw in the bog that was Athletic Park. The crowd of 10,000 were treated to a fine farewell to rugby by Billy Wallace. He fielded expertly at fullback, found touch accurately and, at the game's end, departed bearing the accolade, from one English critic, of 'the prince of all rugby players', and, from two British internationals, 'the finest back who ever wore shoe leather'. Stead was recalled for the final test, which was won 29–0. The occasion was a poignant one for the 12,000 spectators who saw Bob Deans play in an All Black uniform for what proved to be the last time. Disregarding a grumbling appendix, Deans played through the game, returned to his farm without benefit of medical advice and was soon dead of peritonitis.

It was during this tour that there occurred an incident which remains to this day one of the strangest mysteries in the history of rugby. One of the visitors, a front-row forward named F.S. Jackson, who played in the first test, was expelled from the Anglo-Welsh tour and put on a ship for home, having allegedly received money while playing for Leicester. The mystery surrounds the true identity of the man who was so unceremoniously disgraced.

One of the most celebrated of all Yorkshire and English amateur crick-eters was one F.S. Jackson, who was born in 1870 and who died in 1947. Among his distinctions were the captaincy of England and the presidency (1921) of the Marylebone Cricket Club – the MCC. It was generally assumed that this was the man who was a member of Harding's touring rugby team.

In 1990, Fred Jackson, youngest son of the expelled player and a resident of Otahuhu, an Auckland suburb, suggested that his father, in all prob-ability, was not the F.S. Jackson who had played cricket for England. His own detective work over the years had revealed his real father to have been born in 1883 and to have died in 1957. Although Fred had no solid grounds for belief, he thought his father might have been Welsh ('He often called me "Boyo",'), possibly born in Swansea, and that the family name, or his mother's maiden name, was Jones. For some reason, he borrowed the name and initials of one of the cricketing heroes of his childhood.

Fred Jackson found evidence to suggest that his father had played rugby for Swansea, Swinton and Broughton before becoming, in 1906 or 1907, a member of the Leicester club – the famous 'Tigers' of the Midlands. It was after his selection for Harding's team and while in New Zealand that the Rugby Football Union was told, or heard evidence, that Jackson had received payment for his services at Leicester. It reacted at once by re-quiring Jackson's dismissal from the touring team and his return to England.

Fred Jackson found confirmation that his father had boarded the *Matai*, which left Wellington for Sydney on the night before the second test and which carried the New Zealand Universities' team bound for a tour of Australia. Yet F.S. Jackson, the rugby player, never saw Britain again. He was next sighted on the west coast of New Zealand's South Island, working as a coal-miner. By now he had switched to rugby league. His son believes he played for New Zealand against Australia in 1910. In that year, too, Jackson was a delegate from Nelson to the fledgling New Zealand Rugby League.

He was next seen on the east coast of North Island where, soon after-wards, he married a woman of the Maori tribe, the Ngati-Porou, which considers itself the most distinguished of the race. Reverting to rugby, still on the east coast, he became a selector and was either a rival, or close associate, of Tim French, who held many offices in rugby and was eventually made a life-member of the New Zealand Rugby Union.

F.S. Jackson was the father of five children, one of whom, Everard, a prop-forward, won six All Black caps, three of them against the powerful Springbok touring team of 1937.

'In all of the time I knew him,' says Fred Jackson, 'my father expressed hatred of the English. He cultivated the feeling partly because of the indignity of being expelled from Harding's team and partly because, in January of 1909, the Rugby Football Union, at an official inquiry, found no evidence to support the charges of professionalism which had been laid against him. These, apparently, were based on the fact that Leicester at the time was so powerful a team that strong rumours were spread that it must be "buying" players. All charges against F.S. Jackson were dismissed. Dad never forgave. He never forgot.' A strange, sad and disturbing story.

In 1893 there was a meeting of the Rugby Football Union. The point at issue was the desire of clubs in Lancashire and Yorkshire to allow their players to receive compensation for bona-fide loss of working time and earnings. J.A. Millar, of Yorkshire, proposed, and M. Newsome, of the same county, seconded a resolution that players be allowed such reimbursement. Before a vote could be taken, Rowland Hill, honorary secretary of the Rugby Football Union, moved an amendment, supported by R.S. Whalley of Lancashire, to the effect, simply, 'that this meeting decline to sanction the same'. As a direct negative of the resolution, the amendment ought not to have been tabled. In fact, it was carried by 282 votes to 136, no fewer than 120 proxies being cast for it.

Reactions were sharp, sudden and severe. Overnight, 22 rugby clubs in the two counties seceded from the Rugby Football Union. These included Wigan, St Helen's, Leeds, Widnes, Hull, Halifax, Oldham and Bradford. The clubs banded together as the Northern Union, and within three years 100 clubs were affiliated to the rebel union, which functioned as such until 1923, when it changed its name to the Rugby League.

Members of the 1905 All Blacks naturally came to hear of the new union's activities. One who was particularly impressed was the great wing, George Smith, who had not been happy to be described as 'a three bob a day man', the derisive term applied by the northerners to those who were willing, in the cause of amateurism, to play for their country for such a paltry reward. In Sydney, in 1906 or thereabouts, Smith met two prominent cricketing men, J.J. Giltinan, an administrator, and Victor Trumper, the immortal batsman. Together with a shrewd and tough character named Jersey Flegg, these two were badgering amateur rugby players to subscribe to a game in which their skills would be adequately rewarded. According to the *New Zealand Rugby League Annual* of 1933, Smith said to Giltinan: 'What about you getting "Rugby League" [an error here, surely, as the title had not yet been invented] going in Australia and I'll do my best when I get home.' The two men, reports the *Annual*, shook hands on it.

The *Rugby League Annual*, scarcely a disinterested party, said that Gallaher's men had returned to New Zealand to find 'that there was much call for change of the old rules – not to imitate Rugby League, oh, no! – just to speed up the game!' The *Annual* asserted that these men had 'learnt something else – the advantages of the "objectionable" professional code. . . . There was consternation when it became known in 1907 that quite a number of the best All Blacks held, and stood for, decidedly revolutionary action about what they began to term "the old game" and its administrators. More shocking still, these All Blacks held a lively respect for the broadmindedness of various English rugby league clubs which spontaneously had offered ground use and other facilities to their kinsmen from this Colony!'

Cometh the hour, cometh the man. A.H. Baskerville, from Wellington, had written to the Northern Union to urge that they receive 'a special team' for a tour of northern England. Reception of the proposal was so enthusiastic that Baskerville quickly gathered, in secrecy, 28 players, a manager, secretary and treasurer, each of whom was bonded to contribute £50 towards the cost of the expedition. Four of the 1905 team, Smith, Mackrell, Johnston and McGregor, were in the party, which soon was being called the 'All Golds', and which set off for England in August 1907. En route, games were played in Sydney. By a stroke of luck, a 24-year-old Australian, a genius of a threequarter named Dally Messenger, was pledged into the team. He was, and remains, a nonpareil of the league game.

The All Golds, if not quite of the class of the All Blacks, beat England by two tests to one. In a tour of 34 matches, they won 19, lost 12 and drew three. Gate receipts amounted to £8838; total revenue was £9494. At the end, the players, who had been receiving a token £1 a week, whacked up £5461 among them. Sadly, during the course of matches in Sydney and Brisbane on the way home, Baskerville contracted pneumonia and failed to recover. His body was returned to Wellington, and the All Golds staged a benefit match for his mother at the Basin Reserve, the city's cricket ground. Before splitting up, the players each received a bonus of £120.

Herbert Moran's Wallabies toured England and Wales, playing 31 matches in the winter of 1908. At about the same time, the New South Wales rugby league sent a team, known as the Kangaroos, to Britain. In September of that year, the Wallabies were persuaded, for £100 per man, to take on the Kangaroos in Sydney. The matches drew enormous crowds.

Herbert Moran was deep into his post-graduate studies at Edinburgh University at this time. The Wallabies defeated New South Wales by 22 to 16 at the Sydney Cricket Ground and all its players returned to inter-club and inter-state matches. In late July of 1909, secret negotiations were begun with almost all of the team to turn to rugby league. In the *Sydney Sun* of 3 August 1910, Jersey Flegg alleged that it was he who, in 1909, had secured assurance of outside finance to contract Wallabies who were willing to make the switch. The period was late July. Blair Swannell, secretary of the

Metropolitan Rugby Union, wrote on 27 August to players and officials of the team inviting them to attend a meeting on 1 September.

It was too late. On 27 August Sydney newspapers carried stories about eleven Wallabies who had switched. In his revelations, a year later, Flegg said fourteen Wallabies had contracted, during August, to play three matches, on 4, 8 and 11 September, against the Pioneers of the rugby league. One of the men, Flegg said, had received £200, two others had received £150 each and the remaining eleven had each signed for £100. Because the Wallabies had insisted that the matches be played at 15 a side, Flegg secured a club player for £50 and another young man for £27. In all, payments amounted to £1850. Gate-takings for the matches, despite enormous publicity, fell £121 short of the guarantees. Flegg's sponsor, for £500, apparently was a Sydney tycoon, Sir Joynton Smith, who published *Smith's Weekly*, a journal for the lower socio-economic orders. The Pioneers – properly the Kangaroos – won the first match, lost the second and won the third, 8–6. Because the Kangaroos had not received a penny, a fourth match, for which each of them received £15, was staged, the Kangaroos again winning. The biggest gate was 18,000, the smallest 2500.

When, amid bitter political strife, Australia declared against conscription for the First World War, 'the cloth-capped brigade', as it was called by a subsequent secretary of the Australian Rugby League, Keith Sharp, achieved a dominance among the footballing groups of New South Wales and Queensland which it has never relinquished and which has, in recent years, made Sydney the strongest league centre in the world.

Although many rugby men in New Zealand, as in Australia, rushed to the colours, the adoption of conscription by the Massey Government deprived the league of the vast opportunities for expansion that the game enjoyed in Australia. Nevertheless, a crisis arose in 1912 when delegates of the Canterbury Rugby Union recommended to the New Zealand union that it consider adopting the Northern Union game. One Christchurch newspaper commented in an editorial: 'If the Northern Union code is really an improvement on rugby, there should be nothing to stop New Zealand adopting the rules, on the basis of strict amateurism.'

'After all,' said the paper, 'it is the playing, and not the paying, that counts.'

In November 1912, the recommendation was placed before a conference of the New Zealand Rugby Union in Wellington. Despite support from Auckland, Bush Districts, Hawkes Bay, Canterbury, South Canterbury, Otago and Southland, the proposal was defeated by 34 votes to 28. It was the Waterloo of New Zealand rugby history, and the decision had been in the balance.

Less than two years later came the outbreak of war, and the world was torn apart.

CHAPTER FIVE

GIANT STRIDES, TINY STEPS
1920-9

*T*he decade of the 1920s was undoubtedly one of the most memorable of all eras in New Zealand rugby. Three great tours were mounted – and a fourth was quickly buried away in a cupboard kept for Kiwi rugby skeletons.

In the years immediately following the end of the First World War – during which, with 17,000 men killed and almost 100,000 wounded, New Zealand suffered more casualties, proportionate to population, than any other combatant nation – rugby continued to flourish. With talented players and appreciative crowds, the quality of play was as high as ever. However much authorities in other countries might deplore the 2–3–2 scrummage formation and the attendant rover, or wing-forward, the emphasis was always on running, passing, *attacking* rugby. The simple fact that neither scrummage could be sure of heeling the ball, save by the skill of the two hookers, compelled backlines to adopt attacking formation. When heeled through the clear passage formed by the spread feet of the strong men of the scrum, the lock, the ball flew into the hands of the waiting, *stationary* scrumhalf, whose options were almost boundless. He could pass to either flank, into the hands of the first or second five-eighths; or, with some protection from the rover, he could himself break past opposing flank forwards. He could punt the ball into 'The Box' – the more or less vacant area astern of his opposing halfback and forward of the defenders' fullback – or crack it behind the opponents' line. Most importantly, because he was stationary, and unhindered, he could pass accurately, and at *speed*.

So the ball became, as it always should be, King of the Game. But in those postwar years, the Auckland Rugby Union became frightened by the increasing popularity of rugby league in the city and devised what came to be known as 'The Auckland Amendments'. No player might move ahead of the last line of forwards' feet until the ball had been heeled by the opposing side. When a player located anywhere between the 25-yard lines punted the ball into touch on the full, it was returned to a lineout formed at right angles to the spot from which it had been kicked. The wing-forward putting the ball into the scrummage could not be hindered by his marker, who had to stand behind the last line of his forwards' feet.

More or less coincidentally, the Auckland selector-coach, Vincent Meredith, later knighted for his services as Auckland's Crown Solicitor, devised what came to be called 'The Early Pass'. As soon as a player received the ball, he passed it to a support. 'Doc' Nicholls, one of the two halfbacks of a famous Wellington family of three All Blacks, was unaware of the innovation as he followed his forwards chasing the kick-off in the Auckland-Wellington game at Eden Park. Observing Vic Badeley, an Auckland centre, fielding the ball and, on the instant, passing it to his wing, Freddie Lucas, Nicholls sang out in glee. 'Brother,' he chortled, 'have these Aucklanders got the wind up! They're passing when no one's anywhere near them!'

Meredith was such an original that his seven-man Auckland backline at times included five men who normally played at centre threequarter. He plucked out of third grade a teenaged boy named Bert Cooke who, as soon became apparent, was a genius. Cooke was much younger than an Artful Dodger named Karl Ifwerson, Meredith's and Auckland's ideal of a constructive, clever, attacking midfield back. Encouraged by 'Iffy', Cooke had only to reach for the ball to bring the crowd to its feet.

Even more gifted than Meredith was another authority, Norman McKenzie. He tested players by looking, as he said, 'for the unusual'. In the early 1920s no province played more than six to eight representative club or league games in a season which began in mid-April and ended on 30 September. In 1922, McKenzie produced, in the Hawkes Bay province, a team of so little account that only a few thousand attended at Athletic Park on a Wednesday afternoon to watch Wellington defend the Ranfurly Shield. The whole nation virtually stopped breathing when McKenzie's team won.

From then until June 1927, Hawkes Bay resisted no fewer than 24 challenges for the trophy. In 1926 McKenzie had on call ten current, or recent, All Blacks. The team's play was dazzling. Wairarapa, first to challenge, were beaten 77–14 as the Bay scored 17 tries. Wanganui conceded 10 tries as they lost 36–3. Wellington, cock-a-hoop because, with Cliff Porter and Mark Nicholls, they had the brainiest players in the game, swooped down like the Assyrians on the Bay fold; and departed, overwhelmed, 58–8. Mighty Auckland, early pass and all, whimpered all the way home after defeat by 41–11. Only in the grace-and-favour gesture of taking the shield 400 miles to Christchurch, for a challenge by Canterbury, was Hawkes Bay seriously troubled. The team scraped home, 17–15, in a match fit for the gods.

On the international front, it was a time of giant strides, notably as represented by the tours involving another mighty rugby nation, South

Africa, and the well-tested national sides of England, Ireland, Wales and France.

The first tour, in 1921, was by the South African Springboks, captained by Theo Pienaar. Having won all four of their preliminary matches in Australia, the visitors built up a formidable record, in New Zealand, of 15 wins, two draws and two defeats. The All Blacks won the first test 13–5, the Springboks the second 9–5. The third, played in the most abominable conditions, in streaming rain and with much of the field covered by sheets of water, ended in a scoreless draw.

In 1924–5, the Second All Blacks, as they were known, won all 30 matches played in England, Ireland, Wales and France, scoring 721 points and conceding 112. Such was their superiority that they were called 'The Invincibles'. A 19-year-old Maori boy, George Nepia, after being shang-haied in a couple of trials into appearing at fullback, a position he had never played, became the heroic figure of the tour by playing in every match, a unique feat in the history of all major rugby tours.

On the third tour, in 1928, another All Black team, captained by one of the greatest of forwards, Maurice Brownlie, visited South Africa. After the triumphs of 1924, the results of the tour deeply shocked New Zealanders. Of 22 matches played, five were lost and another drawn. The four-match international series was squared, the Springboks winning the first and third tests, the All Blacks the second and fourth.

Perhaps the dice were loaded against Brownlie and his men before they left home. Old hands, classifiable as experts, were united in their paean of praise: 'This is the greatest team ever to leave New Zealand.' Not quite the kiss of death, but a close-run thing.

In another sense – as far as concerned rugby relationships between Australia and New Zealand – the giant strides were interspersed by the pitter-patter of tiny feet. Billy Wallace, a revered figure during and after his playing days, was adamant that close links with Australia were vital to New Zealand rugby. In 1920, 1922, 1924, 1925 and 1926, New Zealand teams visited New South Wales, the only Australian state still faithful to the game. Hospitality was reciprocated in 1921, 1923, 1925 and 1928. In the course of such tours, the two unions engaged in test matches, which were regarded as true internationals. One match, at Auckland's Eden Park in 1925, became celebrated as the greatest exhibition ever given by an All Black team on a home field. Play was dazzling, as might have been predicted. Thirteen of the New Zealanders had been in the Invincibles. New South Wales were defeated by 36 points to 10 – six goals and two tries to two goals.

Years later, the rugby unions of the two countries jointly decided to remove these fixtures from the international list, thus depriving many fine players of the ultimate honour of an international cap. The decision was all the more infuriating because the four Home Unions and France had awarded caps to their players for the matches in 1927–8 against the Waratahs – New South Wales.

Old-time Kiwis still feel a hot flush as they recall the All Black tour of Australia in 1929. Australia, restored at last to true international status, won three of the four matches, the other being drawn. At the Sydney Cricket Ground, the Wallabies, lustily cheered by a handsome gate of 40,000, got home by a point, 9–8. Kiwi spectators were understandably bewildered when sections of the crowd persisted in raising the chant of 'Porter, you bastard!'. Cliff Porter, the All Blacks' captain, had been cut to pieces by the Sydney press for his activities at wing-forward in a previous match, but because of injury was on this occasion not even on the field.

Next time out, at Brisbane, the Wallabies did a more thorough job, winning 17–9; and in the final test, back at the Cricket Ground, Australia skimmed home 15–13. Yet even the most chauvinistic Aussie in the 29,000 crowd had to acknowledge that Porter was by far the finest player in the game.

A clean-out? By the Wallabies? Impossible! There were some excuses. Porter had been kept out of the first test, and injury to Bill Dalley, by far the best of New Zealand's scrumhalves of the time, had forced him to miss all three of the lost matches. Moreover, the last of the Invincibles were disappearing, Nepia, for example, playing only the first half of the initial test. But although New Zealanders blushed at the results, they overlooked the indisputable fact that Australian backs such as Syd Malcolm and Tom Lawton at halfback, Cyril Towers in the centres, and Alex Ross at fullback then ranked among the most outstanding players in world rugby: not to mention back row forwards Wylie Breckenridge and Len Palfreyman, and front men Eddie Bonis and Bill Cerutti.

Cerutti was both a supreme comedian and a very tough cookie indeed. As an 18-year-old in the New South Wales' team which toured New Zealand in 1928, he had been urged by his team-mates to 'bop' a ferocious Aucklander named 'Bubs' Knight at the earliest opportunity. Cerutti obeyed instructions and spent most of the match at full gallop, always a few yards beyond Knight's grasp. In the first of the 'non-tests', the two met again. Cerutti pursued the same tactics but in the meantime Knight had evidently sharpened his sprint. Early on, he grabbed the Aussie. 'What are we going to do, Cerutti?' he demanded, menacingly. 'Play football?' 'Yes, Mr Knight,' replied the youngster, meekly. Upon the instant, the two men became blood brothers for life.

★　★　★

Eight years earlier, Pienaar's Springboks had attracted huge crowds on and off the playing field. In one sense, they were welcomed as comrades in arms. New Zealand, with its own wonderful war record of service in the Dardanelles, on the Western Front and in Palestine, was gratified that no fewer than 23 of the 29 South Africans had also fought for King and Country. The squad travelled the country mainly by train; and unfailingly, at every stopping-point, even the tiniest hamlet, Kiwis turned out to gape at the visitors, not least at 'Baby' Michau and Royal Morkel, both well over 6 ft and weighing more than 17 stone.

The tour came alight in the second game of the 19-match itinerary, when Taranaki, a farming province, played a scoreless draw at Pukehara Park, set in a bowl formed by three steep terraces. Roger Young, an old Taranaki hand, described the game many years later: 'With no score, you might suppose the play to have been dull, just another forward struggle. In fact, it was wonderful. Both teams constantly attacked. The running was fierce, the tackling fiercer. You left the ground hugging yourself, trying not to lose the shivers of excitement you had felt through every minute of play.'

Four matches later, the Springboks were beaten. The Canterbury forwards averaged 12 stone 12 pounds per man, the visitors 14 stone 9 pounds, a discrepancy offset by the kindly intervention of Mother Nature. Rain fell until noon and Lancaster Park was thus soft, heavy and treacherous. With the muddy conditions on their side, the Canterbury players hurried and harried the 'Boks, even forcing Gerhard Morkel, legendary 'Prince of Fullbacks', into unhappy mishandlings. Early on, Colin Deans, younger brother of the man who scored the try that was not a try against Wales in 1905, punted crossfield to David Wilson on the wing, who beat two men to score. Then, as the Springbok backline attacked, Strauss, in the centres, checked, wheeled and, with a lovely drop goal, put his team one point ahead before the half-time break. Within three minutes of the restart, Morkel was hustled by Deans into misfielding and miskicking a slithering ball. It pitched into the arms of 'Jockey' Ford, who sped round three men to score. At 6–4, it was a famous victory.

Interest naturally focused on the three internationals. Springbok Tokkie Scholz summed up the atmosphere of the first match in the series at Dunedin on 13 August when he remarked that 'both teams, for the first 25 minutes, were too scared to open up the play'. The first break came to the Springboks when the ball was passed to the 1920 Olympic Games sprinter, Attie van Heerden, who slashed the defence at blinding speed to score by an upright. Morkel placed the goal and it was 5-nil to South Africa at half-time.

It was time for the All Blacks to summon up the blood. Although it had rained on previous days, Carisbrook's pitch was reasonable, conditions overhead were fine, and there was little excuse for Morkel to drop back behind his goal-line to await, on the bounce, a punt-ahead from Ces Badeley at second five-eighths. The ball skewed. Henry Morkel and Meyer, of the threequarters, went for it, the latter vehemently claiming that he had touched it down for a drop-out 25. But 'Moke' Belliss, running hard, dived at the ball and referee Ted McKenzie (older brother of Norman and, some twenty years later, *sole* New Zealand selector) awarded a try. Mark Nicholls goaled from next to the sticks.

When Badeley thoughtfully punted crossfield, Jack Steel made a sensational catch above his head, worked hard to keep control of it while rounding Henry Morkel and raced 50 yards for a try which Nicholls again goaled. And New Zealand were not yet done. Percy Storey, a wing in both the Army team in South Africa and for the All Blacks in 1920, finished off a fine move with a try in the corner to make it 13–5. Dunedin, which is Gaelic for

Edinburgh, danced the Highland fling, the eightsome reel and all manner of Caledonian celebrations through the night and for some time thereafter.

It testifies to the death-or-glory attitude of the New Zealanders in defence that seldom, during the entire tour, did the South Africans overwhelm the opposition. They narrowly beat Manawatu and Waikato, neither ranked among first class teams, 3–0 and 6–0 respectively. Nevertheless, it was apparent that the second test, at Auckland, would be desperate going.

The All Black selectors, Alf Griffiths, George Nicholson (of the 1905 team) and D.M. Stuart, had caused astonishment by naming the inexperienced George Aitken – later to play for Scotland in the glorious Grand Slam year of 1924–5 – as captain of the first test. 'Ginger' Nicholls, halfback, had been awarded a gold medal for his performance in that match; whereupon he was dropped for the second test. Two changes in the forward pack also seemed strange, although one of them, Les McLean for the flank, was several years later to be chosen (by other selectors!) as New Zealand's fullback.

Everything to do with the match made hot news. The All Blacks holed up in the Auckland's Royal Hotel six days before the game, and in no time it was being rumoured that the 'Old Digs', or war veterans, were not the only players who enjoyed one pint, and then another, and then another. Word passed that the Springboks were snapping at one another over performances at Carisbrook. The players chose their own team, and by popular selection, six men, including the fleet-footed van Heerden, were dumped.

Conditions at Eden Park, before a 40,000 crowd, were glorious, ideal for the South Africans. Spurred by Henry Morkel, the Springbok forwards soon began to roll. Van Rooyen, a lock of 15 stone or more, cleft the defence. Meyer at flyhalf took his pass, sent the ball on immediately to Clarkson in the centres; and Sendin, on the wing, naturally made use of the wide-open field to rush to a try which Gerhard Morkel goaled.

Eden Park gave tongue. For the All Blacks, brilliant little Teddy Roberts, gathering a loose ball, ducked and dodged until he was almost at the tryline. Belliss appeared fairly to catch the pass, and on the instant was down, heavily tackled. McLean, supporting, claimed the loose ball; and Albert Neilson, a referee of stern and set opinions, awarded a try. The Springboks vigorously disputed the decision on the fine point that a tackled ball could only be brought into play with the foot. The referee marched out to the spot from which Mark Nicholls was about to attempt the goal. As the ball sailed over the crossbar, Neilson's signal demonstrated that the scores were even.

Pulses raced when the Springboks' Zeller, a magnificent wing, raced down the touchline. Belliss stopped him and Teddy Roberts had a go at a dropkick. So near, so far. Mark Nicholls claimed a fair catch and tried for goal. The ball swerved past the upright. The Springboks charged, so fiercely that that Steel's saving kick sent the ball dead. A 5-yard scrum. South Africa heeled. Somehow, the New Zealand forwards broke on to the ball and began to dribble it upfield. One booted too hard. Gerhard Morkel, out by the touchline, made the catch. He was 35, perhaps 40, yards from the goal. He took a step or two and let fly with a dropkick. The ball soared and soared. Neilson's signal in effect ended the game, 9–5 to South Africa. A great international was crowned by the presentation of a gold medal to Gerhard Morkel by the Auckland rugby administrators – for the kick that had beaten New Zealand! Life was different in those simple days.

Regrettably, an affair of grave and lasting importance was to dissipate the genial sportsmanship of the Auckland crowd. Travelling on, the Springboks defeated a combined Hawkes Bay-Poverty Bay team 14–8 at Napier. Four days later, on the same field, they beat New Zealand Maoris 9–8 in a match which reeked of ill humour and foul play. The spectators, moreover, protested hysterically against the referee, the touch-judge and the Springboks in general. Insensitive Afrikaners in the team deliberately turned their backs upon a group of Maori girls who were performing a *poi* dance of welcome (the *poi* is a ball of dried flax on a cord, dexterously twisted by the dancers). Chester and McMillan, the New Zealand historians, say in their book, *The Visitors*, that members of the Maori team, observing this discourtesy, were 'seething with anger as we waited for the kick-off'.

The two hookers of the Maori side, Mitai and Korakiko, packed in the scrums with their heads together, so forming a wedge which unbalanced the South African pack. The play built up to two unsavoury climaxes. Jack Blake, a Maori centre, claimed a fair catch from a kick in front of the Springbok goal and from which he could easily have goaled. Jack Peake, the Canterbury referee, disallowed the claim on the unexceptional ground that the ball had cannoned into Blake's arms from the shoulder of a Maori player – and the mob howled for Peake's blood. They screamed the louder when, amid furious disputation by the Maoris, the Springboks claimed the ball and sent it on to Zeller, who crashed down the touchline. By stupendous effort, Blake reached him. Zeller heaved the ball infield. A favourable bounce presented it to Townsend, who skipped over for a try. Many who said they were within yards of the incident swore that Zeller's foot was in touch as he threw the ball infield. An Aucklander of considerable later renown as a sporting journalist, 'Ponty' Jones, was touch-judge. Because his flag remained down, the mob declared war on him as well!

Townsend's try placed the Springboks six points clear, 9–3. Almost at once, a Maori rush was topped off by Garlick, a forward, and Tureia converted the try. This set going a host of 'ifs'. If Blake had been awarded his fair catch and goaled, and if Townsend had been denied his try, and if Blacket and Tureia between them had scored, why then the Maoris would have won the match 11–6. If . . .

Within 24 hours, all these demonstrations and controversies had been surpassed by a scandal – a scandal which is unlikely ever to die. According to the more reliable of two reports, the telegraphist at the Napier Post Office who filed to Cape Town the match report of the South African correspondent, C.W.F. Blackett, was excited and appalled by the message. Excited because he, of all New Zealanders, was the only person to know of it; appalled, because of the contents. The man could not keep the firebrand to himself. He typed several copies. One soon turned up at a nearby billiards saloon where a *Napier Daily Telegraph* reporter, name never disclosed, was playing. He looked, he reflected, he sped. Within little more than an hour, the story was rolling from the newspaper's presses.

Some story. In relevant passages, Blackett had cabled: 'Most unfortunate match ever played. . . . Bad enough having (Springboks) play officially designated New Zealand natives; but spectacle thousands Europeans frantically cheering on band of coloured men to defeat members of own race was too much for Springboks, who frankly disgusted. That was not the worst. The crowd was most unsportsmanlike experienced on tour, especially section who lost all control of their feelings.

'On many occasions,' continued Blackett, 'Africans were hurt. Crowd without waiting for possibility of immediate recovery shouted "Take him off! Take him off!" . . . Maoris flung their weight about regardless of niceties of game.'

This incendiary stuff ignited every journalist, every politician, every civic leader worth his appointment. The South African manager, H.C. Bennett, who never contradicted the remark he was reported to have made to J.M. Brown, of the Hawkes Bay Rugby Union, that 'the Maoris did not come up to the Zulus. There was no comparison between them,' publicly stated that Blackett had 'expressed regret for his action. The cable had been written in the heat of the moment.' Blackett immediately hit back. He was 'astonished' that Bennett 'thought fit so abjectly to apologize'.

A sub-editor of the *Daily Telegraph*, Trevor Geddis, later the paper's chairman of directors, denied years later that there had been a Post Office leak. He maintained he had been handed a copy of the story from a politician who had received it directly from Blackett with the words: 'I have forwarded this message. You can publish it locally if you like.' The irresistible implication is that Blackett was no simpleton; he could have sold the story anywhere in New Zealand without trouble. Despite Geddis's denial of a leak, the department's enquiry resulted in the dismissal of one telegraphist, never reinstated, and three other officials, who were.

Little more need be said of the final test except that the whimsical All Black selectors changed six or seven of their team, that it rained and rained, and that there was no score in the match. Van Heerden appeared not to touch down when Keith Siddells, an All Black newcomer, was hurling himself at the ball in the Springbok in-goal. Jack Steel was heading for a try when he slipped, understandably in those conditions. Mark Nicholls at centre had the Springbok defence beaten with Steel, unmarked, outside him; but, unwilling to share the glory, cut back infield. Referee Albert Neilson, though he became increasingly crusty with each passing year, later described the match as a wonderful, surging, thrilling struggle by men of limitless pride and courage.

All told, the Springboks conceded only 13 tries in their 19 matches. For this they were much abused by their own countrymen, who were in turn slated by Theo Pienaar, a captain too old to play in the tests. 'Go out there yourselves,' he bellowed at his critics, 'and fight a New Zealand team on its own soil. A team that is filled with the consciousness of its own prowess and flushed with great achievements of the past. And if you do not eat humble pie on your return, well – I shall!'

★　★　★

While New Zealand opinion still holds the 1924 All Blacks to be sacrosanct, *sans peur et sans reproche*, there was disagreement on other fronts. When Cyril Brownlie was sent off by referee Albert Freethy in the last match of the tour, against England at Twickenham, the British press descended like vultures on a carcass. 'Brownlie gave backchat,' remarked one critic. 'That settled it. The referee pointed to the pavilion.' Brownlie himself, interviewed by the *Sunday Express*, said: 'It was a piece of sheer ill-luck on my part. I found myself involved in a series of minor altercations and was unfortunate to be dropped upon as the second man in the affair. . . . I do think another man should have gone off the field besides myself.' England's captain, Wavell Wakefield, was quoted: 'Brownlie has only himself to blame. He was cautioned twice or thrice for swinging his arms and legs about, persistently playing the man instead of the ball. We won't stand that behaviour from any team. It is not football.'

Wakefield added: 'It was clear the referee had put his finger on the trouble. Afterwards, there was not a single incident. The game was beautifully clean, hard, fast and enjoyable.' Compare this, however, with the voice of 'The Thunderer', none other than *The Times*: '. . . Even after Brownlie's departure, the match was marred by instances of foul play. Throughout, there was far too much unnecessary roughness.' This last comment could draw attention to the fact that the English pack of the time, led by Ronald Cove-Smith, already had a reputation for foul and unfair play.

Two final observations on the affair. One came from Maurice Brownlie in a subsequent comment to a Poverty Bay referee, Ken Waite: 'The best referee I ever played under was Albert Freethy. He was quite right about Cyril. Cyril did punch Tom Voyce, though this was after Voyce had belted him.' The other was delivered by Voyce himself to a band of Kiwis supporting the All Blacks' tour of the British Isles in the 1960s. 'I have only one regret about my rugby career,' Voyce said. 'When Cyril walked, I should have walked with him.'

By the time of the Twickenham match, the All Blacks were well on the way to their extraordinary record of winning all 28 games of the tour. On the way they had played two remarkable matches, against Oxford University, beaten 33–15, and Cambridge University, 5–0. To the end of their days, the All Blacks judged the Oxford game as the most strenuous and difficult of the tour. Phil Macpherson, George Aitken, 'Johnny' Wallace and 'Pup' Raymond, on the field for Oxford, were four brilliant international backs of remarkable speed and sleight-of-hand; and A.C. Valentine, an American Rhodes Scholar, in the Oxford pack, had captained the United States team which had won the rugby tournament of the 1924

Olympic Games in Paris. With 15 minutes to play, the All Blacks led by no more than four points, but then poured on the pressure to outpace and even outwit the gallant university men.

The All Blacks scrambled to beat Ireland, in driving rain, 6–0, eliciting a typically off-beat conclusion from one Dublin reporter: 'The All Blacks have a rover. He doesn't wear a collar and they don't pay tax on him. Once a bouncing ball nearly knocked out a burly All Black. "That's news," shouted a friend behind me. I looked enquiringly. "When a dog bites a man, that's nothing. When a man bites a dog, that's news. So, too, when a man biffs a ball, that's nothing; but when a ball biffs a man . . ." An enthusiast near me babbled about clever bridge-work. The more I see of rugby, the more I am convinced it must have been invented by dentists and bridge-work mechanics for the good of their kind. The only mouth that has no teeth to lose in the game is the goalmouth.'

One man who remained unimpressed after the Invincibles had defeated Cardiff 16–8 was Rhys Gabe, the great international who had brought off the controversial tackle of Bob Deans back in 1905: 'One had been led to expect,' he wrote, 'thrilling moments in which the ball was passed along the threequarters, ending with the wing racing for the line. There was not a single movement of this sort. Shades of the 1905 All Black team! They are not in the same street as Gallaher's team. In some respects, they compare very favourably. In speed, in physique and physical fitness; and in kicking, they are quite as good. But in the thing that matters, "football brains" – well, one must contrast and not compare them.'

Dr W.G. Williams, a committee-man of the Cardiff club, supported Gabe. 'The present New Zealand team,' he said, 'is not the equal of that of 1905. Wales can beat them next Saturday.' It was not to be. The All Blacks were wound up not only to play better but to avenge that famous defeat. They beat Wales 19–0. In his *Illustrated History of Welsh Rugby*, J.B.G. Thomas wrote: 'Wales fielded an ill-assorted side and so poor was the form, skill and confidence of the national team that any group of fifteen Welsh players would have stood no chance against one of the most efficient teams to leave New Zealand. . . . The Welsh experiment of two five-eighths was a disaster. One of them, the captain, Jack Wetter, of Newport, suffered an injury and played with the forwards in the second half.'

So to England and high drama. Said the *Sydney Sun*: 'The All Blacks introduced a new war-cry: "We are about to slaughter you!" A wag in the grandstand retorted with the Latin quotation: "We who are about to die salute you!" '

Back to *The Times* on the match, won 17–11 by the All Blacks: 'Thus on the historic field of Twickenham where England has but once before tasted defeat, the All Blacks repeated the overseas victory of the 1913 Springboks; and in a manner more convincing; for it was only by a couple of penalty goals that the South Africans marred the otherwise unbroken roll of English victories.' Col. Philip Trevor, in the *Daily Telegraph*, was perceptive in his praise: 'A great side has just brought to a close a wonderful tour and established a great record which has the one essential feature of being a real record. It cannot be beaten. . . . Nepia stands alone among modern full-backs. His pluck is equal to his play, and that is saying a great deal. Nicholls is the brains of the side and Cooke has no rival. . . . I should imagine that Maurice Brownlie is quite the best forward in the world. . . . What are the essentials they have taught us? Chiefly, I think, the value, the combined value, of pace and inter-understanding. Obviously, initial pace is of infinitely more consequence than subsequent pace. "Do it at once" is the essential motto of modern rugby football and these New Zealanders are very much moderns. . . .'

Col. Trevor had a final nasty word for the alickadoos of the Rugby Football Union. 'Some of our rugby supercargo, and some that has long rotted in the hold must be jettisoned. It was after a very extensive tour of the Dominions that the Prince of Wales came home and said: "Wake up, England!" We must get on – or get out.'

★ ★ ★

Professionals had plenty to say about the inaugural tour of South Africa by Maurice Brownlie's All Blacks in 1928. Only two who attended the major matches, including the internationals, were New Zealanders: Syd Nicholls, elder brother of then vice-captain Mark, and Graham Beamish of the *Auckland Star*, whose work serviced all the national dailies. Yet it was an amateur who, in a few words, conveyed a deeper understanding than countless other commentators of the problems of that tour and the reasons for the 'failure' of the All Blacks to prove themselves 'the greatest team ever to leave New Zealand'. His spoken remarks, too, which were never publicized, warranted serious consideration and study.

Early in the 1970s, Bill Dalley, second-string scrumhalf of the 1924 All Blacks and first string of the 1928 side, underwent surgery which compelled a long convalescence. He filled in time by writing memoirs of his career. He had a sharp eye, he wrote simply, and well. At the farewell party of the 1924 team, he observed that after the manager, Stanley Dean, had gratefully received a tantalus from the team, Cliff Porter, the captain, all but broke down when presented with a rose-bowl. Although Dalley did not say so, the explanation for Porter's unaccustomed emotion only emerged years later when, caught on the hop by a young reporter, Porter admitted that as long as Dean held a position in New Zealand rugby, he would never allow himself to be closely associated with the game. Porter's detestation of Dean had been evident from the start of the tour when he warned the manager publicly to mind the administrative side and leave the rugby to him. Porter contended that Dean – an expert conniver – had reserved the captaincy in the internationals for Jock Richardson, leaving Porter only the French match as solace. Most of the players, nonetheless, were loyal to Porter, and the gift expressed their admiration and affection.

Bill Dalley played at scrumhalf in the first test in South Africa, at Kingsmead in Durban, which the Springboks won 17–0. 'This was a very hard game,' Dalley wrote later, in his reminiscences, 'and the might of the Springbok forwards was too good for our pack. Ninety per cent of the game was played on our 25, and we were beaten in the scrums and lineouts. Bennie Osler, the 'Boks' flyhalf, hardly sent his backs away in one passing rush. He either kicked for touch or had pots at goal. He succeeded in potting two goals and two penalty goals – 14 points out of the 17 scored by his team. We did not score at all. Before we left New Zealand, we were playing the kick-into-touch rule which stated that the ball could only be kicked out on the full from inside one's own 25. This encouraged our forwards to play too loosely. We were also playing the 2–3–2 scrum. Our forward play had to be improved.'

A shock as of an earthquake measuring 8.0 on the Richter Scale passed through New Zealand at news of the humiliation. As the tour marched through one difficulty after another – defeat in the second test, a beating by Transvaal, loss of the second halfback, Frank Kilby, with a broken leg, further defeat in the third test – it became evident that a cabal of the Nicholls brothers and Beamish had been formed, and that the tone of the official reports consistently favoured Mark in particular.

The tour committee comprised W.F. Hornig, one of the least effective managers of any All Black team (a searing condemnation, given that the standard has all too often been deficient), Brownlie, Nicholls and two members of the 1924 team, Neil McGregor, a five-eighths, and Ron Stewart, a magnificent loose-forward. Not without cause, Mark Nicholls considered that there was bias against him because of bad blood from the 1924 tour, when he had compelled McGregor to play at first five-eighths. By one means or another, and to the total astonishment of South African observers, Nicholls contrived to keep out of the first three internationals – and the reports home made little of these strange goings-on.

There were other problems. Hornig's ineptness was grimly demonstrated during a formal dinner at Pretoria when, responding to a toast, he joked: 'Actually, the last time I was in this place, we were scrapping against you blokes.' The remark fell like a stone.

The sole surviving member of the tour, Jim Burrows, a loose- or front-row forward who was never capped, said in 1990: 'Brownlie was not a good captain. He was a cold, hard man. He was distant from, and had neither interest in, nor sympathy with, the rank-and-file. I have to admit that, having Hornig as manager, Brownlie had to do too much. Yet his lack of compassion affected the quality and tenor of the team.' Burrows, who went on to a distinguished career in the Army and as headmaster of one of New Zealand's great schools, Waitake Boys High, was not a man to utter a harsh word against his colleagues. His assessment of Brownlie was thus startling, if not damning.

After the initial setbacks in South Africa, the All Blacks went into seclusion, behind locked doors, at the Wanderers ground in Johannesburg. There they practised, in secrecy, an innovation designed to stem the superiority of the Springbok forwards by modifying the standard All Black 2–3–2 scrummage formation. Whether or not Mark Nicholls himself came up with the idea (and it may have originated from someone writing to the team), it was he who recognized the merit of the proposal. The plan was that Stewart, just before the ball was put into the scrummage, would join the New Zealand front row, positioning himself on the loose-head side, or that side where the ball was being put in. This nullified the enormous power and high technical skill of the Springboks' props, Phil Mostert, the team captain, and 'Boy' Louw.

Of the second test, played at Ellis Park in Johannesburg, Graham Beamish wrote: 'In the second half, the Springbok forwards were smitten, hip and thigh. The All Blacks took command to display craft, pace and precision. This surprised the most fervent New Zealand supporters and sent them into ecstasies of joy.' Mostert dropkicked a goal from a mark, Osler placed a penalty and David Lindsay goaled for New Zealand. With 15 minutes to play, the Springboks led 6–3. Then Archie Strang, playing second five-eighths or inside centre outside Dalley and Lance Johnson, dropkicked a superb goal for a thrilling All Black victory, 7–6.

Five minutes after kick-off in the third test at Port Elizabeth, Syd Carleton, a midfield back of indifferent skills, threw to David Lindsay, chosen as a centre but an authentic hero of the tour at fullback, so sloppy a pass that the ball bounced into the All Blacks' in-goal. Philip Nel flopped on it and Osler goaled. The All Blacks responded to this shattering blow with magnificent work by two men at the lineout, Ian Finlayson, who made the break, and Stewart, who capitalized on it. Lindsay's goalkick bounced the wrong way from an upright. Play was rugged. Manus de Jongh retired for attention to a broken nose and, returning, scored a try from a movement in which Jack van Druten, Osler, Rousseau and Van der Westhuizen had all handled. For once, Bennie bungled a kick at goal. Powerful Bert Grenside then galloped to the goal-line for an All Black try. At half-time it was 8–6 to South Africa.

As the two teams continued to charge at each other like Light Brigade cavalrymen, George Daneel crowned a Springbok rush with a try. Osler failed to convert when the ball rebounded from a post across the bar. On the call of time, the All Blacks launched the finest attack of the match from their goal-line. Herbie Lilburne, so short in the leg that he seemed to be scuttling, Bill Hazlett, brawny as a buffalo, and 'Tuna' Swain, a slippery hooker (*tuna* is an eel in Maori), gave Grenside a clear go at the corner-flag and the try that might have tied the match. As the crowd rose to its feet, screaming, Grenside then committed the unforgivable. He looked back. Gerry Brand, racing from somewhere in midfield, profiting from the momentary hesitation, crashed the All Black into touch. 'I would say,' commented Jim Burrows, 62 years later, 'that Bert, at best, was a farmer winger.'

Mark Nicholls shrewdly withheld himself from the last match but one, against mighty Western Province, which the All Blacks lost. But Nicholls was there as the teams lined out for the final test at Newlands, in Cape Town. And the rain fell, and fell. It is still remembered as 'The Umbrella Test'.

Nicholls is immortalized as the man who won the match by placing two penalty goals and dropkicking a goal, thus scoring 10 of New Zealand's 13 points (Swain scored a try); and the Springboks, in the heavy conditions, could manage no more than a Van der Westhuizen try, goaled by Osler. Yet perhaps that cold, hard man, Maurice Brownlie, deserves equal credit. On the Sunday morning after the defeat by Western Province, Brownlie assembled his team. 'These are the rules for this week,' he announced. 'You will not vary them in *any* particular. You will go to bed at a reasonable hour. You will get up at a reasonable hour. Each day, you will each take a decent walk. For the rest, you can do what you like. Under *no* circumstances whatever will any of you touch a rugby ball throughout the week.'

In the dressing-room before the kick-off, Brownlie said: 'We have had a great deal of bad publicity in New Zealand. If we do not win this test match, we might as well not go home.'

Osler put the ball into play. His kick was caught by 'Rube' McWilliams, a great flanker. Instantly, he flung the ball far across to Fred Lucas, his clubmate from Ponsonby, in Auckland. Like snorting racehorses released from the curb, the All Blacks charged into the Springbok quarter. Within little more than two minutes, V.H. Neser, the celebrated South African referee whom the New Zealanders had demanded for every test, awarded the All Blacks a penalty. Nicholls made his mark. He placed the goal.

With Brownlie in the lead, displaying superhuman energy, Stewart nullifying Mostert, Kruger and Louw in the scrummaging, and Dalley revelling in command of the heavy, greasy ball, Nicholls kept on kicking goals. Prior to this crucial game, the All Blacks, exhausted by long train journeys, including an expedition to Rhodesia, the heat of the winter, the thin air of the high veldt and, not least, the power, pride and physical strength of their South African opponents, had been a stale, weary band of men. Now at last – thanks to the week's total rest from rugby, Brownlie's uncompromising 'We might as well not go home', and McWilliams's inspired, javelin-like heave of the ball – everything had come together for New Zealand.

Bill Dalley, a conservative man, said then, and insisted for the rest of his life: 'The 1928 All Blacks were a better team than the Invincibles.'

An arresting thought, worth pondering in the years ahead.

CHAPTER SIX

MEN OF DESTINY
1930-49

New Zealand rugby teams were involved in four major tours between 1930 and 1949. They played host to the British Lions in 1930, visited the British Isles in 1935–6, and received the Springboks again in 1937. After the Second World War, in 1949, the All Blacks made another visit to South Africa. On all these occasions, fortunes were swayed – and fates sealed – by the decisions and actions of the managers concerned, coincidentally representing the teams that were travelling abroad. In 1930 James Baxter's autocratic attitude and biased selections failed to make the most of the Lions' obvious talents; moreover, Baxter's criticism of the home side's tactics led to a radical alteration in the rugby laws, greatly to New Zealand's disadvantage. Vincent Meredith's equally arrogant and autocratic behaviour had much to do with the All Blacks' defeat, four years later, by England at Twickenham. In the pre-war Springbok tour, Percy Day was manager in name only; the fact that the tour was run by five powerful team members set the South Africans well on course for victory in the tests. And the post-war tour of South Africa by the All Blacks was so beset with controversy and ill-feeling among selectors, managers and players that it led to possibly the most crushing New Zealand humiliation of all.

In 1930, the British Lions were beset by problems from the start. Douglas Prentice, the captain, was past his best playing days. Carl Aarvold, who operated as field captain in many important matches, developed high talent as a shadow-tackler but seldom exploited his exceptional pace and swerve. And despite the presence of George Beamish, the great Irish lock, the British lineout play was indifferent. Worst of all, Baxter played favourites. In-form or specially gifted players were so often overlooked that, under the presidency of a Cumberland prop, the genial Sam Martindale, a so-called 'Rank and File Society' was formed during the tour. Except for Beamish and the brilliant Welsh flanker, Ivor Jones, its membership was confined to those who failed to win caps in the international matches.

More than a generation later, Roy Jennings, a staunch R & F man, twice organized team reunions at Twickenham prior to internationals. Aarvold, now a knight, a judge and president of the All England Lawn Tennis & Croquet Club, was prevented, either because of previous or subsequent engagements, from attending, but watched the second party, a wow by any standards and televised by the BBC, through the dining-room window. When he later complained bitterly to the flyhalf genius of the 1930 tour, Roger Spong, that he had not been invited, Spong remarked, without particular warmth, 'You mean you would have come, Carl, if you had known TV was to be there?'

From the beginning of the tour, there were curious goings-on. In the opening match, Wilf Sobey, the Lions' scrumhalf, received such a heavy blow on the knee that he was out for the rest of the tour. (Had ice been applied immediately and the man rushed to hospital, he would almost certainly have missed only a couple of matches.) Early in the same game, Gordon Bonner, the fullback, was taken from the field with a gashed eyebrow. This was patched up. He could see. He could move. Yet, despite the loss of Sobey, he refused to return to the game. In the 21 tour matches, he was played only five times; though perfectly fit, he was dropped for 12 consecutive games.

It was at the dinner following the second match against Taranaki that Baxter proclaimed openly that the wing-forward, or rover, of the New Zealand team formation, was a cheat. Such was his influence, as a former international player and referee, that in 1932 the International Rugby Football Board revised its Laws of Rugby to compel three men to pack in the front row of the scrum – and the rover disappeared.

Baxter, thereafter, remained more discreet in public, although he might well have criticized the play of Cliff Porter in the Wellington match, the fifth of the tour, in which the Lions were beaten. Confronted by Roger Spong, a bouncy ball of a man with sensationally quick reactions, who could break inside or out, and was an attacking flyhalf of highest quality, Porter, pinching a yard here and a couple of yards there, set about his opponent mercilessly. In the first test, too, he continued his constructive-obstructive tactics against Spong, who was not intimidated. Plainly, though, he regarded Porter's play as unsporting. Many Kiwis thought the same.

Despite everything, the Lions won the first test at Carisbrook, 6–3, with a last-minute try, run the length of the field, which demonstrated the team's pace and potentialities. In the first half their tall English wing, Jimmy Reeve, outpaced George Hart to score in the corner. After an excellent move begun by Jimmy Mill from behind the scrum and a brilliant threatening thrust by Bert Cooke, Charlie Oliver squirmed from Reeve's grasp and squared the contest. George Nepia's attempt at goal struck a post and bounced the wrong way.

With a minute of the game to go, the score still 3–3, the All Blacks were on the attack, scrummaging almost on the Lions' goal-line. They heeled. Mill passed, or aimed to pass, to his flyhalf, Herbie Lilburne. Breaking at speed, Ivor Jones intercepted and pelted past Nepia, stationed near half-way. He passed to Jack Morley, the Newport sprinter on the left wing. Cooke, somewhere out in midfield, hurtled on the angle, closing fast, but Morley scored. It was schoolboy stuff, of the highest quality, and certainly one of the greatest tries to be scored in a home international.

Just before half-time of the second test, played at Lancaster Park, Christchurch, New Zealand were leading 8–5 when Paul Murray, the Irish scrumhalf, dislocated his shoulder. He was not to play again on the tour. It was a crushing blow which demonstrated the fatal flaw in Baxter's management of the team. After Sobey had been so seriously injured in the opening match, a replacement ought immediately to have been sought. Arthur Young, who had played on the winning side in 12 of his 18 internationals for England, was at an Army posting in India and easily available. It would have been a proper courtesy for New Zealand to pay Young's passage but when the replacement proposal was broached, the chairman of the New Zealand Rugby Union, S.S. Dean, declined to pay any share of the travelling cost, later relented by offering half, and finally agreed to pay the whole amount. Baxter, an equally difficult, obstinate man, turned him down. Indeed, he would have been justified in demanding that New Zealand cover the entire expense, in default bringing the tour to an end.

With both Murray and Sobey gone, the Lions struggled along with a Welshman, W.C. Powell, who was decidedly substandard. Even so, having lost the second test, 13–10, playing for more than half the game with Ivor Jones at scrumhalf, they made a great game of the third, at Eden Park, before losing 15–10. A new man in the All Black pack, Hugh McLean, later to become one of the two founders of the New Zealand Barbarians club, scored two tries, one from a charge-down of a clearing kick by the topnotch Welsh fullback, Jack Bassett. The third was engineered by the genius of Mark Nicholls who, nipping into flyhalf at a scrummage close to touch, about 25 yards from the goal-line, immediately transmitted the clearing pass from Mervyn Corner into a long punt that flew across the goalmouth and was caught by the speeding Fred Lucas on the left wing. The kick, the catch, the wisp of a sidestep and the try represented consummate artistry.

After this, the Lions, practically speaking, lost interest. They were overpowered in the final test at Athletic Park, 22–8, five tries to one. The tour ended on a sour note. During the formal dinner which followed the match, there was an astonishing outburst from the chairman of the All Black selection committee, Ted McKenzie. Carl Aarvold had paid graceful tribute to the All Blacks, and McKenzie and Cliff Porter had been invited to reply. McKenzie alleged that Baxter, early in the tour, had described the New Zealand captain and wing-forward as the 'wolf of rugby'. For his part, he considered that the British offended the canons by their obstructive play and their proclivity for 'shepherding'. 'I do not go so far,' said McKenzie, 'as to say that this is intentional. At the same time, some of it appears to be part of a deliberate and studied system. There is also a considerable amount of tackling the man without the ball and of catching hold of the jerseys of opponents not in possession.'

At one stage of the speech, following a particularly cutting remark, Aarvold had murmured his dissent, whereupon McKenzie turned towards him and said, 'I am speaking, Mr Aarvold, not you.'

★ ★ ★

Charles Bathurst, Lord Bledisloe, Governor-General of New Zealand during the early 1930s, familiarly known to newspaper proprietors and editors as 'Cheerful Charlie', because of his criticisms over their standards of reporting, was a very wealthy man. His purchase and gift to the nation of the Treaty House, where the Treaty of Waitangi had been signed on 6 February 1840, and the grounds lapped by the waters of the Bay of Islands, was a generous gesture. The noble lord was less fortunate in his decision to award a silver cup, bearing his name, for rugby competition between Australia and New Zealand. The cup is huge, embarrassingly ornate and very heavy. With the passing years, officials of both national unions must often have wished that it were consigned to the bottom of Cook Strait or the Tasman Sea.

Frank Kilby captained one All Black side which won the cup in Australia, in 1932, three matches to one, but he was less fortunate there in 1934, when the Wallabies, with a win and a draw, won it back. Even so, he was by far the most experienced and best captain in the country; and with the tour of the British Isles coming up in 1935, and Scotland at last restored to the fixture list, he was regarded as a certainty for the appointment.

Manager Vincent Meredith thought otherwise. He wanted a captain who could be trained as 'His Master's Voice'. The choice fell upon a Canterbury flanker, Jack Manchester, a man of integrity, earnestness and somewhat simple values, nicknamed 'Lugger'. A more serious selection error was the omission of a powerful Maori wing, Charlie Smith, in favour of an Aucklander, Henry Brown, a comparative lightweight who was only played seven times in the 28 games of the tour. Brown maintained, to the end of his days, that the weakness of the New Zealand forwards was responsible for the match record, in Britain, of 24 games won, three lost (including two internationals) and one drawn, with the All Blacks scoring 431 points against 180 to opponents.

This might, in part, have been true. At Meredith's whim, the All Blacks opened their tour against Devon and Cornwall by packing 3–4, with Hugh McLean, a natural flanker, acting either as a rover or extra halfback. In the second half of the match, as New Zealand ran away with the game 35–6, McLean packed on the back for a 3–4–1 formation. Long afterwards, McLean observed: 'We soon learned that in the UK, all our forwards had to stick their noses as close as possible to the ground and just PUSH!' After this opening win, the All Blacks only twice more topped 30 points, against Abertillery and Cross Keys (31–6) and, late in the tour, against Welsh Mid-Districts at Aberdare (31–10).

'Lugger' Manchester displayed his sterling qualities in the fifth match of the tour, against Swansea. At one point, as the home team surged into the lead, he exclaimed: 'Men, we can't lose this match. We're *New Zealand!*' To which Arty Lambourn retorted: 'Have a look at the bloody scoreboard, "Skip." That'll soon tell you!' Swansea went on to beat the tourists 11–3. Perhaps the real winner, though, was one of the great Swansea characters, Cliff Prosser, who had fought to persuade a local headmaster to allow two of his teenagers, Hayden Tanner, scrumhalf, and Willie Davies, flyhalf, to play. Howard Marshall, of the *Daily Telegraph*, wrote: 'How well the wiry Tanner played, slipping away on his own – where, by the way, was the New Zealand backrow defence? – giving beautiful passes to Davies and kicking with judgement and precision. The 19-year-old Davies has surely a touch of genius, that instinctive eye for the opening which marks the perfectly balanced, running with changes of pace and direction sufficient to carry him through the smallest gap like an elusive ghost.'

Marshall, with prescience of things to come, continued: 'Then there was Claude Davey in the centre, racing up to tackle like a battering ram, shaking the New Zealand backs out of their stride, setting Swansea an example which caused them to nip the rare All Black attacks in the bud.'

New Zealand won the first two internationals, beating Scotland at Murrayfield, 18–9, and Ireland at Lansdowne Road (after a 3–3 draw with Ulster), 17–9. Then came the grim final stages of the tour – the internationals against Wales and England.

At Cardiff Arms Park, the New Zealand pack dominated the first-half scrummages by a remarkable 18 to 6, and scored just before half-time, through Nelson Ball, to lead 3–0. But from the second half kick-off, the All Blacks were awash. Cliff Jones, a strong candidate for the title of the most brilliant flyhalf in history, cut through and, beautifully poised, punted to the goalmouth. Claude Davey picked up the try and Vivian Jenkins goaled. Four minutes later, Wilfred Wooller sliced through from centre and lobbed his punt over the head of Mike Gilbert. Wooller impetuously overran the ball, but Rees-Jones, backing up, claimed it for the try, and Jenkins again converted.

The All Blacks responded with promising moves spoiled by errors. Gilbert (that rock of steadiness who had placed the goal from the sideline and the mud to beat Oxford 10–9) caught a looped kick 35 yards out and deliberately banged home a superb goal. Gilbert skewed another drop and, mysteriously, neither Claude Davey nor Rees-Jones could decide who should gather the ball. Nelson Ball dribbled it, crossed the line and scored; Gilbert's conversion placed New Zealand ahead, 12–10. Wales were shaken, all the more when Tarr was carried off with a serious spine injury. Then Idwal Rees made a half-break, good enough for a clear pass to Wooller. The big man hoisted an enormous punt to the All Blacks' goal-line. At which precise moment, Claude Davey, with an illegal tackle, thoughtfully removed Charlie Oliver from the defensive line, so leaving the field clear for Rees-Jones to dot down.

It was a glorious game, rated among the finest ever played by Wales. As the great English referee, Cyril Gadney, signalled no-side, Cardiff Arms Park was engulfed by a horde of screaming, exultant Welshman – and who could blame them? And, with a notable touch of grace, 'Lugger' Manchester fought his way through the mob to shake Gadney by the hand. 'Thank you, Ref.,' he said. 'It was a wonderful game.'

By now it had become commonplace for New Zealanders to jeer at their team. Dressing up, by order, in dinner jackets for formal occasions, was bad enough. But what about the beating they had taken, earlier on, from a couple of schoolboys? Well, Tanner ranks among the immortal scrum-halves, and Davies, that shy villager who took to rugby league and 'went north', was unlucky that Cliff Jones, Cambridge and all that, held greater appeal for the Welsh selectors.

By omitting three of his finest backs, Joey Sadler, scrumhalf, Jack Griffiths, flyhalf, and George Hart, wing, because they had stayed too long at a New Year's Eve party 48 hours or so before the kick-off, Meredith signed and sealed the death of the All Blacks at Twickenham, where they were beaten 13–0 by an English team captained by Douglas Kendrew, who at the age of 19 had been on the Baxter tour of 1930, and graced by a White Russian prince named Alexander Obolensky, who scored two tries in the first half. The opening try was straightforward, around Gilbert, the second a stupendous exhibition of the hypotenuse in rugby. When Candler, at flyhalf, fielded a ball close to the right-hand touch, Obolensky sizzled infield to take the pass and head for the distant left-hand corner. Once again he rounded Gilbert and evaded Mitchell, the left wing who was covering across from the right. In the second half, Bernard Gadney, brother of Cyril, a towering figure at scrumhalf, sent the backline away, and when Cranmer on the left wing was checked, he sidestepped and dropped a superb goal. Finally, with the All Black defence in tatters, left wing Sever ran 35 yards for a try, putting the finishing touch to a shattering All Black defeat.

Four words uttered by Philip Nel, early on in the final test, spelled the epitaph for the All Black team which lost the three-test series against the 1937 Springboks. Although Percy Day was nominally the manager of the touring side, selection and strategy were virtually dictated by five team members, Philip Nel, captain, Danie Craven, vice-captain, 'Boy' Louw, prop-forward, Louis Strachan, flank-forward, and Gerry Brand, fullback.

The All Blacks made a promising start in the first match at Athletic Park. Although playing for more than half the game with 14 men – Doug Cobden having left the field after being hoisted sky-high by Chris Jennings and dumped – the All Blacks won 13–7. Flyhalf Dave Trevathan, a slow mover, was nevertheless adept at goalkicks; his two penalties and a drop goal, plus a try by John Dick on the right wing, shocked the Springboks. Or most of them, anyway. They had been singing and skylarking in the dressing-room and as the teams took the field, Craven, taking over from Nel as captain, predicted the 'Boks would lose. Craven himself, slow and cumbersome at flyhalf, was partially to blame for the defeat; the threequarters were scarcely in the play.

There was no singing as the Springboks changed for the second test at Lancaster Park; and stern words were spoken, in Afrikaans, after Jack Sullivan, the New Zealand centre, brilliantly intercepting a pass by Louis Babrow, ran in one try, and scored a second after another cut-off, a punt and kicks-ahead, racing the powerful wing, Dai Williams, to the line. Starting the second half 6–0 down, South African class then began to tell. Their new boy at flyhalf, Tony Harris, showed superlative understanding with Craven; and in a backline move the ball was passed out to Freddie Turner on the left wing. Turner, fast and powerful, evaded Dick, fullback Jack Taylor and scrumhalf Harry Simon, and with a magnificent cut-in headed into the wide-open of midfield to score a try which Gerry Brand goaled.

As the forward packs wrestled for control, the All Black flanker, Jack Rankin, who weighed no more than 13 stone, was struck by 'Boy' Louw and fell as if pole-axed. His team colleagues retaliated by hitting out at Louw, knocking him to the ground, partly concussed. After the fracas, Gerry Brand placed a penalty goal. The power of the Springbok scrummage became more menacing. Strachan broke clear and, on the run, cross-checked and passed, intending to find his partner, Babrow. Instead, Ebbo Bastard, the flanker, instinctively grabbed the ball and plunged across the goal-line. Brand placed the conversion for a 13–6 Springbok victory.

The cost, in human terms, proved tragic. Rankin never recovered from the blow, suffering from memory lapses and other problems for the rest of his life. It was not until some 40 years later that he cornered Louw in Cape Town and asked him what had provoked the attack. Louw, not by nature a communicator, eventually replied: 'Craven spoke to me. He said you were being a damned nuisance to him. He said, "Do something about it." I had to do what "Doc" ordered.'

Later in the tour, when the Springboks played Hawkes Bay, which fielded All Black Doug Dalton in the front row and the very powerful 'Snow' Bowman, who became an All Black lock in the following year, Louw was deliberately set upon at every available play, but was too cunning and experienced to be targeted. Louw is still revered in South Africa as one of the great prop-forwards, but it is sad that he inflicted a life injury on an opponent in what was supposed to be a sporting affair.

The strength of the South African pack was demonstrated when the team played Otago, the provincial champions of the year. The Springboks were merciless, winning 47–7. Then, in the opening minutes of the third and final test at Eden Park, as New Zealand punted the ball into touch, Nel made the pronouncement which 'killed' the All Blacks: 'We'll scrum, New Zealand.' As one scrum followed another, the lighter All Blacks were smashed. Ron King, a gallant captain, did everything possible by example to rally his men, but the result was seldom in doubt.

New Zealand's problems were compounded from the beginning by selection decisions which still buzz about the ears of Jim Burrows, the last surviving selector. Although it was plain, from the first test, that the Simon-Trevathan combination was dangerously slow, and that a young

South Canterbury halfback, Charlie Saxton, and a King Country school-teacher, Clive Crossman, would have been faster and more dangerous, the committee could not be persuaded. Had not Trevathan, after all, won that first match? The decision to play Nelson 'Brushy' Mitchell at centre proved even greater folly. After displaying extraordinary brilliance earlier in the season, he had been severely crocked. Because he had not played for some weeks, the selectors, as a precaution, fielded him in a match just prior to the final test. He appeared to weather the experience successfully, but within minutes of the kick-off in the test, the old injury returned and he no longer played an effective role. He went to his grave still exclaiming: 'Never play an unfit man in a test.'

Grasping at straws, the selectors placed Harcourt 'Pat' Caughey, an elegant and stylish back of the English style, at wing. As an executive of a long-established Auckland departmental store, having spent time for the company in the United States, Caughey had played little rugby in the previous weeks and the odds were against him reaching first-class level. In the event, he and Sullivan, who had been chosen for the wing when his ideal position was second five-eighths, turned out to be the only reliable men of the New Zealand line.

From 15-stone 'Boy' Louw at prop to Ferdie Bergh, 17 stone 4 pounds, at number 8, the Springbok forwards were huge. Oddly enough, Nel, a charming individual well remembered for the try he had scored in the 1928 series, was the slowest man in the pack; yet the pack was never so efficient, so coordinated, so aware, as when he played. Nel's partner, Mauritz van den Bergh, was a magnificent thrusting lock in the incessant scrummages. Bergh, packing in between the two, simply had to lean forward and the entire scrum did the same.

The Springboks had been downcast at news that their powerful centre, Jimmy White, one of the *great* tacklers, had to cry off with injury. Reluctantly, because no chances could be taken, they agreed to White's recommendation that 'Floppie' Lochner, a mere 23-year-old, should substitute. Taking the ball on the break, the newcomer burst between Jack Hooper and Mitchell, the All Black centres, before he passed to Babrow, who scored ten yards from the corner-flag. Soon afterwards, on the break, Babrow kicked to the right, to the goal-line, and from the mass of Springbok supporting forwards, Bergh got the try, which Brand goaled.

Joe King, the referee, was often unhappy about the Springbok scrummaging methods, especially the Craven put-in which carried the ball clean through the tunnel. At yet another penalty, Trevathan obliged. It was 8–3 at half-time. The 55,000 Kiwi spectators were hardly clapping their hands with glee; and they were less happy within a few minutes when, at Craven's signal, Harris took station even farther into midfield. Trevathan naturally posted out there, too, leaving a gap wider than the proverbial church-door, into which Turner flashed from the blindside as he took a short pass from Craven. As he was checked, Turner lobbed the ball to Lochner who, jumping, catching and passing in one movement, sent Babrow over for another try near the corner. Then it was Babrow again who ran nearly into the arms of Taylor before passing to Strachan, and wide to Turner, who almost strolled down the touchline to his try. Just six minutes from the end Trevathan dropped another goal. Final score 17–6.

An hour or so later, two of the Invincibles, Bill Irvine and Ces Badeley, were still standing as if carved in stone. 'It's not possible,' they muttered mournfully, 'for an All Black team to concede five tries and itself fail to score. It does not, it CANNOT happen.' 'Boys,' said a friend, 'you have just seen it happen.' The two former All Blacks slumped away.

The Springboks, it has to be recorded, scored 87 tries, no fewer than 50 from the threequarter line. Years later, one bright Kiwi deeply immersed in rugby ventured an answer to the question – 'The greatest team ever to leave New Zealand?' 'The 1937 Springboks, of course,' was his unhesitating opinion.

★ ★ ★

Another devastating world war came and went; and in 1949 the All Blacks prepared for a tour of South Africa, the most fateful in New Zealand rugby history. It began under bad auspices, with unfortunate repercussions over the appointment of manager and coach. One of the national selectors, Alex McDonald, a 1905 immortal, was recommended by the chairman of the New Zealand Rugby Union, A. St C. 'Slip' Belcher, for the post of manager. McDonald immediately – and secretly – urged Otago's great coach Victor G. Cavanagh ('Young Vic') to take on the same job for the national side. Cavanagh delightedly accepted.

During these goings-on, another member of the Rugby Council, Jim Parker, the Canterbury man who had supplanted Cliff Porter as wing-forward in the three vital internationals of the Invincibles' tour, happened to be abroad. On his return, he was outraged and dismayed to learn that Belcher had offered McDonald the managership of the tour. Parker had set his heart on the job and announced he would regard his non-appointment as a breach, by Belcher, of their Masonic brotherhood. Belcher, pleasant but ineffectual, dithered, and resolved the issue by persuading the council to appoint Parker as manager and McDonald as coach. Cavanagh voiced his objection, although not as strongly as was rumoured at the time. When, a few months after the disastrous tour, the New Zealand Council made selection appointments for the 1950 season, the animus against Cavanagh was so bitter that he failed to win one of the three seats of the South Island committee, a minor position. It was a calculated insult which cost New Zealand rugby Cavanagh's services for almost ten years and turned him into a dangerous opponent, a well-informed critic who, as general manager of an influential newspaper, did not hesitate to speak, and write, his mind.

The team to tour South Africa had to be chosen during the 1948 season because of shipping schedules. Reflecting over the terrible punishment exacted by Nel's team of 1937, the All Black selectors – Norman McKenzie, Alex McDonald and Harold Strang, all men in their sixties – concluded that the winning factor for the 'Boks had been the weight of their

THE ILLUSTRATED LONDON NEWS

REGISTERED AT THE GENERAL POST-OFFICE FOR TRANSMISSION ABROAD.

No. 2582.—VOL. XCIII.   SATURDAY, OCTOBER 13, 1888.   WITH EXTRA SUPPLEMENT   SIXPENCE. By Post, 6½d.

THE MAORI FOOTBALL TEAM: FIRST MATCH AT RICHMOND, OCT. 3—AGAINST THE SURREY CLUB.

The New Zealand 'Native Team' took the field for their first match in England at Richmond on 3 October 1888. The British were not quite sure what to make of such Maori traditions as the war dance, as this page of the *Illustrated London News* demonstrates.

Billy Wallace so well served the original All Blacks of 1905 that his record of 224 points on a tour has never been bettered. At the end of his career fellow-Wellingtonians presented him with 400 sovereigns which were sufficient to set up a foundry business that kept him going for life.

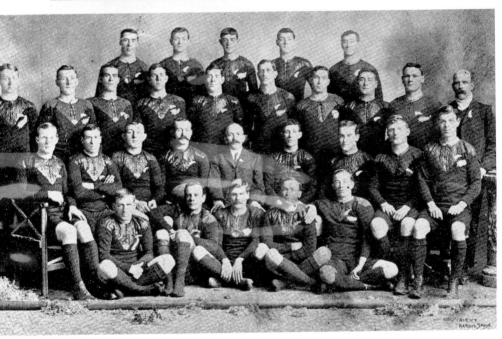

The All Blacks have arrived! The 1905 'Originals' who toured Britain are: *back row left to right:* G. Gillett, S. Casey, D. McGregor, A. McDonald, F. Roberts. *Second row left to right:* E.T. Harper, J. O'Sullivan, C. Seeling. R.G. Deans, W. Johnstone, G.W. Nicholson, J. Corbett, W. Cunningham, F. Newton, J. Duncan (coach). *Third row left to right:* H.L. Abbott, W.J. Wallace, G.A. Tyler, D. Gallaher (captain), G.H. Dixon (manager), J.W. Stead (vice-captain), W. Mackrell, F. Glasgow, W.S. Glenn. *Front row left to right:* J. Hunter, H.J. Mynott, G.W. Smith, E.E. Booth, H.D. Thomson.

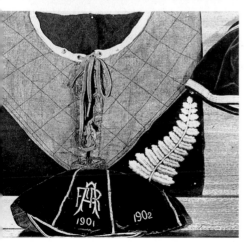

Top: Middlesex's forwards played the 'first up, first down' principle and were completely swamped by the scientific packing of the 1905 All Blacks who routed the county 34-0. They used the 2-3-2 formation invented by Maori Tom Ellison, which completely flummoxed the Middlesex forwards (*above*).

Left: George Nicholson, the tallest of the 1905 All Blacks, always treasured his jersey and his Auckland representative cap.

Left: George Nicholson played in the 1904 international against Britain and was naturally chosen for the great team of 1905.

The 1914 All Blacks are one of the forgotten teams of New Zealand rugby, but at least three players have stalls in Valhalla. 'Ranji' Wilson (third from the right, second row), of English-West Indian stock, was a forward of ferocious physical strength and supreme battle-cunning. Dick Roberts (third from the left, front row), was in mid-career and superb. Teddy Roberts (extreme left, front row) is a strong candidate for the distinction of being New Zealand's finest scrumhalf.

Above: David Gallaher, captain of the 1905 All Blacks, was never too proud to hold the ball while his fullback, George Gillett, was attempting a shot at goal. *Below:* George Nepia had never played fullback when chosen as such for the 1924 All Blacks. He was only nineteen and played so well in the tour that he was an immortal of Kiwi sport before he reached his majority.

Above: Mark Nicholls, the 'captain of the backs', was invaluable to the unbeaten 1924 All Blacks.

The 1924 All Blacks who won all thirty matches in their tour of England, Ireland, Wales and France. (For various pernickety reasons Scotland refused to play them!)

The Welshmen's vigorous tactics on St Helen's field at Swansea in 1924 did them no good whatsoever. The All Blacks scientifically avenged the only loss of the 1905 tour by winning 19-0.

In shame and mortification Cyril Brownlie becomes the first international player ever to be ordered off the field for rough play. Welsh referee Albert Freethy took this drastic action eight minutes into the 1925 international against England at Twickenham.

One of the most famous of all New Zealand's rugby-playing families. From left to right: Cyril, Maurice and Laurence Brownlie. Maurice was arguably New Zealand's greatest forward and captained the 1928 All Blacks.

Dalley
Table 8
All Blacks

Farewell Luncheon given by the Sportsmen of the Motherland

Edward P

Abdicated the Throne

To

THE NEW ZEALAND RUGBY XV.
THE "ALL BLACKS" 1924-25

The Right Hon. The Lord Desborough. K.C.V.O.
In the Chair.

THE PICCADILLY HOTEL
JAN 21st 1925

British sportsmen organised a farewell luncheon for the 1924 All Blacks at London's famous Savoy Hotel. All Black scrumhalf Billy Dalley was immensely proud when the guest of honour, the Prince of Wales, signed his menu.

LIST OF TABLES with Names of

Table A.

THE LORD DESBOROUGH, K.C.V.O. (*Vice-President, British Olympic Association, and President, Lawn Tennis Association*).

In the Chair

MR. C. G. PORTER (*Captain, "All Blacks"*).

H.R.H. THE PRINCE OF WALES, K.G., K.T (*Hunting, Squash Rackets, and Golf*).

THE HON. SIR JAMES ALLEN, K.C.B. (*High Commissioner for New Zealand*).

GENERAL SIR IAN HAMILTON, G.C.B G.C.M.G., K.C.B., D.S.O..

THE VISCOUNT BURNHAM, C.B.E. (*Vice-President, British Olympic Association*).

GENERAL SIR WILLIAM BIRDWOOD, G.C.B. K.C.M.G. (*Commander of the Australian and New Zealand Corps, France*).

GENERAL SIR ALEXANDER GODLEY, K.C.B. K.C.M.G. (*Hunting and Polo*).

THE EARL CADOGAN, C.B.E. (*Chairman British Olympic Council*).

THE REV. R. S. DE COURCY LAFFAN (*British Olympic Association*).

THE LORD RIDDELL (*Vice-President, British Olympic Association*).

THE VISCOUNT CAMPDEN, O.B.E. (*Vice-President, British Olympic Association*).

THE LORD ASHFIELD.

MAJ. GENERAL RT. HON. J. B. SEELY, C.B. C.M.G., P.C.

COLONEL CLIVE WIGRAM, C.B., C.V.O.

MR. J. RICHARDSON, (*Vice-Captain, "All Blacks"*).

BRIG.-GENERAL R. J. KENTISH, C.M.G. D.S.O. (*British Olympic Association*).

VICE - ADMIRAL SIR LIONEL HALSEY G.C.V.O., K.C.M.G. (*Shooting, Fishing Golf*).

THE EARL OF LONSDALE (*Hunting and Racing*).

THE RT. HON. L. S. AMERY, P.C., M.P. (*H.M. Secretary of State for the Colonies*).

MR. S. S. DEAN (*Manager, "All Blacks"*).

Table B.

WING-COMMANDER LOUIS GREIG, C.V.O. (*Scottish Rugby International*).

MR. MAURICE J. BROWNLIE (*The "All Blacks"*).

MR. T. D. S. FRANCIS (*English Rugby International*).

MR. C. F. O. BADELEY (*The "All Blacks"*).

MR. J. MILL (*The "All Blacks"*).

MR. R. D. HAMILTON-WICKES (*English Rugby International*).

MR. B. V. McCLEARY (*The "All Blacks"*).

MR. W. C. DALLEY (*The "All Blacks"*).

MR. I. H. HARVEY (*The "All Blacks"*).

MR. M. F. NICHOLLS (*The "All Blacks"*).

Table C.

MR. HARRY PRESTON (*Boxing*).

MR. J. STEEL (*The "All Blacks"*).

MR. A. C. C. ROBILLIARD (*The "All Blacks"*).

LT.-COMMANDER CECIL KERSHAW (*English Rugby International*).

MR. A. H. WEST (*The "All Blacks"*).

MR. R. T. STEWART (*The "All Blacks"*).

CAPT. G. CRAWSHAY (*President, London Welsh Rugby F.C.*).

MR. A. WHITE (*The "All Blacks"*).

COMMANDER W. J. A. DAVIES (*English Rugby International*).

MR. K. S. SVENSON (*The "All Blacks"*).

MR. J. H. PARKER (*The "All Blacks"*).

MR. L. F. CUPPLES (*The "All Blacks"*).

Wines

Château La Flora Blanche
Étampé

Château Pontet Canet
1917

Port
Dixon's Double Diamond

La Fine Champagne
La Bénédictine D.O.M.

Menu

Les Hors d'Œuvre à la Porter
Le Saumon fumé

-

Le Consommé Richardson en tasse

-

La Timbale de sole à la Nicholls

-

Le Poulet de printemps Wakefield
Les Haricots verts nouveaux de Nepia
La Salade Cooke

-

La Vasque de poires Brownlie
Les Gourmandises

-

Café Dean Special

MR. E. RONEY (*British Olympic Team, Yacht*)
SIR ERNEST RONEY (*Yachting*).
SIR HOWARD FRANK, K.C.B.

Toasts

His Majesty The King
Proposed by
The Chairman

-

The Dominion of New Zealand
Proposed by
The Rt. Hon. L. S. Amery, P.C., M.P.
His Majesty's Secretary of State for the Colonies

Responded to by
Colonel The Hon. Sir James Allen, K.C.B.
The High Commissioner for New Zealand

-

The New Zealand Rugby XV
"The All Blacks"
Proposed by
H.R.H. The Prince of Wales, K.G., K.T. *abdicated*

Responded to by
Mr. S. S. Dean (Manager)
Mr. C. G. Porter (Captain)

-

The Chairman
Proposed by
The Rt. Hon. The Earl of Lonsdale

Left: Jack Griffiths was an invaluable member of the backline of the 1935 All Blacks and, a year later, captained New Zealand.

Right: No one was more surprised than Jack 'Lugger' Manchester himself when he was chosen to captain the 1935 All Blacks for their long tour of the British Isles and France. Although dominated by the team's manager, Vince Meredith, Manchester was fondly remembered by his players for his integrity, devotion to duty and love of the game.

Right: Tom Morrison was fast, powerful and determined. He was a first-choice wing threequarter when the 1938 All Blacks toured Australia.

Left: Charlie Saxton was a brilliant scrumhalf who was capped for the 1938 All Blacks and led the triumphant New Zealand army team in their 1945-6 tour of Britain, France and Germany.

The All Blacks scraped to victory 13-10 in the second
test against the touring British Lions in 1930. Here Bert
Cooke is tackling Tony Novis, the brilliant English wing,
who had just received the ball from Roger Spong.

George Beamish, one of the greatest Irish lock-forwards,
is running with the ball in the first test between the
1930 Lions and the All Blacks at Carisbrook.
His pursuers are Jimmy Mill, Bill Irvine and Cliff Porter.

Above: Having won the massive Bledisloe Cup at its first presentation in 1932 these 1934 All Blacks, captained by Frank Kilby, confidently headed across the Tasman only to lose the cup to the gallant Australians (until the next time).

Keith Arnold, star forward of 'The Kiwis' in 1945-6, was
slim and slight but bowed the knee to no man. A
Combined Northern Counties gets the Arnold
'treatment' in a match won by the Kiwis 25-8.

As was the charming custom in those far off days, the
Irish and All Black players pose together before their
international at Lansdowne Road in 1935. The All Blacks
won 17-9.

In this, the blackest day of New Zealand domestic rugby, Pat Caughey is being tackled by Springbok wing, Dai Williams, who is in turn supported by Danie Craven. The final test of the 1937 series went to the Springboks 17-6.

The 1937 Springboks, captained by Philip Nel, who smote New Zealand rugby from one end of the country to the other and beat the All Blacks 2-1 in the test series.

Nelson 'Brushy' Mitchell, famous All Black winger and a
glorious player at best. Although he played in the vital
final test against the Springboks in 1937, he was too unfit
to contribute. He never forgave himself or the selectors.

As opposing wingers in the second test between the
touring British Lions of 1950 and the All Blacks, Bill
Meates of New Zealand and Malcolm Thomas are
wrestling for possession. The All Blacks won the test 8-0.

Facing page, top: Vince Bevan, the game little scrumhalf who the year before was not allowed to tour South Africa because of his Maori blood, is passing the ball in the dramatic first test of the 1950 series, Lions v All Blacks at Carisbrooke. *Above:* At the last gasp, as the Lions look certain to win, All Black centre Ron Elvidge, breaking to his right and using his powerful fend against the wing-forwards Billy McKay and Peter Kininmonth, heads for the try which draws the game 9-all.

Facing page, bottom: Peter Johnstone, a tough backrow forward, and Bleddyn Williams, one of the legendary players of Welsh rugby, lead out their teams for the final test of the 1950 Lions' tour at Eden Park. Roy Roper, 'Tiny' White and Peter Kininmonth follow. The All Blacks won 11-8.

19

20

Left: Daan Retief, the glorious Springbok flanker, scores the first of South Africa's two tries in the second test at Athletic Park in 1956. All Blacks Ron Jarden, Pat Vincent and Pat Walsh fail to check him. The scoreline: South Africa 8, New Zealand 3.

Facing page, bottom: Dr Danie Craven classed the third test against the Springboks, played at Lancaster Park in 1956, as the dirtiest game he had ever seen. New Zealanders, watching the All Blacks win 11-5, would not agree. Visible from the left are 'Ponty' Reid, 'Tiny' Hill, Peter Johnstone, Johan Claassen (SA), Kevin Skinner, Chris Koch (SA), Ron Hemi and Bertus van der Merwe (SA).

Below: All Black scrumhalf Kevin Briscoe is gathering the ball from a scrummage in the fourth test against the Springboks at Port Elizabeth in 1960. The Springboks won the test 8-3.

Though once held to a draw, the 1967 All Blacks were unbeaten as they faced the Barbarians in the last match of their tour. Here the legendary Colin Meads is passing to scrumhalf Chris Laidlaw. It was a rousing match which the All Blacks won 11-6.

Left: F.R. Allen was perhaps New Zealand's finest coach, first for Auckland and then for the All Blacks. Such was the intensity of his coaching methods that he was called 'Fred the Needle' by an All Black wit – the name stuck!

Facing page: Tough All Black hooker Bruce McLeod, well supported by Colin Meads, dives unstoppably for a try in the second test at Carisbrooke against the 1965 touring Springboks. New Zealand won the match 13-0 and cleaned up the series 3-1.

Colin Meads is heading, meaningfully, at the French forwards Benoit Dauga, Alain Plantefol, Jean-Pierre Bauz and Jean-Marie Esponda in the second test against the touring French Tricolors in 1968. Meads' captain and great friend, Brian Lochore, is rushing to support. The All Blacks won 9-3.

Below right: Two great forwards, Benoit Dauga (France) and Colin Meads, contest the ball in the same match. The All Blacks cleaned up in the internationals 3-0.

Above: Peter Whiting was one of the finest forwards in the world. He suddenly disappeared from the game, seemingly disillusioned by it.

Left: Bryan Williams, aged nineteen, stirred the world with his incredible brilliance during the 1970 All Black tour of South Africa. Williams, playing left wing, commanded a sidestep the width of a barn door and, in addition, would stop anything.

Below: Scrumhalf Chris Laidlaw fires the ball to his backline in the first test, played at Pretoria, of the 1970 series against the Springboks. To his left the Springbok 'loosies' Jan Ellis and Albie Bates await developments and the All Blacks Ian Kirkpatrick and Sam Strahan are on hand. South Africa won the test 17-6 and the series 3-1.

Ian Kirkpatrick is determination personified as he heads into the heart of the British Lions' defence with All Black prop Bill Bush in support. Lions' flanker Terry Cobner (left) and Ian McGeehan are equally determined to stop him. The Lions won the test 13-9 but lost the 1977 series 1-3.

Sid Going, a superstar at best, is breaking past the 'Boks in the first test of 1976 at King's Park, Durban. As usual in All Black-Springbok test matches, there was a row about the refereeing. Also as usual, the All Blacks lost the series.

All Black prop Kent Lambert is being tackled by Kennedy and Willie John McBride while his fellows, Tane Norton, Peter Whiting and Grahame Whiting, rush to support him. All seemed to be going well for the All Blacks in the 1973 international against Ireland until, very late, Irish right wing Tom Grace made a try for a 10-all draw.

Despite a waterlogged ground covered with lakes, through one of which Bryan Williams is now scoring, the New Zealand Rugby Union insisted that the game be played. The touring Scots conceded four goals in a 24-0 defeat in the one international of their 1975 tour.

28

Above: The great All Black wing, Stuart Wilson, is being stopped by the Springbok fullback Gysie Pienaar in the first test of the infamous 1981 Springbok tour of New Zealand. But the 'Boks couldn't stop the All Blacks this day, the final score being 14-9.

Facing page, above: One of the great All Black captains – perhaps even the finest of all – Graham Mourie is showing the way to do things in this match against Monmouthshire in 1978.

Facing page, bottom: In 1980 New Zealand was offered the ultimate distinction of being chosen to play Wales in their Centenary Match. Under the leadership of Graham Mourie the All Blacks triumphed 23-3 in a glorious match. Here Derek Quinnell (Wales), Frank Oliver, Andy Haden and Gary Seear are in contention.

Powerhouse lock Andy Haden surges past Springbok
defenders in the strife-torn tests of the 1981 Springbok
tour of New Zealand.

The brilliant Maori back, Steven Pokere, slices through
the British Lions' defence in the final test of the 1983
series. The Lions lost the match 6-38 and suffered a
clean-out in all four tests.

All Black prop Steve McDowell is on one of his many
crunching runs against Argentina, supported this time by
hooker Sean Fitzpatrick. The All Blacks won the first test
in Dunedin 60-9 and the second test in Wellington 49-12.

Wayne Shelford is facing up to Welsh flanker David Bryant in the second and final test of the Welsh tour in 1988. The scoreline, New Zealand 54, Wales 9, is used as the basis of horror stories told by Welsh parents to their children.

forwards. Sixteen trials were played before the All Black team was named. At each of them, a set of scales was produced and every forward had his weight accurately recorded. Arthur Hughes, much the finer technician, lost the second-string hooking spot to Norman Wilson because he was 5 pounds the lighter. Bert Taylor, a cheerful and capable Auckland flanker, toyed with the idea of putting slivers of steel into his boots before the weigh-in.

Weight was everything – more than everything because, during that summer, many of the forwards eased up on their training and were grossly overweight as they boarded ship; and some never managed to reduce to true fighting level.

Although he held no official position, Vince Meredith was convinced that a comparatively large man, Bill Conrad, would be an ideal scrumhalf. He had Conrad on display for Fred Allen, the logical choice for captain, on the lawn at Mission Bay, on the Auckland Harbour waterfront. Conrad was chosen, played in no more than nine matches and scored a single try. Despite all the subsequent urging of his team-mates to get out there and die for dear old New Zealand, his contribution, due to some peculiar streak of temperament, was negligible.

After four not entirely convincing wins, the All Blacks were beaten 9–0 by Border, brilliantly captained by Basil Kenyon, possibly the finest and warmest person ever to play international rugby. They were to lose six more games – to Eastern Transvaal, 6–5, to Rhodesia, 10–8, and finally, all four tests against the Springboks. Meanwhile they drew three matches, with Orange Free State, with Rhodesia and, in the return game, with Border. All told, this unfortunate team recorded 14 wins, three draws and seven defeats, with a points aggregate of 230 against 146. They were held to be marvellously skilled in defence, conceding only eight tries, but were equally unskilled in attack, scoring no more than 43 altogether, fewer than two a match. The national sprint champion, Peter Henderson, a tough and wiry wing, scored seven tries, Allen scored six, Morrie Goddard five. The rest trailed along.

There was high comedy on arrival of the team in Cape Town, where last in line for presentation to National Party Leader, Dr D.F. Malan, was the masseur, 'Massa' Johnson. 'Sir,' confided Johnson as he grasped Malan's hand. 'I have a message for you.' Dr Malan's eyebrow lifted. 'Really? From whom?' 'From Sir Ernest Davis, sir – he has been Mayor of our Auckland city.' 'Of course,' replied Malan. 'I know well of Sir Ernest. Pray, tell me his message.' 'Sir Ernest says,' 'Massa' leaned forward excitedly, 'stay within the Empire.' 'Well, thank you, Mr Johnson,' rejoined Dr Malan. 'And please thank Sir Ernest from me.'

The mood did not last long. In the first training session at Hermanus, a seaside resort where the All Blacks stayed prior to beginning the tour, as the players duly trooped on to the field, Fred Allen, the captain, called: 'Right-oh, all backs over this way!' Vice-captain Ray Dalton, a prop-forward, echoed: 'Right-ho, forwards, all over here!' By usurping the coach's role. Allen and Dalton were reflecting the players' disgust that Cavanagh had not been sent on the tour, in an open statement of contempt for the 'old man', 67-year-old McDonald. Allen said, many years later, that McDonald had been ill for much of the tour. Maybe. 'Massa' Johnson also remarked that he had been standing with McDonald at one of the seaports as a liner pulled out. 'I would give anything,' McDonald said, 'to be on that ship, going home.' The tour still had some weeks to run.

In the first test at Newlands, Cape Town, the All Blacks led 11–3 at half-time, their forwards having achieved remarkable domination over the enormous Springbok pack. Then the referee, Eddie Hofmeyr, stepped in. On four fatal occasions in the second half he penalized the All Blacks. Winston McCarthy, in his later report of the tour, judged two of the calls legitimate, two home-town. Each time prop 'Okey' Geffin placed goals with superb precision, a total of five for the game. South Africa 15, New Zealand 11. The Springbok captain, du Plessis, asked for a quote at the end of play, remarked: 'They won't smell us!'

Nor did they. The second test, at Ellis Park in Johannesburg, was 13–3 to South Africa, Ralph Burmeister refereeing in a style not much different from Hofmeyr's. The third test, at Durban, 9–3 to the 'Boks, once more starred Geffin and Hofmeyr. In the final test, at Port Elizabeth, South Africa was at it again, 11–8. Not a peep of complaint this time against Burmeister, who was admirable. Indeed, the only peep came from fullback Jack Scott – in Hennie Muller's opinion, 'the greatest footballer I ever saw, in any position'. Sitting on his bench in the dressing-room, Scott said, 'Sorry, fellers,' and, head in hands, burst into tears. The All Blacks did their best to comfort him. Never a great goalkicker, genius though he was in all other aspects of play, his had been the burden of trying to counter the goals that Geffin had been placing so easily. It was a poignant moment.

Several of the All Blacks, Allen among them, gave up rugby on their return. Their bitterness was fuelled by a dispute between Winston McCarthy, whose book on the tour was a searing indictment of South African refereeing, and Dr Danie Craven, coach of the 'Boks, who wrote no fewer than five newspaper articles in an attempt to demolish McCarthy's criticism. No Kiwi could forgive Craven for his invention of 'Mullerism'. Hennie Muller was an exceptionally fast, strong wing-forward who, at 'Doc's' direction, stood in midfield at the lineouts and from this advantageous position hurled down the All Black midfield backs as they tried to move the ball in passing rushes. 'Often enough,' said Allen, 'Hennie was operating behind the referees, who seemed to be a yard or two ahead of him. Thus they could not see that he was "fringing", illegally. When he hit you, he hit damned hard. Our back play was stifled by this tactic – the Craven ploy.'

Allen's summary, 40 years on, was that the All Blacks were hopelessly handicapped by their halfbacks – Conrad, the non-trier, and Larry Savage, the total trier but, sadly, not above club standard in skill. Had the team been served by Percy Tetzlaff, a sturdy Aucklander who had retired from playing in 1948, Wally Cameron, a tough little Taranaki scrumhalf, or, best of all, Vince Bevan, a Wellingtonian who had played for Allen's 1947 All Blacks in Australia, the series could, in Allen's view, have been shared or probably won. 'It was a tough break for us,' remarked Allen, 'that Bevan was a Maori. The 'Boks are hard enough to beat anyway. When they've got race on their side, they're even harder.'

CHAPTER SEVEN

MERRY MEN AND MOPERS

1950-9

*T*he 1950s saw a stream of home triumphs for the All Blacks against touring teams. The decade began and ended with visits by the British Lions, both high spirited and largely successful tours. In between came sweet revenge against the Springboks in a rather more sour and controversial series.

The 1950 Lions were captained by a 23-year-old Dublin gynaecologist, Karl Mullen, and contained a wealth of characters ranging from an Irish prop, Tommy Clifford, who sang O'Reilly's Daughter' in so broad a brogue that an axe would have been needed to separate the syllables, to Cliff Davies, a Welsh coalminer who, when greeted by the New Zealand Prime Minister, S.G. Holland, with a genial 'Glad to meet you, Cliff', responded with an equally jovial 'Glad to meet you, Sid'.

The 1956 Springboks were coached by the recently elected president of the South African Rugby Board, Dr Danie Craven, vice-captain of the 1937 side. At the first formal gathering of the tour, Craven replied to the welcome of the Lord Mayor of Sydney by declaring, bang-off: 'We have come here to win!'. After the three-one defeat by the All Blacks in the test series, Craven said to Kiwi newspaperman, Wallie Ingram: 'They sacrificed Christ. Now, they have sacrificed me.'

The tour of the British Lions in 1959 ended in yet another convincing test series victory for New Zealand, but the home crowds were vastly entertained by the sterling qualities of the opposition. And the Marx Brothers antics of two Irishmen, Tony O'Reilly and Andrew Mulligan, added off-field spice to the presence of a widely popular side.

The quality of the rugby was often inspired, producing three immortal matches, all of them, coincidentally, at Auckland's Eden Park. In the final test of 1950, the Lions, down 11–3, heeled the ball on their own goal-line. It was whipped into the hands of the 19-year-old Llanelli genius, Lewis Jones, a tour replacement for George Norton, the Irish fullback, who had broken an arm. Jones tricked Tanner with a dummy and, bearing slightly right, raced upfield. At about halfway, under threat, he lobbed the ball over Bob Scott's head to Ken Jones, a member of Britain's 4 × 100 metres relay team in the 1948 Olympic Games. The ensuing contest had the 58,000 spectators screaming. Peter Henderson, a Commonwealth Games sprinter, Bob Scott, emphatically no sprinter, Roy Roper, a dazzling centre, and Bill Meates, from the far wing, gave chase. Jones veered infield, toward the goalposts. He was a few yards from the tryline when Roper despairingly dived, attempting to clip his heels. Roper undershot; and when one Jones scored, under the bar, and the other Jones placed the goal over it, the park was in turmoil.

Not even a true-blue Kiwi would have complained if, a few minutes from no-side, Bleddyn Williams, the great Welsh centre, had succeeded in his desperate charge for the line; but Peter Henderson nailed him. The Lions had narrowly failed to win, but for weeks afterwards the whole town was buzzing with excitement over the Jones boys.

Six years later, the 61,240 spectators at Eden Park – the largest crowd in New Zealand's sporting history – were again roused to ecstasy by the performance of another Jones boy: a professional fisherman from the Far North of New Zealand and hulking number 8 whose full name was Peter Frederick Hilton-Jones, known to his team-mates as 'Kumara' (sweet potato). The occasion was the rubber test between the All Blacks and Craven's Springboks who, although 3–0 down at half-time, through a penalty by Don Clarke, looked an even-money bet to square the series, two games apiece. At a lineout, with 37 minutes to play, 'Popeye' Strydom, at scrumhalf, mishandled his clearance 10 yards inside the South African half. The All Blacks' hooker, Ron Hemi, swooped from the short end of the line to knock the ball down. From the far end, the Jones boy charged. As he gathered the bouncing ball, the goal-line was almost 40 yards distant – and Basie Viviers, the Springbok captain, waited.

As Jones moved slightly left toward the goalposts, Viviers seemed to veer slightly left as well, toward touch. 'Kumara' pounded on; and as he crashed to his try, he yelled and raised his arm in appeal to Bill Fright, the referee. But there was no doubt about the try – in the circumstances, one in a million. Don Clarke placed the goal, and then struck his second penalty to put the result beyond doubt. Roy Dryburgh's try for South Africa, minutes from the end, and the conversion by Viviers were just a formality. The 'Boks had been beaten in a test series. Fred Allen's Forty Niners were avenged. Over the public address system, Danie Craven announced: 'It's all yours, New Zealand. You know how it feels.' The All Blacks were back on top of world rugby.

There was to be another memorable moment. Peter Jones was hauled from the dressing-room, an All Black blazer over his playing gear. Grasping the Radio New Zealand microphone, he spoke to the nation. 'Well, ladies and gentlemen,' he whispered, in his soft tenor, 'I hope never to play in a tougher game. I'm absolutely buggered!'

61

Seldom does a Kiwi sporting crowd, least of all a rugby crowd, turn against its own representatives. Yet early in the fourth and final test of the series, already won by the All Blacks, against the 1959 British Lions, a chant went up from the sunlit terraces at Eden Park, of 'Red! Red!' (the Lions' colour). It was repeated, fortissimo, at what proved to be the most dramatic moment of the game. With half an hour gone in the first half, after Don Clarke had put New Zealand ahead with a penalty, the Lions heeled. O'Reilly, from the blindside, whizzed into the backline, took a pass from Bev Risman at flyhalf and slashed upfield. Outside ran the Scottish waif, Ken Scotland, master of all the talents, who created all manner of confusion before tossing the final pass to Peter Jackson, the wing threequarter, whose furrowed, impassive features earned him the nickname of 'The Commissar'. What Jackson lacked in speed he amply made up for in incredibly skilled weaving and footwork. 'Jacko!' roared the Lion supporters as he swerved and sidestepped his way toward Clarke and the goalline, appearing to slip through the eye of a needle as he dived for his try.

In the second half the Lions scored two more tries to a second Clarke penalty goal, and were leading 9–6 when, with five minutes from no-side, they were penalized and Clarke again came forward for the attempt at goal. His mark was about 15 yards in from the right-hand touch, almost on the 25-yard line. The conversion would tie the score, 9–9. Once more the chant 'Red! Red! Red!' echoed from the terraces. By Clarke standards, the kick was a sitter. He had already placed 39 points during the series.

Perhaps the unpatriotic call unsettled him. Perhaps, secretly, he still agonized over his part in the first test at Carisbrook in Dunedin when, near the end of play, he placed his sixth penalty goal which beat the Lions (four tries) 18–17 – a result which Kiwi journalists labelled a 'day of shame' in New Zealand rugby history. In any event, Clarke's kick slewed across the goalmouth to end a memorable match.

Inevitably, amidst these extraordinary events, New Zealand's matches against other rugby nations made a lesser impact. The Australians were entertained three times, in 1952, 1955 and 1958; and in 1951 and 1957 the visiting Fijians beat New Zealand Maoris three out of three in the Grand Polynesian Championship.

During their first tour, the Fijians listened respectfully to their baggage-master, a tiny, muscular Welshman, 'Taffy' Davies, who related to them the drama in the dressing-room at Eden Park before the Springboks took the field for the final test of 1937. After Philip Nel had summoned his men passionately to die for South Africa, Louis Strachan stood up and vowed: 'They can only win over our dead bodies!'

The Fijian hooker was a little man, Ponipate ('Napoleon') Baba. After one member of the team was hurt, Baba, muttering something to his comrades on the reserves' bench, darted on to the field. In the very next play, he himself was kayoed. As he was carried from the field, his colleagues on the bench rocked and rolled with laughter. The New Zealand liaison officer, Norman McKenzie, appalled at this heartless reaction, remarked crossly: 'I don't see much fun in having a team-mate knocked out of a game.' 'You may, if we tell you,' said the Fijian coach, Pat Raddock, 'that just as Ponipate was taking the field, he called out to us, "They can only win over my dead body!" '

In 1949, while the All Blacks were suffering defeat in South Africa, their second-string team was being beaten in two home tests by a Wallabies' side brilliantly captained by Trevor Allen. The gloom deepened in 1952 and again in 1957 when another superb Wallaby centre, John Solomon, led teams which defeated the All Blacks in individual tests, though not in the series. Yet the second loss, in 1957, at Christchurch, by a score of 6–3, was epochal. It marked the appearance of Wilson Whineray, then just turned 23, as New Zealand captain; and although assured that life would go on, much as before, he chose to interpret the defeat as an absolute disgrace. Had a firing-squad been handy, he would have paraded before it and personally given the rifles the order to blaze.

Whineray's time was to come. Back in 1950 New Zealand rugby was licking its wounds after the South African disaster. Selectors Norman McKenzie, Harold Strang and Alex McDonald had immediately tendered their resignations, and the newcomers, Tom Morrison (convenor-coach), Mervyn Corner and Arthur Marslin, stuck pretty faithfully to Fred Allen's principal players. These were John Simpson and Kevin Skinner in the front row, Jack McNab, Lester Harvey and Pat Crowley in the second, and Peter Johnstone at the back. The scrummage was strengthened with Arthur Hughes at hooker and, particularly, Richard 'Tiny' White at lock, who used his weight and height to rise at lineouts, caught the ball securely and frequently breached the opposing line in a style reminiscent of Maurice Brownlie. Laurie Haig, the Otago flyhalf, may have lacked agility but, being a coalminer, he was exceptionally strong and a calm, calculating tactical kicker. The great find in the backline was the centre, Roy Roper, not least in his ability to burst from a standing start into sprint speed.

By winning the test series, albeit narrowly, against the 1950 Lions, the All Blacks recovered much of the pride they had left strewn over the fields of South Africa. True, they had been lucky to draw the first match, 9–9, at Dunedin. The Lions, having recently lost 23–9 to Otago and 11–0 to Southland, came in as underdogs and showed tremendous character. The immortal Irish flyhalf, Jackie Kyle, whose genius alone was worth the price of admission, scored one try with blinding speed and, with a magically precise punt to the corner, had presented the flying Welsh wing, Ken Jones, with another. With only five minutes to play, the Lions led 9–6. At a 5-yard scrum, Vince Bevan from scrumhalf passed to the powerful centre, Ron Elvidge, bearing right. Elvidge used his effective left hand to fend off Ivor Preece for the try.

In the second test, at Christchurch, Pat Crowley opened the scoring by diving over as the All Black pack pushed back the Lions inch by inch after they had heeled from a scrummage on their own goal-line; and it was

Roper, beginning on the blindside and swinging to the open, who made the match safe for New Zealand with an excellent try, converted by Haig.

The Lions' selection table virtually gifted the third test, at Athletic Park, to the All Blacks. The British team contained no fewer than 14 Welshmen, who ganged up against Karl Mullen in favour of their own hooker, Dai Davies. Mullen, conscious of the discontent, carried out a medical self-examination and pronounced himself unfit to play. (He did the same in the fourth test, and the team's manager, 'Ginger' Osborne, felt he lacked the authority, never having won an international cap, to stop the nonsense.)

The match developed into a tragedy of ineptitude. After 20 minutes, the All Blacks lost their 'iron man', Simpson, with a heavily twisted knee. Seven minutes before half-time, when the Lions led 3–0, Elvidge, on the burst, was tackled with ferocious strength by Jack Matthews, in a head-on charge which virtually ended the All Black captain's career. Elvidge, refusing to go to hospital, bravely returned to the field, placing himself somewhere behind the backline, his arm held painfully across his chest. The All Blacks attacked. Peter Henderson surged into midfield, supported by Peter Johnstone who, receiving the ball, obeyed old instincts and passed, with the goal-line a few yards away, to Elvidge. With an extraordinary display of courage, Elvidge dived through and over the tackle of the Lions' fullback, Billy Cleaver, for the levelling try, creating a position of advantage which the All Blacks exploited, late in the game, when Scott, from 30 yards, placed the winning goal. The series was over, although the fourth test at Eden Park, as already described, set a memorable seal on the proceedings.

Two blunders cost the Lions the game. The first was to believe Mullen when he said, of both the third and final tests, 'I *could* have played.' Had he been more forceful and had the Lions kept him as captain there is little doubt that they would have won the third and possibly the fourth test. The second was the failure of the substitute captain, Bleddyn Williams, to understand that with one forward lost and one back all but totally disabled, the All Blacks could not withstand a running game. Dutifully, the Lions' forwards fought for the ball in lineouts of normal length when, at every chance, it should have been hurled clean over the top. Dutifully, they heeled to Gordon Rimmer who, time after time, was nabbed either by Crowley, or Harvey, or both – probably no two All Black forwards have played better in a single test. For want of sheer tactical common sense, the Lions permitted the All Blacks to score one of their more glorious victories.

The Lions lost five and drew one of the 23 matches on their tour; and they scored 81 tries, a magnificent effort. Not only were they perhaps the most popular team ever to visit New Zealand, they were ranked by Jack Sullivan, the prewar All Black who was later chairman of the New Zealand Rugby Union, as a side of rare accomplishment, superior even to the 1937 Springboks. Although Mullen's packs never approached the forward strength of Nel's forwards, Sullivan was adamant. 'Show me,' he would say, 'backs of finer quality than Kyle, Matthews, Williams or Ken and Lewis Jones; or a better lineout player than Roy John. I would take them, any day, as the best side I have seen tour New Zealand.'

★ ★ ★

By 1953, when selections were being made for the Fourth All Blacks to tour the British Isles and France, all but Bob Scott and Kevin Skinner of the Forty-Niners had disappeared. Scott actually had to be coaxed out of retirement to become available. His selection proved a bonus. The All Blacks were quartered at Eastbourne for a week of training before their first match. Newspapermen gaped in amazement as Scott, with a bare right foot, calmly placed goals from the halfway mark. As a boy growing up in a railway camp in a wild area of North Island, he had learned to bend his right toe almost vertical, and this bare-footed kick was his speciality. 'My one regret,' he admitted, 'was that in test matches I couldn't take off my right boot and have a go with the toe.' Scott's exhibition, well publicized, stirred interest in the team and the tour.

The All Blacks' record of 25 matches, four lost and two drawn, with a points aggregate of 446 (including 90 tries) to 129 conceded, might have been even better had Johnnie Simpson captained the side. The big man would have exercised a more commanding presence with the players than the two managers, Norman Millard, a 67-year-old secondary schoolmaster, and Arthur Marslin, a back-country farmer from Central Otago, who had been an assistant selector in the great days of Cavanagh's Otago Ranfurly Shield teams. Millard had a profound knowledge of rugby, but his humour was heavy and his pronouncements pontifical. Marslin, whose shyness stemmed partly from the fact that he had not won a cap, placed too high an importance on defence as the basis of the game.

Simpson cried off immediately he learned that his wife, Iris, was bearing their first child. Bob Stuart, his replacement, was 32 years old, with a distinguished naval record in the Second World War. He was a hard physical specimen, lacking the speed of an ideal number 8, but magnificent in lineout support and as a tough, driving forward. He, too, placed stress on a defensive approach, and was inevitably caught up in the row that simmered and blazed during the tour, and which resulted in Laurie Haig, essentially a defensively minded flyhalf, being chosen in preference to 20-year-old Guy Bowers, a sturdy, speedy youngster with a penchant for the attacking game. Because the two Kiwi correspondents covering the tour, McLean for the Press Association, and McCarthy for Radio New Zealand, hitched their wagons to the Bowers' star, the public at home were deeply divided on the issue.

The team toppled in Wales, being beaten 8–3 by Cardiff, drawing 6–6 with Swansea and losing to Wales 13–8. The fault was not entirely theirs. Dr Peter Cooper, an Englishman, refereed the Cardiff match in such a state of excitement that he permitted Sid Judd, the Cardiff loose-forward, to sit at the back of the All Blacks' scrum, between the number 8 and the scrumhalf, without penalizing him – the spot was perhaps 15 yards in front of the Cardiff goal. Swansea was one of those dreadful affairs every touring team suffers. The Welsh international, again with Cooper in command, was poised at 8-all until Clem Thomas gathered the ball by the left touch and, after a considerable pause, booted it far across the field. Two fliers, Ken Jones, Wales, and Ron Jarden, New Zealand, converged as the ball hit the turf and rebounded. The bounce was kind for Jones and he scored.

From the start, Rex Willis, Morgan's partner, harried his opposing scrumhalf, Keith Davis, relentlessly; and Ken Jones, charging on to a loose ball, kicked it downfield. Scott trapped it. Three Welshmen trapped Scott. In an agonizing replay of the second test of 1928 when Sid Carleton had passed to a David Lindsey who was not there, Scott passed to a Fitzpatrick who was not there. Sid Judd, however, was; and Gwyn Rowlands placed the goal. Wales 5, New Zealand 0. Fifteen minutes played. Jarden placed a penalty for the All Blacks. Scott booted high into the goalmouth and Bill Clark turned side-on to skip past Welshmen to a try which Jarden converted, giving New Zealand an 8–5 half-time advantage.

After the break the All Blacks' pack were here, there and everywhere. But Clark, trying to extricate himself from a heap of bodies 20 yards from the All Blacks' goalmouth, was adjudged by Peter Cooper to have played the ball on the ground. Rowlands kicked the penalty goal to level the scores.

Then, for New Zealand, came that terrible moment which meant defeat. Rees Stephens headed a Welsh charge. The ball fell loose, lying about a yard from the left touch. The players seemed to stare at it, mesmerized. Eternities came and went. Except in the mind of the touch-judge, Ivor Jones, he who had broken the All Black defensive line in the first test of 1930 and sent Jack Morley hurtling to his magical try. 'Kick it! Kick it!' yelled Ivor. As if in slow motion, Clem Thomas obliged, and kicked the ball crossfield. Everything thereafter occurred at top speed. Ken Jones gathered the bounce, raced for the line, and Rowlands placed the goal.

Even the Welsh crowd admitted that the All Blacks should have won. Although Haig and Brian Fitzpatrick as a midfield combination were too slow and unadventurous, the forwards, brilliantly inspired by Stuart, were in absolute control for at least 25 minutes of the second half. Quality support behind would have sewn up the match. It was not there. When Fitzpatrick charged on the blindside, he was well held, despite his size, by Gerwyn Williams at fullback, with Bleddyn Williams soon lending a hand. Haig had the strength to break past the superlative Cliff Morgan and he knocked over two or three others as well; but each check slowed him down, and the cover gathered.

Ireland were comfortably beaten, 14–3, even though Jarden, against orders, had received a leg injection that morning. Kyle soon saw him hobbling, and the bombardment of the left wing compelled Stuart to detach Des Oliver from the scrum to roam in a defensive role. Bowers, in his first international, weathered the experience pretty well; but he was clearly too flighty for the selectors who reverted to Haig for the England and Scotland matches.

Douglas Wilson, sharpish but not entirely committed, supplanted Fitzpatrick for the Twickenham international; and the one really dangerous midfield back, Jim Fitzgerald, was sadly overlooked. But the All Blacks won 5–0, the only try coming after Hemi broke from a lineout with kicks ahead and lock forward Nelson Dalzell, butting the huge English right wing, Ted Woodward, with his head, scored near the corner. Scott placed the goal. England might later have saved, or won, the match when their powerful left wing, Phil Davies, started a run just beyond his 25. He was *very* fast. Young Peter Jones, first cap, cut across on the slant. Placing his hand on Davies's collar, he stopped him cold.

At the Marine Hotel, North Berwick, the All Blacks listened to Scots bewailing their 44–0 defeat by South Africa three years previously. At every 'Please, please, don't do that to us again!' they grew more suspicious. Obviously the campaign was designed to soften both their hearts and morale. During the game, 'Duggie' Elliot, the Scottish skipper, clearly intended to soften their bodies as well. When Stuart courageously dived at the feet of Elliot and the other Scottish forwards to check a blinding rush, Scott, 10 yards distant, admitted later that he was astonished, as a result of Elliot's solid thrust, not to receive both ball and Stuart in his arms.

Aided though they were by a slushy field, the Scottish pack were the finest encountered in all the internationals. A new cap in the centres, Elgie, might have won the game. He twice kicked, with support to hand, when only Scott barred his way. It was Scott's penalty goal, early in the second half, so low in flight that it almost scraped the crossbar, which won the match for New Zealand. Then, near the end, Haig, himself Scottish born, ran desperately for a try on the blindside, and undoubtedly scored. The Welsh referee, Ivor David, the best of the tour, ruled against it.

A huge crowd gathered at Cardiff Arms Park to enjoy the final match of the tour against the Barbarians. The All Blacks' lineup was Davis, Bowers, Fitzpatrick, Fitzgerald, Jarden and Dixon. Three of the four tries in a splendid 19–5 All Blacks' victory were scored by the backs. Norman McKenzie wept with pleasure when Scott was carried shoulder-high from the field – 'the finest fullback display I have ever seen' – and a tear for 'Tiny' White, Stuart, Fitzgerald, Bowers, the whole bang lot, would have been merited. This was running, attacking rugby, in excelsis: and, at the end, the Welsh raised their voices to the All Blacks in song.

★ ★ ★

Dr Danie Craven's blunt statement that his 1956 Springboks had come to win was borne out by their record in Australia. But although both tests against the Wallabies were won 9–0, they pointed to deficiencies in the team performance that were surprising after the 29–9 defeat of New South Wales in the second match of the tour. Some writers took the view that the failings were more pronounced when the ball was behind rather than in front of the forwards; and Movietone news-clips seemed to confirm that weakness. Craven's worries were compounded by the opening game of the much more important tour of New Zealand, against Waikato.

Dick Everest, the selector coach of the Waikato team, had played in the Waikato-Thames Valley side which narrowly lost, 6–3, to Nel's Springboks of 1937 – the game which restored Gerry Brand as an international, match-winning fullback. The Waikato team spirit was legendary, a quality which at one stage sustained them through several tough challenges for the Ranfurly Shield. At Dunedin, in 1948, he had gazed upon the mighty Otago forward pack and had himself been complimented and encouraged in his methods by the master-coach, Vic Cavanagh.

Having read the reports and studied the film-clips of the 'Boks in Australia, Everest believed that there were shortcomings behind the pack and that the forwards themselves might not be adapted to the New Zealand style of rucking perfected by Cavanagh. He noted, too, that the blindside wing, in defensive situations, often appeared to drift toward the open side behind his scrumhalf.

What to do? The Laws of Rugby required the throw-in to be made from right-angles to touch, but they did not specify or mention the speed at which the ball could or should be thrown. Everest delivered his plans to his team: the throw-in must be low and firm and Waikato had to win the kick-off to start play. It must also win the first ruck which would develop as the opposing forwards, having caught the kick-off, massed to the ball. Jack Bullick would then hoist another towering punt toward the Springbok left-hand corner and Tommy van Vollenhoven, the star sprinter who guarded their left touch. The forwards must again win the ruck; and 'Ponty' Reid from scrumhalf would then use his right wing, Malcolm McDonald.

The plan worked to perfection. As the second Waikato punt headed downward, Johnny Buchler, the Springbok fullback, waited to catch it. He was immediately overwhelmed by the advancing Waikato forwards. The ball came to Reid, thence to McDonald. Not having to deal with van Vollenhoven, who had drifted across, McDonald made sure of his try with a leaping dive.

The more than capacity crowd of 30,000 roared its approval of this first-minute try, the sound echoing over the great basin of the Waikato River. For the next quarter of an hour, McDonald on the right and Grant Carrington on the left hurled in their throws at a height of some 5 feet and at extreme velocity. The Waikato forwards, duly warned, took evasive action, and the Springboks performed startled leaps to avoid decapitation. Most times, the ball bounded behind their lines; and 'Rag-Mop' Nola, Rex Pickering and Johnny Mauger, the loose forwards, hurtled after it.

Springbok morale, already dented, drooped further when, after 19 minutes, Donald Clarke dropkicked a left-foot goal from 40 yards. Eight minutes later, Reid passed to Gordon Brunskill on the blindside and 'Brunny', noting that the 'Boks' right wing, Jan du Preez, had drifted infield, tossed it out to Pickering on the left wing, who scored. Don Clarke goaled. Eight minutes from half-time, he placed another penalty.

Fourteen to nil to Waikato at the break! It had been a staggering exhibition of intelligent team play and powerful forward rushes. Now the Springboks prepared to make effective use of the brisk wind behind them and a team advantage after Bullick had left the field because of an accidentally crushed cheekbone, and Nola had been reduced to walking pace following a lineout clash with 'Butch' Lochner. Jan Pickard, captain for the day, sensibly switched Jimmy Nel to flyhalf in place of 'Peewee' Howe, who had committed unfortunate blunders. Soon after, Nel powerfully burst past Brunskill, and van Vollenhoven's try, although far out, was well converted by Pickard. In the 26th minute, van Vollenhoven broke into midfield and passed to Nel, who with great skill timed a pass which du Preez caught just beyond Don Clarke's reach. Again Pickard goaled the try to make the score 14–10.

'Even then,' said Craven, 'I wasn't worried.' If Buchler, having caught a kick, had appreciated that Nel and du Preez, ten yards ahead, were perfectly placed to outflank the defence for the winning try, Danie, that night, would have been a happy man. But Buchler punted for touch and the South Africans, in their opening game, handed over the springbok head reserved for the first team to beat them.

Indeed, well before the end, the tour had turned into a nightmare for Craven. The Springboks beat North Auckland 3–0 on a gluepot of a pitch and Auckland 6–3 in glorious conditions. There was an appalling moment in the latter game when an Auckland prop, Geoff Perry, was mercilessly booted by Jan Pickard. Newspapers preferred not to name the miscreant, and even a book about the tour sidestepped the issue. But 'Peewee' Howe, one of the few Springboks with a sense of humour, put matters right. Warned that the next game, against Wellington, would be a hard one because Wellington, in 1955, had beaten Auckland 37–11, 'and it was a massacre', more or less chortled: 'That's nothing. We beat Auckland 6–3 – and that was a massacre, too!'

Narrow, unconvincing victories, all of them, and hardly the best of preparations for the first test at Dunedin. On the Wednesday, four days beforehand, the selected players went into total retreat, segregated from their team-mates and harangued by Craven, morning, noon and night. Required to pledge, so it seemed, that each would sacrifice everything, starting with his life, for South Africa, they trooped from the writing-room of Wain's Hotel as if they had been slung from a catapult; and in the peace and quiet of the hotel lounge, they behaved as if released from servitude. There were, so their attitude implied, superior joys in life to playing test rugby.

With hindsight, it seems certain that the Springboks would have won if the 30 players who awaited kick-off had been spared injury. Six All Blacks were laid out at various stages of the game and Mark Irwin had to go off at half time. For the Springboks, du Preez and Dawie Ackermann were both stretchered off, the former gallantly staying on until a kick which saved his side from serious difficulty smashed his right fibula.

The first onslaught of the Springboks was staggering. Manifestly, the New Zealand selectors had been at fault to choose 21-year-old Irwin at tight-head prop. The combined power of the South African scrummage was directed at him – and what a scrum: Jaap Becker, Bertus van der Merwe, Newton Walker in the front row, Salty du Rand and Johann Claassen in the second, Daan Retief, 'Butch' Lochner and Ackermann in the back. Their pressure from the very first scrum hurled the All Blacks back almost 15 yards. Ron Hemi, the hooker, was beaten pointless by van der Merwe. But White, after a shaky start, established himself as an incomparable lineout forward, and received strong support from Stan Hill and Don McIntosh on the flanks; and from half-time, John Buxton proved a number 8 of true fury.

Referee Frank Parkinson penalized the All Blacks in the first minute and from 43 yards Roy Dryburgh, a magnificent fullback, struck an upright with his fine kick. A few minutes later, from a mere 30 yards, he goaled with ease. Nearing half-time, Buxton slid past 'Popeye' Strydom at scrum-half and hacked the ball onward, into the goalmouth. Amid a vast clamour of Carisbrook sound, White pressed down the bouncing ball for a try which Ron Jarden, showing supreme confidence, goaled with a standing kick. As cold, heavy rain briefly swept the field, Dryburgh, Ackermann, Howe and Paul Johnstone began a dangerous move from about halfway. When Ackermann passed to Howe, Jarden, with the breakaway of an Olympic sprinter, darted forward to intercept. He caught the ball, stumbled, recovered and began to run. It was a 40-yard gallop, but thanks to that phenomenal initial burst, he was clear of all when he crossed the goal-line for a try which he himself converted.

New Zealand 10, South Africa 3. Twenty-seven minutes to play. Howe, a little man, very fast, broke the defence in a move to the right before passing to Johnstone. Instantly, Johnstone returned the pass, and Howe flew in for a superb try. Dryburgh missed the goal. Towards the end Carisbrook yelled its rage at Parkinson when he refused Jarden a try from a move begun by Robin Archer with a lobbed punt that Bill Gray caught before making a high pass, which was ruled forward. Resisting South African pressure to the last, the relieved All Blacks left the field, first up, 10–6. It is doubtful if this would have been the score if 15 fit men from either side could have played out the game.

From then on, it was mostly downhill for the Springboks. A week after Carisbrook, they were beaten by Canterbury, 9–6, in circumstances so controversial that Craven publicly complained to the New Zealand Rugby Union about the quality of Kiwi refereeing ('Sour grapes, Dr Craven – very sour grapes indeed' was the editorial comment of Greymouth's tiny *Grey River Argus*). Then, at Athletic Park, Wellington, in a furious, cold southerly gale, with squalls gusting up to 40 miles per hour, the Springboks won the second test, 8–3. Winning the toss, the 'Boks astutely gave the All Blacks first use of the wind, whereupon the New Zealanders, earnestly and enthusiastically, proceeded to kick the ball, mostly out of play.

Calculated aggression of a disagreeable and at times disgusting nature, mostly initiated by the Springboks, set the tone for play. The South African scrum pinpointed the new prop, Frank McAtamney, so violently that he was projected several feet in the air. As the scrum reformed, the All Blacks concentrated on van der Merwe, who received similar treatment. Third time was unlucky for McAtamney. Once more, he rose like a rocket and crashed. He remained on the field, but only to make up the numbers.

Ross Brown's try after eight minutes gave the All Blacks a 3–0 half-time lead. A misfortune. Pat Vincent, a cool, experienced captain, immediately placed the team's eggs in the kick-and-chase basket, with futile results. In the second half, with the wind at their backs, the Springboks were soon ahead. Tommy Gentles slipped round the blindside to put Daan Retief, a great player, in for a stunning try which Viviers goaled. The Springboks aimed many kicks, either from place or drop, at goal, but were foiled by the vile, cruel wind. Then Gentles again ran the blind, and du Rand, another fine forward, scored the try. If not a match to remember, it contained one tiny gem. Morrie Dixon, a hard, tough railwayman, after a brush with Johnstone, a Rhodes Scholar of sombre manner and offhand gesture, stood back: 'Your trouble, mate,' he remarked, 'is – you're yeller!'

Thereafter, the 'Boks marched forward to doom: a 3–3 draw with Taranaki, who were denied a try because the in-goal area was only 10 yards deep and the scorer slithered over it; a 17–10 defeat in the third test at Christchurch, which Craven maintained was the dirtiest game in international rugby history, but which other observers felt was rather more refined than the second test; a hammering by New Zealand Universities, 22–15, in which the second-string South African pack was overwhelmed; and, finally, subjection, 11–5, in the final test at Eden Park, and Craven's public admission of New Zealand's restored supremacy.

Scandal and controversy in the Kiwi establishment brought about a remarkable change in the All Blacks' team for the third test at Lancaster Park. Vincent, dropped both as captain and player, was replaced by the tiny but durable Waikato man, 'Ponty' Reid, whose coolness under fire in the second half of the Waikato game had been vital to that victory. Pat Walsh, the Maori man of all positions, was displaced at fullback by the Waikato giant, Don Clarke; and, most remarkably, the great Otago prop, Kevin Skinner, officially retired, was returned to the pack – obviously, alleged the Springboks sourly, because he had once been amateur heavyweight boxing champion of New Zealand and the All Blacks needed thuggery.

Hard words, not many of them spoken in jest. In the second minute of play, the Springboks were penalized close to the All Blacks' right touchline. The distance from goal was at least 45 yards. Don Clarke, apparently nerveless, placed the ball, moved back a few yards, sighted and kicked – and the ball was well above the crossbar as it carried between the posts. Sensation! And more was soon to come.

Skinner, an observer of the first two tests, had noticed that the Springboks were still at their crafty 'slim' lineout game, dating back to 1949, of breaking through the All Black line to get at the scrumhalf. Taking the field for the third test, he was determined, even at the risk of being ordered off, to stop the practice, especially by Chris Koch, a master of the art. In the first lineout, New Zealand seemed to have won possession when Koch darted through the Kiwi line. The second lineout was an action replay, except that as Koch plunged through the line, Skinner caught him a thunderous right-fisted punch in the face, smearing it with blood. Shortly afterwards, as a scrummage was breaking up, Koch threw a right uppercut to Skinner's jaw, which missed its target. Police sergeant Bill Fright, the referee, awarded New Zealand a penalty, dead in line with the centre-point of the crossbar. No trouble for Clarke. Two goals inside eight minutes delighted the 51,000 spectators.

Eight minutes later Reid picked up a bouncing ball and flung it at least 15 yards to Gray. He offered the ball to Brown, then on to Dixon, a home-town boy, who made the 15 yards to the goal-line at frantic speed and scored in the corner. Don Clarke, superhuman, placed the goal, signalled by referee Fright only after consultation with the touch-judges.

At half-time, Ian 'Chutney' Clarke, the loose-head prop, who had been getting worked over quite a bit by the heavier, stronger Bekker, swapped places with Skinner. The change soon produced another '49 reunion, and after ten minutes or so of the second half, Fright called the captains together to tell them he expected rugby, not rough-house.

Within seven minutes Jarden's flykick was caught by van Vollenhoven, who broke to the left and carved clean through until confronted by Dixon. Lochner was on hand for a superb try, and Viviers's goalkick from the touchline was even better. Robin Archer was now a passenger with a severe shoulder injury, which may have helped the Springboks when Gentles began another startling breakaway. Forwards, rather than backs, offered support: first Ackermann, then Bekker, and finally du Rand who, wanting a yard or two of pace, was glad of a call from Wilf Rosenberg. The try, by the posts and goaled by Viviers to reduce the All Blacks' lead to a bare point, 11–10, demonstrated that the Springboks had too often failed to deliver their potential because they under-estimated the importance of support-play.

The ball was now all over the place and counter-attacks were a dime a dozen. With no more than two minutes of play remaining, and tension almost unbearable, Brown gathered a loose ball and punted low and hard to the left-hand corner. The ball pitched on its point and rebounded. Jarden, travelling fast, and Briers, leaping high, went for it. Jarden won and scored with a flying dive which no defender could have hoped to check.

Four points advantage. Was it enough for New Zealand? Peter Jones charged, harassing Rosenberg, scooped up the ball and flung it to Dixon, 'Tiny' White was there outside to take the pass a few yards from the tryline, and score, sealing the match.

The South African tour excited greater interest, hysteria and, among home spectators, pride, than any other in New Zealand history. Yet the Springbok team displayed strange and conflicting qualities. Craven himself inspired awe rather than affection, and his intensive physical training programme was demonstrably inefficient. Nor did he recognize the latent, and sometimes patent, discord between his English and Afrikaans players. Du Rand might have turned the squad into a happy band of brothers, but Viviers, a cheery chap but hardly a natural leader, either on or off the field, was Hobson's Choice. Pickard, later a first-rate administrator, too often indulged his vanity. Clive Ulyate, overpraised for his performance against the 1955 British Lions, proved the most disappointing player of all. Brian

Pfaff, superlative when in form, was prevented by injury or ill health from playing in more than three games; and Rosenberg, the key man of the third test, managed only five. The stalwarts were Jeremy Nel in midfield, Bertus van der Merwe at hooker, 17 games apiece, and Claassen and Walker, 15 each.

★ ★ ★

The atmosphere was entirely different when the 1959 Lions toured. True, they had their problems as well. The large Welsh contingent, as in 1950, intrigued against the captain, Ireland's Ronnie Dawson, when he was played at hooker instead of their man, Bryn Meredith. 'Alf the Manager' Wilson increasingly lost the confidence of his players as the tour wore on, admitting later that he had been a 'bloody fool' not to see his own faults. And the loss, for all but nine games in New Zealand, of the Irish lock, Bill Mulcahy (severely injured in a country match in New South Wales), badly affected the balance and strength of the scrum and may even have determined the series for the All Blacks. When fit, he was an ideal partner for the great Welsh lock, Rhys Williams.

Yet the wit, the style, the *speed* of the Lions made their tour a joy to behold. They were thoroughly beaten, 22–6, in the third of their four tests with the All Blacks. Given a sound goalkicker, they would, very likely, have won the other three. Although they scored 113 tries in New Zealand, they converted no more than 60 of these; and their 36 penalty goals precisely matched the penalties placed by New Zealand teams.

Those 113 tries demonstrated the quality of the backline. The combination fielded in the final test, at Auckland – Andy Mulligan and Beverley Risman, halfbacks, Ken Scotland and David Hewitt, centres, Tony O'Reilly and Peter Jackson, wings, and Terry Davies, fullback – may have been equalled but never surpassed by an international visiting team. The speed of Hewitt was phenomenal, O'Reilly, powerful and aggressive, was little slower. Scotland wafted his way out of tackles and was a tower of reliability in any position. Jackson's genius in evasion, feint passes and feint plays, was incredible. Early on, Mulligan, a replacement, looked suspect under pressure, but soon developed confidence, reading the flow of play superbly. Risman, son of a truly great exponent of English rugby league, played only nine games, and his absence from the second and third tests, allegedly due to ill health, was probably the factor which determined the series.

Sadly, a controversy raged over the standards of refereeing. It was then the habit of many New Zealand referees to go overboard in awarding penalties. In the first test, more than 20 went against the Lions. With fewer than 12 minutes of play left, the Lions led 17–9. When Don Clarke placed a 50-yard goal and, five minutes later, another from 45 yards, the mood of the crowd changed dramatically. The chants of 'Black! Black!' turned to 'Red! Red!' At Clarke's sixth and final penalty, two minutes from no-side, the jeering of the All Blacks was almost venomous. The experience jarred Wilson Whineray, just settling into his long reign as captain. And it angered the Lions, too, some of whom grossly misbehaved at the formal dinner that evening, throwing oyster shells and salted peanuts about the dining-room and mocking the accent of Gordon Brown, president of the New Zealand Rugby Union, as he declared that, 'within the framework of the rules', the referee had done his duty.

Unfortunately, the result of the second test at Athletic Park likewise hinged on a refereeing decision, though not so blatantly. Despite Risman, Scotland, Jackson, Mulligan and Ken Smith being declared unfit, the All Blacks were only six points clear at half-time, thanks to two beautifully executed tries by the new left wing, Ralph Caulton, but engineered by Terry Lineen, one of the topnotchers of Kiwi midfield play in postwar years. With the wind behind them, the Lions' forwards asserted their superiority. O'Reilly broke clear into midfield with only Clarke ahead. Rather than use his considerable speed, he chose to kick over the defender's head and follow up. Clarke laid him low with a perfectly timed late charge which produced three points from a Terry Davies goalkick but which should, without any doubt whatsoever, have been a penalty try. Then Malcolm Price, on the slant, drew Clarke before offering a high pass to John Young, a flier who, for a wonder, held the ball, running for the try which Davies goaled. So the Lions took the lead, 8–6.

Then followed a series of controversial incidents. Davies, arguing to be allowed a penalty shot at goal from 60 yards, was overruled by his captain, Ronnie Dawson, and instructed to put the ball into touch. This was the first mistake. Placing of the ball and preparations for the kick would have absorbed time, just what the Lions needed. Worse still, Davies failed in the simple task of finding touch, criminal folly in the circumstances. Clarke fielded the ball and, amid tension and rising excitement, began the moves which cost the Lions the game.

As New Zealand mounted the attacks set up by Clarke, Lineen placed a low, raking punt to the left. The ball came to Davies's hands at about the Lions' 25-yard line. Davies fumbled the catch, recovered the ball and found touch. In calling the fumble a knock-on, Waikato referee Roy Gillies was undoubtedly at fault. Davies and the ball had been heading for the corner flag. The ruling that he had projected the ball forward was more than a misfortune, it was tragic. A scrummage was formed. A tackle. A ruck formed over 'Tiny' Hill and Malcolm Thomas. The ball, loose, sped from Kevin Briscoe to his flyhalf, John McCullough, and thence, at an urgent cry, to Don Clarke, who zoomed for the catch and cleared the goal-line for a try which he easily converted.

An hour or so after the match, Gillies asked a newspaperman: 'How did I do?' 'For a start,' answered the reporter, 'the knock-on call against Davies was wrong. The ball was heading toward the Lions' goal-line, not the All Blacks'.' The chairman of the New Zealand Rugby Referees Association, 'Brit' Matthews, chipped in. 'I would agree with that,' he said. 'Davies did not knock the ball on.'

There was only one might-have-been to the 'massacre' which the Lions suffered in the third test, 22–8, on the pavement-hard pitch at Lancaster

Park. Early on, Hewitt blazed down the left touch with O'Reilly in support. Clarke was the only defender. Ecstatically, the Lions' reserves awaited the try and the goal. But they groaned when Hewitt swerved infield and, inevitably, was floored by Clarke. It was not the youngster's fault. O'Reilly, over-eager, had run ahead of him in the chase, a massive blunder, and Hewitt had no alternative.

For the rest, Wilson Whineray and Colin Meads led a forward pack of tremendous strength, stamina . . . and fury. But there was one dissenting voice. The correspondent of the London *Sunday Times*, Vivian Jenkins of Oxford, Wales and the 1938 Lions in South Africa, wrote in the *Christchurch Star*, on test-match eve, that international forwards who wore padding under their jerseys must be 'softies'.

'Softies!' The All Blacks' coach, Jack Sullivan, dwelt lovingly on the word as he gazed at the eight powerhouses of the All Black pack. Could it be that they were young puppies rather than hardened mastiffs? Had his New Zealanders lost their manliness?

One thing was certain. There were greater pleasures in life than playing for the British Lions on that Saturday afternoon of 1959.

CHAPTER EIGHT

'NODDY', 'GRUMPY' AND 'NEEDLE'
1960-9

*T*he achievements of the 1960s, by and large, were truly remarkable. From 42 matches played in New Zealand, Australia, the British Isles, France and South Africa, the All Blacks scored 35 wins, were beaten four times and were held to three draws. In these matches, they scored 99 tries, 63 conversions, 49 penalty goals, 14 drop goals and one goal from the mark, while their opponents scored 32 tries, 14 conversions, 41 penalty goals and 10 drop goals. The total tally of points was thus 714 points against 277.

This success record, which established New Zealand rugby as the best in the world, owed much to the endeavours of four individuals, two outstandingly gifted players and two remarkable coaches, who bore somewhat whimsical nicknames: Wilson Whineray, familiarly known as 'Noddy' (although he preferred 'Skip'), Neil McPhail, dubbed 'Grumpy', Fred Allen, 'Needle' and – playing a walk-on-part – Colin Meads or 'Piney'.

Wilson Whineray, born in 1935, was to play 77 matches in the All Black uniform, 32 of them internationals. He was captain in 30 of these and winning leader 25 times. He led the great tour of the Fifth All Blacks of 1963–4 in a series of triumphs marred only by a scoreless draw with Scotland, and made his last appearances against the arch-foe, South Africa, in 1965, when the chance of the All Blacks cleaning out the 'Boks in all four tests was lost in the fateful second half of the third match at Christchurch.

As a teenager Whineray played at scrumhalf, learning to use both hands and both feet equally naturally. Weighing about $15^1/_2$ stone, he also won the New Zealand Universities' heavyweight boxing championship, an invaluable experience. Although he did not look for fights on the field, he could be a rugged peacemaker. Against Ireland at Lansdowne Road in December 1963, the All Blacks were desperately holding on to a 6–5 lead when their champion lock, Colin Meads, was fetched a tremendous blow by Willie

John McBride. As Meads practically went down for the count, Whineray hissed: 'For Christ's sake, stand on your feet. If you go down, we'll lose. Get to the next lineout and lean on somebody. Your head will clear.' At that lineout, McBride was struck a thunderous blow. No one saw Whineray's punch, but McBride terminated his aggressive attitudes. The All Blacks scraped home by a whisker.

Despite that incident, Whineray was remarkable for never losing his temper. He was a man of most excellent humour, with a gift for exaggerated stories. Yet, deep down, there was a trace of uncertainty. He found captaincy a lonely experience. At a critical moment of the tour of South Africa in 1960, doubts had developed concerning his field play as a loose-head prop. While the All Blacks trained in brilliant sunshine on the vast stadium at Bloemfontein, the All Blacks' managers, Tom Pearce and Jack Sullivan, discussed with Whineray whether he should be replaced by Ian Clarke, an All Black since 1953. It was a delicate situation. When a majority vote was finally taken to play Whineray, Clarke, fine man that he was, shook his hand. 'That's the way I'd have voted,' he said.

The All Blacks had been beaten pointless in the first test at Ellis Park, Johannesburg, 13–0, Don Clarke plainly lacking the speed to nail the flying Springbok left wing, Hennie van Zyl, as he ran in two tries. A masterful team display, sparked by Colin Meads, enabled the All Blacks to tie the series by winning 8–3 at Newlands in Cape Town; and the Springboks, with peerless sportsmanship, spread out in arcs on either side of the tunnel as they applauded their opponents from the field.

The Press Corps men of both countries bet a dollar a head on the likely result and score of the third test. Reg Sweet, senior reporter of the South African *Argus* Group, plumped for an 11–11 draw, and must have spent the last ten minutes of the game torn between loyalty for his team, heading for victory, and regret that he was not going to win the sweep. The 'Boks were leading 11–3. Dickie Lockyear, the scrumhalf, had placed a penalty just before halftime. One minute into the second half, Don Clarke cracked over an equalizer from 48 yards, and Lockyear responded with a goal almost immediately. Martin Pelser, one of the truly great Springbok flankers, then charged down a clearing kick by Don Clarke and the ball skidded on the bounce into the arms of Ian Kirkpatrick, who cut back against the swarming tide to send flyhalf Keith Oxlee in for a try under the crossbar, which Lockyear converted.

More in hope than certainty, Whineray called up Clarke for a shot at a penalty fully 60 yards from the goal, then turned his back, not daring to watch. Concentrating most of his 230 or so pounds on to the toe of his left boot, Clarke let fly. The ball was still soaring well above the bar as it crossed between the posts.

Five points behind and still time for things to happen. Whineray commands a tap-kick from a penalty and the All Blacks win the heel from the ruck. Briscoe heaves an awful pass along the ground and Terry Lineen picks it up and feeds a grub-kick into the Springbok in-goal area. If left-wing Frank McMullen can do one thing well, it is to run; and he is going like the clappers, past Michael Antelme, as he gets his hand to the ball and presses down for a try.

Clarke has to kick for the goal from a spot five yards in from the left touch. With the stiff breeze blowing in from the corner-flag, it is a hellishly difficult proposition. Whineray cannot bear to watch this one either. But over she goes, and over so surely that, long before the ball has reached the uprights, New Zealand touch-judge Ian Clarke is signalling his brother's goal with flag held high and a mighty leap in the sky. Over she goes so cleanly that Reg Sweet, with a broad grin on his face, is already holding out a hand for his winnings.

The fourth test, New Zealand 3, South Africa 8, at Port Elizabeth, bred bitter controversy because the referee, Ralph Burmeister, involved in the '49 disputes, ruled tackled-ball against McMullen when the latter, heel-tapped by Oxlee, had gone to ground just short of the goal-line and, regaining his feet, had crossed the line to score. Burmeister's ruling was a blunder, for McMullen had not been held, and it was not a tackled-ball situation.

The misfortune probably cost the All Blacks five points and their only chance ever to win a series against the Springboks in South Africa. Yet the capital blunder was the choice of Tony Davies for flyhalf. A footballer of skill and courage, Davies had an excellent record at fullback but had only played once previously at flyhalf. His inclusion was a desperate gamble by a selection committee which had lost faith in Adrian Clarke (too flighty) and Steve Nesbit (a coloured Pacific Islander whose confidence had been sapped by the rampaging South African loose-forwards). Nesbit, if necessary with the off-field assistance of a faith-healer, should have been required to play. The selectors misfired again by playing the light-framed 'Red' Conway at number 8.

In the match, Clarke goaled one of several attempts and Lockyear equalized with his first kick. Downwind, the 'Boks surged. 'Monkey' Briscoe, who gallantly played on after a mighty swipe from Pelser, conceded a 5-yard scrum, and when Avril Malan called for the wheel with the ball held in the second row, Conway lacked the nous to stop Pelser falling on the ball for the try which Lockyear goaled.

The first French team ever to tour Down Under, in 1961, was memorably involved in the international at Wellington which never should have been played. The match was won 5–3 by the All Blacks, with a try to each side and yet another extraordinary conversion by Don Clarke.

The French manager, Marcel Laurent, and the coach, Guy Basquet, were a casual, ineffectual pair and François Moncla, the captain, was from the start a Lone Ranger. That supremely gifted rugby writer, Denis Lalanne, of *Équipe*, author of the splendid book, *The Great Fight of the French Fifteen*, on the successful Tricolors' tour of South Africa in 1958, remarked that Moncla would return home 'alone – all, all alone', to shoulder the blame, undeservedly, for France's defeat. Such a pity. Moncla was a nice man even if, on the field, his incessant braying appeared to irritate rather than encourage. He had some fine troops. The brothers Boniface, André and Guy, were midfield backs of speed and subtlety. Jean Dupuy, who scored the try in the teeth of the Wellington gale, was equally fast and courageous. Amedée Domenech, a veteran of the South African tour, was a prop highly gifted in setting up and participating in swirling movements of a close-knit pack which mysteriously transferred the ball from man to man. Less positively, Michel Crauste's villainies at loose-forward included kicking one man on the ground and knocking another stiff; and by these and similar efforts he carved a niche when, at Timaru, he was fiercely and repeatedly struck in the back by a brolly-wielding grand-mother who darted furiously from the sideline on to the field.

The French lost the first test at Auckland, 13–6, largely because, with one of their backs being treated for injury and the pack a man short, the All Blacks won a heel against the head. Des Connor's perfect pass gave Don Clarke another moment of glory when he dropkicked the goal which effectively turned the game.

Conditions for the second test at Wellington were atrocious. The south-erly blizzard was icy, surging between the old grandstand and the new, high one on the opposite side of the field with melancholy sounds suggestive of departing souls crossing the Styx. In Cook Strait, the liner *Canberra* could not make Wellington harbour. Never had two international rugby teams been compelled to play in such adversity. Laurent, very properly, requested postponement. The request was refused. The New Zealand Rugby Union had sold out the ground and, gale or no gale, the match would go on.

When Moncla won the toss and elected to play with the wind, Whineray gravely nodded. It was a gift from Heaven. He immediately detached John Graham from the flank to position himself behind the backline as a second fullback, assisting Don Clarke. Against a massive and magnificent pack consisting of forwards such as Victor Yates at number 8, Graham and Tremain on the flanks, Colin Meads and Neven MacEwen at lock, Whineray, Dennis and Ian Clarke up front, and the superb Australian-turned-Kiwi, Des Connor, at scrumhalf, the French had no hope of winning and controlling the ball sufficiently to breach the defence. Any kick, tactical, speculative or intentional, flew like a rocket beyond the deadball line. Taking placekicks for penalties in the field, Don Clarke could only cut off, with his great boot, 10–15 yards of the touchline.

It was nil-nil at half time; and when Clarke missed a penalty kick, dead in front of the goalmouth, from only 20 yards out, a mighty groan went up from the crowd. Colin Meads, it is true, was denied a try because referee Alan Farquhar was unsighted by a mass of bodies. Time marched on. The French were displaying courage worthy of Verdun. At a heel, Connor passed the ball to his tiny flyhalf, Neil Wolfe, who juggled and finally dropped it. On the instant, Jan Pique darted forward, gathered and sped into a gap. He bore out to the left, toward Dupuy. Clarke and right-wing

Don McKay stood guard. Subtly, Pique coaxed McKay to abandon his point of defence, marking Dupuy, and to rush, instead, at him. At the vital moment, Pique launched the perfect pass. Clarke and centre Paul Little were infield, too far distant to check Dupuy, but too wise to give him the ghost of a chance of scoring his try in the goalmouth.

Then the French did silly things. They were rushed to their goal-line where, at a scrum, they heeled. Scrumhalf Pierre Lacroix flung the ball to Claude Lacaze, the young fullback. The ball was rising as Kevin Tremain, the mighty flanker, raised his arms as a barrier. At the rebound, Tremain pounced and scored. If the 21-year-old Lacaze wept, he must have howled at the sight of Clarke's conversion kick. Taking the ball back to the 25-yard line, close to the touchline, Clarke booted for goal. Carried by the wind, the ball broke freakishly on the right angle and sailed between the posts. Of all winning kicks in the history of international rugby, this was surely the most astonishing of all.

The following evening, the Tricolors sat down for dinner at the Grand Hotel, Invercargill, still seething at having been forced to play in a gale and, naturally, at losing the match. Their spirits rose gradually as they were served bowls of Stewart Island oysters, followed by Southland lamb chops, all washed down by very decent claret. Some hours later, they were aglow. Someone carelessly mentioned the test match. Test? Test? What test? The French can be the finest of rugby players and teams. They can also be the worst, or near to it. Because, fundamentally, for them, there are more important things in life than playing rugby.

Building up, in mid-season of 1963, for the tour which would establish him, in many eyes, as New Zealand's greatest captain, Whineray led the All Blacks in two tests against the first team ever sent by England to a country not of the Five Nations' Championship. The five-match itinerary, including two internationals, was sheer lunacy. On 18 May, the English, captained by a most gifted threequarter, Michael Weston, beat Wellington. Four days later, they lost to Otago at Dunedin. The flight by Friendship aircraft to Auckland occupied much of 23 May. Yet only two days later, the first test was staged at Eden Park – and predictably, the English were beaten, 21–11. Three days later they lost again, to Hawkes Bay, at Napier.

In the final test, on 1 June, at Christchurch, Michael Davis, lock-forward, dislocated his shoulder after only eight minutes but gallantly returned to the field and played on. Perhaps his team-mates were inspired by his example, or perhaps they were tired of being pushed around by one Kiwi team after another. Five minutes from no-side, this team of $14^1/_2$ men were level with the All Blacks, an extraordinary achievement. Against tries for New Zealand by Don McKay and Pat Walsh, Malcolm Phillips, of Fylda, had scored a try and Roger Hosen, a fine Cornishman, had placed a penalty goal. Sixty five yards from England's goal-line, Don Clarke claimed a mark. His brother, Ian, held the ball. Three Englishmen stood on the mark. Don Clarke baulked – deliberately; and 'Badger' Jacobs, for all his experience of more than 20 caps, 'did his scone', as the Kiwis say. He charged. Clarke now had a free kick for goal. It was a magnificent effort, struck with unerring precision, and it won the match 9–6.

It was at about this stage that 'Grumpy' joined 'Noddy' to form the partnership which embellished the growing successes of the All Blacks of the Sixties. Neil McPhail, at the age of 50, brought excellent credentials to his appointment as coach to the team. In the late 1930s he had been playing so well for Canterbury that he looked a sitter for the All Black team that never was – the one scheduled to tour South Africa in 1940. Instead, he found himself heading for Europe as platoon commander of the 20th Infantry Battalion, part of the 2nd New Zealand Division led by the legendary General Freyberg, VC, which established a reputation as one of the great fighting units of the war.

McPhail's part was comparatively brief. In the winter of 1941, after distinguished service in Crete and Libya, he was taken prisoner in fierce fighting around Sidi Rezegh. His natural sense of humour, belying his subsequent nickname (awarded him because of the strict discipline he imposed), sustained him through weary years in prisoner-of-war camps in Italy and Germany. 'Recalled to life', as it were, when Germany capitulated in May 1945 he learned of plans to stage a rugby tour of the British Isles, France and Germany by a team drawn from Freyberg's division. 'The Kiwis', as they were called, won 29 of the 33 matches played, demonstrating a spirit of attack instilled into them by their captain, the great scrumhalf Charles Saxton, who preached the gospel of 'Possession, Position, Pace' to a willing, cheerful band of talented players.

The partnership of McPhail and Whineray during the 1963–4 All Blacks' tour of 36 games through the British Isles, France and Canada, helped to produce 34 wins, one loss and one draw. There was disagreement over the plea by one selector, Ronald Bush, of Auckland, to include at scrumhalf the former Australian Wallaby, Desmond Connor, who from 1960 onward was the mastermind of the Auckland Ranfurly Shield teams which defied 24 consecutive challenges. McPhail and fellow-selector Jack Feilding demurred, arguing that Connor's inclusion would place too many Aucklanders in the team. On a split vote, a Taranaki man of lesser quality, Kevin Briscoe, was picked.

Had Connor been chosen, the All Blacks would almost certainly have been undefeated or, at least, achieved a Grand Slam in the five internationals. An all-round player of exceptional skills, Connor was one of the greatest scrumhalves ever fielded by New Zealand; in tactical intelligence he probably ranks with Freddy Roberts of the 1905 side and Charlie Saxton, of 1938, in Australia.

That record was dented when, in only the third match of the tour, the All Blacks were beaten 3–0 by Newport. A chancy drop at goal by a student named John Uzzell floated out of the mud and over the bar while the 25,000 spectators in the shabby but historic Rodney Parade ground whirled about in joy. Blame was attached like a limpet to the 'new boy' at flyhalf, Earle

Kirton, playing in the black for the first time. After his magnificent performance for South Island versus North in the later stages of the tour selection, Whineray had remarked: 'Because rugby is essentially a team game, I make it a rule never to single out individuals. But, today, "the boy Kirton" . . .'

Kirton, paired with Briscoe, did not play well against Newport, but it was a sign of McPhail's perception and independent mind that he did not concentrate his criticism on the new boy. Instead, he informed Don Clarke, by now a sainted figure, that if he wished to retain his place in the first team, he would do well to concentrate on such a simple matter as finding touch whenever he kicked for it. Indeed, in a late All Black surge, Clarke dropped the pass which might have tied and, with a goalkick, won the match. Clarke's high opinion of his own abilities – his vanity, to put the point more precisely – perhaps tempted him into essaying kicks of enormous distance which, regrettably, failed to enter touch. They may have been early symptoms of a waning self-confidence which, late in the tour, so affected his play that when he tried to place-kick a penalty in a match at Lyon, the ball, struck a few yards infield from the left touchline, skewed so badly off his foot that it found touch only a yard or two from the French goal-line. The spectators marvelled at yet another instance of Clarke genius. If only they had known. . . . This was a humiliating come-down for the mighty 'Camel'.

McPhail's upbraiding of Clarke stemmed from his belief that the highest duty of a rugby team, especially one of international status, was perfection. He was sore as a boil, for example, when the All Blacks beat Ireland at Lansdowne Road only by 6–5, a try by Tremain and a penalty goal by Clarke against a try by winger Johnny Fortune and a conversion by that fine fullback, Tommy Kiernan. The result could well have gone the other way. A furious late Irish rush into the goalmouth seemed certain to yield a try. The chairman of the New Zealand Rugby Union, Cuthbert Hogg, a man easily stirred to great passions when his team was in danger, leapt to his feet. 'Knock-on, Ref!' he bellowed. The President of Eire, Eamon De Valera, touched Hogg on the arm. 'I quite agree with you, Mr Hogg,' he said. Mr De Valera was blind; he had been sightless for years.

McPhail's sour and bitter words to his players found justification in the comments made the following day in the London *Observer* by one of the game's finest critics, H.B. Toft, who noted that whereas Briscoe had handled the ball 56 times, Ireland's scrumhalf, James Kelly, had received it only 27 times. From all those heels, taps or passes, the All Blacks managed a try, a dropkick from flyhalf Mack Herewini which rebounded from an upright, and a clean miss when Herewini passed to Derek Arnold just as the latter was being early-tackled by an over-conscientious Irishman. Malcolm Dick and Ralph Caulton on the wings and Paul Little in the centres – all skilled, swift operators – were not given the ball.

Nor was McPhail overjoyed when the All Blacks beat Wales at Cardiff Arms Park 6–0, with two penalty goals by Don Clarke. He would dearly have loved at least one try as a tribute to Bob Deans, denied the equalizing try back in 1905. But there was glory, all the same, in a tough, grim match.

This was the first time in four attempts that an All Black team had defeated Wales on the Arms Park. The result was not appreciated by the 50,000 or so fervid Welsh fans. When, shortly before no-time, Colin Meads charged into the Welsh captain, Clive Rowlands, as the latter was claiming a mark and, so it appeared, planted his knee in Rowlands's back, the reaction was venomous. In fact, it was the Welsh players, especially the forwards, who told Meads to take no notice of Rowlands's writhing and groaning. 'Clive's just doing a "Hollywood",' they remarked. 'Don't give the affair a second thought.' Nevertheless, as the two teams amiably swapped jerseys on their way to the tunnel, the crowd's hissing and booing of the Kiwis expressed the bitterest hostility.

McPhail should have been delighted with Clarke's extraordinary achievement in concealing from the Welsh (surely the shrewdest of all rugby appraisers) that from his first gigantic 70-yard penalty kick at goal, which rebounded from an upright, he had so strained an upper thigh muscle that for the rest of the game he had to make almost every kick with his left foot. He did, in fact, place a goal, but it was a tiddler from 15 yards or so, and even then he skewed the ball. And with a fine drop goal by Bruce Watt, the All Blacks made international history. They might have had that try, indeed many tries, but for the superb backrow play of Alan Thomas, Ray Pask and Dai Hayward, who covered and commanded Briscoe, Watt and Arnold behind the Kiwi pack, and the tigerish tackling of fullback Graeme Hodgson, who stopped some of the great All Black forwards, Whineray, Tremain, Meads, Ken Gray and Alan Stewart, in their tracks.

After conveying his opinion, decisively, that nothing but the best was good enough, McPhail soon recovered his humour. 'The Man with the Hooded Eyes', as the prop, Ian Clarke, called him, helped to make the tour as enjoyable as possible. Before the start of each training session, there was a soccer game between the Youngies (under 25) and Oldies, and played with such enthusiasm and competitiveness that a day or two before the final match against the Barbarians at Cardiff, a full international, with proper team uniforms, was staged. The entire tour was great fun; and the perfect relationship between Whineray and McPhail was strengthened by the intelligence and pride of senior players such as Graham, Gray, Meads and Tremain.

They needed all their humour after they had beaten England 14–0 at Twickenham. Except for one man, Uel Titley of *The Times*, Fleet Street set about the All Blacks as if they were a pack of curs. Toft, in the *Observer*, wrote of the match that it was 'all brilliantly logical, it was virile, it was successful, it was boring'. J.B.C. Thomas, in Cardiff's *Western Mail*, said the All Blacks 'technically infringed more persistently than any touring team I have ever seen'.

The leader of the English forwards, Nicholas Drake-Lee, told the *Daily Express* that England's white strip was a cause of their defeat. 'We were unable to counter their obstructive lineout wedge with a similar tactic,' he complained, 'because the referee could spot us so easily.' Said Titley in *The Times*: 'Afterwards it was said that the England backs never had a chance because of New Zealand's flat lining up, which was not the most glowing compliment to England's backs. It was said in the second half the All Blacks were content to sit on a lead of 14 points, which was unjust in the first place and less than a compliment to England in the second. The simple truth was that New Zealand were much too good.'

Wise words. Despite the ranting of the critics, the match proved of climactic importance. Members of the International Board at last appreciated the absurdity of a Law which permitted opposing backlines, in effect, to stand chest to chest. At their next meeting, they introduced the compulsory 10-yard gap at the lineout. Many times in later years it seemed that the change had made little difference: cunning backs or backlines pinched yards of ground to check or destroy a promising attack. What the Law needed was vigilant refereeing – and that, alas, is easier said than found.

Whineray and McPhail now stood on the brink of glory – masters of the first All Black team to score a Grand Slam of victories in the four internationals of a great tour, something the Springboks had done four times out of five. Wales, 1905, was a might-have-been, Scotland's obduracy in 1925 had prevented a match, both Wales and England had settled the hash of Manchester's men in 1935, and Wales had again delivered the knockout punch in 1953. Now, surely, the time had come.

So near and yet so far. The Scotland match was a scoreless draw. Initially, McPhail and Whineray were at fault for choosing Herewini, who was superlative at flyhalf and no sluggard at fullback, to play at five-eighths, or inside centre, leaving Bruce Watt to partner Briscoe. In the wide open spaces of midfield, Herewini was lost. It soon became evident, too, that Briscoe, a key man, was out of form. His heart pumped as vigorously as ever, he would stand up to any man; but his fingers had turned into thumbs, and for want of celerity in clearing the ball through the backline, the backs were doomed to individual efforts. Of these, the most spectacular was a 60- perhaps 70-yard run by Don Clarke, bearing left to right and, with his enormous bulk, cutting a bow-wave as he ran. Sadly, no one ran with him; and poor 'Camel', built for 10-yard dashes rather than 100-yard sprints, could eventually do no more than punt and hope for the best. As no-time approached, Malcolm Dick made three urgent solo charges, all to no avail.

All credit to the Scots, especially Christopher Elliot, a wing who caught one of Clarke's dropkicks and who, had he run and run, as opportunity offered, must have scored. Sad to see a man kicking to shut out his chance of glory. Jim Telfer and Clarke raced after a ball bouncing in the All Blacks' 25, and with no other challenge to hand, Jim was the quicker. How he failed to score remains a mystery that would have baffled even Sherlock Holmes.

If the draw was a disappointment, the performance of the All Blacks at the most critical moment of the game established, conclusively, that McPhail's men were worthy of their predecessors. In only the 16th minute of play, the Scottish scrumhalf, Tremayne Rodd, broke on the blindside past the Kiwi backrow, past Briscoe and into open ground. Elliot and Stuart

Wilson, the fullback, kept him company. At one check, Rodd passed to Elliot; at another, Elliot passed to Wilson. By now, Tom Grant, the eighth man, had joined the hunt. Amid all the tension and excitement, Wilson was caught and Grant persuaded to kick; whereupon Paul Little scuttled to the bouncing ball, grabbed it and hurtled into the safety-net of touch-in-goal.

The Irish referee, Ray Williams, ordered a scrum five yards, Scotland with the put-in. Norman Bruce, with 28 caps already for Scotland, was just the man to win the heel, snap the ball back to Rodd and, very likely, initiate a score. Dennis Young, his opponent, was much lighter, although vastly experienced. Size alone argued that Scotland must win this crucial scrummage.

At this supreme moment of opportunity, Bruce missed the bus. Young, powered by the craggy All Black scrum, won the heel, and Briscoe cleared. Scotland made other attempts to score, Wilson fumbling a reasonable chance of a penalty goal; and with men such as Telfer, David Rollo and Peter Brown, they stood firm to every New Zealand assault.

The Grand Slam was once more a chimera. Yet the memory of that heel against the head at the scrum five yards endures forever.

So the All Blacks sailed off to France for three victories. The most significant, naturally, was against the national side, 12–3, notable, too, in that the Kiwis tried out their new scrumhalf, Chris Laidlaw, against a French pack whose second row, André Herrero, Benoit Dauga, Jean le Droff and Michel Crauste, compared with the world's best. Whineray tried on Herrero's blazer. 'It was like a horse-blanket,' he said. 'The skirt reached down to about my knees.' Magnificent players whose effort, at the lineout, was pretty well wasted because the backline, with Pierre Albaladejo, André Boniface, Jean Gachassin, Jean-Claude Darrouy and Claude Lacaze, argued incessantly with one another and with everyone else.

Then back to Cardiff Arms Park for the final match against the Barbarians, who seemed to have chosen their team more by guess than by God, with a place of honour in their front-row for Ian Clarke, already unique in being the first All Black twice to visit the British Isles in full-length tours. After 20 minutes Ian claimed a mark from a drop-out 25 by his famous brother Don. The spot was about 45 yards from goal, and he invited referee Gwynne Walters to position the touch-judges at the goalposts. He then took two or three steps and let fly with a dropkick which had 'Goal' written on it from the first yard of flight.

Tries by Tremain and Meads, neither converted, gave the All Blacks a 6–3 lead at half-time. The Barbarians were not running the ball, and play was stodgy and humdrum. Five minutes into the second half, the game was transformed. Graham beat Simon Clarke to a Barbarian heel on their own goal-line, diving for the try. Then a pass from Clarke pitched awkwardly in front of Barbarians' flyhalf Richard Sharp, and Wake Nathan pounced on it to score. Don Clarke placed both goals. After this, the All Blacks, while running in four more tries, played with such crazy abandon that the Welsh crowd, no less, was roaring, 'More!' The climax came when Little and Graham cut through midfield and, 20 yards from the posts, passed to

Whineray. Meads was running to Whineray's left, certain the ball would be his. That was how Stuart Wilson, the Scottish fullback, read the situation. As he flashed across Whineray's bows, 'Noddy' offered Meads a truly superb dummy pass, sidestepped to the right and dotted the ball down behind an upright.

The try lives on forever in television news-clips, flashbacks and fortunate spectators' memories. With a final scoreline of 36–3, the roars of 'Whineray! Whineray!' boomed over Cardiff city as 'Skip' was carried shoulder-high from the field. And at the banquet, Glyn Hughes, only the fourth president of the Barbarians in its 60-plus years, said that as the crowd chanted 'More, more, more!', his Baa-Baas were yelling back, 'Yeah, yeah, yeah!'

★　★　★

The tour of New Zealand by the Springboks, captained by Dawie de Villiers, in 1965, saw the All Blacks win the test series three matches to one. The possibility that the 'Boks would be cleaned out in all four of their matches, even more decisively than the Forty-Niners had been, looked as near as dammit at half-time of the third test at Christchurch. With a masterful lead of 16–5, Whineray seemed to have a team ready to do to the 'Boks what the 'Boks had done to Scotland in 1951. The field was muddy – a surface that the South Africans treat as if it were a field of poisonous snakes. Yet with a sensational goalkick by lock-forward 'Tiny' Naude late in the game, the Springboks won the match by 19 to 16 and Kiwis still think it a shame Dawie de Villiers's 'Boks didn't get it where the chicken got the axe. On the morning of the fourth test in Wellington, when the 'Boks were demolished 20–3, Dr Danie Craven had three words to explain their deplorable performance. 'Too much poking,' he reiterated. Kobus Louw, the South African manager, took a more dispassionate view of things, declaring at every opportunity that 'rugby was a winner', but the crown went to the All Blacks. And Wilson Whineray, that great captain, retired from the international rugby scene.

The British Lions, on their visit in 1966, were led by Michael Campbell Lamerton, who had neither the background nor the intellectual grasp of high-level captaincy. He was only one part of a triad which turned out to be so ineffective that a full-scale investigation followed the end of the tour. The team's manager, Desmond O'Brien, a former Irish wing-forward, was unhappy about his captain and apparently incapable of supporting his coach, John Robins, a 1950 Lions' prop-forward, in the strife which developed over training and tactics. When the Lions lost three of their first five matches, disintegration set in. In all, the team won no more than 15 of its 25 matches and, appallingly, scored only 300 points while yielding 281.

The one real misfortune was the loss of the second test at Athletic Park, 16–12. At a critical moment when a Scottish back, Hinshelwood, was making a run which seemed certain to produce a try, referee Pat Murphy, for unfathomable reasons, blew his whistle. That, practically speaking, was the end for a side which mustered players of the quality of Michael Gibson, one of the greatest backs of all time, David Watkins, a tiny Welshman of enormous speed and guile, Ray McLoughlin, a master of the art of scrummaging, and Willie John McBride, famous among lock-forwards.

'Grumpy' had now been replaced by 'Needle', thanks to whom New Zealand's style and brand of rugby came to be acknowledged as the finest. Fred Allen had coached the Auckland team which between 1960 and 1963 defended the Ranfurly Shield a record-equalling 24 times; and it was during this period that Neil Wolfe, an All Black flyhalf standing little more than 5 ft, remarked to a watching group: 'There goes old Fred, needling the boys again.'

The name stuck. It was perfect. Allen ended his training runs with what he called 'The Arse-Knocker'. The players, a yard or so apart, lined up on one goal-line and, on command, ran to the opposite end of the field. As each man passed the ball, he sprinted to the end of the line, ready for another pass. At a mistake, a dropped ball or even a bobble, the 'Knocker' restarted. At Carisbrook one day, the troops had been battered by hard work. As they headed for the dressing-room, Tremain, an old buddy, remarked, 'Bless you, Allen.' 'Fred the Needle' raised his head. 'Right-oh,' he shouted, 'Everyone back on the field!'

As a selector and coach, Allen achieved enduring success with teams and players. Considering that Colin Meads, the great forward of the time, was trading on his reputation, he dropped him for the second of three tests against the Wallabies, breaking the chain of 55 record caps Meads won in an international career extending from 1958 to 1971. (Meads refused to speak to Allen for two seasons). Of greater significance was Allen's belief that New Zealand rugby had become sterile. Partnered by his friend, Charles Saxton, in the management of the '67 All Blacks in the British Isles and France, Allen produced an unbeaten team which to this day is ranked with the 1951–2 Springboks and the 1984 Wallabies as one of the greatest touring teams ever. They beat England 23–11, Wales 13–6, France 21–15 and Scotland 14–3; but a potential Grand Slam was prevented by the cancellation, due to a foot-and-mouth outbreak in Cheshire, of the Irish section of the tour. In a magnificent finale, the Barbarians were defeated 11–6 at Twickenham.

In fourteen internationals between 1966 and 1968, Allen's All Blacks won every match, although there was one close shave in the second and final test of the 1968 tour of Australia, at Brisbane. With two minutes to go, the Wallabies, ahead 18–14, seemed sure to win. Bill Davis, the New Zealand outside centre, hoisted a punt and was well into pursuit of the ball when his marker, Barry Honan, crashed him to the ground. Kevin Crowe, Queensland's pride among referees, headed for the ball as it bounced, then turned and ran, blowing his whistle hard, indicating, at the goalposts, that he was awarding New Zealand a penalty try. As most of the 12,000 spectators offered Mr Crowe information concerning his ancestry, Fergie McCormick came up from fullback and kicked the goal. New Zealand 19, Australia 18.

The French Tricolors of 1968, captained by the charming Christian Carrère, could have been a great team had they been disciplined by 'The Needle'. As it was, they were beaten in all three tests. In the second match, Brian Lochore, the All Blacks' captain, remarked to the referee: 'If you don't fix things up, Ref., we will.' The quarrelsome little scrumhalf, Marcel Puget, had been snarling and shrieking while men kicked and punched one another, and Lochore, a peaceable man, was enraged by what the French called 'the severities'. The celebrated French critic, Denis Lalanne, wrote in the New Zealand *Weekly News*: 'The New Zealand referees control in great degree the destiny of the All Blacks and have an exorbitant influence on the style of New Zealand rugby. When that day comes on which they no longer deem it necessary to whistle up 30 penalties against each team, then there will be more time in which, perhaps, to play rugby well. And try for tries.'

M. Lalanne was both right and wrong – right to exclaim against the tendency of Kiwi referees to dominate a game, wrong to complain that New Zealand was not going for tries.

That, indeed, was the genius of 'The Needle'. In the 17 games of the 1967 tour, including two in Canada, 71 tries were scored, no fewer than 13 in internationals: five against England, two against Wales, four against France, two against Scotland and two against the Barbarians. Allen had no time for defensive, win-at-all-costs rugby. He encouraged the running game. Thus, in that '67 tour, Bill Davis scored twelve, Bill Birtwhistle nine, Tony Steel eight, Malcolm Dick seven and Grahame Thorne four – all of them playing in the threequarters.

Allen was gifted in his judgement of players, particularly the young. For the 1967 French international in Paris, he replaced his first-stringers at scrumhalf and flank, Laidlaw and Tremain, by two youngsters, the Maori Sid Going and Ian Kirkpatrick, both to emerge as among the world's finest. 'Kirkie' had his nose smashed early in play, and Going was harried continuously by the French. Both lads scored a try. Next year, at the team-talk before the last test against France at Eden Park, Allen repeatedly urged Going: 'Sid, you can do it. You can SCORE. I WANT you to score.' Twice did Going, built low to the ground, immensely strong, instinctive in all his responses, react to sloppy French concentration by sneaking around the blindside of scrums and plunging to tries.

In the 1967 international against Scotland at Murrayfield, Colin Meads suffered the supreme misfortune of being ordered from the field. The incident occurred late in play. New Zealand, having scored, were leading 14–3 when Scotland again put the ball into play. Inevitably, it descended into a mass of All Black forwards. The Scottish pack, maddened at the imminence of defeat, arrived in a smouldering bunch. Meads, on the fringe of the maul, was hurled from it by 'Sandy' Carmichael, a powerful prop. As Meads recovered balance, he saw the ball emerging, on the ground, into the hands of David Chisholm, the Scottish flyhalf. Meads stepped forward and, according to his own testimony, swept at the ball with his right boot.

The whistle sounded. Kevin Kelleher, the distinguished referee, informed Meads he was sending him off. Brian Lochore protested and Ken Gray angrily shouted at Kelleher. Sensing the decision, the gallery in the great grandstand close by took up a passionate chant of 'Off! Off!' Meads hung his head to one side, left hand on hip, as he began to march. He straightened as he passed into the tunnel and the dressing-room.

Afterwards, all hell broke loose. Saxton and Allen, interviewed on BBC television and shown the incident in slow motion, over and over, declared there had been injustice. Most critics shouted blue murder. Against the fact of the Tours Agreement, which specified that any case of ordering-off would be judged by a panel comprising representatives of the Home Union (Scotland), the Visiting Union (New Zealand) and an independent party, the International Board entered the fray, nominating Cyril Gadney, of the Rugby Football Union, and Glyn Morgan, president of the Welsh Union, to sit with Saxton in judgement. The board's honorary secretary, Eddie Kirwan, was called from Dublin to announce to the British and New Zealand Press Associations the finding that because, earlier in the game, Meads had been formally warned for foul play and misconduct, his dismissal was fully supported by the panel. 'Meads,' said genial Eddie, 'has been severely admonished and warned as to his future conduct and is suspended for the next two games on the tour.'

The rumpus might never have died had not T.P. McLean, the *New Zealand Herald*'s critic, telephoned Kelleher on the last day of the All Blacks' stay in Britain. Kelleher then made the momentous statement: 'I did not send Meads off for foul play. I sent him off for dangerous play.'

There was no doubting he was right. The formal warning had been issued in the first half after Meads – wearing brown headgear to cover the white bandage around his scalp after having been deliberately kicked by Alain Plantefol in the French international – had jumped with both feet on to a ruck as the ball was issuing to Laidlaw. A *Glasgow Herald* picture demonstrated the grimness of the leap. It was then that Kelleher offered the formal warning, which compelled him, in terms of the Law, to order Meads from the field at any further visible act of misconduct. 'I hope,' Kelleher told McLean, 'that I may some day be able to shake Colin's hand.' In fact, the two struck up a correspondence, and the rapport between them was evident when Kelleher visited South Africa in 1970 to watch some of the All Black matches.

Meads was 'Pinetree' or 'Piney'. At 6 ft 4 in and 16 stone 8 pounds, he was incredibly strong. He had risen to greatness as a player during his association with Whineray, McPhail and Allen, and had become virtually a saintly figure with the New Zealand public.

Regrettably, the picture had flaws. Meads had a harsh side to his nature. In the second test on the Sydney Cricket Ground, in 1962, he dragged the great Wallabies' halfback, Ken Catchpole, by one leg from a ruck, ignoring the shrieks of pain as the latter's groin muscles tore – an injury that ended his career. In 1963 he smashed the side of Campbell-Lamerton's face at Twickenham; and in 1969, at the Christchurch test match, his blow broke the jaw of the Welsh hooker, Jeff Young.

Such a pity that a man who exercised so much influence on New Zealand and world rugby through the 1970s could commit such acts. In due course, he was made a foundation member of the New Zealand Sports Hall of Fame. Many hailed him as the greatest player in New Zealand rugby history. Great player, yes. Greatest, no. Dangerous play which produces cervical spinal injuries and which turns men, especially young men, into cripples paralyzed for life, is the intolerable aspect of a sport which, if it is to endure, must remain unblemished.

CHAPTER NINE

DECADE OF DISASTERS
1970-9

During the tour of New Zealand in 1965 by the Springboks, the South African Prime Minister, Dr Hendrik Verwoerd, delivered a speech at the tiny dorp of Loskolp Dam, in which he said that Maoris would not be welcomed as members of touring All Black teams. The statement was noted by the council of the New Zealand Rugby Union. Just before Christmas 1966, the South African Rugby Board invited an All Black tour of South Africa in 1967 'under the old terms'. To the chairman of the New Zealand union, Tom Morrison, the phrase had only one meaning: no Maoris could be included.

Morrison and his councillors were outraged and decided under no circumstances to accept the tour. In March 1967, Morrison and his deputy chairman, Cecil Blazey, stopped off, on their way to London, in Cape Town to inform the president of the South African board, Dr Danie Craven, that never again would the All Blacks visit South Africa unless the Maoris were considered eligible for selection. It later pleased New Zealand's Prime Minister, Sir Keith Holyoake, to claim that it was at his Government's direction that the tour was cancelled – a superlative illustration of the gift shrewd politicians possess for jumping on a convenient band-wagon.

Largely at the behest of one of rugby's great administrators, Sir William Ramsey, in London, the Four Home Unions hastily organized a substitute tour for 1967. Thus, out of politics, was born the great tour which Fred 'the Needle' Allen and Charlie Saxton commanded.

After Dr Verwoerd's assassination at his desk in the Parliamentary chamber in Cape Town, his successor, Mr J.B. Voerster, hinted that *his* Government would not object to the presence of Maoris or Polynesians in a touring All Black side, and preparations were made by the New Zealand union for a tour in 1970. Three Maoris, Sid Going, scrumhalf, Blair Furlong, flyhalf, and 'Buff' Milner, utility back, and the 19-year-old part-

Samoan, Bryan Williams, were chosen for a team captained by Brian Lochore.

The tour proved the first of several disasters to afflict New Zealand rugby during the 1970s. In only the seventh game, against Eastern Transvaal, Colin Meads, down on the ground, had his arm broken with a deliberately aimed kick. Under sensible management he would have been packed off home; but a month or so later, he played again, with an arm-guard, at a level perhaps 75 per cent of his best. The management of the team by Ron Burk, an able referee and outstanding administrator, left much to be desired. Ivan Vodanovich's profound belief in the efficacy of long training-runs predictably blunted the firepower of the attack; and apart from victory in a singularly ill-tempered second test, when fullback Fergie McCormick dislodged a front tooth, with a well-aimed elbow jolt, from the jaw of Sid Nomis, just as this gifted centre was bursting into the clear, the All Blacks lost the test series, three matches to one.

In the first test at Pretoria, Chris Laidlaw left the field, carrying an injury which medical inspection failed to detect, and was replaced by Going in the second half. At that stage the Springboks, powered by flyhalf Piet Visagie's superb tactical punting and Joggie Jansen's immensely positive tackling in midfield, led 12–0.

Going transformed the New Zealand team. His scudding, breaking runs baffled the Springbok midfield defence. McCormick, having missed a couple, at last landed a penalty goal. Then Going broke on the blindside, throwing Nomis off the scent as he passed to Williams. The youngster bolted at fullback Ian McCallum and, with a stupendous left-footed sidestep, broke clear for a gallop to the goal-line. Even so, the Springboks were winners by 17–6.

Despite the evidence of Going's amazing talent in evasive running, the team's selectors stuck with Laidlaw until he was stricken with stomach problems resolved only by an appendectomy. The All Blacks narrowly won the second test at Cape Town, 9–8, then lost the third, 14–3, at Port Elizabeth. Going was brought back for the final international at Johannesburg, even though he had suffered a severe wrenching of the knee and ought not to have played. He bravely battled until, at half-time, the All Blacks won a heel against the head at a scrummage a few yards from the Springboks' goal-line. By strength and supple sidestep, Going pierced the first line of defence. At his pass, Williams again used spectacular sidesteps to reach the goal-line, then turned infield for the posts, evading four more tacklers for a brilliant try, the climactic moment in a match which eventually went South Africa's way, 20–17.

From his first dazzling appearance at Bethlehem – a township in the wilds of Orange Free State – Williams played with a skill no All Black wing has surpassed and few have emulated. In 14 games he scored as many tries, three fewer than Grahame Thorne's record for all South African tours, but Thorne played four more matches.

★ ★ ★

The manager of the British Lions' team to tour Australia and New Zealand in May-August 1971 was Dr Douglas Smith, a Scottish international wing threequarter of the late 1940s. After long consideration, Carwyn James, a flyhalf whose career had coincided with that of the Welsh wonder-man, Cliff Morgan, and who only won the first of two Welsh caps at the age of 29, was chosen as coach. They made a strong partnership and planned exhaustively for the tour, watching club and country rugby in addition to home internationals, liaising constantly with the selectors and urging the team to restore the prestige which had been lost by Campbell-Lamerton's touring side of 1966.

On the verandah of a Brisbane hotel on 10 May, in brilliant sunshine, the questions at the Press conference rather limped along until Doug Smith casually remarked that the Lions would probably lose their opening match against Queensland in two days' time. How come? he was asked. 'Circadian dysrhythmia,' answered Dr Smith. 'In God's name,' cried one reporter, 'what IS that?' 'Jet-lag,' replied Smith, smiling serenely.

'Then, of course, as to New Zealand,' he continued, 'the Lions in the test matches will win two, lose one and draw one.' There was uproar. One or two older hands surmised that Smith was deliberately taking the mickey out of the group, perhaps indulging the same type of humour as when, after the first test in New Zealand, he announced and reiterated that the All Blacks had a weakness, a one-man weakness in their side. Very shrewd, that. Who could it be?

Four months and four days later, the Lions and the All Blacks moved on to Eden Park in Auckland for the last of their four tests. By now, Duggie Smith was being vetted for appointment as junior assistant to Nostradamus. His team had won the first test at Dunedin 9–3 when their shortest forward, Ian McLauchlan, had brought off the unlikely feat of charging down a clearing punt from the All Blacks' goal-line and following the rebound for a try. The Lions had lost the second test at Christchurch, 22–12, when Sid Going and a new partner, Robert Burgess, had jointly scored three brilliant tries. In the third test at Wellington, where Burgess might have died after swallowing his tongue had not someone promptly reacted, the Lions had emerged victors, 13–3.

Soon enough, the All Blacks were ahead in the final test, 8–0, after a try by Wayne Cottrell, replacing Burgess, goaled by Laurie Mains, and a penalty by Mains. It had not been pretty stuff. At only the third lineout, Peter Whiting, alleging he was being deliberately obstructed by the Scot, Robert Brown, flung a punch which tore a strip, six stitches long, in Brown's face. 'Jas' Muller kicked McLauchlan, and Tom Lister moved off rapidly as Willie John McBride began chucking haymakers at him. Increasingly, as play proceeded, the Lions formed a defensive backline loop at the lineouts. Their flyhalf stood back the required ten yards, the inside centre edged forward a couple of yards and the open-side wing stood level with the lineout. This cunning formation was of inestimable help, in the second half, to David Duckham. From his illegal station, his tackling was so consistent and severe that he almost qualified as the finest player in the game.

In those injury-time minutes before the half-time break, Richie Guy, a running prop-forward, conceded a penalty which Barry John goaled. Duckham made a dangerous run which Bryan Williams gallantly stopped. At the lineout, almost on the All Blacks' goal-line, Colin Meads called for a long throw. The ball dropped into the arms of Gareth Edwards, who immediately handed it to Peter Dixon, of the flankers. Spying a broad lead through the tail-end of the All Blacks' line, Dixon swept in and, unimpeded, scored a try which John converted.

Three minutes into the second half, Jas Muller balefully put the boot into Brown, causing a wound which required 14 stitches and ought to have led to Muller's dismissal. It gave John the opportunity to kick a glorious penalty from 48 yards. Seven minutes later, New Zealand equalized as the Lions unbelievably called for a long throw-in on their goal-line and Lister, catching the ball, fell over the line for the try.

The Lions attacked, left, and Duckham thoughtfully chucked the ball infield to J.P.R. Williams, 48 yards from goal, who took two or three steps and let fly with a colossal dropkick. Amid the cheering and groaning that accompanied the goal, J.P.R. turned to his parents in the grandstand and punched his fist triumphantly in the air.

For most of the final 20 minutes, the field belonged to the Lions, although Mains briefly stemmed their ardour by placing the penalty goal which tied the score at 14–14. More significantly, Barry John – now reverently dubbed 'The King' by his team-mates – used one fine Edwards pass after another, 13 in all, to put the ball safely to touch. None of the All Blacks attended the party that night to which John Dawes had invited them. When the Lions departed next day for London, with a record of 23 victories, two losses (one attributable to Circadian dysrhythmia) and one draw, with an aggregate of 570 points against 231 yielded, no member of the All Black team was present to offer a farewell hand.

Duggie Smith came in for attack at the last of his many Press conferences. He had already had fun and games with his extraordinary forecast of results and his allegation that the All Blacks had a weakness (it was assumed he meant Meads, no longer the great man of old). And he had echoed, repeatedly, his severe criticisms that New Zealand rugby, even under Fred Allen, had been 'very physical'. Moreover, Smith and his brother-Brits implied, New Zealand had lost its former enthusiasm for the running game.

Some of the Press now snarled back. Why, seeing that in the last quarter of the final test, the All Blacks, especially forward, were tuckered out and could have been cut to pieces, had 'The King' played a totally defensive game? 'We HAD to win,' Smith replied, in a dark, heavy voice. 'We HAD to win.' A sad remark, exemplifying the growing trend toward a win-at-all costs attitude as the foundation of international rugby.

Yet, as far as New Zealand was concerned, the Lions' tour turned out to be a children's tea-party compared with 1972–3, when the All Blacks played 32 tour matches in Vancouver, New York, the British Isles and France. In only the second match in Britain, Ian Kirkpatrick's team was beaten, 9–3, by the Llanelli club side coached by Carwyn James. Six matches later, in a fiery affair at Workington, it was beaten by North-Western Counties, 16–14. Then, at Cardiff Arms Park, against Wales, in a match which often hovered on the brink of ferocity, the All Blacks scraped home, 19–16. Keith Murdoch, the huge prop-forward, scored the only try; and Joe Karam placed five penalty goals, untroubled by the atmosphere of 'hate' which erupted in the crowd in the later stages of the game. The single Welsh try was scored by John Bevan, the sprint winger who had the torso and shoulders of Atlas; he simply shrugged off Duncan Hales as the latter went for him ten yards short of the tryline. Phil Bennett placed four penalty goals. Towards the end, the crowd's screams of rage reached an ugly climax as the English referee, Johnny Johnson, refused to award J.P.R. Williams a last-minute try which would have drawn, and perhaps won, the match.

Not pretty stuff, and hardly a convincing argument for rugby as the greatest of footballing team-games. Nor did things simmer down off the field.

Throughout the tour there had been vexatious happenings which eventually established the All Blacks as the least popular New Zealand side ever to tour Britain. And there was a sensation later that night, in the kitchen of the Angel Hotel in Cardiff, where the Welsh Rugby Union had earlier hosted an official dinner-dance. Keith Murdoch, scorer of the All Blacks' winning try, who had been involved in a number of previous unseemly brawls and rampages, punched a security guard. Ernie Todd, the All Blacks' manager, decided within 30 hours to expel Murdoch from the tour.

Boys being boys? Hardly. To a man, the players said at the tour's end that they had had a great time. There had been no dissension among them. They did not mention the heavy drinking. They did not say, as Chris Laidlaw was to remark in his book *Mud and Glory*, that many of Kirkpatrick's team became players by day and stayers at night.

In the entire story of the All Blacks in New Zealand's sporting history, immense sympathy was generated and is still felt for two of the largest and most powerful men who ever wore the Silver Fern. But whereas the sending off of Colin Meads at Murrayfield in 1967 occurred in full view of thousands of spectators and the television cameras, the disgracing of Keith Murdoch was a secretive, rumour-ridden business, the true facts of which were known only to a few active participants and witnesses. The author of this book, T.P. McLean, was present when the alleged offence took place and was involved in subsequent events resulting from the affair. He discussed these at length in his book about the tour, *They Missed the Bus*, and it seems appropriate to digress briefly here to consider certain aspects of the incident, only recently revealed, which may be relevant and interesting.

From the first night of the tour, on the outward-bound flight from Auckland to Vancouver, dispute was already simmering between Murdoch and manager Todd. Murdoch was drinking too much and his noisy conduct was proving a nuisance to other passengers. No fewer than four times did he disregard Todd's instruction to settle down and sleep.

On 23 October, the day after the All Blacks arrived in London, the team and officials were guests of the Four Home Unions at a formal dinner at the East India Club. It was a cheerful show, the company was genial, the wine first-rate, the atmosphere agreeable. The account of what happened comes in part from the team's assistant manager and coach, Robert H. Duff, an outstanding Canterbury and All Black lock of the 1950s, and in part from John Brooks, gifted, balanced rugby critic of the Christchurch *Press*.

Duff returned by cab to the team's hotel, the Britannia, in Mayfair, and joined a group of players who were having one for the road. He recalls Murdoch, Alex Wyllie, Alan Sutherland, Hamish Macdonald, Graham Whiting and Brooks. 'They were senior guys, having a pleasant talk,' Duff said, years later. 'All were relaxed. A pleasant session. I was astounded when Ernie Todd joined us – astounded because Todd took sighting shots, in turn, at Murdoch, Wyllie and Sutherland. He referred to something "Sully" had done during the All Blacks' internal tour a few months before. He took a crack at Wyllie's tendency to play too hard. He hit Murdoch hardest. He told Keith he knew the full story behind the fact that he had played only eight games for Brian Lochore's team in South Africa. If he were not prepared to do better on our tour, Todd said, Murdoch could be assured of an air-ticket home.'

Todd's manner, according to Brooks, was 'very objectionable'. After he had left the room, Sutherland pounded an angry fist into Brooks's suitcase with such force that the dent was irreparable. Murdoch disappeared for a few minutes. When he returned, he said, according to Brooks: 'That bloody chump Todd, picking on me like that. I have just told him, "If you don't want me on this tour, say so, now. I'll go home. I could be a dead loss, playing the tour under a bloody cloud."'

Macdonald, a level-headed, sober-sided man, offered what in time became the team's judgement of their manager. 'Todd's behaviour was disgraceful,' he said. 'He lost our respect in that one incident. During the rest of the tour, most of us ignored him.'

After the All Blacks had been beaten by the Llanelli club team, the players returned for the night to their quarters at the Grand Hotel, Swansea. Murdoch and others found some plastic bags, filled them with water and tied them tightly. They tossed these makeshift water-bombs into the street outside, where they produced sharp, violent explosions. This was late 1972, three years since the beginning of the troubles in Belfast. The blasts caused the staff rapidly to close the hotel doors and make a thorough inspection of the premises.

During the Llanelli game, Murdoch was involved in argy-bargy with the Welsh cap, Denis Quinnell. In the next match against Cardiff, an ill-tempered game for which the home side were principally responsible, Murdoch was set upon by three Cardiff forwards. In the Press Box, the famous Welsh flyhalf of the 1950s, Cliff Morgan, bellowed in rage. 'Look at those stupid bastards,' he said. 'Three of them smashing Murdoch. Why aren't they chasing Kirkpatrick to stop him scoring his try?'

One week later, following the game with London Counties, Murdoch was asked by his neighbour at the dinner-table, Sir William Ramsay, the one and only 'Bill', to venture his opinion of the Twickenham match and such-like. Murdoch snarled: 'It was for the birds. Playing those bloody Poms in front of all those other bloody Poms. And then they bring us here and give us all this bloody fancy stuff to eat. Screw them.' Ramsay had been too long in rugby to be dismayed or displeased. 'Well, Murdoch,' he remarked, 'It's a long way from here to your farm. But I happen to think that, in ten years' time, you will look back on this as the greatest day of your life.' A few minutes later, Ramsay told T.P. McLean of the incident. 'If I want to,' he said, 'I can swear a bloody sight better than he can. Anyway, I intend to invite him to my place for Christmas dinner.' He did, too, by letter, within a day or two – but Murdoch was well gone by Christmas.

That was Saturday evening. On each of three succeeding Saturday evenings, Murdoch got into strife. The match with Ulster, at Belfast, was played amidst a more emotional atmosphere than any previously encountered by an All Black team in the British Isles. Because of 'The Troubles' there was much discussion as to whether the New Zealanders should fulfil their engagement. In the end, Todd took the decision to go. Ravenhill Park was ringed with British troops and armed vehicles as the All Blacks took the field. For almost two minutes, the 25,000 spectators stood to the Kiwis, clapping and cheering.

Sad, therefore, that after so stirring an experience, followed by a dinner and dance at the Dunadry Inn, 14 miles west of Belfast, Murdoch and two companions, Graham Whiting, his fellow-prop, and Michael Parkinson, a midfield back, should somehow procure from the hotel porter the security key which allowed admission to all the hotel rooms. At about 2 o'clock in the morning, they charged into several bedrooms, hustling and manhandling the occupants. The reporter of the *Auckland Star*, Roy Williams, was asleep when the three men grabbed him, hoisted him high and dropped him to the floor. 'I still have a chipped bone in my left elbow,' Williams said, years later. 'I didn't really mind. I remembered that as a youngster I had done some pretty stupid things. It's part of growing-up, I guess.'

Murdoch, Whiting and Parkinson carried on. Only with extreme difficulty were they stopped from hurling the hotel's piano through a first-floor window on to the concrete yard outside. On the Sunday morning, the manager of the Inn confronted Todd, listing the damage to the property and demanding a cheque for £500 before he would allow the team to leave the hotel.

Saturday night, so the song goes, is the loneliest night in the week. Not for Murdoch. One week after Dunadry, the All Blacks were at the Peebles Hydropathic Hotel in the Scottish Border district. They had that day played the Borders at Hawick, and won 26–6. At a late hour in the hall of the Hydro, Murdoch was pretending to be Graham Whiting and demanding from the porter the key to Whiting's room. Standing close by was a Kiwi expatriate, Norman Harris, formerly in the sports-writing department of the *New Zealand Herald* and now on the sports staff of the London *Sunday Times*. As a man of saturnine humour, Harris joined the conversation. 'Actually,' he informed the hall-porter, 'this gentleman is Mr K.A. Murdoch.'

At these words, Murdoch whipped about, placed both hands on the crown of Harris's head, grasping him by the hair and pressing his huge weight downward. Harris fell violently to the floor. Money from his pockets rolled about the hallway. He was dimly aware, as he fell, that Murdoch called him a filthy word. Harris and T.P. McLean, who had been his sports editor on the *Herald*, sat together in the coach which next day bore the Press to Edinburgh's airport. Harris was silent, but did remark at one stage: 'That is the first time in my thirteen adult years that anyone has struck me.' In the All Blacks' coach, Murdoch asked: 'Who was that joker I knocked down last night?' Told that Harris was a Kiwi newspaperman who now worked in London, Murdoch commented casually: 'Well, he wouldn't care much, would he?'

On the contrary, Harris cared a good deal. Back in the *Sunday Times* sports-room, he mentioned the fracas to John Lovesey, the editor, and several others, including Dudley Doust, who wrote a column, 'Inside Track'. Doust was enraged by the assault on his friend and, against Harris's protests, called McLean, who was now with the All Blacks at the Angel Hotel, Cardiff, awaiting the international with Wales at the Arms Park a couple of days hence. McLean could not offer much. The incident had passed into the All Blacks' domain of secret information.

Soon enough, after the match in which the All Blacks narrowly got home 19–16, it was Saturday night again. In the course of the dance that followed the dinner, McLean and Murdoch exchanged a genial greeting as they waited to pay for drinks at the bar. At some stage Murdoch entered the room of Peter Bush, the eminent New Zealand rugby photographer, and ordered them both beer and sandwiches. Later, Murdoch expressed irritation that the bar had been closed.

Todd remembers being called to the hotel kitchen at about 1.15 on the Sunday morning, on reports of a bust-up there, though at that stage there had been no physical violence. Murdoch had entered the kitchen, demanding drink. Peter Grant, of the Gwent Security Guard, whose members behaved, that night, like SS types, told him there was none. When Todd came in, he held a piece of paper in his hand. He flicked it, menacingly. 'Right, Murdoch,' he was reported to have said. 'This time you *are* going home.' 'Well, if I'm going,' replied Murdoch, 'some of these bastards are coming with me.' He fetched Grant a heavy blow, and all hell broke loose.

McLean became aware of the situation when, returning from the Angel carpark at about 1.30 am after seeing some dinner guests to their car, he encountered Graham Whiting at the front-door of the hotel. 'Have you seen Keithie?' Whiting asked. 'There's been a hell of a row. That chump Ernie is talking of sending him home.' McLean prospected down one street, Whiting the other. They met at the door. No sign.

Next morning, McLean grabbed an early copy of the *Sunday Times*, which carried a searing piece by Doust suggesting that many former friends of New Zealand would be glad when the All Blacks went home. McLean sat in the foyer waiting for Todd to return from Mass. The two men greeted each other. 'Ernie,' said McLean, 'I am told there is a good chance Murdoch may be sent home. Is there any truth in this?' 'Too bloody right,' answered Todd. They walked to the foot of the stairs. 'Putting it on the line, Ernie,' McLean said, 'I would be entitled to report there is a good chance Murdoch could be sent home?' Todd agreed. McLean sped to a telephone to call his office in Auckland. Next morning, the *Herald* carried a billboard, 'Murdoch May Be Sent Home.' Twenty-four hours later, Murdoch was on his way.

From the moment Murdoch poked his head, outside a Birmingham hotel, into the coach which was to convey the All Blacks to training for the next match, remarking 'Hooray, boys. I'm off', until his departure from Heathrow Airport within a couple of hours, the Press and television had a meal of the man. The caption to one picture mentioned that Murdoch had torn from his blazer the pocket with its Silver Leaf monogram. Peter Bush managed to wheedle his way past guards to the aircraft door and pleaded for permission to shake hands with Murdoch. The air hostess was sympathetic but firm. 'I'm sorry,' she said, 'Mr Murdoch does not want to see anyone.'

Murdoch, a silent passenger, demanded to be let off the plane at Singapore. Later, he flew to Darwin. Then he disappeared into the blue. In 1974, T.P. McLean, of the *New Zealand Herald*, tracked him down to a small encampment of railwaymen who tended the line bearing iron from Newman, in the fastnesses of Western Australia, to Port Hedland, whence it was shipped to Japan. Murdoch did not greet the reporter enthusiastically. 'Who brought this So-and-so up here?' he shouted to the driver of the Scammell truck which had carried him to the work-site, some distance from the camp. After informing McLean that he had written many lies, Murdoch offered a threat. If McLean did not leave immediately, he would be cast into a slowly running pool of black oil, a foot wide, an inch deep, which lay between them. McLean, although sizeable enough to qualify as a light-heavyweight, could see neither point nor profit in a punch-up and declined the invitation.

For the next 16 years, Murdoch vanished from view. It was often rumoured, especially in the early days, that he had turned down very large sums of money to play rugby league in Australia. Publishers bit their fingers to the bone, dreaming of presenting to the world the *real* story. At least two of New Zealand's most prominent rugby writers, Lindsay Knight, variously of the Wellington *Dominion*, the *Auckland Star* and the *Dominion* again, and Bob Howitt, editor of the national weekly, *Rugby News*, happened upon him. Murdoch greeted them fairly; but he declined, courteously, the request of each man for an interview, which, conducted in the right humour, might even have led to a book.

Murdoch sometimes returned to his Dunedin home to visit his mother. His wish that his visits be private were respected. McLean, who had perhaps been closer than any journalist to the developing story of a latter-day Greek drama, sometimes thought of the man as rugby's Flying Dutchman, condemned forever to sail the seas of solitude.

Murdoch might have remained in that situation had it not been for the enterprise of an independent television producer named Julie Christie, of Auckland. Communicado, for which she worked, sold Television New Zealand the idea for a series called *Mud and Glory*, conveying profiles of a number of especially celebrated All Blacks. TVNZ jumped at the idea. Given the go-ahead for the programme, Christie appreciated that the biggest catch of all would be Murdoch. She hired Margot McRae, an experienced researcher and interviewer, to track him down.

McRae discovered that Murdoch was working in a small town, Tully, in northern Queensland. She later told Barry Shaw, television editor of the *New Zealand Herald*, that she had found her man in a small pub. 'I just approached him, softly, softly,' she said, 'I knew that he would never speak to reporters. He just hates them. He agreed to a chat with me. He was willing to be filmed. The agreement was that I was to do the voice-over, to say what he had said to me.'

McRae said Murdoch cleared up a few points about the punch-up; but the interview was not the ultimate – 'the one in which Murdoch tells all'. Her impression was that the whole story would never be told, not least because Murdoch was never going to write, or have published, a book. Comely, young and sympathetic, she thought Murdoch basically was 'very shy, not given to words. He had a fear of sounding, or looking, foolish. When we ran the tape back, we could hear Keith saying, "Why am I doing this?" '

She returned to the hotel, with her cameraman, the following day. Murdoch 'saw us coming. He disappeared into the bush.'

The programme, which was nationally televised in June of 1990, aroused intense interest. Yet again the public sympathy for Murdoch was evident. Although a substantial part of the story had been told by T.P. McLean in *They Missed the Bus*, there was a feeling that Murdoch had been ill-used, and that Todd, who had ended the tour as one of New Zealand's least successful managers, had either made an unfortunate personal decision or had been pressured by authorities of the Four Home Unions into sending him home.

Not unnaturally, therefore, *Mud and Glory* stirred mud. Reviewing the programme, McLean wrote in the *Herald* that 'Murdoch was not sent home for the one act of punching the guard. His dispatch was the culmination of a series of events which began on the flight from Auckland at the start of the tour.'

After expelling Murdoch, Todd had sent home to his wife, Pat, in Wellington, a tape-record, the contents of which were not made generally known until an excellent special writer for the Wellington *Evening Post*, Alex Veysey, published them on 26 June 1990, two days after the showing of the television programme.

According to Todd, Lin Colling, Murdoch's room-mate, rushed in, saying: 'You've got to come down below. Keith's in trouble. He's going mad.' Todd spoke in the tape of Murdoch as being 'in some ways a wonderful guy. . . . I think that if he drinks spirits the way he drinks beer . . . he just runs off the rails and I don't think he knows what he is doing. . . . He has been in quite a bit of trouble – not quite a bit but on three or four occasions he has been in trouble and John Tallent, the chairman of the Four Home Unions, has virtually demanded I send him home.'

This last remark coincided with opinions voiced at the time of the expulsion by Kirkpatrick as captain of the team and, many years later, by Duff, the coach who, astonishingly, was not interviewed for *Mud and Glory*. Kirkpatrick said: 'I am convinced the Four Home Unions demanded that Todd send Murdoch home. I was there. I could hear Todd talking on the telephone. I have been of a mind to stand up and speak about this. The Home Unions wanted Keith out. It was a bad business. The fellers all liked Keith, you know.'

Duff said: 'I have always been under the impression the Four Home Unions exerted pressure. At a meeting at the Angel, the morning after the shindig, Tallent, Albert Agar, of the Rugby Football Union, and the treasurer of the Welsh union and member of the International Board, Ken Harris, were present. Each of these men said, in effect: "You can't have this sort of thing, you know."

'Kirkpatrick, Going (the vice-captain) and I had a meeting with Todd. We decided, after discussion, that Murdoch must be severely reprimanded. We had to choose the team for the next match, against West Midlands, a tough game. We put Murdoch in. Later, we paraded Murdoch to secure an undertaking that he would not again misbehave. He refused to speak while Todd was in the room. When Todd left, he gave the three of us the assurance.

'When we set off for Birmingham, everything, so far as "Kirkie", "Sid" and myself were concerned, had been cleaned up. During the night, something transpired. At 8 in the morning, or thereabouts, Todd told me he was sending Murdoch home. Kirkpatrick was told, too. We were both deeply shocked. Within the hour, Murdoch was gone. I have always been under the impression that the "something" which happened and which evidently caused Todd to change his mind was pressure from the Home Unions.'

In his tape to his wife, Todd said that the chairman of the Home Union's committee (Tallent) had virtually demanded Murdoch be sent home. At the time, McLean had confronted Tallent with this allegation. Was there truth in the statement? Tallent, a charming, silver-haired London stockbroker, an England cap many times and (so McLean assumed) a good friend, smoothly replied: 'My dear fellow, of course we didn't demand that Todd send Murdoch home. We merely said that if Ernie did decide on expulsion, we would offer no objection to Murdoch's immediate replacement.'

During the furore over the *Mud and Glory* programme, McLean telephoned Tallent. The man was in distress. His wife, Helen, had collapsed and died a few days before. He was preparing to leave for her memorial service. Naturally, in these grievous circumstances, it took Tallent a while to concentrate on McLean's question. Had the Four Home Unions demanded Murdoch's expulsion? 'Decidedly not,' he replied at last. 'The situation was as I told you at the time – we would offer Todd every help in securing a replacement if he decided that he must send Murdoch home.'

Let us end this saddening tale which has bitten so deeply into the New Zealand rugby mind that a huge majority of Kiwis still appear to believe that Murdoch was unjustly dismissed, with two revelations, one a sorry self-confession by Murdoch, the other a devastating remark by Cecil Blazey, who for many years was chairman of the New Zealand Rugby Council until his retirement in 1987. On the night of the team's first game in the British Isles, Murdoch was seated at dinner with a member of the Western Counties' team. He was unusually talkative. He knew, Murdoch said, that it had been and would be a policy of opposing players to nibble and needle him, to get at him, to put him off-balance; and he added: 'I am not the same as you ordinary blokes, you know. Nine-tenths of the time, I am OK. On the other tenth, I have got to blow. I can't take it. I have got to stand up for myself and explode.'

Three months after *Mud and Glory*, Ces Blazey and T.P. McLean were seated next to each other at a meeting of the Board of Governors which had been set up to establish a National Sports Hall of Fame. The two men were old friends and greatly trusting of each other. McLean told Blazey he had been in touch with Tallent. The Murdoch case came up. McLean repeated what Tallent had said.

Blazey is too polite ever to say such a damning word as 'Nonsense'. But he did say, positively: 'Tallent caused Murdoch to be sent home. I was dining with him and Helen. The subject came up. John said: "Of course, we sent him home. I told Todd that if he did not send Murdoch home, the Four Home Unions would immediately cancel the All Blacks' tour."'

'They would never have done that,' observed McLean.

'Of course they wouldn't have,' said Blazey. 'But that was Tallent's ultimatum. That was the climax of the pressure that the Home Unions brought to bear on Todd.'

Although he has deeply admired Murdoch's reticence, his refusal ever to tell his side of the story, which would naturally cast heavy doubt on Todd's competence for managing an international rugby team on a long tour, McLean has never wavered in the belief that Murdoch's behaviour on the tour justified his expulsion, dreadfully severe though the punishment was. Three eminent men of New Zealand rugby, V.G. Cavanagh, the famous Otago coach, Jack Manchester, captain of the 1935 All Blacks, and Dudley Manning, sports editor of the *Otago Daily Times*, great friends all, had individually, before the selection of Kirkpatrick's team, urged the New Zealand Rugby Council to instruct selectors not to choose Murdoch. Their opinions were based on his play for Otago club rugby and his curious behaviour during the tour of the 1971 British Lions when, on the morning of the match, he declined to turn out for Otago against the tourists. Subsequently, although chosen three times in All Black teams to play the

Lions, Murdoch each time failed to show up. Was it not Murdoch himself who had remarked to a stranger at a formal dinner: 'I am not the same as you ordinary blokes, you know.'?

★ ★ ★

A fortnight after the dramatic scenes in Cardiff, Scotland was defeated, 14–9, and then England, 9–0. So now, in spite of everything, this unlikely, cross-grained, ill-managed, ill-disciplined side was offered the chance, against Ireland, of the Grand Slam, the supreme prize.

Taking the wind with the toss, the Irish blew into the match with Celtic fury. They soon had the lead from a penalty by their burly flyhalf, Barry McGann. Meantime the fine All Black front five of Graham Whiting, Tane Norton, Kent Lambert and, in the second row, Peter Whiting and 'Toby' Macdonald, were stemming the Irish tide. Macdonald, in particular, was gaining the upper hand over Willie John McBride. Going wrestled himself clear of the powerful Irish number 8, John Moloney, to score a try which Joe Karam converted. So it was 6–3 at half-time – not great rugby, but hellishly exciting stuff – and a quarter of an hour into the second half it was 10–3 from superb support play. Lambert gathered the loose ball. From him, it went to Burgess and thence, 15 yards short of the tryline, to Alex Wyllie, who stormed through to score.

Then, in three crashing blunders, the All Blacks kissed goodbye to the Grand Slam. Karam made a very long punt which he failed to follow up – a crime because Tom Kiernan, making the catch, produced a powerful counter-attack which the great Mike Gibson carried into the All Blacks' 25. When Tom Grace threw the ball in crookedly at the lineout, Kirkpatrick ordered a scrum. Second blunder: Joseph penalized Going for putting the ball under the feet of his front row. McGann goaled. Karam then initiated the final blunder. He punted the ball into touch on the full. From the heels at the scrum at halfway, the Irish surged into the All Blacks' 25. Moloney sucked Grant Batty away from his station by the left touch to pass to Grace, who, running within a yard or two of the touchline, lofted the ball past Karam.

Two All Blacks, Burgess and Going, and one Irishman, Grace, raced for the ball bumbling in the All Blacks' in-goal. It seemed certain to bounce over the deadball line. Did Burgess, thinking so, slightly slacken his run? As the players dived, the ball hopped up by Grace's right shoulder – and Burgess was to his left. Inches from the deadball line, Grace fairly grounded the ball to level the score 10–10. Many a heart the length and breadth of Ireland was broken when McGann failed to place the goal across the wind.

Going was penalized four times by Welsh referee, Meirion Joseph, for his put-ins at the scrummage. Going was adamant that after the second offense, Joseph issued him a general warning. In terms of this Law, the referee was required, at the next infringement, to order Going from the field. It was at the fourth offense that Ireland, with admirable spirit, saved the game.

Despite all the criticism, the All Blacks ended their tour of the British Isles on a high note, contributing strongly to what has been called the most exhilarating, exciting and enchanting match in the history of the game, against the Barbarians at Cardiff Arms Park.

True to their policy of encouraging promising players, the Baa-Baas played one uncapped man, Robert Wilkinson, a Cambridge lock. He was surrounded, in the pack, by such notables as John Pullen at hooker, Ray McLoughlin and 'Sandy' Carmichael at prop, McBride in the second row and Derek Quinnell, Tom David and Fergus Slattery in the back. The backline teemed with talent – Gareth Edwards and Phil Bennett at halfback, David Duckham, Dawes, Gibson and John Bevan in the threequarters, and J.P.R. Williams at fullback.

In the third minute, Bryan Williams kicked very deep. Bennett fielded, a yard or two forward from his goal-line. Hurtling at him came a raw country youth named Alistair Scown; he had physique, he had speed, he had everything – except know-how. Bennett shrugged to his right and Scown swerved that way. Instantly, Bennett broke to his left. An utterly fantastic movement developed. Bearing upfield and toward the left touchline, Bennett passed to J.P.R. Williams, who moved on a few yards before passing to Pullen. Getting on for halfway, Dawes took the pass and sent on to David. At about 45 yards from the All Blacks' goal-line, David passed to Edwards. Kent Lambert, a Clydesdale type, gave chase to Edwards, who was Thousand Guineas' stuff. Whether the try was the greatest ever, as is still contended, is unimportant. Simply, it was perfection.

Not uncharacteristically, the All Blacks had blundered in choosing their team. Going had taken the field suffering serious leg problems. After about ten minutes he received another crack which placed him in agony. He kept on and on, less effective every minute, and finally had to go.

By half-time, the Barbarians were 17 points clear from tries by Edwards, Slattery and Bevan, and a conversion and penalty goal by Bennett. They had raged all over the field in glorious, sweeping runs. Seven minutes into the second half, the All Blacks, stirred by Kiwi pride, had scored seven points from a penalty by Karam and a try by Grant Batty, made for him when Bryan Williams streaked into the attack from the blindside to beat Gibson cold. Ian Hurst placed a superb punt across the Barbarians' defensive line and Batty, gathering, faced J.P.R. Williams, tackler incomparable. So simple to score a try when everything is well done. Batty lobbed a punt over Williams, ran around him, and with perfect judgement gathered the bounce for a try which put the Barbarians, at 17–11, in some difficulty.

This was soon resolved. Duckham set off one of his runs, blond hair streaming. Gibson joined him. J.P.R. was ready for the final pass. Phil Bennett topped off the movement, the game and the thrilling qualities of true Barbarianism with his fine converting goal. The final score was 23–11.

The rest was anti-climax. The All Blacks toddled off to the munificent Parc des Princes stadium in Paris to receive a come-uppance from France, 13–6. A dollop of sour cream on the coffee of a sour tour.

★ ★ ★

The All Black team of 1974 visited Australia before travelling to Ireland to play six matches in celebration of the centenary of the Irish Rugby Union. The new captain was a modest, genial Wellingtonian, Andy Leslie, and the coach a former schoolmaster, J.J. Stewart, a man of lively, original mind, much loved by the players, whose belief in individual freedom in expression bore fruit in the Australian test series, which the All Blacks took with two wins and one draw. In the slush and mud of the third test at the Sydney Cricket Ground, Duncan Robertson, an all-weather flyhalf, lashed the sodden, heavy ball far across the goalmouth where Grant Batty, the 'Gingerbread Man', that pugnacious threequarter, ran on to a superb catch and a lovely try. Although the All Black scrummage was not playing consistently to a superior international standard, Jay Jay was encouraged by the magnificent backrow play of the flankers Ken Stewart and former captain Ian Kirkpatrick, and of Leslie himself, a fast, light-footed player with perfect hands. The drill of these three was an education: Stewart first to the ball-handler in the opposing backline, catching him, and the ball, in the act; second, Kirkpatrick, thundering into the play to take a pass or gather the ball and plunge onward; third, Leslie, acting, as he whimsically put it, 'as a sweeper who just arrives to tidy things up'.

Except on the field, the Irish extended hospitality with a capital H. The Irish union presented each of the All Blacks with a Waterford crystal pint holder, decorated with the union's arms. It also struck a tie of black background, green stripes and decorated with shamrock and silver ferns, distributed only to members of the opposing teams. And its Leinster branch gave every New Zealand player a 21-piece teaset.

On field, however, the Irish celebrated their centenary with a will that far exceeded the bounds of sporting play. T.P. McLean reported to the *New Zealand Herald* that Ireland had become 'the land of the flying footwear'. Of the match with Leinster, a hummer won by the All Blacks 8–3, Ned van Esbeck, a senior man of the *Irish Times*, wrote that 'regrettably it must be said that persistent and deliberate late-tackling and indiscriminate use of the boot in the rucks will do nothing to enhance the reputation of New Zealand as a great rugby nation'. David Irvine told readers of the *Guardian* that the All Blacks' energies were 'usually manifested in late tackles, dangerous footwork in the rucks and, eventually, the incongruous squaring up of Lambert to all comers, as though in a boxing ring'. A young New Zealand expatriate, Robert Messenger, whose brother was to become president of the New Zealand Rugby Union but who had become more Irish than the Irish, wrote in the *Irish Press* that 'the All Blacks cannot take as good as they give. When a man lies on the ball on their side of the ruck, kick him off it. But if an All Black lies on the opposition side, fists up if he is touched. If an All Black tackles, it is hard and meant to hurt. If an opponent tackles, fists up again.'

The listed injuries to All Blacks in this match read like an agony column: Peter Whiting had to be put to sleep with pethidine to kill the pain of the wound below his knee – from a kick; Macdonald could not train the next day because of the pain of a shoulder wound – from a kick; the backside of

the Maori prop, Bill Bush, naturally brown, was, after the match, black –
from a kick; during play, Leslie rolled in agony – from a kick; Kevin
Eveleigh, loose-forward, was heavily bruised over back and chest – from
kicks; Sid Going, the fullback, was deeply scraped on the leg – from kicks;
Lambert's body was a catalogue of bruises and gashes. Jay Jay summed the
match up perfectly: 'The All Blacks undoubtedly must be the maddest of all
time; after all, it was apparent that they spent their time either kicking each
other, or themselves.'

The All Blacks overcame Ireland in the lone international, 15–6. The
only try came from Joe Karam, who entered *Guinness* by scoring all his
team's points with that try, a conversion and three penalties. Michael Quinn
inadvertently aided the All Blacks by lofting four drop-outs from the 25 into
the arms of the unmarked Whiting, who, claiming fair catches, hosted
return kicks of enormous altitude which troubled the Irish defence considerably. Yet such was the Irish spirit overall that in their six matches, the
All Blacks managed no more than 18 tries against two, eight conversions
against none, 13 penalty goals against 13 conceded, and no drop goal
against one.

So, for the rest of the short tour, across the water to Cardiff, where
strange things happened. Two years before, the mob had threatened to tear
Todd's team into strips. Yet now, as the Kiwis marched on to the field at
Arms Park to play a Welsh XV, 50,000 spectators greeted them as if they
were prodigal sons. 'God Save the Queen' and 'Land of Our Fathers' were
sung with tremendous verve and after performing their *haka*, the All Blacks
were wildly cheered.

The wind was tearing downfield, from the River Taff end, and Gareth
Edwards (there is many a sucker, even in international rugby) took it. At
half-time it was a penalty goal apiece. Phil Bennett looked harried and
careworn, incapable of placing penalty shots, neglectful of backs as talented
as Gerald Davies, J.J. Williams, J.P.R. Williams and Ray Bergiers.
Extraordinary. Another back, Ian Hall, a 28-year-old policeman, lay with
his legs in a tangle as Kirkpatrick was shoved over him. 'Kirkie', a farmer
accustomed to blood and gore, rose and gazed, horrified, at the fractured
bones of Hall's leg, jutting through the stocking; and Bruce Robertson,
who had been marking Hall, shouted for the doctors and ambulance-men.

Spirit and pride are prime elements of Welsh rugby at all levels; and the
All Blacks, with the wind, took 25 minutes to take charge of the game.
Going, Robertson and Whiting all figured in a mix-up and maul 20 yards or
more from the Welsh goal. Kirkpatrick was arriving fast when the ball was
squirted along the ground at him. With an expert pick-up, his sidestep,
right, may have coincided with a Bennett sidestep to *his* right, and he was
off. Ball in hand, goal-line looming, 'Kirkie' at speed was no sight for the
timorous, and nothing was going to stop his run for the try which Karam
goaled with his third successful shot of the game.

All Wales, astonishingly, agreed that the 12–3 victory of the All Blacks
was well deserved. After the match, J.J. Stewart, a compassionate man,
came across a little boy named Hunter who had recently lost a leg in an

accident. Jay Jay took him to the All Blacks' dressing-room, introducing him to each of the players. Thence to the Welsh dressing-room where Gareth Edwards, emerging from his shower, steaming and streaming, did the rounds with his team. At the banquet, Edwards preached one of the verities. 'We were very dis-ap-pointed,' he said, stringing out the syllables in the Welsh fashion, 'to lose that test match today. So far as we were concerned, it was a test match; and because it was against our great friends and rivals, we wan-ted to win it very badly. But then I must tell you that this little boy, Hunt-ter, came into our dressing-room; and when I last saw, he had around his neck one pair of All Black socks and one pair of Welsh; and I thought, loooking at that little boy, that the los-ing of a test match is not such a very serious mat-ter, after all.'

Now these All Blacks had one more river to cross. Their match with the Barbarians at Twickenham was celebrated in the official programme by Dr Tony O'Reilly, whose record of 17 tries for the British Lions against the Springboks in South Africa, in 1955, had been beaten by one point by Graham Thorne of the 1970 All Blacks. O'Reilly had described the spirit of Barbarians' football – 'the willingness to take risks and the enduring friendships, summarized in the simple qualifications of anyone who is asked to wear the great Black and White jersey, that he be a Footballer and a Gentleman'. Warming up, he looked at the prospects for the coming match: 'Today will be a contrast in styles – the Barbarians determinedly amateur, playing the game for fun, upholding in my view (without being unctuous) the finest traditions of rugby football. . . . Today's equation is: tank v cavalry; rapier v claymore.'

What fun to be entertained by O'Reilly, telling amusing stories in countless dialects, so unconsciously solemn and sober-sided. In fact, the Barbarians were today fielding the same forward pack, scrumhalf Edwards and fullback Andy Irvine, stalwarts of the Lions' team, captained by Willie John McBride and coached by Syd Millar, which, a few weeks beforehand, had achieved the seemingly impossible – an undefeated tour of South Africa and a test-match series of three wins and a draw. That amazing feat, by a pack of the quality and strength of Ian McLauchlan, Bobby Windsor and Frank Cotton in the front row, McBride and Gordon Brown in the second, and Roger Uttley, Mervyn Davies and Fergus Slattery at the back, with Gareth Edwards and Phil Bennett, had, so some critics noted, been hewed with the religious fervour to a battle-plan of nine- or ten-man rugby; win the ball, belt it over the top, chase, compress, win again, place the penalties or score the tries.

In yet another instance of non-Barbarianism, McBride lashed the club for refusing to allow him to bring in Syd Millar to coach the team. What was plain, in any event, was that the All Blacks, despite the 13–13 result, and despite doing some remarkably silly things - late-charging twice at the cost of two penalties, and swinging punches (Kirkpatrick and Macdonald) which were not admired by French referee Georges Demercq, or by their own team either, but which were surely responses rather than sallies – were decidedly the better team: better as cavalry, better with the rapier.

After just over an hour's play, the Barbarians, with penalty goals by Irvine, led 9–7, Leslie having scored a try and Karam placing a lone penalty from seven attempts. Then Sid Going lofted a punt so high that as Irvine caught it, he was brought down fairly by Batty. As the ball was played back to him by the forwards, Batty punted. It was caught on the bounce, far to the right, beyond Duckham, by Bryan Williams, who set off full-steam and would have reached the goalposts had not Duckham clipped his heel with a despairing dive. Karam's goalkick cannoned from the upright over the bar.

Now, with eight or nine minutes left, battle was fairly joined. Preece, slight, shortish, sprinted at speed, Irvine took his pass and lofted a tremendous punt to the goal-line. Karam, for only the second time on the tour, failed to make a clean catch, and as the ball bounded high, Mervyn Davies, a magnificent number 8, caught it and dived over for the equalizing try.

Peter Robbins, perhaps the coolest of all the British critics, wrote in the *Financial Times*: 'The attractions of this well-led and well-coached party have been the involvement of all of the team. I wrote earlier in the season of signs that British rugby is reverting to forward power. This would be disastrous for us, as well as foreign to our nature. Having shown New Zealand the way in 1971, are we in very real danger of losing that way ourselves?'

★　★　★

Not the least arresting features of this Decade of Disasters were the proliferation of short tours and the intrusion of politics. They resulted in the appearance of promoters and/or entrepreneurs who, in various ways, set about nibbling away at the Regulations Relating to Amateurism which had long been declared sacrosanct by the International Rugby Board. Extraordinary developments followed. In the late 1970s, positive steps were taken toward the formation of a professional troupe which would tour the world, holding exhibition games where appropriate. Famous players from the Four Home Unions, New Zealand, Australia and other countries were said to be interested; but the longer talk about the troupe went on, the more surely such funds as had been available dribbled away.

During the 1980s, David Lord, an Australian entrepreneur, caused wild alarm by building up, so he claimed, a professional troupe which would suck from amateur rugby many of its finest players. His apparent New Zealand agent, Andy Haden, a prominent All Black and later a severe critic of the Establishment, at one stage produced a statement that 28 All Blacks had signed letters of intent, held by his bank, to join the organization.

Who could these players be? The guessing went on and on. Later, Haden and Lord appeared to fall out, sharp words were spoken, and another sensation was laid to rest. But the movement for enticing leading players to become quasi-professionals soon became irresistible. In 1990, the International Board accepted that it was proper for prominent players to

108

earn money by writing books or articles, making public appearances and being paid for addressing gatherings. No sooner had this resolution been approved than the Rugby Football Union in London began querulously to question that it had been correctly framed. By the late 1980s, the demands upon leading players had become extreme. All Blacks were on call to play, mostly at first-class level, for eight, nine, even ten months of the year.

Meanwhile politics gnawed away at the New Zealand game. As the young Bryan Williams developed his glorious talents during the 1970 tour of South Africa, he became an idol of the Coloured population, players and spectators alike, of Cape Province, and, to a lesser degree, of Blacks who preferred the game of rugby to Association Football. Near the end of the game against Griqualand West, in Kimberley, a large number of Blacks moved forward, obviously just to gaze upon, or maybe touch, Williams. Whites in the crowd resisted the surge; a box was thrown, a blow struck, a curse uttered, and in no time a riotous situation had developed. New Zealand spectators in the grandstand and All Black players still on the field watched with horror the parading of racial hatred.

The Prime Minister of the Third Labour Government of New Zealand, Norman Kirk, doubtless had Kimberley in mind when he told the Rugby Union to 'postpone' their invitation for the Springboks to tour the country in 1973. He was reviled in rugby circles. Sadly, he was dead by the time of the General Election of 1975. Although Robert Muldoon, leader of the National Party, did not campaign on the South African issue and the Kirk veto, as a pragmatist, he knew the depth of feeling, especially in rural districts, against the Labour Party's attitude to South Africa. The issue became important; and National swept to power.

One year later, its Parliamentarians may have wondered whether they had caught a tiger by the tail in not vehemently criticizing the regime of President J.B. Vorster. Despite many warnings, the All Blacks, captained by Andy Leslie, had set off to play 24 games in South Africa. They left Auckland amid extraordinary security restrictions and were driven straight to their aircraft. Since the Australian Government had refused transit to a national sporting team heading for South Africa, they flew by Singapore Airlines to Singapore. The roundabout route then took them, in a squalid plane of Olympic Airways, to Bahrein and Athens: whence they departed, after a dutiful inspection of the Acropolis, for Lisbon, Abijan and Jan Smuts Airport in Johannesburg.

Their reception, by Dr Danie Craven and a good many Whites who, like him, had spent much of their lives in rugby, was in stark contrast to the welcome given to Wilson Whineray's team by excited thousands of all races at the same airport 16 years previously. The city was seething with rage and bitterness. Only five days before the All Blacks had left Auckland, thousands of Black schoolchildren in Soweto had met to protest against the obligatory teaching of Afrikaans. They wanted English, the children shrilled. There may have been stirrers – who knows? But a stone was thrown, then another and another, until a hail was being chucked at the police. As on that fateful day at Sharpeville, in 1960, the police, in panic, opened fire. By the end of the riot, 176 lay dead on the ground, with many more wounded.

Early on, the All Blacks learned that the great loose-forward, Jan Ellis, had refused the captaincy of a South African Invitation XV to play the All Blacks. The Johannesburg *Sunday Times* carried the full story. Ellis had turned down the offer because his team was to include two Coloureds and two Blacks, saying: 'Multiracial sport anywhere else in the world is OK. I have played against, and socialized with Fijians, Maoris, and all other kinds. But that was in Europe. When in Rome, you do as the Romans tell you. Here, in South Africa, the same thing holds – and I am a White South African.'

On the All Blacks' arrival, Kit Fawcett, a young fullback who was to bring pain and despair to Leslie, to Jay Jay and to many team-mates, chatted his head off to a charming (and smart) reporter of the *Johannesburg Star*. The topic of sex was raised. Fawcett suggested the Kiwis would score more off the field than on it. Such candour rocked South Africa and disgusted his fellow All Blacks.

All this might have been diverting or humorous. Sadly, the atmosphere of the tour, on and off the field, was deadly serious. Once more, the All Blacks came up against a controversial decision, this time from Ian Gourlay, in the first of the four tests at Durban, won by the Springboks 16–7. Two All Blacks, Duggie Bruce and Leslie, were clasped in a maul, Bruce at the back, holding the ball, Leslie at the front, being held by the Springboks. It was a well-constructed maul, moving remorselessly toward the goal-line and the try by Bruce which would be converted to tie the score. Of a sudden Gourlay ruled that Leslie was offside because he had joined the maul ahead of a team-mate holding the ball. When Leslie pointed out that, according to the relevant Law, it is impossible for a player in a maul to be declared offside, Gourlay marched the All Blacks ten yards up the field. Dannie Craven, later, said there had been no infringement; and when Jay Jay harried the referee, instructing him on the Laws of Rugby, Gourlay remarked, 'I'll look it up.' Gourlay was never again asked to referee an All Black match: and with good reason.

Three men won for the All Blacks the second test, played at Bloemfontein. One was Joe Morgan, a modest midfield back from North Auckland, who from 20 or 25 yards sliced clean through the Springbok defence for a try which Going converted. The second was a lock, Peter Whiting, who, as the superb 'Bok flanker, Boland Coetzee, was plunging to score, hit him so precisely with his shoulder – and feet off the ground in a daredevil dive – that both men and the ball finished in touch, yards beyond the line.

The third hero, the great man, was Going. It was biting cold in Bloemfontein. Snow had fallen. As a teetotaller, Going found no solace in liquor. He went over the play of the first test, particularly the All Blacks' misdeeds and mistakes. He talked things over with Leslie. A film of the match was procured. Shown at a team gathering, it turned into a kind of inquest. Gerhard Burgher, of the Johannesburg Afrikaans daily, *Die*

Vaderland, on match morning visited the hotel occupied by the All Blacks. He spoke to one, nodded to another. 'I knew then,' he said, 'that there was no way the Springboks were going to win this test.'

The third test, won by South Africa at the famous Newlands ground in Cape Town, 15–10, was a chronicle of nastiness, principally on the part of the Springboks. The All Blacks called in, as replacement for Brad Johnstone – supposedly invalided from the tour but playing superbly for Auckland one week later – an inexperienced loose-head prop named Perry Harris. He was money for jam for the huge, powerful South African prop, Johan Strauss, who bore him down so far that one scrummage after another collapsed. Referee Gert Bezuidenhout made no attempt to check the illegality – and Harris, as he admitted later, was so afraid of conceding penalties that he dared not risk settling the situation either by fist or Liverpool Kiss. At one ruck, the Springbok lock, 'Moaner' van Heerden, ruthlessly booted Going in the head. Going did not offer the other cheek. He chased van Heerden, belting him with punches. A half-hour later, Whiting was strapped on the ground in a ruck. Van Heerden stamped him, so violently that one ear was almost split from the head, a wound that required six stitches. Bezuidenhout did not react. ('You must NEVER,' said a South African who had been a member of the 1938 British Lions, 'go into a test match with a member of the National Party as referee.')

These were events too shocking to bear in the name of sport, an amateur *team* sport. Early on in the tour, Danie Craven had told the All Blacks that rugby, because of its physical hardness, was a dying game. Some 24 hours after the test, Jay Jay Stewart glumly forecast: 'Rugby will be dead in South Africa inside 15 years and in New Zealand in 20.' Both men could be right. At the end of the match of blood and gore and failed kicks at goal, Stewart entered the referee's dressing-room and presented him with an All Black blazer. Why, then did Bezuidenhout burst into tears?

The last test, at Ellis Park in Johannesburg, won by the Springboks 15–14, again demonstrated the All Blacks' inability to place goals, whether from penalties or after tries. Kirkpatrick and Going both scored tries and Bruce dropped a goal; but apart from a penalty by Williams from inside the quarter-line, the All Blacks failed with four more attempts. In contrast, Gerald Bosch, a great kicker, placed the three penalty chances he was offered and goaled Kritzinger's try. At least two penalty tries should have been awarded the All Blacks, and at the last whistle the rage of Kirkpatrick was all too manifest.

It was sad, sad stuff, echoed all too frequently off the field. Between the second and third tests, against South Africa's great provincial team, the 'Blue Bulls' of Northern Transvaal, the All Blacks had just pulled ahead with a brilliant try. At a lineout formed some 32 yards from the New Zealand goal-line, Thys Lourens, Northern's captain, muttered in Afrikaans to the pedantic referee, Piet Robbertse; '"Uncle" Piet,' he said, 'I am dropping out of the lineout. Watch it.' Because of a swift throw-in, the two forward lines had been higgledy-piggledy; and Kenny Stewart, unquestionably, was in the open field as the ball was being played. Robbertse immediately blew his whistle, marched downfield and ordered a penalty against Stewart. South Africans never miss sitters; and the game was lost 29–27.

At the formal dinner, Andy Leslie, replying to a toast, strung off a list of Maori place-names, pausing occasionally to remark: 'And that means, Mr President, that we are delighted to be in your beautiful city.' And so on. Had they known it, the 'Blue Bulls' were being deliberately, grossly insulted. Would they have cared? At the same dinner, the wife of Dr Fritz Eloff, President of Northern Transvaal, explaining the South African situation to her neighbour at table, said: 'Of course, Blacks are different from Whites. They smell.' Her companion happened to be Jay Jay Stewart, who stood up, mumbled a word and abruptly left the room. He did not return.

As a selector of the touring team, along with Jack Gleeson and Eric Watson, Stewart had been unhappy from the start. He had no faith in either Laurie Mains or Kit Fawcett at fullback, and had wanted Bob Barrell, of Wanganui, a fine goalkicker, or Doug Rowlands, of Bay of Plenty, small but very reliable. Although his forward pack was accomplished, backed by excellent halfbacks in Going and Lyn Davis, there was want of topnotch quality at flyhalf, where Duncan Robertson, at 29, failed to recover the brilliance of former years. There were other problems. Although he scored nine tries, Neil Purvis looked out of place on the wing; and Bill Osborne in midfield somehow failed to reproduce the form of his partnership with Bruce Robertson in their best years. The ultimate tragedy was the choice of Grant Batty for the tour. He had torn the lateral ligament of his right knee in a pre-season game and, very late in the first test, crashed to the ground and felt the knee 'go'. A South African orthopedic specialist fitted him with a plastic gate, and somehow 'Bats' struggled along, but not within ten points of his real self.

The team was beaten six times in 24 matches, scoring 610 points, including 89 tries. The last figure reflected the decline of the All Black attacking standards. Lochore's 1970 team scored 135 tries in an aggregate of 687 points.

After three months, the All Blacks set off for home. They were tired, sickened and shamed by the memories of Kirkpatrick and two or three others having been tear-gassed during a riot in Cape Town, shamed at the daily reports of carnage. The Christian Institute, a compassionate, non-racial organization, later reported that at least 3000 young people, mostly Blacks and Coloureds, had been shot by the police, many fatally. More than 300 had been detained, incommunicado, without hope of trial or writs for habeas corpus.

This was not sport. This was, as near as dammit, civil war. For New Zealand rugby it was the dismal climax of the Decade of Disasters.

EXPANSION OF THE UNIVERSE
1975-80

*T*he catalyst for the broadening of New Zealand's international rugby interests both at home and abroad was probably a most unhappy tour Down Under by the 1977 British Lions. The team's achievements, on the face of it, were impressive. Of the 25 matches, most were played in diabolical weather – cold, wind and rain – and three of the four games lost were in the internationals. Moreover, it was only by a freakish, fluky charge-down of a clearing punt in the last few minutes of play in the final test which cost the Lions their merited achievement of a squared series.

Yet the 19 members of the team who were from Welsh clubs gave the impression of carrying the banner for their colleagues of 1969 who had whimpered and whinged their way home after their dreadful beating in the second test. Furthermore, the kindest word which could be said about the manager, George Burrell, a Scot, was that he had entirely lost the apparently brilliant form that he had brought to the pioneering Scottish team of two years before (although insiders pointed out that in 1975 Burrell had the great Bill Dickinson as coach).

John Dawes, of London Welsh, who coached the 1977 team, had looked ideal as captain and supportive midfield back, superb in his judgement and timing of passes, with the great Lions' side of 1971. Now he was revealed as a man of bitter attitudes. The Irish genius, Michael Gibson, not only was refused a cap but was even accused of feeding the enemy, the New Zealand Press, with secret information because his wife, Moyra, was spared the horrors of touring alone by being welcomed in the Auckland home of T.P. McLean and his wife, Carol.

The extraordinary men who have at times run British rugby gave the captaincy of the tour to the Llanelli wonder-man Phil Bennett; and if ever a player was unsuited to wear that cap, it was the unfortunate Bennett. Too shy to accept the warmth and friendship offered him by Kiwis who, from earlier acquaintance, had placed him among the great flyhalves of the era, aware of schisms in the party, saddened by the want of a shoulder (such as that of Carwyn James) to lean or cry on, Bennett's playing form steadily deteriorated. As to his strength of leadership, much could be inferred from the fact that he was not even invited to the final Press conference of the tour.

What a misfortune that tour turned out to be! Furious rows blazed between the Press, especially the British contingent, and Burrell and Dawes. Duels would once have been fought as a result of Dawes accusing John Reason, of the *Daily Telegraph*, and Clem Thomas, of the *Observer*, of using Gibson as a spy. And there would have been a firing squad at dawn, with some fellow writers manning rifles, for Chris Lander, of the *Daily Mirror*, for filing, against general Press corps advice, an especially grim piece from that purveyor of pornography, the weekly *New Zealand Truth*, in which a young Kiwi woman claimed to have participated in 'groupies' with certain Lions, describing them as 'lousy lovers'. The story was carried on the *Mirror* front page.

Burrell rounded off the tour by telling the 57,000 spectators of the fourth test at Eden Park that he was disappointed at the Lions' defeat because they had outplayed the All Blacks. He had, he added, one consolation: the crowd behaviour was an improvement on that of other matches of the tour. 'This was,' commented Peter Devlin, sports editor of the *Auckland Star*, 'a remark in bad taste. This was neither the time nor the place for it. It fully deserved the booing it received.'

Not all the buffeting was one-sided. Ray Dellabarca, a player and later selector-coach of Wellington teams, told Alex Veysey, of the Wellington *Dominion*, that 'rugby in New Zealand has been transformed from an essentially simple game into an ego trip for theorists and administrators'. He followed this with the riveting statement that 'rugby has to accept that it is a business. If it is not well run, as such, only one group will suffer – the players. There is too much pressure on them. If administrators would get out and talk to them, instead of regarding them as appendages, they would be startled – frightened, maybe – at the intensity by which the players are disturbed. Players have their personal lives, their business lives, to cope with. Rugby is a sport, an unpaid hobby to be enjoyed. Administrators would do well to remember this when they place unreal demands on players.'

This tour may have influenced the decision, within the next few years, to scale down pretty well all rugby tours. The practical reduction of tours from 18 to 20 matches to about a dozen, or fewer, somehow diminished the sparkle, the fun and the humour both for visiting teams and their hosts.

Prior to this, in 1975 and 1976, Scotland and Ireland respectively had made short tours, Scotland losing 24–0 (four tries, all goaled) when Eden Park was inundated, and Ireland being beaten 11–3. Of special distinction, too, in 1975, was a visit by a Romanian team captained by Alexandre Pop, who, sensible fellow, later migrated to the United States. These charming men, one of whom, Dmitru, a lock, looked topnotch, were granted only a match with New Zealand Juniors. They drew this, 10–10, at Athletic Park, Wellington, in heavy conditions, and would have won if their flyhalf had taken the trouble, now and then, to pass the ball, bearing out the observation by that sage of the Invincibles of 1924, Mark Nicholls, that 'the two worst things in life are a kicking five-eighths and a nagging wife'.

In late 1977, an All Black team played the first official match at Rovigo, in Italy, and shared a test match series in France. Its manager, a fiery type from Auckland named Ronald Don, screamed blue murder about the incompetence of the tour arrangements. The great wing threequarter, Bryan Williams, suffered a dreadful hip injury in one match and would certainly have been lost to the game forever had it not been for the presence in the side of a qualified medical man, Laurie Knight. The All Blacks, captained by Mourie, recovered remarkably from their 18–13 defeat at Toulouse to win, most convincingly by 15–3, the second test in Paris.

The Wallabies more than repaid various savagings by All Blacks when at Eden Park, in 1978, they won by the massive score of 30–16. Greg Cornelson, a lanky, bearded loose-forward, scored four tries, one of them from a throw-in over the top by Andy Dalton on his own goal-line. By and large, however, the All Blacks continued their overlordship of Australia. Hard to take, therefore, were their defeats: Sydney, 1979, by 12–6 (and Kiwis snarled as the Wallabies, Bledisloe Cup aloft, did a triumphant lap of honour around the Cricket Ground); Sydney, 1980, by a whopping 26–10; and Sydney, yet again in 1984, by the narrowest of margins, 25–24.

Italy toured, Fiji toured, Tonga toured, and the relationship with France developed until, in the eyes of the New Zealand Rugby Council, this country had supplanted South Africa as the Kiwis' most conspicuous and, to an extent, feared rival. Even the United States and Canada were played at international level in 1980, while the All Blacks were en route to Wales as celebrants-in-chief of the Welsh Rugby Union centenary.

The United States were beaten at San Diego, 53–6, a result less remarkable than the fact that the gallery numbered 10,000 – a sign that the game was making genuine progress in California, where, because of the climate, rugby flourishes most strongly. The Canadians lost at Vancouver, 43–10. Although the weather is kindest to rugby in British Columbia, it is played throughout that vast country with a quite wonderful enthusiasm. The two props hailed from Vancouver, the hooker from New Brunswick, 3800 miles eastward. It was stirring to encounter such a genuine and passionate love of the game.

★ ★ ★

After 1977, Phil Bennett had ample cause to brood about New Zealand rugby. Yet it was this modest and charming man who instantly appreciated what was in the mind of the Scottish referee, Alan Hosie, when Llanelli played the All Blacks before the great centennial game with Wales at the Arms Park on 1 November 1980. Hosie's blast on the whistle and arm projected toward the touchline signalled, without any doubt, the imminent departure from the field of Graeme Higginson for a gross breach of sporting play. On the instant, Bennett was at Hosie's side, pleading that no unfortunate incident should mar this centennial year. Bennett was joined by Ray Gravell, a centre, along with Mourie. The long debate was ended as Hosie blew for no-side, saying later, not too convincingly, that he had not issued the final order, but had merely warned Higginson that anything more of that kind would produce the chop.

The centenary match was one of the great distinctions of New Zealand rugby, principally because the All Blacks were the only team to be considered for the occasion, but also because, inspired by Mourie, the New Zealanders played with a divine fury.

At the centenary dinner, the union's president, Cliff Jones, that immortal flyhalf of the 1930s, bellowed, 'Welcome to you all – whether you come from the south or from the north!' In the hard times between the two World Wars, in the hard times when, in the 1970s and 1980s, one coal-mine after another in Wales was closing, when the vast Abbey steel works were sliced to the bone, when unemployment at one stage was almost 13 per cent, many a Welsh cap had, of necessity, gone north. To be welcomed by Jones was an emotional experience both for the players attending the dinner and all rugby men present who appreciated the circumstances.

What a game it was for a celebration, and, for New Zealand, what a victory over so great a rugby nation! The All Blacks won it by 23 points to 3, four tries, two conversions and a penalty to one penalty by Steve Fenwick. The satisfaction was to be there, to feel the pulse of the 55,000 spectators, to sense the pride in the New Zealand team, to see moments of play so exhilarating that the imprint remains forever.

Mourie, quite possibly New Zealand's finest captain at international level, at one point made a desperate effort to stop a ball entering touch – it was in slow motion about a foot from the line. Succeeding, he lifted up and sent off a pass which, an instant later, turned into an attack raging down the other side of the field. Later in the game, scrumhalf David Loveridge, a leading candidate in any contest for New Zealand's best player ever in this position, broke at the field end of a lineout – an all but impossible achievement by a scrumhalf. Out in midfield he 'found' Mourie, who sped a few yards before returning the ball. They had started just outside the quarter-line at the city end of the park and were now racing toward the distant corner at the River Taff end. Loveridge hurled the ball out to his right, Bill Osborne picked it up on the bounce and wonderful Bruce Robertson appeared to have drawn both the fullback, J.P.R. Williams, and the left wing, Robert Ackerman, before he passed to Stuart Wilson on the right wing.

The park was in frenzy now from the speed and excitement. Ackerman brilliantly got to Wilson, his tackle tipping the All Black on his back, the ball held in both arms, clear of his body. Taking a gander, Wilson observed that Hika Reid, the Maori hooker, was hurtling toward him from the front of the lineout, so far distant. Impossible! With a whip of the hands, Wilson put the ball into Reid's arms; and there was the try. Glory Hallelujah!

Sadness lingers from another special memory of the match. Great was the hullabaloo when the All Blacks' flyhalf, Nicky Allen, spearing down the grandstand touchline on the blindside, dived for a try. Clearly enough, he had bounced the ball up and down, and hand, ball and ground were not in contact when the try was signalled. Terraces and grandstand resounded with shouts and chants of disapproval.

It was Allen's second international and his last game for the All Blacks. He had not been much appreciated at the highest levels and, somehow or other, drifted off to Australia. Playing in a club match at Wollongong, a steel town south of Sydney, on 10 July 1984, he was tackled. He went down, hard. His head struck a pitch almost as firm as concrete. He was deeply concussed. He did not recover.

It is interesting to speculate what Allen's career might have been if he had been under the care of coaches of the quality of Fred Allen and John Hart. His was a rare, blithe spirit. He was cheeky and polite, amusing and serious, careful and unconcerned. His playing gifts were quite exceptional. He had the panache of such Frenchmen as Jo Maso and Jean Gachassin who, too, dared to free themselves from the shackles of conventional wisdom. It is possible, faintly possible, that Nicholas Houghton Allen could have qualified for the company of Billy Stead, Mark Nicholls, Trevor Berghan and Steven Pokere in the gallery of the greatest All Black flyhalves. It is cause for mourning that he was not more greatly encouraged. Yet there is exquisite pleasure in associating him with the team which, at the Arms Park in 1980, reaffirmed the contention of a great Australian captain, 'Chilla' Wilson, that 'New Zealand back-play is as good as any in the world – when it is uninhibited.'

CHAPTER ELEVEN

BLEMISH ON THE THREE P'S
1980-90

*I*t was a tragedy for New Zealand, indeed for world, rugby that over a period of forty years a great playing doctrine, once an inspiration, threatened to become a disaster.

The original Three P's – Position, Possession and Pace – were the concept of Charles Saxton, captain and master-mind of the Kiwis, a team culled from the ranks of the 2nd New Zealand Division, which made a triumphant tour of the British Isles, France and Germany in the winter of 1945–6, immediately following the Second World War. Saxton, a cheery, thoughtful and earnest lover of the game, had played for South Canterbury against Philip Nel's all-powerful Springbok team of 1937 and was hailed as New Zealand's finest scrumhalf by South Africa's best, Danie Craven.

After Nel's team had won the three-test series against the All Blacks with a massive 17–6 victory, five tries to none, in the final test, the nation was still in a state of shock as it bid farewell to the team which in 1938 was to visit Australia.

Behold! Solid, powerful, tough forwards (who also liked to run with the ball) were backed by first-stringers in Saxton at scrumhalf, Trevor Berghan at flyhalf, Jack Sullivan and Nelson Mitchell (captain) in the centres, Tom Morrison and Bill Phillips on the wing, and Jack Taylor at back. The line could fairly be compared with the finest ever sent abroad in a touring team. The nine matches, including three tests, were won, a high proportion of the team's total of 279 points being scored by the backs from combined movements of pace and skill; and when Saxton broke – like Haydn Tanner, great Welsh scrumhalf of the time – it was to score.

Saxton thus set off to war as a proven international of the highest class and, as squadron commander of an armoured regiment in the Italian Campaign, inspired the trust and respect of the men with whom he shared the stress of battle. As skipper of the Kiwis, with a reputation for being 'as

118

straight as a gun barrel', he was much-loved, keeping his players in a fine state of companionable good humour.

The doctrine preached by 'Charlie' – Position, Possession and Pace – was, he insisted, the basis of an attacking game. Players must be in place to receive the ball; they must be sure to hold it, not least when passing on the dead run; and they must commit themselves to the dash which would breach a defence or turn its flank.

The Kiwis loved the concept, and its corollary that the object of rugby was for fourteen men to give the fifteenth a start of half a yard. If Saxton himself was unable quite to reach his pre-war form, he managed to turn many of his companions from good players into topnotchers. Fred Allen, best at flyhalf but preferring inside centre, had exceptional strength, on the run or the tackle. Ron Dobson, in midfield, was said to play like a demented butterfly. An apparently sloth-like Maori centre, J.B. Smith, packed behind an impassive countenance a football brain, an all-round vision, of the highest quality; seldom has New Zealand fielded a back with a mind so subtly attuned to the possibilities of attack. As a move developed, Johnnie's heavy legs moved like pistons; time after time, he gave his wings – powerful Jim Sherratt and Wally Argus, and high-spirited Eric Boggs – that half-yard start. Behind the line, two fullbacks of genius, Bob Scott, superb in fieldcraft and cunning, and Herbie Cook, who twinkled like a ballerina in size $4^{1}/_{2}$ boots that delivered a kick of staggering power, competed for first place while never permitting personal ambition to obtrude upon the Musketeer spirit of the side – All for one and one for all.

★ ★ ★

Forty years on, a change had occurred. By the 1980s, the gold had turned to dross with the emergence of the new Three P's: Politics, Penalties and Payments.

Labour Prime Minister Norman Kirk had pledged, during his election campaign of 1972, not to allow politics to intrude into sport. Within a year, and doubtless influenced by the horrors of the Springboks' tour of Australia in 1971, with riotous public behaviour in Melbourne and Brisbane, Kirk did a U-turn. He required the New Zealand Rugby Union to 'postpone' its invitation for the Springboks to tour New Zealand in 1973.

Kiwi rugby men went into a slow burn. Notwithstanding the violent background to the All Blacks' tour of South Africa in 1976, punctuated by student riotings and police shootings, the New Zealand union solidly backed the invitation for the Springboks to tour in 1981. It was, without doubt, the crassest decision it had ever made. The South African Rugby Board abetted the blunder by appointing, as manager of the team, a great lock forward of the 1950s, Johan Claassen. Slow-speaking and sometimes, it seemed, slow-witted, Claassen was cut to pieces, mainly by tough Aussie reporters, at his first Press conference. His contention that his team had come to play sport, not to indulge in politics, became strained. Nor did he make adequate use of his trump card – that the presence in the side of two coloured players, Errol Tobias at centre and Abe Williams as assistant-

119

manager, argued that the South African authorities implicitly accepted that their national team must be non-racial.

Claassen was a total failure, as was the tour. Not since the strike by Waihi gold-miners in 1913 and the urban hunger riots during the Depression of the 1930s had New Zealand come closer to mass civic disorder. The well-organized anti-apartheid movement in the late 1960s, represented by CARE (Citizens Association for Racial Equality) and HART (Halt All Racist Tours), had many adherents, especially among students and Maoris. A substantial portion of the public, too, was dismayed at the presence of a team chosen by a sporting body which for years had practised a Whites-only selection policy. Dr Danie Craven, president of the South African Rugby Board, had put it bluntly: 'No Black,' he declared, 'will ever play rugby for South Africa.'

Public reaction was strong and not confined to words. Two notorious street battles were fought in Wellington streets, Molesworth and Rintoul, by police wearing protective helmets, carrying shields and wielding long batons. The second match of the tour, against Waikato at Hamilton, was abandoned after a threat by a decorated Spitfire pilot, Pat McQuarrie, to fly his light plane into the crowded grandstand. A warning by the Commissioner of Police, Robert Walton, that the tour could be cancelled was quickly scotched by the National Party Prime Minister, Robert Muldoon, abroad at the time but fully appraised of developments. Eventually, after 13 matches and a win and a loss in the first two tests, the Springboks arrived at Eden Park for the decider.

A Maori woman who produced a film of the tour (which the State-owned television broadcasting service refused to show) recorded the turbulence in the surrounding streets before kick-off. Specially arresting shots were of a large group of young men of various races, wearing crash helmets and chest protectors, and carrying long fence-battens clearly capable of being used as weapons. The film showed the group approaching police officers who, sensibly, turned and ran hard away.

The party was not yet over. The police – 50 per cent of whom were said to be opposed to the tour – did not appear to have covered all possible contingencies inside the ground. During the match, a man named Marx Jones, with a companion, flew a light plane (hired from the local North Shore Aero Club) no fewer than 62 times over Eden Park. At times the plane swooped down to goalpost level and either Mr Jones or his friend tossed flour-bags, nets or burning objects on to the field. One flour-bomb struck an All Black prop, Gary Knight, on the shoulders and knocked him to the ground. Meanwhile, conscious of the risk that the plane might, accidentally or otherwise, crash into the steep, crowded terrace at the eastern end, a senior police officer, Graham Perry, piloting a second light plane, maintained radio communication with Jones, using every possible means, short of ramming, to persuade him to desist.

Despite the interruptions, the game went on. The All Blacks led 19–9. The 'Boks fought back to 19–15, 19–18. New Zealand reached 22 when Doug Rollerson scored a drop-goal resembling the flight of a wounded

One of the great All Black lock-forwards, Peter Whiting, goes for the ball in the first test of the 1970 All Blacks' tour of South Africa at King's Park, Durban. Luck was not with the Blacks. By ruling Duggie Bruce to be offside in a maul – an impossibility – the referee Ian Gourlay cost the Kiwis a try and a likely goal.

2

Above left (facing page): Magnificent Murray Mexted, one of the great Number 8s, is tigerishly on the move against the Argentinian Pumas. David Loveridge, one of the great scrumhalves, is to hand. The two men had a fine understanding but it was later said of Mexted that he tried to do more than his share of work at the back of the scrum or ruck.

Left (facing page): Though he scored one of the four tries by which the All Blacks beat Scotland 20-6 at Murrayfield in 1979, Stuart Wilson is involved here in a real party. Not only is one Scot firmly grasping but another four, in extended formation, are set to deny him any further part in the current Kiwi attack.

Above: Two famous men in lock-forward history, Andy Haden of the All Blacks and Moss Keane of Ireland, are in battle for the ball as the New Zealanders build up to a last-minute victory during the international at Lansdowne Road in 1978.

Above: Nicky Allen is vigorously fending off Welsh scrumhalf Gareth Williams in the historic match against Wales at Cardiff Arms Park which celebrated the centenary of Welsh rugby. Sadly, Allen was dead within two years from a contusion of the brain suffered in a club match at Wollongong in New South Wales. Given a normal career he might have become established as one of the greatest of All Black flyhalves.

Above right (facing page): Stuart Wilson, superlative at his best, is on the burst against the Wallabies in the second test of 1982. Faithful support is being offered by David Loveridge and Murray Mexted but Steve Tuynman is determined none shall pass – and the All Blacks, at 16 points, failed to pass the Wallabies' score of 19.

Right (facing page): In perishing cold on a Carisbrook pitch David Loveridge looks as if he is about to score against the 1983 Lions. He didn't – and John Rutherford, the bonny Scot who is playing for once at centre, is making sure of the check.

Mark Shaw, one of the tougher hombres of All Black rugby during the 1980s, is on the charge against the British Lions at Carisbrook in 1983. The valiant Pontypool prop, 'Staff' Jones, looks well positioned to stop him.

Left: As he has done dozens of times in All Black service, blindside flanker Alan Whetton is about to command the ball in New Zealand's second Cup match. Fiji were thrashed 74-13 this day, 27 May 1987, at Lancaster Park in Christchurch.

Below: John Kirwan, as powerful as the village blacksmith, is bursting on to a pass from his scrumhalf David Kirk. The All Blacks are playing the last of their matches in the World Cup Pool Round and Argentina is feeling the lash by no side, 15-46 at Wellington's Athletic Park on 1 June 1987.

Facing page: Day in, match out, Gary Whetton is a nifty hand at the short end of the lineout – and in the opening match of the World Cup tournament at Eden Park, Auckland, on 22 May 1987, he has a dream ride against the Italians. The scoreline tells the story – New Zealand 70, Italy 6.

Above: Powered by their Number 8, Wayne 'Buck' Shelford, the All Blacks are surging in an attack against Scotland at Lancaster Park in Christchurch on 6 June 1987. The Scots gave it their all, but still were outclassed, 30-3, in the Cup quarter-final.

Above: Midfielder Warwick Taylor has hit the deck but Alan Whetton and Grant Fox are racing in support; and the Welsh, playing in the semi-final of the World Cup at Ballymore in Brisbane on 14 June 1987, are heading for a hiding – an unbelievable 49-6 All Black victory.

Above right (facing page): Flyhalf Grant Fox, keenly supported by his midfield men, Warwick Taylor and 'Smokin' Joe' Stanley, is giving the French defenders the slip in the grand final of the World Cup. Fox certainly made a mark on the match, scoring 17 of the All Blacks' 29 points from a conversion, 4 penalty goals and 1 drop goal. The French scored 9 points in the glorious sunshine over Eden Park on 20 June 1987.

Right (facing page): Playing the game of his life, the All Blacks' scrumhalf and skipper David Kirk is on the break for the try that put the seal on New Zealand's achievement in winning the Webb Ellis Trophy in the first World Cup tournament in rugby history. Brothers-in-law, as well as brother All Blacks, Wayne Shelford and Steve McDowell are belting along ready for instant support. The day was New Zealand's – All Blacks 29, France 9.

Above: Bearer of an immortal rugby name – and a fine player in his own right – Bruce Deans (great-nephew of Bob Deans whose try against Wales in 1905 was disallowed) is fending off his scrumhalf marker, Nick Farr Jones, in the drawn test at Ballymore in Brisbane in 1988. Beanpole Steve Cutler, for the Aussies, and Alan Whetton, for the All Blacks, are in support. Until they lost to the touring Wallabies in the final test in 1990, the Ballymore result was the only smudge on a run of fifty victories for the All Blacks.

Left (facing page): As a judo expert since boyhood, Maori Steven McDowell is an awfully hard man to stop. Here he is demonstrating his strength in a charge against the Welsh at the National Stadium in Cardiff in 1989. Experts have no doubt that he is the finest loose-head prop in the game at the moment.

Above: Despite the challenge of Craig Innes, Michael Lynagh, currently holder (with Argentina's Hugo Porta) of the world record for point-scoring in rugby internationals, is leaping high in the sky during the Australian-New Zealand test at Eden Park in 1990.

Above: Only the brave and true of heart would hurtle into the great French fullback, Serge Blanco. Young Craig Innes had these qualities in abundance, and with Michael Jones and Zinzan Brooke hanging about he is pushing ahead.

Right: Alan Whetton and the Scot Derek Turnbull are scrapping for the ball in the first test of 1990 between the touring Scots and the All Blacks. Steve McDowell (No. 1) and Gary Whetton (No. 5) are poised to assist.

Those fine Scottish front-row men, Colin Deans and Iain Milne (No. 3), are prominent as their fellows battle the All Blacks for the ball in the second test of the 1990 tour. Scotland lost, 18-21, by a last-minute penalty and despite their superiority in the run of play. All Blacks Richard Loe, Sean Fitzpatrick and Kieran Crowley look on.

Overleaf: Which is the greater achievement – to captain New Zealand to victory in the inaugural World Cup tournament or to be invited to take up a Rhodes Scholarship at Oxford? David Kirk, here holding the Webb Ellis Trophy, might be the only one able to say. He copped both distinctions.

duck. Then the Springboks' right wing, Ray Mordt, in devastating form, got his third successive try by racing around Bernie Fraser and scampering clean away from fullback Allan Hewson. At 22-all, Naas Botha, the all but infallible Springbok goalkicker, attempted the winning conversion. The scene and tension recalled Ellis Park, Johannesburg, in 1955 when Johan van der Schyff saw his potential winning goal against the British Lions veer to the left of the far upright. Now 'Nasty Naas' suffered the same humiliation. His goalkick missed.

South Africans will never share the glowing opinion that Kiwis had of Clive Norling, a heavyweight among international referees, who had charge of matches played by Grahame Mourie's Grand Slammers in 1978. What with the constant interruptions, Norling must have allowed at least 11 minutes of overtime. During the last dramatic moments, scrumhalf David Loveridge had been removed, concussed, and his replacement, Mark Donaldson, was soon on the job. When Norling penalized the Springboks some 45 yards out, Donaldson tap-kicked and began to run. Norling whistled. Majestically, he marched upfield 10 yards. The 'Boks, he indicated, had not retired that requisite distance. Andrew Dalton, the All Blacks' skipper, summoned Hewson. The penalty kick cleared the bar, between the posts. The All Blacks had won the series, two to one.

Marx Jones, who was sentenced to two years' jail, spent only six months in confinement, reflecting on his part in the most dramatic rugby international ever played.

The tour did considerable damage to New Zealand rugby. Coincidentally, the New Zealand Football Association was successfully steering its national team, the All Whites, into a place among the 16 teams to qualify in the World Cup of soccer in Spain in 1982. Countless Kiwi parents, disgusted by a rugby administration which was sightless, thoughtless and dumb, turned their sons to soccer. Auckland Grammar School, headed by an outstanding loose-forward of the Whineray era, John Graham, had always been one of *the* great rugby schools of the country; now, perforce, it was fielding more soccer than rugby teams.

In 1985, the Rugby Union, in the face of substantial evidence that the racial situation in South Africa was neither good nor bad but plain terrible, proposed sending the All Blacks on a full-scale tour to that unfortunate country. Two youngish Auckland lawyers, Philip Recordon and Paddy Finnegan, invited, so it was reported, 38 of their city colleagues to prepare a suit against the Rugby Council, aiming to stop the tour by High Court injunction. The case was masterfully argued by a Queen's Counsel, E.W. or Ted Thomas (later elevated to the Bench of the High Court). A special witness, the Reverend Arnold Stofile, a member of the Xhosa peoples of the Ciskei homeland and chaplain of the Black University of Fort Hare, recounted the simple, painful tale of the injustices of South African society. On a Saturday afternoon, not a normal working time, Judge Casey granted the injunction. The tour was off.

A former High Court Judge and Governor-General, Sir David Beattie, scorned the timid reaction of the Rugby Council. 'They should,' he said, 'have sped into the Court of Appeal on Monday morning. On a proper application, Casey J. must have been overturned.' Instead the Rugby Council, after agonizing discussions, appealed to the Privy Council, and in due course argued its case before the Law Lords, who were not in the least impressed. Mr Justice Casey's ruling was upheld. It had cost the council prestige and a great deal of money to learn that, in certain circumstances, politics and sport are indivisible.

In 1985, Labour Prime Minister David Lange decided to make a grand stand against another All Black tour. Parliament had already unanimously endorsed a resolution urging the Rugby Union to stop the tour, but two days later, Mr Lange, preferring to throw his not inconsiderable weight around, summoned the council to his office and read out a letter reviewing the proposal to send the All Blacks. His peroration was majestic. 'I order you,' he declared, 'to stop the tour.'

At a Press conference in the afternoon, astonishment and merriment were caused when the chairman, Cecil Blazey, a man of high intelligence and utter probity, announced that, Lange or no Lange, the tour was proceeding. One Pressman, an Old Dig of the Second World War, protested that the council, or Blazey, or both were 'shilly-shallying' in the belief that they could disregard an order from the highest personage in the land. In a scene that might have come from *Alice in Wonderland*, the old joker addressed Blazey. 'From your very long experience in the Army,' he said, 'you *must* be aware that orders, when properly given, must be obeyed.' 'Ah,' replied Blazey, 'but has this order been properly given? Has it been properly framed?' Et cetera.

Because the final decision rested, not on Mr Lange's direction but on the superior authority of the Privy Council, whose orders had to be obeyed even if those of a Kiwi Prime Minister did not, the tour was aborted.

Temporarily. Amid secrecy as massive as that which produced, in cricket, the phenomenon initially called Kerry Packer's Circus and now known as World Series Cricket, All Blacks, including the reigning captain, Andy Dalton, the senior Pro., Andrew Haden, and some South Africans, set about promoting a tour of that country in 1986. Two potential team members, John Kirwan and David Kirk, turned the proposal down. When the news broke of the secret congregation of the team members in Johannesburg, the scandal was prodigious. Having refused an offer – said to be a fee of $10,000 – to coach the side, Fred Allen was replaced by Colin Meads. One of the Corinthians of Kiwi rugby, Ian Kirkpatrick, took on the managership. Dalton was made captain – and in the first match of the tour was so brutally assaulted by an opposing forward that he was unfit to play thereafter.

The tour had been organized without the knowledge of the South African Rugby Board, which was ordered, or requested, by the International Board, meeting in London, to have it immediately abandoned. Dr Craven accepted the direction but, when he returned to Cape Town, instructed his board instead to take control of the remainder of the tour, a decision which ended his relationship with Russell Thomas, chairman of the New Zealand

Rugby Council. Thomas was so outraged by the tour that he wrote more than 700 letters to officials and personalities all about the world in search of something like the truth of the matter. Charlie Saxton spoke for a great many when he said he could not believe that All Blacks – *All Blacks!* Sainted people! – would deliberately neglect the loyalty and discipline of rugby to play on a rebel tour.

The team was called the Cavaliers, and wild rumours circulated about the amount of money paid. Mark Shaw, a loose-forward, was said to have returned home 'drenched with money'. As for Shaw, so for the others. In his book *Boots 'n All*, Andy Haden mentioned the Tour Fund set up some years previously by touring teams, made up of money raised from the sale of tickets, fees paid for the appearance of players at gatherings, contributions from sponsors and the like.

At the end of each tour, the fund was equally divided among the players, and presumably, officials of the party. Payments, in New Zealand, at any rate, were tax-free. As to the Cavaliers' tour, the inferences to be drawn from veiled references in Haden's book was that substantial South African corporations, led by the enormously wealthy Yellow Pages, had tossed substantial sums into the kitty. It was surmised that the gross Tour Fund, in this instance, could have amounted to at least 2 million South African rands.

The Cavaliers came marching home. They were not greeted with bands, trumpets, flags and bunting. They were hauled before the Rugby Council and, one by one, swore an oath that they had not been financially reimbursed for taking part in the tour. All they received, they said, was the daily allowance of about $50 laid down by the International Board, to which, incidentally, they were not entitled, their team not being nationally representative.

One upshot, the judgement that the Cavaliers be suspended for two international matches, caused mocking laughter. This intensified after a New Zealand team called the 'Baby Blacks', because ten of them had not played international rugby, beat France 18–9 and Australia 13–12, in the first of three tests, and was then totally changed in the forwards and in three of the backs for the two remaining matches with the Wallabies. In the event, the All Blacks lost the second test 13–12 and the third, along with the Bledisloe Cup, 22–9.

So much for the separation of politics and sport. The announcement of the two-match suspension and the decision to dump the Babies fostered an even greater measure of cynicism among bystanders of Kiwi rugby.

As for the ever increasing incidence of penalty goals, consider that when the 1905 All Blacks scored 976 points, exactly 12 of these came from the tour's four penalty goals. One year later, Paul Roos's Springboks also scored four penalty goals in an aggregate of 608 points. The '24 Invincibles scored 10 penalties for a total of 721 points; and the scoring situation was still rational when Bob Stuart's 1953 team tallied no more than 17 goals. Even Wilson Whineray's side of 1963–4 recorded 118 tries and 32 penalty goals, although this team had a profusion of drop-kickers.

After this, and because of various changes made to the Laws of the Game by the International Board, things, from an All Black viewpoint, rather went haywire. Fred Allen's 1967 team scored 30 penalty goals in 17 matches. In the last long All Black tour of 1972–3 the number had jumped to 422, and during Mourie's Grand Slam tour of 1978, 33 goals were placed in 18 matches.

During the tours of South Africa of 1960, 1970 and 1976, Dickie Lockyear, Ian McCallum and Gerald Bosch were supreme goalkicking marksmen. After the final test of '76, the All Blacks' coach, J.J. Stewart, remarked that whereas the Kiwis had outplayed their opponents, the Springboks, by superior goalkicking, had won the series. 'Let's all go surfing,' Stewart said. He was not smiling.

Yet this was kids' stuff compared with the rugby internationals of the 1980s. In eight games in France in 1986, the All Blacks placed 21 penalties against 29 tries. In 14 games in Canada and the British Isles in 1989, 28 penalties were placed.

It was not until after the Second World War that New Zealand produced goalkickers of outstanding skill, comparable to Billy Wallace of 1905 and Mark Nicholls of the 1920s, both of whom kicked under forbidding rules which required the ball to be held off the ground until the kicker began his approach run and which also demanded the kicker's retirement, usually by about ten yards, after a penalty had been awarded. Don Clarke kicked the 1956 Springboks and many other teams to kingdom come with his enormous slashes. Fergi McCormick in time exceeded Clarke's tally at first-class level, though he was never as daunting as 'Camel' at his best.

Both these men were toe-kickers. As and when the round-the-corner style of kicking with the instep was displayed in New Zealand and, ultimately, accepted, a vast change occurred. Robbie Deans was of paramount importance as Canterbury won match after match in the Ranfurly Shield competition of the early 1980s.

Then, in the mid-1980s, came New Zealand's greatest-ever goalkicker: Grant Fox, an Auckland flyhalf, who in 27 internationals reached the colossal aggregate of 445 points, all but three from goals after tries and penalties. During seven internationals in 1990, Fox placed 14 goals from tries and 20 from penalties, while scoring one try and two drop goals. In the last two tests of the year, against France, the All Blacks scored 54 points. Fox scored 34 of them. The man was a genius – but what were those words on the wall plaque of Rugby School? 'First picked up the ball and ran with it, thus originating the distinctive feature of the rugby game'.

Payments – professionalism – had gradually crept in as a silent and sinister aspect of rugby. Until hard evidence was produced from other countries, notably South Africa, where sums of several hundred rands were being paid to players appearing in provincial matches, it seemed that New Zealand led the rest in this practice. True, there had been scandals over the years. G.V. Travers, the BBC's commentator in Wales, alleged in a book that it was commonplace for players of the first rank to find the toes of their boots stuffed with money – £500 for the best. 'Geevers', a cheery chap, was not at all disturbed to be sent to Coventry.

The New Zealand public has a passion for books, biographical or otherwise, about their All Black heroes. Sir William Collins paid double what was offered by other publishers for Alex Veysey's biography of Colin Meads, which sold about 60,000 copies in hardback. Andy Haden (describing himself as 'writer' to be on the safe side) cracked the market for some 45,000 copies with *Boots 'n All*, though he did less well with the follow-up, *Lock, Stock 'n Barrel*. Both books fired more than a few whiffs into administrators, writers and other unfortunates.

Because so many books were ghosted by professionals, the New Zealand Rugby Union seemed happy to believe that silver had not greased any players' palms. The situation toughened when various touring teams expressed amazement at the flouting of Amateur Regulations by the All Blacks, and things became decidedly sticky from the mid-1980s onward. Graham Mourie was mightily admired for announcing, after the publication of his biography, that he had accepted royalties and therefore was in breach of the regulations. Under severe pressure, the International Board relaxed its by-laws; and in 1990, the recently deposed All Black captain, Wayne Shelford, brought out a ghosted autobiography which sold 20,000 hardback copies in a fortnight and a reprint of 5000 in next to no time. His amateur status was not imperilled.

More disturbing, on the New Zealand front, was the trading of players. Men were lured from club to club, the cheque-book was always to hand for ambitious committees, and sponsorship reached such a pitch that in 1989 the chairman of the New Zealand union, Russell Thomas, acknowledged openly that his union had during the year profited to the tune of at least $2 million. What was good for the goose must be good for the gander, said the players. One union, Wanganui, pleaded at an annual general meeting of the New Zealand union that an investigation be made into the trafficking. The suggestion won support and, immediately, was ignored.

In January 1991, E.J. Tonks, who in a palace revolution a year previously had ousted Thomas from the chairmanship, raised the eyebrows only of a few old-timers when he announced that hereafter, the council of the union was to act as agent in procuring players' fees for articles, books, lecture appearances and public speeches. The council would charge a fee, Tonks said, and parcel it out to players according to the terms of the engagement.

'Times have changed,' declared the players and/or promoters, sponsors and employers.

They have indeed. It was Jeff Butterfield, a great English and British Lions centre of the 1950s who remarked, many years later: 'I used to get a great deal of pleasure out of reporting, at midday on Friday, to play for England on Saturday.'

What a quaint old game rugby was when a farmer named Bill Phillips, of the 1938 All Blacks, rode his horse over hill-country, across creeks and rivers, for 20 or 30 miles to catch transport into Hamilton for a training run with the Waikato team. What a quaint old game it still was when that ornament of Cardiff and Welsh scrummages, Cliff Davies, walked 23 miles from the city to Kenfig Hill, the little village where he was part-time coalminer and part-time keeper of a funeral parlour. Cliff would not have dreamed of cadging a ride or demanding a taxi. Sufficient for him the glory of playing for club and country.

One of these days, someone in *real* authority might ask, of himself and of as large an audience as possible, 'Have we allowed the glory to pass from our game?'

CHAPTER TWELVE

'SIR KIRWAN' AND THE WORLD CUP 1980-91

*F*ollowing the shock of the Cavaliers' tour to South Africa, New Zealand rugby decided on a shake-up from stem to stern. In concert with the Australian Rugby Union, the Kiwi councillors had for some time been advocating a World Cup international tournament. There had been strong resistance, particularly from the British, heedful of the warning by Sir Stanley Rous, of the Football Association, that it was a recipe for disaster. 'In football,' said Sir Stanley, 'we have had foul play, cheating, ultra-nationalism, every sort of ill you don't want in sport. You rugger fellows would be best advised to stick to your international tours and matches and forget all about the flummery of a World Cup.'

The Aussies and Kiwis were not persuaded. The game, they contended, must develop a focal point, and a World Cup would help to spread the game's growth and popularity. Reluctantly, the International Board granted permission for a working study and found no cause for objection when this was presented. But they directed, peevishly, that this should not be the World Cup tournament. Instead, it would be designated the International Rugby Football Board Tournament for the Webb Ellis Cup.

At some point during the build-up to the tornament, an Australian and several Kiwis were driven by taxi-cab to an Auckland hotel. They talked much of a young Auckland wing-threequarter, John Kirwan, who, in their opinion, could become the greatest ever fielded by the All Blacks. As the attentive driver, a West Samoan turned New Zealander, held open the car door on arrival, he delivered the ultimate tribute, in a caressing tone: 'Ah,' he said, ' "Sir Kirwan".'

In 1983, the British Lions opened their tour of New Zealand with a match against Wanganui, in the presence of Prince Edward, then a master at the city's famous school, Wanganui Collegiate. The Lions, speedy, with weight and power in the pack, won stylishly 47–15.

The next match was against Auckland which, as the largest union in the country, would certainly offer pace, strength and special qualities communicated to the players by a coach of exceptional talent, John Hart. Yet the Lions were international, the Aucklanders provincial. There was a world of difference.

Hart had been tipped off that an 18-year-old boy playing lower-grade inter-club matches for the Marist club had 'real' possibilities. Unobrusively, Hart looked the lad over. Tall, powerful, strong in the chest and shoulders, genuinely fast for a big man – and apparently quite fearless. But would he possess the resolution, the physical willingness to stand up to the strongest opposition? Hart called on his father, a butcher by trade, and put the question to him.

'Ah, you'll have no worries,' he replied. 'Young John's tough. He can look after himself. He won't be worried about facing big names.'

Not without a qualm, Hart named Kirwan for the team. Auckland gasped. A teenager against the Lions?

Early on, the attempt of an Auckland back, in midfield, to loft a clearing kick from his quarter into touch misfired. The kick was charged down. It spurted and rolled, irresistibly, into the Auckland goalmouth. A 27-year-old centre, Clive Woodward, Harlequins, Leicester, 16 caps, aquiline of feature, aristocratic of bearing, was clear of the field as he strode, at a comfortably relaxed hand-gallop, for the ball, the try, the goal and the psychological break which would decide the match. A moment of glory awaited. Six points on a plate.

Of a sudden, something between a hiss and a roar was heard in the crowd. From far away on the right, perhaps 30 yards distant, a figure streaked across the turf. Some ten yards from the line, John Kirwan dived and clasped the ball in a touchdown drop-out 22, an instant before Woodward could make contact.

The effect on the Lions was profound. Instead of romping to an easy victory, here they were back at the lineout, battling for the ball. They were beaten in the match 13–12. During their 18-game tour they lost six times, including the four internationals with the All Blacks. They were defeated 9–0 in the second test at Wellington because they allowed the superlative scrumhalf David Loveridge to break, time after time, past their loose-forwards at the scrum, thus initiating, like so many Lions' teams of the past, a process of self-destruction. It is not too much to claim that disintegration set in after the shock of seeing an 18-year-old boy robbing them of a gift try.

The following year, Kirwan was an All Black on tour in Australia, but a fracture of his arm in an early match ensured he would make little impression. Yet by June 1984 he was ready for his first cap, against the French at Christchurch. It was a scary affair, because the All Blacks' 10–9 win would assuredly have been a defeat if the French flyhalf, Jean-Patrice Lescarboura, had not attempted, four times in the last five minutes, to dropkick a goal. The Kiwi historians, Rod Chester and Neville McMillan, wrote in their *Men in Black*, which records every international: 'Kirwan made a fine test-match debut. He showed great determination when given the chance to run with the ball. He was also very sound on defence.' For 'Sir Kirwan' these were early days.

World Cup or not, and politics aside, New Zealand rugby during the 1980s was busy keeping more than 200,000 players of all ages fruitfully occupied for up to six months of the season, usually devoting the other months to the activities of the All Blacks. The Springbok visit of 1981, in which the All Blacks triumphed two tests to one, was followed by a lone international in dankest Romania, won with difficulty 14–6. The two tests in France were a little easier, but not by much. Graham Mourie wrote his book and retired, branded as a professional, to be succeeded by Stuart Wilson, who was too far removed from the combat zone to exercise sufficient authority. The match at Murrayfield, late in 1983, in which Scotland and New Zealand each scored 25 points, was lamentable; and after England had been beaten 15–9 at Twickenham, the tour was stowed away as quickly as possible in a dark corner which bore the label, 'Not to be dragged out, under *any* circumstances'.

A more promising feature of this period was the rise of Australian rugby to the stage where, in 1984, the Wallabies scored a Grand Slam in their wonderful tour of the British Isles, rounding it off with a magnificent match against the Barbarians, the final try being scored by a lock-forward, Steve Williams, who appeared to have run half a league before he reached out for the last crucial pass. Great credit for the improvement in Wallaby standards was due to the extraordinary vitality of the team's coach, Alan Jones. The backline of the 1984 side, Philip Cox and Mark Ella at halfback, Michael Hawker and Andrew Slack in the centres, David Campese and Brendan Moon on the wings, and Richard Gould at fullback, would rank among the finest in rugby history.

In 1986, the All Blacks lost a home series, two tests to one, against Australia, facing yet another great scrumhalf in Nick Farr-Jones. Indeed, during the post-war decades, a succession of great Wallaby scrumhalves – Cyril Burke, Des Connor, Ken Catchpole, John Hipwell, Peter Carson and Farr-Jones – ranked as the best in the game.

The All Black team of 1985, denied South Africa, was awarded a consolatory tour of Argentina. A Wellington lawyer, Michael Hobbs, led his side to a fine 33–20 victory in the first test, bringing off more than his fair share of tackles. But the burly Argentinian flyhalf Hugo Porta, with prodigious goalkicking (four penalty and three drop-kick goals) in the second test brought off a draw, 21 points all. Powerful in the legs, with a chest of a champion weightlifter, he was also remarkably sinuous and balanced; and by deft movement of hand or foot he could throw off even a Hobbs on the tackle before slashing the ball at goal.

In 1986, the French arrived to play three matches, one of them against the All Blacks, at Lancaster Park, Christchurch. Since most of the All Blacks who should have faced them were then unofficially in South Africa (only John Kirwan and David Kirk had refused to join the so-called

Cavaliers) the selectors had to scout around. Daringly, they named ten players, five forwards and five backs, who were unblooded at international level. Captained by Kirk, the Baby Blacks, as they were christened, were led on to the park as lambs to the slaughter.

Yet because these young men had been born to the game and had lived all their lives in the peculiar, and perhaps unique, rugby atmosphere of New Zealand, they stood to arms and brought off a thrilling victory by 18 points to 9, albeit, sorrowfully, scoring only one try to none. The French fielded such magnificently gifted players as Serge Blanco, Jean-Patrice Lescarboura, Philippe Sella, Pierre Lagisquet and Pierre Barbizier in the backs, and Daniel Dubroca, Jean-Pierre Garuet, Jean Condom and François Haget in the forwards. Chester and McMillan remarked sympathetically that the French 'didn't do themselves justice on the day'. They were not allowed to. Someone wound up the Baby Blacks and set them ticking all over the field.

Later that year, the official All Blacks took off to France, gaining a comfortable victory, 19–7, in the first test at Toulouse, and being defeated, shatteringly, 16–3, at La Beaujoire Stadium in Nantes. Kiwis brooded about that one until the World Cup, next year, wiped away all tears.

★   ★   ★

Alex Wyllie, John Hart and Brian Lochore now had to select the All Black team for the World Cup. Wyllie, coach of the Canterbury team which defended the Ranfurly Shield 25 times, had heard of the reputation as trainer of a Glaswegian physical education graduate of the world-famous Loughborough College, James Blair, who had migrated to New Zealand. He mentioned Blair's name to John Hart, whose Auckland team had just lifted the Shield from Canterbury in September 1985, scraping home 28–23 in an incredible match. Hart sniffed around, and soon enough had Blair training his team. When it came to choosing the World Cup side, Wyllie and Hart urged Lochore to sign Blair as trainer.

'It didn't matter,' Hart said, years later, 'that Jim Blair was born to soccer. He had, and has, two special skills. One was the devising of individual programmes for individualized training by each man in the team. The other was the presentation of a number of training skills in grid activities, using balls, which improved the agility and speed of players.

'He attacked every player, assessing his strengths and failings and offering means of improving the one and eradicating the other. Bit by bit, you could see the players responding. Their speed improved, in some cases quite remarkably. Their agility grew like a mushroom. When he immersed them in training groups . . . their development was extraordinary. . . . I have no doubt that the All Blacks succeeded in the World Cup because in physical fitness and ball-skills they were far ahead of all opponents. They played each match at a sustained speed beyond the reach of any opposing side.'

First match, for New Zealand, of the World Cup: versus Italy, at Eden Park, on 22 May 1987. The All Blacks won 70–6 (eight goals, two penalty goals and four tries, one of them a penalty, to a penalty goal and a drop goal). The game was thus an unlikely occasion for the birth of a legend. Yet it was here, late, that John Kirwan became 'Sir Kirwan'. David Kirk, well inside the All Blacks' quarter, passed the ball to him. Kirwan could have kicked, passed or even dropped it. Instead, he ran. By power and pace, by feint and fend, by dodge and sidestep, he bore upfield. Six, perhaps eight Italians came at him. He bypassed them all. Twenty yards beyond halfway, he was clear. An Italian made a last, desperate, flying tackle, but Kirwan was himself diving, and over for the try that stood New Zealand on its ear.

Then, with overwhelming victories against Fiji (74–13), Argentina (46–15), Scotland (30–3) and, incredibly, Wales (49–6) in one semi-final, the All Blacks swept on to win the tournament and the Webb Ellis Trophy. With their irresistible power, speed and stamina, they scored 43 tries in six matches. In the second semi-final, Australia appeared to have France by the throat. From somewhere, the French conjured the spirit of Napoleon's Old Guard. Almost every man in the team handled the ball before Serge Blanco scored a sensational try for victory by 30 points to 24.

This, undoubtedly, was the great match of the tournament, expressing the finest qualities of attack and defence. Yet the combined strengths and skills of the All Blacks prevailed in the final, in which they defeated France 29–9, a memorable and exhilarating display. Sadly, Andrew Dalton, injured in the first match, missed the remainder of the tournament; but so highly did Lochore, Wyllie and Hart value his experience and skill in team management that they retained him in their 26-man squad.

In the event, David Kirk, the field captain, emerged as virtually the most dynamic player in the final. Two of his blindside breaks, begun almost from halfway, were superlatively judged and run. He himself scored one of the New Zealand tries, Kirwan the second (his sixth of the tournament) and Michael Jones, a sensational Samoan open-side flank-forward, the third. Old-timers might have preferred less evidence of the remarkable goal-kicking qualities of Grant Fox, who scored 17 of the All Blacks' points tally. (In the six matches, he notched no fewer than 126 of New Zealand's 298 points, with 30 goals from tries, 21 penalty goals and one drop goal). Perhaps it was apposite to recall the heavy words of Dr Duggie Smith after being chided for conservative play in the final test of the 1971 Lions, who drew the match and won the series. 'We HAD to win,' he said. If the final of the World Cup tournament ranked as the most important international ever played, victory, whatever the means, had to be accounted the ultimate glory.

After the defeat by France at Nantes in 1986, All Black teams, variously captained by David Kirk, Wayne Shelford and Gary Whetton, racked up an unbeaten string of 50 matches, international, State and club, before Farr-Jones, in the middle of 1990, led the Wallabies to victory in the last of three tests of their New Zealand tour and so broke the spell.

International rugby has seldom known shocks of the magnitude to compare with those registered when the Welsh, in 1988, played at Christchurch and Auckland. In conjunction with the earlier crushing All Black win in the

World Cup, these two victories, 52–3 (six goals and four tries to a penalty goal) and 54–9 (eight goals and two penalty goals to a try by Jonathan Davies and a conversion and a penalty goal) emphasized the decline, both on and off the field, of Welsh rugby, culminating in England's smashing win at Cardiff in 1991 and other terrible indignities.

Wayne Shelford, a dynamic leader, was soon to become only the second All Black captain since the war to be dumped both in that capacity and as a player; and considerable bitterness was expressed against Alex Wyllie, convenor of the selection committee, who was adjudged, rightly or wrongly, to have been the principal agent. Gary Whetton, as a lock, had been a fixture in teams since 1981, and commanded an Auckland Ranfurly Shield side which had resisted some 40 challenges. He was a very fast runner and had a remarkable ability at kick-outs from the halfway or quarter-line, either to make the catch or to be the first player following up to touch it. But Shelford had that rare quality, fire. It was not easy to understand why he was dropped.

It was Whetton, nevertheless, who closed out the decade of the 1980s by leading the All Blacks to a sweep of the two-test series at Nantes and Paris after the team had been beaten in two matches against 'French Selection XVs', which so often seem to be very closely related to the French national side. After the first test, one All Black official drank a bottle of Scotch, unaided, in little more than an hour. He seemed unshaken, but probably slept well. Kiwi rugby had travelled a long, long way from the days of 1905 when the Boys from Way Under paid three pennies for a pint of finest bitter. Times change, as do habits.

Was the victorious World Cup team the greatest All Black side in history? Demonstrably, there could be quibbles. For all his genius as a match-winner, Fox at flyhalf could never be regarded as other than a reliable link. And for want of early pace, the All Black backlines against Scotland, Wales and France could never be compared favourably, as an attacking unit, with such lines as Freddie Roberts, Billy Stead, Jimmy Hunter, Bob Deans, Billy Wallace and George Smith or Duncan McGregor of the 1905 side, or with Jimmy Mill, Neil McGregor, Mark Nicholls, Bert Cooke, Fred Lucas, 'Snowy' Svenson and George Nepia, of 1925. The latter group formed part of the team which demolished New South Wales at Eden Park by 36 points to 10, scoring eight tries, six of them converted by Nicholls. Moreover, 'Ginger' Nicholls, Mark Nicholls, Ces Badeley, George Aitken, Percy Storey, Jack Steel and 'Nipper' Kingstone displayed high qualities of savvy and speed, too, in the first test of 1921 against the Springboks.

It is interesting, too, to pick up the point made by Bill Dally – steeped in rugby, and a wise judge of the game – in his memoirs that the 1928 All Black side, which shared the series with the Springboks and which, according to Mark Nicholls, would have won had Bert Cooke been able to tour, was stronger than the unbeaten, hallowed 1924 team, of which Dalley was also a member.

The temptation is strong to rank, primarily, those All Black teams which have made long tours either to the British Isles or South Africa. In terms of overall performance, therefore, David Gallaher's 1905 team must forever hold first place. By today's standards, its forwards would be considered laughably small. Yet the merit of their achievements was that they were almost wholly inexperienced in rugby at international level. Gathered from small and isolated settlements in a land of fewer than 100,000 souls, they were, essentially, country bumpkins. Yet the level of individual and team skills was extraordinarily high. John Hart rightly praised the ball-handling of the Webb Ellis Trophy team; but it was not superior to that of the likes of Stead, Wallace, Hunter, Roberts and Gallaher, whose intellectual grasp of the technical demands of individual and team play have never been surpassed in any international side.

Although held to a draw by East Wales on a field scraped clear of snow, and denied a Grand Slam because the Irish segment of their tour was abandoned as a result of foot-and-mouth disease in Cheshire, the 1967 All Blacks might well be considered for second placing among touring sides. They were expertly managed, coached and captained by Charlie Saxton, Fred Allen and Brian Lochore respectively. They had great forwards in Colin Meads, Ken Gray, Kelvin Tremain, Bruce McLeod, Waka Nathan, Ian Kirkpatrick and Graham Williams. Their two scrumhalves, Chris Laidlaw, a passer of excellence, and Sid Going, an instinctive genius, served backs the likes of Mack Herewini, Ian MacRae, Grahame Thorne, Tony Steel, Malcolm Dick and Bill Birtwistle, who were either unusually fast or very strong, or both; and their fullback, Fergi McCormick, a player whose qualities have never been fully appreciated at home, brought off, against the Barbarians, two match-saving tackles, one of Keri Jones (the Welsh Commonwealth Games sprinter), the other of Gerald Davies (arguably the greatest back ever developed in the British Isles), which were magical in their skill and power.

Two All Black teams of the 1920s must surely be in contention: the 1924 Invincibles and Maurice Brownlie's 1928 touring side of South Africa. It has to be said, however, that the Invincibles were denied an international against Scotland, which was fielding, at the time, its greatest-ever team. In favour of Brownlie's men, it should be remembered that although they suffered five losses, two of them in the four test matches, they were subjected to endless train journeys and the unprecedented torture of playing at high altitude. Years later, Tane Norton, of the 1976 All Blacks, said that as you ran out of the tunnel at Ellis Park on to the field, you felt yourself gasping for air like a mountaineer at extreme heights.

Wilson Whineray's team of 1963–4, which toured for four and a half months, had greatness at forward, especially with Whineray, Dennis Young and Gray in the front row, Colin and Stanley Meads at lock, and Tremain, John Graham and Waka Nathan at back; but it was handicapped in both scrumhalf and flyhalf positions, and for all the fright aroused by the mere appearance of giant fullback Don Clarke, the backs in front of him were too uneven in quality to place the team among the foremost.

Graham Mourie's Grand Slammers of 1978 had brilliance in a backline which included Bryan Williams, Stuart Wilson, Bruce Robertson, Bill Osborne and the great scrumhalf David Loveridge to support fine forwards such as Brad Johnstone, Andrew Dalton and Gary Knight up front, Andy Haden and Frank Oliver at lock, and Mourie and Lester Rutledge at the back. But, England excepted, the team scraped home in the internationals and only beat the Barbarians in the last minute with a flick of a drop goal.

So, as a challenge, let us list the finest All Black touring teams in the following order: 1905, 1967, 1978, 1928, 1924 and 1963; and retire, immediately, to a bombproof shelter.

Although judgement as to the comparative ranking of All Black teams might lead to dispute and even fisticuffs, there can be no argument on a more vital topic, the quality of New Zealand rugby. This reached its peak after the invention, by the Maori genius Tom Ellison, of the 2–3–2 scrummage, with the eighth forward acting as wing or rover. The formation, admittedly, has been criticized. David Gallaher, in 1905, was accused by the president of the Welsh Rugby Union of playing 'an absolutely unfair and dirty game'. Mark Nicholls condemned as fools New Zealanders who claimed that their 1928 All Black scrum of seven men could outplay the great eight-man South African packs. (He was supported by figures: in the 22 games of the tour, the All Blacks won 491 clean heels from scrummages, their opponents 615.) Then came the tour of the 1930 Lions when the All Black captain, Cliff Porter, an india-rubber build of a man, set about nullifying the skills of the brilliant English flyhalf, Roger Spong. Merry by nature, Spong was disgusted by Porter's attacks on him, either by compelling him to take the inside break, the killer highway for flyhalves, or by deliberately shepherding him before he had received the ball.

Reuter's correspondent with the team, Gordon McLean, in his review of the tour in the *Auckland Sun*, wrote: 'Spong's *bête noire* was Porter. There was never any reason to doubt it. He and the Irish scrumhalf, Paul Murray, frankly disliked the methods of the All Black captain and although the statement that after the Wellington match (which was played early in the tour) some of the British team refrained from congratulating Porter was denied, it was nevertheless true. The New Zealand selectors were well aware of the moral effect Porter had on the British inside backs, and in the early tests, when he was showing poor form, he probably owed his retention to this factor. By the time the last test had been played and lost, the British teams had got to know Porter better, and appreciated his good points. But for all their outward cordiality, some of them never forgave him for the part he played in the Wellington match and the first test.'

James Baxter thus carried a quiver full of sharpened arrows when he reported on the tour to the Rugby Football Union and the Four Home Unions. The 'Colonial countries' of South Africa, Australia and New Zealand were denied seats on the board. No protests could be lodged, and the modification of the scrummage law, early in the 1930s, which required that henceforth the front row must comprise three men, effectively killed the New Zealand formation.

Tears were shed in Kiwi rugby circles. They flowed more copiously when the 1935 All Blacks, losing to both England and Wales, discovered that decades of the running game had not adequately prepared their forwards for the simple task of putting their noses as close to the ground as possible and pushing – pushing as hard as they could. Two years later, Philip Nel's great Springbok pack permitted New Zealanders to see for themselves that fine, powerful forward play was fundamental to rugby, whatever the accompanying style of attack. When Fred Allen's Forty-Niners were walloped, fore and aft, in South Africa, mortification set in.

Yet things gradually improved. What with the subsequent long supremacy in world rugby of the teams captained by Wilson Whineray, the brilliance of Fred Allen's side of 1967, and the wonderful finish in overdrive which Graham Mourie so often compelled from his team in important matches, New Zealand rugby was well on balance. Despite the High Court injunctions, despite rebel Cavalier tours, despite payments under the table and other problems, the All Blacks moved forward to the crowning glory of the World Cup.

★ ★ ★

It was simply a matter of going back to the grass roots. The passion, the enthusiasm had always been there, not least among the impressionable young. The Rugby Union and the wealthier provincial unions sent players of the eminence of Bruce Robertson, Sid Going, Peter Goldsmith and many more as coaches to the more fortunate schools and clubs. Elsewhere, all over the country, Saturday morning by Saturday morning, parents – usually the mothers – drove their sons, aged anywhere from six to twelve, to play in matches (the very young barefooted), controlled by referees who explained their rulings, and as often as not coached by fathers who milled among the children, urging them to catch, pass, run, kick and tackle (the five fundamentals). 'Did you kick the ball today?' a grandfather asked his six-year-old grandson. 'No fear,' said the boy, decisively. 'I wasn't the captain.'

Love of the game, that was the implicit lesson everywhere. At the well-established secondary schools, whether State or private, rugby was the prime sport. Four colleges, principally attended by Maori youths – two were Anglican, one Wesleyan, one Catholic – regularly turned out fine players and teams. And throughout the twenty-seven provincial unions affiliated to the New Zealand Rugby Union, the passion for the game, despite the influence of television and the impact of what Sir Donald Bradman has called the greatest enemy of sport, the motor-car, remained much the same as in those far-off days of the pony-trap and the horse-drawn cart.

Backed by hefty sponsorships, the big unions, New Zealand, Auckland, Canterbury, Wellington, made healthy profits. Smaller unions were less fortunate, some so impoverished that they staggered from one season to the next. A national provincial championship staged in three or four divisions made hay while the sun shone for the top dogs and plunged the lesser fry into debt, simply from the costs of travel and accommodation.

Rugby league, expertly presented on television, not least with the matches in Sydney's formidable Winfield Cup competition, posed threats; and when several All Blacks in 1990 departed for the professional game, there were fears New Zealand rugby might suffer, like its Australian counterpart, from raids on its finest talent. League, too, tended to exercise a baleful influence on playing techniques, even All Black midfield backs at times being persuaded that, ball in hand, their solemn duty was to run headlong at an awaiting tackler. Yet fears that rugby union was losing its popularity were dissipated by the experience of a British rugby league team of highly rated internationals, Jonathan Davies and Martin Offiah among them, which played through New Zealand in the winter of 1990 to such abysmally poor galleries that a good deal of money was lost.

Throughout the land, the true sporting heroes continued to be the All Blacks at national level and leading players at provincial and club levels. In early 1991, New Zealand's population had reached 3,400,000. It was still a small community, still isolated, far distant in the Southern Seas. It was now made up of many races. Auckland, for example, was now the largest Polynesian city in the world. Yet the catalytic agent in sport remained, as it had always been from the days when 'The Lunatics' boarded their ship for Wellington, the game which had begun life on the field of an English public school and which had spread irresistibly all around the world, because of its appeal to courage, skill, craft, manliness. In the development of rugby from infant to international level, New Zealand could proudly claim to have led the rest. What other country could field such as 'Sir Kirwan?'

INDIVIDUAL RECORDS – INTERNATIONALS

Most capped player – 55
C.E. Meads (King Country) 1957–71.

Highest points scorer – 430
G.J. Fox (Auckland) 27 matches, 1985–90.

Most tries – 30
J.J. Kirwan (Auckland) 37 matches, 1985–90.

Most conversions – 90
Fox 27 matches, 1985–90.

Most penalty goals – 76
Fox 27 matches, 1985–90.

Most dropped goals – 6
Fox 27 matches, 1985–90.
NB: in 144 matches for Auckland Province, Fox has scored 2078 points. The former record-holder, S. Watt, scored 400-plus.

Most points in international series – 46
A.H. Hawson (Wellington) v British Lions, 1983.

Most tries in international series on tour – 5
K. Svenson (Wellington) 4 matches, 1924–5.

Most points on tour – 230
W.J. Wallace (Wellington) 25 matches, 1905–6.

Most tries on tour – 42
J. Hunter (Taranaki) 23 matches, 1905–6.

Most tries in an international – 4
D. McGregor (Canterbury) v England, 1905, Crystal Palace.
C.I. Green (Canterbury) v Fiji, 1987, Christchurch.
J.A.Gallagher (Wellington) v Fiji, 1987, Christchurch.
J.J. Kirwan (Auckland) v Wales, 1988, Christchurch.

Most appearances as captain
W.J. Whineray (Auckland, 1958–65) – 30.
G.N.K. Mourie (Taranaki, 1977–82) – 19.
B.J. Lochore (Wairarapa, 1966–70) – 18.
A.G. Dalton (Counties, 1981–5) – 17.
W. Shelford (North Harbour, 1988–90) – 16.

Most appearances in each position
Fullback
D.B. Clarke (Waikato, 1956–64) – 31.
A.R. Hewson (Wellington, 1981–4) – 19.

Wing three-quarter
J.J. Kirwan (Auckland, 1985–90) – 37.
B.G. Williams (Auckland, 1970–8) – 36.

Centre three-quarter
B.J. Robertson (Counties, 1972–81) – 34.
J.T. Stanley (Auckland, 1986–9) – 25.

Second five-eighths
W.T. Taylor (Canterbury, 1983–7) – 22.
I.R. MacRae (Hawkes Bay, 1966–70) – 16.

First five-eighths
G.J. Fox (Auckland, 1985–90) – 27.
W.R. Smith (Canterbury, 1982–5) – 17.

Scrumhalf
S.M. Going (North Auckland, 1967–77) – 29.
D.S. Loveridge (Taranaki, 1978–85) – 24.

Number 8
M.G. Mexted (Wellington, 1979–85) – 34.
B.J. Lochore (Wairarapa, 1963–70) – 24.

Flanker
K.R. Tremain (Hawkes Bay, 1959–68) – 36.
I.A. Kirkpatrick (Poverty Bay, 1967–77) – 36.

Lock
C.E. Meads (King Country, 1957–71) – 48.
A.M. Haden (Auckland, 1977–85) – 41.

Prop
G.A. Knight (Manawatu, 1977–86) – 35.
W.J. Whineray (Auckland, 1957–65) – 32.

Hooker
A.J. Dalton (Counties, 1977–85) – 35.
S.S.T. Fitzpatrick (Auckland, 1986–90) – 30.

Leading try-scorers in internationals

	Matches	Tries
J.J. Kirwan	37	30
S.S. Wilson	34	19
I.A. Kirkpatrick	39	16
F.E. Mitchinson	11	10

137

Leading points-scorers in internationals

	Matches	Tries	Conversions	Penalty goals	Drop goals	Goals from mark	P
G.J. Fox	27	1	90	76	6	–	430
D.B. Clarke	31	2	33	38	5	2	207
A.R. Hewson	19	4	22	43	4	–	201
W.F. McCormick	16	–	23	24	1	–	121

ALL BLACK INTERNATIONAL TEAM RECORDS

Highest score
74 v Fiji (74–13) 1987 Christchurch

Country by country
60 v Argentina (60–9) 1989 Dunedin
38 v Australia (38–3) Auckland 1972
38 v British Isles (38–6) 1983 Auckland
42 v England (42–15) 1985 Wellington
74 v Fiji (74–13) 1987 Christchurch
38 v France (38–8) 1906 Paris
23 v Ireland (23–6) 1989 Dublin
70 v Italy (70–6) 1987 Auckland
14 v Romania (14–6) 1981 Bucharest
40 v Scotland (40–15) 1981 Auckland
25 v South Africa (25-22) 1981 Auckland
51 v United States (51–3) 1913 Berkeley, California
54 v Wales (54–9) 1988 Auckland

Winning margins
64 v Italy (70–6) 1987 Auckland

Country by country
51 v Argentina (60–9) 1989 Dunedin
35 v Australia (38–3) 1972 Auckland
32 v British Isles (38–6) 1983 Auckland
27 v England (42–15) 1985 Wellington
61 v Fiji (74–13) 1987 Christchurch
30 v France (38–8) 1906 Paris
17 v Ireland (23–6) 1989 Dublin
64 v Italy (70–6) 1987 Auckland
8 v Romania (14–6) Bucharest 1981
27 v Scotland (30–3) 1987 Christchurch
17 v South Africa (20–3) 1965 Auckland
48 v United States (51–3) 1913 Berkeley, California
49 v Wales (52–3) 1988 Christchurch

Highest score against
30 Australia (16–30) 1978 Auckland

Country by country
21 Argentina (21–21) 1985 Buenos Aires
30 Australia (16–30) 1978 Auckland
17 British Isles (18–17) 1959 Dunedin
16 England (10–16) 1973 Auckland
13 Fiji (74–13) 1987 Christchurch
24 France (19–24) 1979 Auckland
10 Ireland (10–10) 1973 Dublin
6 Italy (70–6) 1978 Auckland
6 Romania (14–6) 1981 Bucharest
25 Scotland (25–25) 1983 Murrayfield
24 South Africa (12–24) 1981 Wellington
3 United States (51–3) Berkeley, California
16 Wales (19–16) 1972 Cardiff

Largest losing margin
17 v South Africa (0–17) 1928 Durban

Country by country
16 v Australia (10–26) 1980 Sydney
10 v British Isles (3–13) 1971 Wellington
13 v England (0–13) 1936 Twickenham
13 v France (3–16) 1986 Nantes
5 v Wales (8–13) 1953 Cardiff

Most tries by New Zealand
13 v United States (51–3) 1913 Berkeley, California

Most tries against New Zealand
5 v South Africa (6–17) 1937 Auckland
5 v Australia (16–30) 1978 Auckland

Most points scored by an All Black team on tour
868 in British Isles & France (33 matches), 1905–06

Most tries on an overseas tour
215 in British Isles & France 1905–06

NEW ZEALAND INTERNATIONAL PLAYERS

Key: A – Australia; Arg — Argentina; AW – Anglo Welsh; BI – British Isles; E – England; F – France; Fj – Fiji; I – Ireland; It – Italy; R – Romania; S – Scotland; SA – South Africa; US – United States of America; W – Wales; (R) – Replacements. Entries in square brackets denote appearances in the inaugural World Cup tournament.

Note: In the case of a series, figures denote the test matches in which players have figured. Thus BI 1971 3, 5 indicates that the player appeared in the third and fifth tests of the tour.

NB. All Blacks who did not play in internationals are not included in this record.

Abbott, H.L. (Taranaki), 1906 F.

Aitken, G.G. (Wellington), 1921 SA 1, 2.

Allen, F.R. (Auckland), 1946 A 1, 2, 1947 A 1, 2, 1949 SA 1, 2.

Allen, N.H. (Counties), 1980 A 3, W.

Alley, G.T. (Canterbury), 1928 SA 1, 2, 3.

Anderson, A. (Canterbury), 1983 S, E, 1984 A 1, 2, 3, 1987 [Fj]

Anderson, B.L. (Wairarapa-Bush), 1986 A 1.

Archer, W.R. (Otago, Southland), 1955 A 1, 2, 3, 1956 SA 1, 3.

Argus, W.G. (Canterbury), 1946 A 1, 2, 1947 A 1, 2.

Arnold, D.A. (Canterbury), 1963 I, W, 1964 E, F.

Ashby, D.D.L. (Southland), 1958 A 1, 2.

Asher, A.A. (Auckland), 1903 A.

Ashworth, B.G. (Auckland), 1978 A 1, 2.

Ashworth, J.C. (Canterbury, Hawkes Bay), 1978 A 1, 2, 3, 1980 A 1, 2, 3, 1981 SA 1, 2, 3, 1982 A 1, 2, 1983 BI 1, 2, 3, 4. A, 1984 F 1, 2, A 1, 2, 3, 1985 E 1, 2, A.

Atkinson, H. (West Coast), 1913 A 1.

Avery, H.E. (Wellington), 1910 A 1, 2, 3.

Bachop, M.J.T. (Canterbury), 1989, W, I, 1990 S 1, 2, A 1, 2, 3, F 1, 2.

Badeley, C.E.O. (Auckland), 1921 SA 1, 2.

Baird, J.A.S. (Otago), 1913 A 2.

Ball, N. (Wellington), 1931 A, 1932 A 2, 3, 1935 W, 1936 E.

Barrett, J. (Auckland), 1913 A 2, 3.

Barry, E.F. (Wellington), 1934 A 2.

Batty, G.B. (Wellington, Bay of Plenty), 1972 W, S, 1973 E, I, F, E, 1974 A 1, 3, I, 1975 S, 1976 SA 1, 2, 3, 4, 1977 BI 1.

Batty, W. (Auckland), 1930 BI 1, 3, 4, 1931 A.

Beatty, G.E. (Taranaki), 1950 BI 1.

Bell, R.H. (Otago), 1951 A 3, 1952 A 1, 2.

Belliss, E.A. (Wanganui), 1921 SA 1, 2, 3.

Bennet, R. (Otago), 1905 A.

Berghan, T. (Otago), 1938 A 1, 2, 3.

Berry, M.J. (Wairarapa-Bush), 1986 A 3 (R).

Bevan, V.D. (Wellington), 1949 A 1, 2, 1950 BI 1, 2, 3, 4.

Birtwistle, W.M. (Canterbury), 1965 SA 1, 2, 3, 4, 1967 E, W, S.

Black, J.E. (Canterbury), 1977 F, I, 1979 A, 1980 A 3.

Black, N.W. (Auckland), 1949 SA 3.

Black, R.S. (Otago), 1914 A 1.

Blake, A.W. (Wairarapa), 1949 A 1.

Boggs, E.G. (Auckland), 1946 A 2, 1949 SA 1.

Bond, J.G. (Canterbury), 1949 A 2.

Booth, E.E. (Otago), 1906 F, 1907 A 1, 3

Boroevich, K.G. (Wellington), 1986 F 1, 3 (R), A 1.

Botica, F.M. (North Harbour), 1986 F 1, A 1, 2, 3, F 2, 3, 1989 Arg 1(R).

Bowden, N.J.G. (Taranaki), 1952 A 2.

Bowman, A.W. (Hawkes Bay), 1938 A 1, 2, 3.

Bowers, R.G. (Wellington), 1954 F, I.

Braid, G.J. (Bay of Plenty), 1983 S, E.

Bremner, S.G. (Auckland, Canterbury), 1952 A 2, 1956 SA 2.

Brewer, M.R. (Otago), 1986 F 1, A 1, 2, 3, F 2, 3, 1988 A 1, 1989 A W 1, 1990 S 1, 2, A 1, 2, 3, F 1, 2.

Brooke, Z.V. (Auckland), 1987 [Arg], 1989 Arg 2 (R), 1990 A 1, 2, 3.

Briscoe, K.C. (Taranaki), 1959 BI 2, 1960 SA 1, 2, 3, 4, 1963 I, W, 1964 E, S.

Brooke-Cowden, M. (Auckland), 1986 F 1, A 1, 1987 W.

Brown, C. (Taranaki), 1913 A 2, 3.

Brown, R.H. (Taranaki), 1955 A 3, 1956 SA
1, 2, 3, 4, 1957 A 1, 2, 1958 A 1, 2, 3, 1959 BI
1, 3, 1962 A 1.
Brownlie, C.J. (Hawkes Bay), 1924 w,
1925 E, F.
Brownlie, M.J. (Hawkes Bay), 1924 I, w,
1925 SA 1, 2, 3, 4.
Bruce, J.A. (Auckland), 1914 A 1, 2.
Bruce, O.D. (Canterbury), 1976 SA 1, 2, 4,
1977 BI 2, 3, 4, F 1, 2, 1978 A 1, 2, I, W, E, S.
Bryers, R.F. (King Country), 1949 A 1.
Budd, T.A. (Southland), 1946 A 2, 1949 A
2.
Bullock-Douglas, G.A.H. (Wanganui),
1932 A 1, 2, 3, 1934 A 1, 2.
Burgess, G.A.J. (Auckland), 1981 SA 2.
Burgess, G.F. (Southland), 1905 A.
Burgess, R.E. (Manawatu), 1971 BI 1, 2, 3,
1972 A 3, w, 1973 I, F.
Burke, P.S. (Taranaki), 1955 A 1, 1957 A 1,
2.
Burns, P.J. (Canterbury), 1908 AW 2, 1910
A 1, 2, 3, 1913 A 3.
Bush, R.G. (Otago), 1931 A.
Bush, W.K. (Canterbury), 1974 A 1, 2,
1975 S, 1976 I, SA 2, 4, 1977 BI 1, 2, 3, 4(R),
1978 I, w, 1979 A.
Buxton, J.B. (Canterbury), 1955 A 3, 1956
SA1.

Cain, M.J. (Taranaki), 1913 US, 1914 A 1,
2, 3.
Callesen, J.A. (Manawatu), 1974 A 1, 2, 3,
1975 S.
Cameron, D. (Taranaki), 1908 AW 1, 2, 3.
Cameron, L.M. (Manawatu), 1980 A 3,
1981 SA 1(R), 2, 3(R).
Carleton, S.R. (Canterbury), 1928 SA 1, 2,
3, 1929 A 1, 2, 3.
Carrington, K.R. (Auckland), 1971 BI 1, 3,
4.
Casey, S.T. (Otago), 1905 S, I, E, w, 1907
A 1, 2, 3, 1908 AW 1.
Catley, E.H. (Waikato), 1946 A 1, 1947 A 1,
2, 1949 SA 1, 2, 3, 4.
Caughey, T.H.C. (Auckland), 1932 A 1, 3,
1934 A 1, 2, 1935 S, I, 1936 E, A, 1937 SA
3.
Caulton, R.W. (Wellington), 1959 BI 1, 2, 3,
4, 1960 SA 1, 4, 1961 F 2, 1963 E 1, 2, I, W,
1964 E, S, F, A, 1, 2, 3.
Cherrington, N.P. (North Auckland), 1950
BI 1.
Christian, D.L. (Auckland), 1949 SA 4.
Clamp, M. (Wellington), 1984 A 2, 3.
Clark, D.W. (Otago), 1964 A 1, 2.

Clark, W.H. (Wellington), 1953 w, 1954 I,
E, S, 1955 A 1, 2, 1956 SA 2, 3, 4.
Clarke, A.H. (Auckland), 1958 A 3, 1959 BI
4, 1960 SA 1.
Clarke, D.B. (Waikato), 1956 SA 3, 4, 1957
A 1, 2, 1958 A 1, 3, 1959 BI 1, 2, 3, 4, 1960
SA 1, 2, 3, 4, 1961 F 1, 2, 3, 1962 A 1, 2, 3, 4,
5, 1963 E 1, 2, I, w, 1964 E, S, F, A 2, 3.
Clarke, I.J. (Waikato), 1953 w, 1955 A 1, 2,
3, 1956 SA 1, 2, 3, 4, 1957 A 1, 2, 1958 A 1,
3, 1959 BI 1, 2, 1960 SA 2, 4, 1961 F 1, 2, 3,
1962 A 1, 2, 3, 1963 E 1, 2.
Clarke, R.L. (Taranaki), 1932 A 2, 3.
Cobden, D.G. (Canterbury), 1937 SA 1.
Cockerill, M.S. (Taranaki), 1951 A 1, 2, 3.
Cockcroft, E.A.P. (South Canterbury),
1913 A 3, 1914 A 2, 3.
Codlin, B.W. (Counties), 1980 A 1, 2, 3.
Collins, A.H. (Taranaki), 1932 A 2, 3, 1934
A 1.
Collins, J.L. (Poverty Bay), 1964 A 1, 1965
SA 1, 4.
Colman, J.T.H. (Taranaki), 1907 A 1, 2,
1908 AW 1, 3.
Connor, D.M. (Auckland), 1961 F 1, 2, 3,
1962 A 1, 2, 3, 4, 5, 1963 E 1, 2, 1964 A 2, 3.
Conway, R.J. (Otago, Bay of Plenty), 1959
BI 2, 3, 4, 1960 SA 1, 3, 4, 1965 SA 1, 2, 3, 4.
Cooke, A.E. (Auckland, Wellington), 1924
I, w,, 1925 E, F, 1930 BI 1, 2, 3, 4.
Cooke, R.J. (Canterbury), 1903 A.
Cooper, G.J.L. (Auckland), 1986 F, I, A 1,
2.
Corner, M.M.N. (Auckland), 1930 BI 2, 3,
4, 1931 A, 1936 E.
Cossey, R.R. (Counties), 1958 A 1.
Cottrell, A.I. (Canterbury), 1929 A 1, 2, 3,
1930 BI 1, 2, 3, 4, 1931 A, 1932 A 1, 2, 3.
Cottrell, W.D. (Canterbury), 1968 A 1, 2, F
2, 3, 1970 SA 1, 1971 BI 1, 2, 3, 4.
Couch, M.B. (Wairarapa), 1947 A 1, 1949
A 1, 2.
Coughlan, T.D. (South Canterbury), 1958
A 1.
Creighton, J.N. (Canterbury), 1962 A 4.
Crichton, S. (Wellington), 1983 S, E.
Cross, T. (Canterbury), 1904 BI, 1905 A.
Crowley, K.J. (Taranaki), 1985 E 1, 2, A,
Arg, 1, 2, 1986 A 3, F 2, 3, 1987 [Arg], 1990 S
1, 2, A 1, 2, 3, F 1, 2.
Crowley, P.J.B. (Auckland), 1949 SA 3, 4,
1950 BI 1, 2, 3, 4.
Cummings, W. (Canterbury), 1913 A 2, 3.
Cundy, R.T. (Wairarapa), 1929 A 2(R).
Cunningham, G.R. (Auckland), 1979 A, S,
E, 1980 A 1, 2.

Cunningham, W. (Auckland), 1905 s, i, 1906 f, 1907 A 1, 2, 3, 1908 AW 1, 2, 3.

Cupples, L.F. (Bay of Plenty), 1924 i, w.

Currie, C.J. (Canterbury), 1978 i, w.

Cuthill, J.E. (Otago), 1913 A 1, us.

Dalley, W.C. (Canterbury), 1924 i, 1928 SA 1, 2, 3, 4.

Dalton, A.G. (Counties), 1977 f 2, 1978 A 1, 2, 3, i, w, e, s, 1979 f 1, 2, s, 1981 s 1, 2, SA 1, 2, 3, R, F 1, 2, 1982 A 1, 2, 3, 1983 BI 1, 2, 3, 4, A, 1985 E 1, 2, A.

Dalton, D. (Hawkes Bay), 1935 i, w, 1936 A 1, 2, 1937 SA 1, 2, 3, 1938 A 1, 2.

Dalton, R.A. Wellington), 1947 A 1, 2.

Dalzell, G.N. (Canterbury), 1953 w, 1954 I, E, S, F.

Davie, M.G. (Canterbury), 1983 E(R).

Davies, W.A. (Auckland, Otago), 1960 SA 4, 1962 A 4, 5.

Davis, K. (Auckland), 1952 A 2, 1953 w, 1954 I, E, S, F, 1955 A 2, 1958 A 1, 2, 3.

Davis, L.J. (Canterbury), 1976 i, 1977 BI 3, 4.

Davis, W.L. (Hawkes Bay), 1967 A, E, W, F, S, 1968 A 1, 2, F 1, 1969 w 1, 2, 1970 SA 2.

Deans, I.B. (Canterbury), 1988 w 1, 2, A 1, 2, 3, 1989 F 1, 2, Arg 1, 2, A.

Deans, R.G. (Canterbury), 1905 s, i, e, w, 1908 AW 3.

Deans, R.M. (Canterbury), 1983 s, e, 1984 A 1(R), 2, 3.

Delamore, G.W. (Wellington), 1949 SA 4.

Dewar, H. (Taranaki), 1913 A 1, us.

Diack, E.S. (Otago), 1959 BI 2.

Dick, J. (Auckland), 1937 SA 1, 2, 1938 A 3.

Dick, M.J. (Auckland), 1963 i, w, 1964 E, S, F, 1965 SA 3, 1966 BI 4, 1967 A, E, W, F, 1969 w 1, 2, 1970 SA 1, 4.

Dixon, M.J. (Canterbury), 1954 I, E, S, F, 1956 SA 1, 2, 3, 4, 1957 A 1, 2.

Dobson, R.L. (Auckland), 1949 A 1.

Dodd, E.H. (Wellington), 1905 A.

Donald, A.J. (Wanganui), 1983 s, e, 1984 F 1, 2, A 1, 2, 3.

Donald, J.G. (Wairarapa), 1921 SA 1, 2.

Donald, Q. (Wairarapa), 1924 i, w, 1925 E, F.

Donaldson, M.W. (Manawatu), 1977 F 1, 2, 1978 A 1, 2, 3, I, E, S, 1979 F 1, 2, A, S(R), 1981 SA 4(R).

Dougan, J.P. (Wellington), 1972 A 1, 1973 E.

Downing, J. (Auckland), 1913 A 1, us, 1914 A 1, 2, 3.

Drake, J.A. (Auckland), 1986 F 2, 3, 1987 [Fj, Arg, S, W, F], A.

Duff, R.H. (Canterbury), 1951 A 1, 2, 3, 1952 A 1, 2, 1955 A 2, 3, 1956 SA 1, 2, 3, 4.

Duncan, J. (Otago), 1903 A.

Duncan, M.G. (Hawkes Bay), 1971 BI 3(R), 4.

Duncan, W.D. (Otago), 1921 SA 1, 2, 3.

Dunn, E.J. (North Auckland), 1979 s, 1981 s, i.

Dunn, I.T.W. (North Auckland), 1983 BI 1, 4, A.

Dunn, J.M. (Auckland), 1946 A 1.

Earl, A.T. (Canterbury), 1986 F 1, A 1, F 3(R), 1987 [Arg], 1989 w, i.

Eastgate, B.P. (Canterbury), 1952 A 1, 2, 1954 s.

Elliott, K.G. (Wellington), 1946 A 1, 2.

Elsom, A.E.G. (Canterbury), 1952 A 1, 2, 1953 w, 1955 A 1, 2, 3.

Elvidge, R.R. (Otago), 1946 A 1, 2, 1949 SA, 1, 2, 3, 4, 1950 BI 1, 2, 3.

Erceg, C.P. (Auckland), 1951 A 1, 2, 3, 1952 A 1.

Evans, D.A. (Hawkes Bay), 1910 A 2.

Eveleigh, K.A. (Manawatu), 1976 SA 2, 4, 1977 BI 1, 2.

Fanning, A.H.N. (Canterbury), 1913 A 3.

Fanning, B.J. (Canterbury), 1903 A, 1904 BI.

Farrell, C.P. (Auckland), 1977 BI 1, 2.

Fawcett, C.L. (Auckland), 1976 SA 2, 3.

Fea, W.R. (Otago), 1921 SA 3.

Finlay, B.E.L. (Manawatu), 1959 BI 1.

Finlay, J. (Manawatu), 1946 A 1.

Finlayson, I. (North Auckland), 1928 SA 1, 2, 3, 4, 1930 BI 1, 2.

Fitzgerald, J.T. (Wellington), 1952 A 1.

Fitzpatrick, B.B.J. (Wellington), 1953 w, 1954 I, F.

Fitzpatrick, S.B.T. (Auckland), 1986 F 1, A 1, F 2, 3, 1987 [It, Fj, Arg, S, W, F], A, 1988 W 1, 2, A 1, 2, 3, 1989 F 1, 2, Arg 1, 2, A, W, I, 1990 S 1, 2, A 1, 2, 3, F 1, 2.

Fleming, J.K. (Wellington), 1979 s, e, 1980 A 1, 2, 3.

Fletcher, C.J.C. (North Auckland), 1921 SA 3.

Fogarty, R. (Taranaki), 1921 SA 1, 3.

Ford, B.R. (Marlborough), 1977 BI 3, 4, 1978 i, 1979 e.

Fox, G.J. (Auckland), 1985 Arg I, 1987 It, Fj, Arg, S, W, F, A, 1988 w 1, 2, A 1, 2, 3, 1989 F 1, 2, Arg 1, 2, A, w, I, 1990 S 1, 2, A 1, 2, 3, F 1, 2.

Francis, A.R.H. (Auckland), 1905 A, 1907 A 1, 2, 3, 1908 AW 1, 2, 3, 1910 A 1, 2, 3.

Francis, W.C. (Wellington), 1913 A 2, 3, 1914 A 1, 2, 3.

Fraser, B.G. (Wellington), 1979 S, E, 1980 A 3, W, 1981 S 1, 2, SA 1, 2, 3, R, F 1, 2, 1982 A 1, 2, 3, 1983 BI 1, 2, 3, 4, A, S, E, 1984 A 1.

Frazer, H.F. (Hawkes Bay), 1946 A 1, 2, 1947 A 1, 2, 1949 SA 2.

Fryer, F.C. (Canterbury), 1907 A 1, 2, 3, 1910 A 1, 2.

Fuller, W.B. (Canterbury), 1910 A 1, 2.

Furlong, B.D.M. (Hawkes Bay), 1970 SA 4.

Gallagher, J.A. (Wellington), 1987 [It, Fj, S, W, F], A, 1988 W 1, 2, A 1, 2, 3, 1989 F 1, 2, Arg 1, 2, A, W 1.

Gallaher, D. (Auckland), 1903 A, 1904 BI, 1905 S, E, W, 1906 F.

Gard, P.C. (North Otago), 1971 BI 4.

Gardiner, A.J. (Taranaki), 1974 A 3.

Geddes, H.J (Southland), 1929 A 1.

Geddes, W.McK. (Auckland), 1913 A 2.

Gemmell, B.McL. (Auckland), 1974 A 1, 2.

George, V.L. (Southland), 1938 A 1, 2, 3.

Gilbert, G.D.M. (West Coast), 1935 S, I, W, 1936 E.

Gillespie, C.T. (Wellington), 1913 A 2.

Gillespie, W.D. (Otago), 1958 A 3.

Gillett, G.A. (Canterbury, Auckland), 1905 S, I, E, W, 1907 A 2, 3, 1908 AW 1, 3.

Gillies, C.C. (Otago), 1936 A 2.

Gilray, C.M. (Otago), 1905 A.

Glasgow, F.T. (Taranaki, Southland), 1905 S, I, E, W, 1906 F, 1908 AW 3.

Glenn, W.S. (Taranaki), 1904 BI, 1906 F.

Goddard, M.P. (South Canterbury), 1946 A 2, 1947 A 1, 2, 1949 SA 3, 4.

Going, S.M. (North Auckland), 1967 A, F, 1968 F 3, 1969 W 1, 2, 1970 SA 1(R), 4, 1971 BI 1, 2, 3, 4, 1972 A 1, 2, 3, W, S, 1973 F 1, I, F, E 2, 1974 I, 1975 S, 1976 I(R), SA 1, 2, 3, 4, 1977 BI 1, 2.

Graham, D.J. (Canterbury), 1958 A 1, 2, 1960 SA 2, 3, 1961 F 1, 2, 3, 1962 A 1, 2, 3, 4, 5, 1963 E 1, 2, I, W, 1964 E, S, F, A 1, 2, 3.

Graham, J.B. (Otago), 1913 US, 1914 A 1, 3.

Graham, W.G. (Otago), 1979 F 1(R).

Grant, L.A. (South Canterbury), 1947 A 1, 2, 1949 SA 1, 2.

Gray, G.D. (Canterbury), 1908 AW 2, 1913 A 1, 2, US.

Gray, K.F. (Wellington), 1963 I, W, 1964 E, S, F, A 1, 2, 3, 1965 SA 1, 2, 3, 4, 1966 BI 1, 2, 3, 4, 1967 W, F, S, 1968 A, F 2, 3, 1969 W 1, 2.

Gray, W.N. (Bay of Plenty), 1955 A 2, 3, 1956 SA 1, 2, 3, 4.

Green, C.I. (Canterbury), 1983 S(R), E, 1984 A 1, 2, 3, 1985 E 1, 2, A, Arg 1, 2, 1986 A 2, 3, F 2, 3, 1987 [It, Fj, S, W, F], A.

Grenside, B.A. (Hawkes Bay), 1928 SA 1, 2, 3, 4, 1929 A 2, 3.

Griffiths, J.L. (Wellington), 1934 A 2, 1935 S, I, W, 1936 A 1, 2, 1938 A 3.

Guy, R.A. (North Auckland), 1971 BI 1, 2, 3, 4.

Haden, A.M. (Auckland), 1977 BI 1, 2, 3, 4, F 1, 2, 1978 A 1, 2, 3, I, W, E, S, 1979 F 1, 2, A, S, E, 1980 A 1, 2, 3, W, 1981 S 2, SA 1, 2, 3, F 1, 2, 1982 A 1, 2, 3, 1983 BI 1, 2, 3, 4, A, 1984 F 1, 2, 1985 Arg 1, 2.

Hadley, S. (Auckland), 1928 SA 1, 2, 3, 4.

Hadley, W.E. (Auckland), 1934 A 1, 2, 1935 S, I, W, 1936 E, A 1, 2.

Haig, J.S. (Otago), 1946 A 1, 2.

Haig, L.S. (Otago), 1950 BI 1, 2, 3, 4, 1951 A 1, 2, 3, 1953 W, 1954 E, S.

Hales, D.A. (Canterbury), 1972 A 1, 2, 3, W.

Hamilton, D.C. (Southland), 1908 AW 2.

Hammond, I.A. (Marlborough), 1952 A 2.

Harper, E.T. (Canterbury), 1904 BI, 1906 F.

Harris, P.C. (Manawatu), 1976 SA 3.

Hart, A.H. (Taranaki), 1924 I.

Hart, G.F. (Canterbury), 1930 BI 1, 2, 3, 4, 1931 A, 1934 A 1, 1935 S, I, W, 1936 A 1, 2.

Harvey, B.A. (Wairarapa-Bush), 1986 F 1.

Harvey, I.H. (Wairarapa), 1928 SA 4.

Harvey, L.R. (Otago), 1949 SA 1, 2, 3, 4, 1950 BI 1, 2, 3, 4.

Harvey, P. (Canterbury), 1904 BI.

Hasell, E.W. (Canterbury), 1913 A 2, 3.

Hayward, H.O. (Auckland), 1908 AW 3.

Hazlett, E.J. (Southland), 1966 BI 1, 2, 3, 4, 1967 A, E.

Hazlett, W.E. (Southland), 1928 SA 1, 2, 3, 4, 1930 BI 1, 2, 3, 4.

Heeps, T.R. (Wellington), 1962 A 1, 2, 3, 4, 5.

Heke, W.R. (North Auckland), 1929 A 1, 2, 3.

Hemi, R.C. (Waikato), 1953 W, 1954 I, E, S, F, 1955 A 1, 2, 3, 1956 SA 1, 3, 4, 1957 A 1, 2, 1959 BI 1, 3, 4.

Henderson, P. (Wanganui), 1949 SA 1, 2, 3, 4, 1950 BI 2, 3, 4.

Herewini, M.A. (Auckland), 1962 A 5, 1963 I, 1964 S, F, 1965 SA 4, 1966 BI 1, 2, 3, 4, 1967 A.
Hewson, A.R. (Wellington), 1981 S 1, 2, SA 1, 2, 3, R, F 1, 2, 1982 A 1, 2, 3, 1983 BI 1, 2, 3, 4, A, 1984 F 1, 2, A 1.
Higginson, G. (Canterbury, Hawkes Bay), 1980 W, 1981 S, I, SA 1, 1982 A 1, 2, 1983 A.
Hill, S.F. (Canterbury), 1955 A 3, 1956 SA 1, 3, 4, 1957 A 1, 2, 1958 A 3, 1959 BI 1, 2, 3, 4.
Hines, G.R. (Waikato), 1980 A 3.
Hobbs, M.J.B. (Canterbury), 1983 BI 1, 2, 3, 4, A, S, E, 1984 F 1, 2, A 1, 2, 3, 1985 E 1, 2, A, Arg 1, 2, 1986 A 2, 3, F, 2, 3.
Holder, E.C. (Buller), A 2.
Hook, L.S. (Auckland), 1929 A 1, 2, 3.
Hooper, J.A. (Canterbury), 1937 SA 1, 2, 3.
Hopkinson, A.E. (Canterbury), 1967 S, 1968 A 2, F 1, 2, 3, 1969 E 2, 1970 SA 1, 2, 3.
Hore, J. (Otago), 1930 BI 2, 3, 4, 1932 A 1, 2, 3, 1934 A 1, 2, 1935 S, 1936 E.
Horsley, R.H. (Wellington), 1960 SA 2, 3, 4.
Hotop, J. (Canterbury), 1952 A 1, 2, 1955 A 3.
Hughes, A.M. (Auckland), 1949 A 1, 2, 1950 BI 1, 2, 3, 4.
Hughes, E. (Southland, Wellington), 1907 A 1, 2, 3, 1908 AW 1, 1921 SA 1, 2.
Hunter, B.A. (Otago), 1971 BI 1, 2, 3.
Hunter, J. (Taranaki), 1905 S, I, E, W, 1906 F, 1907 A 1, 2, 3, 1908 AW 1, 2, 3.
Hurst, I.A. Canterbury), 1973 I, F, E, 1974 A 1, 2.

Ifwersen, K.D. (Auckland), 1921 SA 3.
Innes, C.R. (Auckland), 1989 W, I, 1990 S 1, 2, A 1, 2, 3, F 1, 2.
Innes, G.D. (Canterbury)), 1932 A 2.
Irvine, I.B. (North Auckland), 1952 A 1.
Irvine, J.G. (Otago), 1914 A 1, 2, 3.
Irvine, W.R. (Hawkes Bay, Wairarapa), 1924 I, W, 1925 E, F, 1930 BI 1.
Irwin, M.W. (Otago), 1955 A 1, 2, 1956 SA 1, 1958 A 2, 1959 BI 3, 4, 1960 SA 1.

Jackson, E.S. (Hawkes Bay), 1936 A 1, 2, 1937 SA 1, 2, 3, 1938 A 3.
Jaffray, J.L. (Otago, South Canterbury), 1972 A 2, 1975 S, 1976 I, SA 1, 1977 BI 2, 1979 F 1, 2.
Jarden, R.A. (Wellington), 1951 A 1, 2, 1952 A 1, 2, 1953 W, 1954 I, E, S, F, 1955 A 1, 2, 3, 1956 SA 1, 2, 3, 4.
Jefferd, A.C.R. (East Coast), 1981 S 1, SA 1.

Jessep, E.M. (Wellington), 1931 A, 1932 A 1.
Johnson, L.M. (Wellington), 1928 SA 1, 2, 3, 4.
Johnston, W. (Otago), 1907 A 1, 2, 3.
Johnstone, B.R. (Auckland), 1976 SA 2, 1977 BI 1, 2, F 1, 2, 1978 I, W, E, S, 1979 F 1, 2, S, E.
Johnstone, P. (Otago), 1949 SA 2, 4, 1950 BI 1, 2, 3, 4, 1951 A 1, 2, 3.
Jones, I. (North Auckland), 1990, S 1, 2, A 1, 2, 3, F 1, 2.
Jones, M.G. (North Auckland), 1973 E.
Jones, M.N. (Auckland), 1987 [It, Fj, S, F], A, 1988 W 1, 2, A 2, 3, 1989 F 1, 2, Arg 1, 2, 1990 F 1, 2.
Jones, P.F.H. (North Auckland), 1954 E, S, 1955 A 1, 2, 1956 SA 3, 4, 1958 A 1, 2, 3, 1959 BI 1, 1960 SA 1.
Joseph, H.T. (Canterbury), 1971 BI 2, 3.

Karam, J.F. (Wellington, Horowhenua), 1972 W, S, 1973 E, I, F, 1974 A 1, 2, 3, 1975 S.
Katene, T. (Wellington), 1955 A 2.
Kearney, J.C. (Otago), 1947 A 2, 1949 SA 1, 2, 3.
Kelly, J.W. (Auckland), 1949 A 1, 2.
Kember, G.F. (Wellington), 1970 SA 4.
Ketels, R.C. (Counties), 1980 W, 1981 S 1, 2, R, F 1.
Kiernan, H.A.D. (Auckland), 1903 A.
Kilby, F.D. (Wellington), 1932 A 1, 2, 3, 1934 A 2.
Killeen, B.A. (Auckland), 1936 A 1.
King, R.R. (West Coast), 1934 A 2, 1935 S, I, W, 1936 E, A 1, 2, 1937 SA 1, 2, 3, 1938 A 1, 2, 3.
Kingstone, C.N. (Taranaki), 1921 SA 1, 2, 3.
Kirk, D.E. (Auckland), 1985 E 1, 2, A, Arg 1, 1986 F 1, A 1, 2, 3, F 2, 3, 1987 [It, Fj, Arg, S, W, F], A.
Kirkpatrick, I.A. (Canterbury, Poverty Bay), 1967 F, 1968 A 1(R), 2, F 1, 2, 3, 1969 W 1, 2, 1970 SA 1, 2, 3, 4, 1971 BI 1, 2, 3, 4, 1972 A 1, 2, 3, W, S, 1973 E 1, 2, I, F, 1974 A 1, 2, 3, I, 1975 S, 1976 I, SA 1, 2, 3, 4, 1977 BI 1, 2, 3, 4.
Kirton, E. W. (Otago), 1967 E, W, F, S, 1968 A 1, 2, F 1, 2, 3, 1969 W 1, 2, 1970 SA 2, 3.
Kirwan, J.J. (Auckland), 1984 F 1, 2, 1985 E 1, 2, A, Arg 1, 2, 1986 F 1, A 1, 2, 3, 1987 [It, Fj, Arg, S, W, F], A, 1988 W 1, 2, A 1, 2, 3,

143

1989 F 1, 2, Arg 1, 2, A, 1990 S 1, 2, A 1, 2, 3, F 1, 2.

Kivell, A.L. (Taranaki), 1929 A 2, 3.

Knight, A. (Auckland), 1934 A 1.

Knight, G.A. (Manawatu), 1977 F 1, 2, 1978 A 1, 2, 3, E, S, 1979 F 1, 2, A, 1980 A 1, 2, 3, W, 1981 S 1, 2, SA 1, 3, 1982 A 1, 2, 3, 1983 BI 1, 2, 3, 4, A, 1984 F 1, 2, A 1, 2, 3, 1985 E 1, 2, A, 1986 A 2, 3.

Knight, L.G. (Poverty Bay), 1977 BI 1, 2, 3, 4, F 1, 2.

Koteka, T.T. (Waikato), 1981 F 2, 1982 A 3.

Kreft, A.J. (Otago), 1968 A 2.

Laidlaw, C.R. (Otago, Canterbury), 1964 F, A 1, 1965 SA 1, 2, 3, 4, 1966 BI 1, 2, 3, 4, 1967 E, W, S, 1968 A 1, 2, F 1, 2, 1970 SA 1, 2, 3.

Laidlaw, K.F. (Southland), 1960 SA 2, 3, 4.

Lambert, K.K. (Manawatu), 1972 S(R), 1973 E, I, F, E, 1974 I, 1976 SA 1, 3, 4, 1977 BI 1, 4.

Lambourn, A. (Wellington), 1934 A 1, 2, 1935 S, I, W, 1936 E, 1937 SA 1, 2, 3, 1938 A 3.

Le Lievre, J.M. (Canterbury), 1962 A 4.

Lendrum, R.N. (Counties), 1973 E 2.

Leslie, A.R. (Wellington), 1974 A 1, 2, 3, I, 1975 S, 1976 I, SA 1, 2, 3, 4.

Leys, E.T. (Wellington), 1929 A 3.

Lilburne, H.T. (Canterbury, Wellington), 1928 SA 3, 4, 1929 A 1, 2, 3, 1930 BI 1, 4, 1931 A, 1932 A 1, 1934 A 2.

Lindsay, D.F. (Otago), 1928 SA 1, 2, 3.

Lineen, T.R. (Auckland), 1957 A 1, 2, 1958 A 1, 2, 3, 1959 BI 1, 2, 3, 4, 1960 SA 1, 2, 3.

Lister, T.N. (South Canterbury), 1968 A 1, 2, F 1, 1969 W 1, 2, 1970 SA 1, 4, 1971 BI 4.

Little, P.F. (Auckland), 1961 F 2, 3, 1962 A 2, 3, 5, 1963 I, W, 1964 E, S, F.

Little, W. (North Harbour), 1990 S 1, 2, A 1, 2, 3, F 1, 2.

Loader, C.J. (Wellington), 1954 I, E, S, F.

Lochore, B.J. (Wairarapa), 1964 E, S, 1965 SA 1, 2, 3, 4, 1966 BI 1, 2, 3, 4, 1967 A, E, W, F, S, 1968 A 1, F 2, 3, 1969 W 1, 2, 1970 SA 1, 2, 3, 4, 1971 BI 3.

Loe, R.W. (Waikato), 1987 [It, Arg], 1988 W 1, 2, A 1, 2, 3, 1989 F 1, 2, Arg 1, 2, W, I, 1990 S 1, 2, A 1, 2, 3, W, I.

Long, A.J. (Auckland), 1903 A.

Loveridge, D. (Taranaki), 1978 W, 1979 S, E, 1980 A 1, 2, 3, W, 1981 S 1, 2, SA 1, 2, 3, R, F 1, 2, 1982 A 1, 2, 3, 1983 BI 1, 2, 3, 4, A, 1985 Arg 2.

Lucas, F.W. (Auckland), 1924 I, 1925 F, 1928 SA 4, 1930 BI 1, 2, 3, 4.

Lunn, W.A. (Otago), 1949 A 1, 2.

Lynch, T.W. (South Canterbury), 1913 A 1, 1914 A 1, 2, 3.

Lynch, T.W. jnr (Canterbury), 1951 A 1, 2, 3.

McAtamney, F (Otago), 1956 SA 2.

McCahill, R.J. (Auckland), 1987 [Arg, S(R), W(R)], 1989 Arg 1(R), 2(R).

McCaw, W.A. (Southland), 1951 A 1, 2, 3, 1953 W, 1954 F.

McCool, M.J. (Wairarapa-Bush), 1979 A.

McCormick, W.F. (Canterbury), 1965 SA 4, 1967 E, W, F, S, 1968 A 1, 2, F 1, 2, 3, 1969 W 1, 2, 1970 SA 1, 2, 3, 1971 BI 1.

McCullough, J.F. (Taranaki), 1959 BI 2, 3, 4.

McDonald, A. (Otago), 1905 S, I, E, W, 1907 A 1, 1908 AW 1, 1913 AI, US.

Macdonald, H.H. (Canterbury, North Auckland), 1972 W, S, 1973 E 1, I, F, E 2, 1974 I, 1975 S, 1976 I, SA 1, 2, 3.

McDowell, S.C. (Auckland, Bay of Plenty), 1985 Arg, 1, 2, 1986 A 2, 3, F, 2, 3, 1987 [It, Fj, S, W, F], A, 1988 W 1, 2, A 1, 2, I, 1989 F 1, 2, A, W, I, 1990 S 1, 2, A 1, 2, 3, W, I, F 1, 2.

McEldowney, J.T. (Taranaki), 1977 BI 3, 4.

MacEwan, I.N. (Wellington), 1956 SA 2, 1957 A 1, 2, 1958 A 1, 2, 3, 1959 BI 1, 2, 3, 1960 SA 1, 2, 3, 4, 1961 F 1, 2, 3, 1962 A 1, 2, 3, 4.

McGrattan, B. (Wellington), 1983 S, E, 1985 Arg 1, 2, 1986 F 1, A 1.

McGregor, A.J. (Auckland), 1913 A 1, US.

McGregor, D. (Canterbury, Southland), 1903 A, 1904 BI, 1905 E, W.

McGregor, N.P. (Canterbury), 1924 W, 1925 E.

McGregor, R.W. (Auckland), 1903 A, 1904 BI.

McHugh, M.J. (Auckland), 1946 A 1, 2, 1949 SA 3.

McIntosh, D.N. (Wellington), 1956 SA 1, 2, 1957 A 1, 2.

McKay, D.W. (Auckland), 1961 F 1, 2, 3, 1963 E 1, 2.

McKechnie, B.J. (Southland), 1977 F 1, 2, 1978 A 2 (R), 3, W(R), E, S, 1979 A, 1981 SA 1(R), F 1.

McKellar, G.F. (Wellington), 1910 A 1, 2, 3.

McKenzie, R.J. (Wellington), 1913 A 1, US, 1914 A 2, 3.

McKenzie, R. McC. (Manawatu), 1934 A 1, 1935 S, 1936 A 1, 1937 SA 1, 2, 3, 1938 A 1, 2, 3.

McLachlan, J.S. (Auckland), 1974 A 2.

McLaren, H.C. (Waikato), 1952 A 1.

McLean, A.L. (Bay of Plenty), 1921 SA 2, 3.

McLean, H.F. (Wellington, Auckland), 1930 BI 3, 4, 1932 A 1, 2, 3, 1934 A 1, 1935 I, W, 1936 E.

McLean, J.K. (King Country, Auckland), 1947 A 1, 1949 A 2.

McLeod, B.E. (Counties), 1964 A 1, 2, 3, 1965 SA 1, 2, 3, 4, 1969 W 1, 2, 1970 SA 1, 2.

McMinn, A.F. (Wairarapa, Manawatu), 1903 A, 1905 A.

McMinn, F.A. (Manawatu), 1904 BI.

McMullen, R.F. (Auckland), 1957 A 1, 2, 1958 A 1, 2, 3, 1959 BI 1, 2, 3, 1960 SA 2, 3, 4.

McNab, J.R. (Otago), 1949 SA 1, 2, 3, 1950 BI 1, 2, 3.

McNaughton, A.M. (Bay of Plenty), 1971 BI 1, 2, 3.

McNeece, J. (Southland), 1913 A 1, 2, 3, 1914 A 1, 2, 3.

McPhail, B.E. (Canterbury), 1950 BI 1, 4.

Macpherson, D.G. (Otago), 1905 A.

MacPherson, G.L. (Otago), 1986 F 1.

MacRae, I.R. (Hawkes Bay), 1966 BI 1, 2, 3, 4, 1967 A, E, W, F, S, 1968 F 1, 2, 1969 W 1, 2, 1970 SA 1, 2, 3, 4.

McRae, J.A. (Southland), 1946 A 1(R), 2.

McWilliams, R.G. (Auckland), 1928 SA 2, 3, 4, 1929 A 1, 2, 3, 1930 BI 1, 2, 3, 4.

Mackrell, W.H.C. (Auckland), 1906 F.

Macky, J.V. (Auckland), 1913 A 2.

Maguire, J.R. (Auckland), 1910 A 1, 2, 3.

Mahoney, A. (Bush), 1935 S, I, W, 1936 E.

Mains, L.W. (Otago), 1971 BI 2, 3, 4, 1976 I.

Major, J. (Taranaki), 1967 A.

Manchester, J.E. (Canterbury), 1932 A 1, 2, 3, 1934 A 1, 2, 1935 S, I, W, 1936 E.

Mason, D.F. (Wellington), 1947 A 2(R).

Masters, R.R. (Canterbury), 1924 I, W, 1925 E, F.

Mataira, H.K. (Hawkes Bay), 1934 A 2.

Matheson, J.D. (Otago), 1972 A 1, 2, 3, W, S.

Max, D.S. (Nelson), 1931 A, 1934 A 1, 2.

Meads, C.E. (King Country), 1957 A 1, 2, 1958 A 1, 2, 3, 1959 BI 2, 3, 4, 1960 SA 1, 2, 3, 4, 1961 F 1, 2, 3, 1962 A 1, 2, 3, 5, 1963 E 1, 2, I, W, 1964 E, S, F, A 1, 2, 3, 1965 SA 1, 2, 3, 4, 1966 BI 1, 2, 3, 4, 1967 A, E, W, F, S,

1968 A 1, 2, F 1, 2, 3, 1969 W 1, 2, 1970 SA 3, 4, 1971 BI 1, 2, 3, 4.

Meads, S.T. (King Country), 1961 F 1, 1962 A 4, 5, 1963 I, 1964 A 1, 2, 3, 1965 SA 1, 2, 3, 4, 1966 BI 1, 2, 3, 4.

Meates, K.F. (Canterbury), 1952 A 1, 2.

Meates, W. (Otago), 1949 SA 2, 3, 4, 1950 BI 1, 2, 3, 4.

Metcalfe, T.C. (Southland), 1931 A, 1932 A 1.

Mexted, G.G. (Wellington), 1950 BI 4.

Mexted, M.G. (Wellington), 1978 S, E, 1980 A 1, 2, 3, W, 1981 S, 1, 2, SA 1, 2, 3, R, F 1, 2, 1982 A 1, 2, 3, 1983 BI 1, 2, 3, 4, A, S, E, 1984 F 1, 2, A 1, 2, 3, 1985 E 1, 2, A, Arg 1, 2.

Mill, J.J. (Hawkes Bay, Wairarapa), 1924 W, 1925 E, F, 1930 BI 1.

Milliken, H.M. (Canterbury), 1938 A 1, 2, 3.

Milner, H.P. (Wanganui), 1970 SA 3.

Mitchell, N.A. (Southland, Otago), 1935 S, I, W, 1936 E, A 2, 1937 SA 3, 1938 A 1, 2.

Mitchell, T.W. (Canterbury), 1976 SA 4(R).

Mitchell, W.J. (Canterbury), 1910 A 2, 3.

Mitchinson, F.E. (Wellington), 1907 A 1, 2, 3, 1908 AW 1, 2, 3, 1910 A 1, 2, 3, 1913 A 1(R), US.

Moffitt, J.E. (Wellington), 1921 SA 1, 2, 3.

Moore, G.J.T. (Otago), 1949 A 1.

Moreton, R.C. (Canterbury), 1962 A 3, 4, 1964 A 1, 2, 3, 1965 SA 2, 3.

Morgan, J.E. (North Auckland), 1974 A 3, I, 1976 SA 2, 3, 4.

Morris, T.J. (Nelson Bays), 1972 A 1, 2, 3.

Morrison, T.C. (South Canterbury), 1938 A 1, 2, 3.

Morrison, T.G. (Otago), 1973 E 2 (R).

Morrissey, P.J. (Canterbury), 1962 A 3, 4, 5.

Mourie, G.N.K. (Taranaki), 1977 BI 3, 4, F 1, 2, 1978 I, W, E, S, 1979 F 1, 2, A, S, E, 1980 W, 1981 S 1, 2, F 1, 2, 1982 A 1, 2, 3.

Muller, B.L. (Taranaki), 1967 A, E, W, F, 1968 A 1, F 1, 1969 W 1, 1970 SA 1, 2, 4, 1971 BI 1, 2, 3, 4.

Mumm, W.J. (Buller), 1949 A 1.

Murdoch, K. (Otago) 1970 SA 4, 1972 A 3, W.

Murdoch, P.H. (Auckland), 1964 A 2, 3, 1965 SA 1, 2, 3.

Murray, H.V. (Canterbury), 1913 A 1, US, 1914 A 2, 3.

Murray, P.C. (Wanganui), 1908 AW 2.

Myers, R.G. (Waikato), 1978 A 3.

Mynott, H.J. (Taranaki), 1905 I, W, 1906 F, 1907 A 1, 2, 3, 1910 A 1, 3.

145

Nathan, W.J. (Auckland), 1962 A 1, 2, 3, 4, 5, 1963 E 1, 2, W, 1964 F, 1966 BI 1, 2, 3, 4, 1967 A.

Nelson, K.A. (Otago), 1962 A 4, 5.

Nepia, G. (Hawkes Bay, East Coast) 1924 I, W, 1925 E, F, 1925 A 1, 1930 BI 1, 2, 3, 4.

Nesbit, S.R. (Auckland), 1960 SA 2, 3.

Newton, F (Canterbury), 1905 E, W, 1906 F.

Nicholls, H.E. (Wellington) 1921 SA 1.

Nicholls, M.F. (Wellington) 1921 SA 1, 2, 3, 1924 I, W, 1925 E, F, 1928 SA 4, 1930 BI 1, 2, 3.

Nicholson, G.W. (Auckland) 1903 A, 1904 BI, 1907 A 2, 3.

Norton, R.W. (Canterbury) 1971 BI 1, 2, 3, 4, 1972 A 1, 2, 3, W, S, 1973 E 1, I, F, E 2, 1974 A 1, 2, 3, I, 1975 S, 1976 I, SA 1, 2, 3, 4, 1977 BI 1, 2, 3, 4.

O'Brien, J.G. (Auckland), 1914 A 1.

O'Callaghan, M.W. (Manawatu), 1968 F 1, 2, 3.

O'Callaghan, T.R. (Wellington), 1949 A 2.

O'Donnell, D.H. (Wellington), 1949 A 2.

Old, G.H. (Manawatu), 1981 SA 3, R(R), 1982 A 1(R).

O'Leary, M.J. (Auckland), 1910 A 1, 3, 1913 A 2, 3.

Oliver, C.J. (Canterbury), 1929 A 1, 2, 1934 A 1, 1935 S, I, W, 1936 E.

Oliver, D.J. (Wellington), 1930 BI 1, 2.

Oliver, D.D. (Otago), 1954 I, F.

Oliver, F.J. (Southland, Otago, Manawatu), 1976 SA 4, 1977 BI 1, 2, 3, 4, F 1, 2, 1978 A 1, 2, 3, I, W, E, S, 1979 F 1, 2, 1981 SA 2.

Orr, R.W. (Otago), 1949 A 1.

Osborne, M.W. (Wanganui), 1975 S, 1976 2(R), 4 (R), 1977 BI 1, 2, 3, 4, F 1(R), 2, 1978 I, W, E, S, 1980 W, 1982 A 1, 3.

O'Sullivan, J.M. (Taranaki), 1905 S, I, E, W, 1907 A 3.

O'Sullivan, T.P.A. (Taranaki), 1960 SA 1, 1961 F 1, 1962 A 1, 2.

Page, J.R. (Wellington), 1931 A, 1932 A 1, 2, 3, 1934 A 1, 2.

Palmer, B.P. (Auckland), 1929 A 2, 1932 A 2, 3.

Parker, J.H. (Canterbury), 1924 I, W, 1925 E.

Parkhill, A.A. (Otago), 1937 SA 1, 2, 3, 1938 A 1, 2, 3.

Parkinson, R.M. (Poverty Bay), 1972 A 1, 2, 3, W, S, 1973 E 1, 2.

Paterson, A.M. (Otago), 1908 AW 2, 3, 1910 A 1, 2, 3.

Paton, H. (Otago), 1910 A 1, 3.

Phillips, W.K. (King Country), 1937 SA 2, 1938 A 1, 2.

Pickering, E.A.R. (Waikato), 1958 A 2, 1959 BI 1, 4.

Pierce, M.J. (Wellington), 1985 E 1, 2, A, Arg 1, 1986 A 2, 3, F 2, 3, 1987 [It, Arg, S, W, F], A, 1988 W 1, 2, A 1, 2, 3, 1989 F 1, 2, Arg 1, 2, A, W, I.

Pokere, S.T. (Southland, Auckland), 1981 SA 3, 1982 A 1, 2, 3, 1983 BI 1, 2, 3, 4, A, S, E, 1984 F 1, 2, A 2, 3, 1985 E 1, 2, A.

Pollock, H.R. (Wellington), 1932 A 1, 2, 3, 1936 A 1, 2.

Porter, C.G. (Wellington), 1925 F, 1929 A 2, 3, 1930 BI 1, 2, 3, 4.

Procter, A.C. (Otago), 1932 A 1.

Purdue, C.A. (Southland), 1905 A.

Purdue, E. (Southland), 1905 A.

Purdue, G.B. (Southland), 1931 A, 1932 A 1, 2, 3.

Purvis, N.A. (Otago), 1976 I.

Quaid, C.E. (Otago), 1938 A 1, 2.

Rangi, R.E. (Auckland), 1964 A 2, 3, 1965 SA 1, 2, 3, 4, 1966 BI 1, 2, 3, 4.

Rankin, J.G. (Canterbury), 1936 A 1, 2, 1937 SA 2.

Reedy, W.J. (Wellington), 1908 AW 2, 3.

Reid, A.R. (Waikato), 1952 A 1, 1956 SA 3, 4, 1957 A 1, 2.

Reid, H.R. (Bay of Plenty), 1980 A 1, 2, W, 1983 S, E, 1985 Arg, 1, 2, 1986 A 2, 3.

Reid, K.H. (Wairarapa), 1929 A 1, 3.

Reid, S.T. (Hawkes Bay), 1935 S, I, W, 1936 E, A 1, 2, 1937 SA 1, 2, 3.

Reside, W.B. (Wairarapa), 1929 A 1.

Rhind, P.K. (Canterbury), 1946 A 1, 2.

Richardson, J. (Otago, Southland), 1921 SA 1, 2, 3, 1924 I, W, 1925 E, F.

Rickit, H. (Waikato), 1981 S 1, 2.

Ridland, A.J. (Southland), 1910 A 1, 2, 3.

Roberts, E.F. (Wellington), 1914 A 1, 2, 3, 1921 SA 2, 3.

Roberts, F. (Wellington), 1905 S, I, E, W, 1907 A 1, 2, 3, 1908 AW 1, 3, 1910 A 1, 2, 3.

Roberts, R.W. (Taranaki), 1913 A 1, US, 1914 A 1, 2, 3.

Robertson, B.J. (Counties), 1972 A 1, 3, S, 1973 E 1, I, F, 1974 A 1, 2, 3, I, 1976 I, SA 1, 2, 3, 4, 1977 BI 1, 3, 4, F 1, 2, 1978 A 1, 2, 3, W, E, S, 1979 F 1, 2, A, 1980 A 2, 3, W, 1981 S 1, 2.

Robertson D.J. (Otago), 1974 A 1, 2, 3, I, 1975 S, 1976 I, SA 1, 3, 4, 1977 BI 1,

Robilliard, A.C.C. (Canterbury), 1928 SA 1, 2, 3, 4.

Robinson, C.E. (Southland), 1951 A 1, 2, 3, 1952 A 1, 2.

Rollerson, D.L. (Manawatu), 1980 W, 1981 S 2, SA 1, 2, 3, R, F 1(R), 2.

Roper, R.A. (Taranaki), 1949 A 2, 1950 BI 1, 2, 3, 4.

Rowley, H.C.B. (Wanganui), 1949 A 2.

Rutledge, L.M. (Southland), 1978 A 1, 2, 3, I, W, E, S, 1979 F 1, 2, A, 1980 A 1, 2, 3.

Ryan, J. (Wellington), 1910 A 2, 1914 A 1, 2, 3.

Sadler, B.S. (Wellington), 1935 S, I, W, 1936 A 1, 2.

Salmon, J.L.B. (Wellington), 1981 R, F 1, 2(R).

Savage, L.T. (Canterbury), 1949 SA 1, 2, 4.

Saxton, C.K. (South Canterbury), 1938 A 1, 2, 3.

Schuler, K. (Manawatu), 1990 A 2(R).

Schuster, N.J. (Wellington), 1988 A 1, 2, 3, 1989 F 1, 2, Arg 1, 2, A, W, I.

Scott, R.W.H. (Auckland), 1946 A 1, 2, 1947 A 1, 2, 1949 SA 1, 2, 3, 4, 1950 BI 1, 2, 3, 4, 1953 W, 1954 I, E, S, F.

Scown, A.I. (Taranaki), 1972 A 1, 2, 3, W(R), S.

Scrimshaw, G. (Canterbury), 1928 SA 1.

Seear, G.A. (Otago), 1977 F 1, 2, 1978 A 1, 2, 3, I, W, E, S, 1979 F 1, 2, A.

Seeling, C.E. (Auckland), 1904 BI, 1905 S, I, E, W, 1906 F, 1907 A 1, 2, 1908 AW 1, 2, 3.

Sellars, G.M.V. (Auckland), 1913 A 1, US.

Shaw, M.W. (Manawatu, Hawkes Bay), 1980 A 1, 2, 3(R), W, 1981 S 1, 2, SA 1, 2, R, F 1, 2, 1982 A 1, 2, 3, 1983 BI 1, 2, 3, 4, A, S, E, 1984 F 1, 2, A 1, 1985 E 1, 2, A, Arg 1, 2, 1986 A 3.

Shelford, F.N.K. (Bay of Plenty), 1981 SA 3, R, 1984 A 2, 3.

Shelford, W.T. (North Harbour), 1986 F 2, 3, 1987 [It, Fj, S, W, F], A, 1988 W 1, 2, A 1, 2, 3, 1989 F 1, 2, Arg 1, 2, A, W, I, 1990 S 1, 2.

Siddells, S.K. (Wellington), 1921 SA 3.

Simon, H.J. (Otago), 1937 SA 1, 2, 3.

Simpson, J.G. (Auckland), 1947 A 1, 2, 1949 SA 1, 2, 3, 4, 1950 BI 1, 2, 3.

Simpson, V.L.J. (Canterbury), 1985 Arg 1, 2.

Sims, G.S. (Otago), 1972 A 2.

Skeen, J.R. (Auckland), 1952 A 2.

Skinner, K.L. (Otago, Counties), 1949 SA 1, 2, 3, 4, 1950 BI 1, 2, 3, 4, 1951 A 1, 2, 3, 1952 A 1, 2, 1953 W, 1954 I, E, S, F, 1956 SA 3, 4.

Skudder, G.R. (Waikato), 1969 W 2.

Sloane, P.E. (North Auckland), 1979 E.

Smith, A.E. (Taranaki), 1969 W 1, 2, 1970 SA 1.

Smith, B.W. (Waikato), 1984 F 1, 2, A 1.

Smith, G.W. (Auckland), 1905 S, I.

Smith, I.S.T. (Otago, North Otago), 1964 A 1, 2, 3, 1965 SA 1, 2, 4, 1966 BI 1, 2, 3.

Smith, J.B. (North Auckland), 1946 A 1, 1947 A 2, 1949 A 1, 2.

Smith, R.M. (Canterbury), 1955 A 1.

Smith, W.E. (Nelson), 1905 A.

Smith, W.R. (Canterbury), 1980 A 1, 1982 A 1, 2, 3, 1983 BI 2, 3, S, E, 1984 F 1, 2, A 1, 2, 3, 1985 E 1, 2, A, Arg 2.

Snow, E.M. (Nelson), 1929 A 1, 2, 3.

Solomon, F. (Auckland), 1931 A, 1932 A 2, 3.

Sonntag, W.T.C. (Otago), 1929 A 1, 2, 3.

Speight, M.W. (Waikato), 1986 A 1.

Spencer, J.C. (Wellington), 1905 A, 1907 A 1(R).

Spiers, J.E. (Counties), 1979 S, E, 1981 R, F 1, 2.

Spillane, A.P. (South Canterbury), 1913 A 2, 3.

Stanley, J.T. (Auckland), 1986 F 1, A 1, 2, 3, F 2, 3, 1987 [It, Fj, Arg, S, W, F], A, 1988 W 1, 2, A 1, 2, 3, 1989 F 1, 2, Arg 1, 2, A, W, I, 1990 S 1, 2.

Stead, J.W. (Southland), 1904 BI, 1905 S, I, E, 1906 F, 1908 AW 1, 3.

Steel, A.G. (Canterbury), 1966 BI 1, 2, 3, 4, 1967 A, F, S, 1968 A 1, 2.

Steel, J. (West Coast), 1921 SA 1, 2, 3, 1924 W, 1925 E, F.

Steele, L.B. (Wellington), 1951 A 1, 2, 3.

Steere, E.R.G. (Hawkes Bay) 1930 BI 1, 2, 3, 4, 1931 A, 1932 A 1.

Stephens, O.G. (Wellington), 1986 F 3.

Stevens, I.N. (Wellington), 1972 S, 1973 E 1, 1974 A 3.

Stewart, A.J. (Canterbury, South Canterbury), 1963 E 1, 2, I, W, 1964 E, S, F, A 3.

Stewart, J.D. (Auckland), 1913 A 2, 3.

Stewart, K.W. (Southland), 1973 E 2, 1974 A 1, 2, 3, I, 1975 S, 1976 I, SA 1, 3, 1979 S, E, 1981 SA 1, 2.

Stewart, R.T. (South Canterbury, Canterbury), 1928 SA 1, 2, 3, 4, 1930 BI 2.

Stohr, L.B. (Taranaki), 1910 A 1, 2, 3.

Stone, A.M. (Waikato, Bay of Plenty), 1981 F 1, 2, 1983 BI 3(R), 1984 A 3, 1986 F 1, A 1, 3, F 2, 3.

Storey, P.W. (South Canterbury), 1921 SA 1, 2.

Strahan, S.C. (Manawatu), 1967 A, E, W, F, S, 1968 A 1, 2, F 1, 2, 3, 1970 SA 1, 2, 3, 1972 A 1, 2, 3, 1973 E 2.

Strang, W.A. (South Canterbury), 1928 SA 1, 2, 1930 BI 3, 4, 1931 A.

Stringfellow, J.C. (Wairarapa), 1929 A 1(R), 3.

Stuart, K.C. (Canterbury), 1955 A 1.

Stuart, R.C. (Canterbury), 1949 A 1, 2, 1953 W, 1954 I, E, S, F.

Stuart, R.L. (Hawkes Bay), 1977 F 1(R).

Sullivan, J.L. (Taranaki), 1937 SA 1, 2, 3, 1938 A 1, 2, 3.

Sutherland, A.R. (Marlborough), 1970 SA 2, 4, 1971 BI 1, 1972 A 1, 2, 3, W, 1973 E 1, I, F.

Svenson, K.S. (Wellington), 1924 I, W, 1925 E, F.

Swain, J.P. (Hawkes Bay), 1929 SA 1, 2, 3, 4.

Tanner, J.M. (Auckland), 1950 BI 4, 1951 A 1, 2, 3, 1953 W.

Tanner, K.J. (Canterbury), 1974 A 1, 2, 3, I, 1975 S, 1976 I, SA 1.

Taylor, H.M. (Canterbury), 1913 A 1, US, 1914 A 1, 2, 3.

Taylor, J.M. (Otago), 1937 SA 1, 2, 3, 1938 A 1, 2, 3.

Taylor, M.B. (Waikato), 1979 F 1, 2, A, S, E, 1980 A 1, 2.

Taylor, N.M. (Bay of Plenty, Hawkes Bay), 1977 BI 2, 4(R), F 1, 2, 1978 A 1, 2, 3, I, 1982 A 2.

Taylor, R. (Taranaki), 1913 A 2, 3.

Taylor, W.T. (Canterbury), 1983 BI 1, 2, 3, 4, A, S, 1984 F 1, 2, A 1, 2, 1985 E 1, 2, Arg 1, 2, 1986 A 2, 1987 [It, Fj, S, W, F], A, 1988 W 1, 2.

Tetzlaff, P.L. (Auckland), 1947 A 1, 2.

Thimbleby, N.W. (Hawkes Bay), 1970 SA 3.

Thomas, B.T. (Auckland, Wellington), 1962 A 5, 1964 A 1, 2, 3.

Thomson, H.D. (Wellington), 1908 AW 1.

Thorne, G.S. (Auckland), 1968 A 1, 2, F 1, 2, 3, 1969 W 1, 1970 SA 1, 2, 3, 4.

Thornton, N.H. (Auckland), 1947 A 1, 2, 1949 SA 1.

Tilyard, J.T. (Wellington), 1913 A 3.

Tindill, E.W.T. (Wellington), 1936 E.

Townsend, L.J. (Otago), 1955 A 1, 3.

Tremain, K.R. (Canterbury, Hawkes Bay), 1959 BI 2, 3, 4, 1960 SA 1, 2, 3, 4, 1961 F 2, 3, 1962 A 1, 2, 3, 1963 E 1, 2, I, W, 1964 E, S, A 1, 2, 3, 1965 SA 1, 2, 3, 4, 1966 BI 1, 2, 3, 4, 1967 A, E, W, S, 1968 A 1, F 1, 2, 3.

Trevathan, D. (Otago), 1937 SA 1, 2, 3.

Tuck, J.M. (Waikato), 1929 A 1, 2, 3.

Turtill, H.S. (Canterbury), 1905 A.

Twigden, T.M. (Auckland), 1980 A 2, 3.

Tyler, G.A. (Auckland), 1903 A, 1904 BI, 1905 S, I, E, W, 1906 F.

Udy, D.K. (Wairarapa), 1903 A.

Urbahn, R.J. (Taranaki), 1959 BI 1, 3, 4.

Urlich, R.A. (Auckland), 1970 SA 3, 4.

Uttley, I.N. (Wellington), 1963 E 1, 2.

Vincent, P.B. (Canterbury), 1956 SA 1, 2.

Vodanovich, I.M.H. (Wellington), 1955 A 1, 2, 3.

Wallace, W.J. (Wellington), 1903 A, 1904 BI, 1905 S, I, E, W, 1906 F, 1907 A 1, 2, 3, 1908 AW 2.

Walsh, P.T. (Counties), 1955 A 1, 2, 3, 1956 SA 1, 2, 4, 1957 A 1, 2, 1958 A 1, 2, 3, 1959 BI 1, 1963 E 2.

Ward, R.H. (Southland), 1936 A 2, 1937 SA 1, 3.

Waterman, A.C. (North Auckland), 1929 A 1, 2.

Watkins, E.L. (Wellington), 1905 A.

Watt, B.A. (Canterbury), 1962 A 1, 4, 1963 E 1, 2, W, 1964 E, S, A 1.

Watt, J.M. (Otago), 1936 A 1, 2.

Watt, J.R. (Wellington), 1958 A 2, 1960 SA 1, 2, 3, 4, 1961 F 1, 3, 1962 A 1, 2.

Watts, M.G. (Taranaki), 1979 F 1, 2, 1980 A 1, 2, 3(R).

Webb, D.S. (North Auckland), 1959 BI 2.

Wells, J. (Wellington), 1936 A 1, 2.

West, A.H. (Taranaki), 1921 SA 2, 3.

Whetton, A.J. (Auckland), 1984 A 1(R), 3(R), 1985 A(R), Arg 1(R), 1986 A 2, 1987 [It, Fj, Arg, S, W, F], A, 1988 W 1, 2, A 1, 2, 3, 1989 F 1, 2, Arg 1, 2, A, 1989 F 1, 2, Arg 1, 2, A, 1990 S 1, 2, A 1, 2, 3, F 1, 2.

Whetton, G.W. (Auckland), 1981 SA 3, R, F 1, 2, 1982 A 3, 1983 BI 1, 2, 3, 4, 1984 F 1, 2, A 1, 2, 3, 1985 E 1, 2, A, Arg 2, 1986 A 2, 3, 1987 [It, Fj, Arg, S, W, F], A, 1988 W 1, 2, A 1, 2, 3, 1989 F 1, 2, Arg 1, 2, A, W, I, 1990 S 1, 2, A 1, 2, 3, F 1, 2.

Whineray, W.J. (Canterbury, Waikato, Auckland), 1957 A 1, 2, 1958 A 1, 2, 3, 1959

BI 1, 2, 3, 4, 1960 SA 1, 2, 3, 4, 1961 F 1, 2, 3, 1962 A 1, 2, 3, 4, 5, 1963 E 1, 2, I, W, 1964 E, S, F, 1965 SA 1, 2, 3, 4.

White, A. (Southland), 1921 SA 1, 1924 I, 1925 E, F.

White, H.L. (Auckland), 1954 I, E, F, 1955 A 3.

White, R.A. (Poverty Bay), 1949 A 1, 2, 1950 BI 1, 2, 3, 4, 1951 A 1, 2, 3, 1952 A 1, 2, 1953 W, 1954 I, E, S, F, 1955 A 1, 2, 3, 1956 SA 1, 2, 3, 4.

White, R.M. (Wellington), 1946 A 1, 2, 1947 A 1, 2.

Whiting, G.J. (King Country), 1972 A 1, 2, S, 1973 E 1, I, F.

Whiting, P.J. (Auckland), 1971 BI 1, 2, 4, 1972 A 1, 2, 3, W, S, 1973 E 1, I, F, 1974 A 1, 2, 3, I, 1976 SA 1, 2, 3, 4.

Williams, B.G. (Auckland), 1970 SA 1, 2, 3, 4, 1971 BI 1, 2, 4, 1972 A 1, 2, 3, W, S, 1973 E 1, I, F, E 2, 1974 A 1, 2, 3, I, 1975 S, 1976 SA 1, 2, 3, 4, 1977 BI 1, 2, 3, 4, F 1, 1978 A 1, 2, 3, I(R), W, E, S.

Williams, G.C. (Wellington), 1967 E, W, F, S, 1968 A 2.

Williams, P. (Otago), 1913 A 1.

Williment, M. (Wellington), 1964 A 1, 1965 SA 1, 2, 3, 1966 BI 1, 2, 3, 4, 1967 A.

Willocks, C. (Otago), 1946 A 1, 2, 1949 SA 1, 3, 4.

Wilson, B.W. (Otago), 1977 BI 3, 4, 1978 A 1, 2, 3, 1979 F 1, 2, A.

Wilson, D.D. (Canterbury), 1954 E, S.

Wilson, H.W. (Otago), 1949 A 1, 1950 BI 4, 1951 A 1, 2, 3.

Wilson, N.A. (Wellington), 1908 AW 1, 2, 1910 A 1, 2, 3, 1913 A 2, 3, 1914 A 1, 2, 3.

Wilson, N.L. (Otago), 1951 A 1, 2, 3.

Wilson, R.G. (Canterbury), 1979 S, E.

Wilson, S.S. (Wellington), 1977 F 1, 2, 1978 A 1, 2, 3, I, W, E, S, 1979 F 1, 2, A, S, E, 1980 A 1, W, 1981 S 1, 2, SA 1, 2, 3, R, F 1, 2, 1982 A 1, 2, 3, 1983 BI 1, 2, 3, 4, A, S, E.

Wolfe, T.N. (Wellington, Taranaki), 1961 F 1, 2, 3, 1962 A 2, 3, 1963 E 1.

Wood, M.E. (Canterbury, Auckland), 1903 A, 1904 BI.

Woodman, F.A. (North Auckland), 1981 SA 1, 2, F 1.

Wrigley, E. (Wairarapa), 1905 A.

Wright, T.J. (Auckland), 1986 F 1, A 1, 1987 [Arg], 1988 W 1, 2, A 1, 2, 3, 1989 F 1, 2, Arg 1, 2, A, W, I, 1990 S 1, 2, A 1, 2, 3, W, I, F 1, 2.

Wylie, J.L. (Auckland), 1913 A 1, US.

Wyllie, A.J. (Canterbury), 1970 SA 2, 3, 1971 BI 2, 3, 4, 1972 W, S, 1973 E 1, I, F, E 2.

Yates, V.M. (North Auckland), 1961 F 1, 2, 3.

Young, D. (Canterbury), 1956 SA 2, 1958 A 1, 2, 3, 1960 SA 1, 2, 3, 4, 1961 F 1, 2, 3, 1962 A 1, 2, 3, 5, 1963 E 1, 2, I, W, 1964 E, S, F.

1987 INAUGURAL WORLD CUP TOURNAMENT

Pool One:
Australia 19, England 6 (Sydney)
United States 21, Japan 18 (Brisbane)
England 60, Japan 7 (Sydney)
Australia 47, United States 12 (Brisbane))
Australia 42, Japan 23 (Sydney)
England 34, United States 6 (Sydney)

Pool Two:
Canada 37, Tonga 4 (Napier, NZ)
Wales 13, Ireland 6 (Wellington)
Wales 29, Tonga 16 (Palmerston North, NZ)
Ireland 46, Canada 19 (Dunedin)
Wales 40, Canada 9 (Invercargill, NZ)
Ireland 32, Tonga 9 (Brisbane)

Pool Three:
Fiji 28, Argentina 9 (Hamilton, NZ)
Argentina 25, Italy 16 (Christchurch)
Italy 18, Fiji 15 (Dunedin)
New Zealand 70, Italy 6 (Auckland)
New Zealand 74, Fiji 13 (Christchurch)
New Zealand 46, Argentina 15 (Wellington)

Pool Four:
France 20, Scotland 20 (Christchurch)
Romania 21, Zimbabwe 20 (Auckland)
France 55, Romania 12 (Wellington)
Scotland 60, Zimbabwe 21 (Wellington)
Scotland 55, Romania 28 (Dunedin)
France 70, Zimbabwe 12 (Auckland)

Quarter-Finals:
New Zealand 30, Scotland 3 (Christchurch))
Australia 33, Ireland 15 (Sydney)
France 31, Fiji 16 (Auckland)
Wales 16, England 3 (Brisbane)

Semi-Finals:
France 30, Australia 24 (Sydney)
New Zealand 49, Wales 9 (Brisbane)

Play-Off, Third Placing:
Wales 22, Australia 21 (Rotorua, NZ)

Grand Final
New Zealand 29 (one goal, four penalty goals, one drop goal, two tries), France 9 (one goal, one penalty goal) (Auckland)

MATCH RECORDS BY COUNTRY

Against Australia

Matches played 90

New Zealand 61 wins, Australia 23 wins, 6 drawn

1903 NEW ZEALAND 22 points (one goal, one penalty goal, two goals from marks, [4 points], two tries), AUSTRALIA 3 (one penalty goal). Sydney Cricket Ground.

1905 NEW ZEALAND 14 (one goal, three tries), AUSTRALIA 3 (one try). Tahuna Park, Dunedin.

1907 NEW ZEALAND 26 (four goals, two tries), AUSTRALIA 6 (one penalty goal, one goal from mark). Sydney Cricket Ground.
NEW ZEALAND 14 (one goal, three tries), AUSTRALIA 5 (one goal).

Woolloongabba Ground, Brisbane.
AUSTRALIA 5 (one goal), NEW ZEALAND 5 (one goal). Sydney Cricket Ground.

1910 NEW ZEALAND 6 (two tries), AUSTRALIA 0. Sydney Cricket Ground.
AUSTRALIA 11 (one goal, two tries), NEW ZEALAND 0. Sydney Cricket Ground.
NEW ZEALAND 28 (two goals, six tries), AUSTRALIA 13 (two goals, one penalty goal). Sydney Cricket Ground.

1913 NEW ZEALAND 30 (three goals, five tries), AUSTRALIA 5 (one goal). Athletic Park, Wellington.
NEW ZEALAND 25 (three goals, one drop goal, two tries), AUSTRALIA

13 (two goals, one try).
Carisbrook, Dunedin.
AUSTRALIA 16 (two goals, two tries),
NEW ZEALAND 5 (one goal).
Lancaster Park, Christchurch

1914 NEW ZEALAND 5 (one goal),
AUSTRALIA 0. Sydney Sports
Ground.
NEW ZEALAND 17 (one goal, four
tries), AUSTRALIA 0. Brisbane
Cricket Ground.
NEW ZEALAND 22 (2 goals, four
tries), AUSTRALIA 7 (one drop
goal, one try). Sydney Sports
Ground.

1929 AUSTRALIA 9 (two penalty goals,
one try), NEW ZEALAND 8 (one
goal, one penalty goal). Sydney
Cricket Ground.
AUSTRALIA 17 (one goal, two
penalty goals, two tries, NEW
ZEALAND 9 (one penalty goal, two
tries). Exhibition Ground,
Brisbane.
AUSTRALIA 15 (three penalty goals,
two tries), NEW ZEALAND 13 (two
goals, one try). Sydney Cricket
Ground.

1931 NEW ZEALAND 20 (one goal, four
penalty goals, one try),
AUSTRALIA 13 (two goals, one
try). Eden Park, Auckland.

1932 AUSTRALIA 22 (two goals, two
penalty goals, two tries), NEW
ZEALAND 17 (two goals, one drop
goal, one try). Sydney Cricket
Ground.
NEW ZEALAND 21 (one goal, one
penalty goal, one drop goal, three
tries), AUSTRALIA 3 (one try).
Exhibition Ground, Brisbane.
NEW ZEALAND 21 (three goals, two
tries), AUSTRALIA 13 (two goals,
one try). Sydney Cricket Ground.

1934 AUSTRALIA 25 (two goals, three
penalty goals, two tries), NEW
ZEALAND 11 (one goal, two tries).
Sydney Cricket Ground.
AUSTRALIA 3 (one try), NEW
ZEALAND 3 (one try). Sydney
Cricket Ground.

1936 NEW ZEALAND 11 (one goal, two
tries), AUSTRALIA 6 (one penalty
goal, one try). Athletic Park.

NEW ZEALAND 38 (four goals, one
penalty goal, five tries),
AUSTRALIA 13 (two goals, one
penalty goal). Carisbrook.

1938 NEW ZEALAND 24 (three goals, two
penalty goals, one try),
AUSTRALIA 9 (three penalty
goals). Sydney Cricket Ground.
NEW ZEALAND 20 (two goals, one
drop goal, two tries), AUSTRALIA
14 (one goal, one penalty goal,
two tries). Exhibition Ground,
Brisbane.
NEW ZEALAND 14 (one goal, two
penalty goals, one try),
AUSTRALIA 6 (one penalty goal,
one try). Sydney Cricket Ground.

1946 NEW ZEALAND 31 (five goals, two
tries), AUSTRALIA 8 (one goal,
one try). Carisbrook.
NEW ZEALAND 14 (one goal, three
penalty goals), AUSTRALIA 10
(two goals). Eden Park.

1947 NEW ZEALAND 13 (two goals, one
penalty try), AUSTRALIA 5 (one
goal). Exhibition Ground,
Brisbane.
NEW ZEALAND 27 (three goals, four
penalty goals), AUSTRALIA 14
(one goal, three penalty goals).
Sydney Cricket Ground.

1951 NEW ZEALAND 8 (one goal, one
penalty goal), AUSTRALIA 0.
Sydney Cricket Ground.
NEW ZEALAND 17 (one goal, one
drop goal, three tries),
AUSTRALIA 11 (one goal, one
penalty goal, one try). Sydney
Cricket Ground.
NEW ZEALAND 16 (two goals, two
tries), AUSTRALIA 6 (two penalty
goals). Brisbane Cricket Ground.

1952 AUSTRALIA 14 (one goal, one drop
goal, two tries), NEW ZEALAND 9
(one penalty goal, two tries).
Lancaster Park.
NEW ZEALAND 15 (two penalty
goals, one drop goal, two tries),
AUSTRALIA 8 (one goal, one
penalty goal). Athletic Park.

1955 NEW ZEALAND 16 (two goals, one
penalty goal, one try), AUSTRALIA
8 (one goal, one penalty goal).
Athletic Park.

NEW ZEALAND 8 (one goal, one drop goal), AUSTRALIA 0. Carisbrook.

AUSTRALIA 8 (one goal, one try), NEW ZEALAND 3 (one try). Eden Park.

1957 NEW ZEALAND 25 (two goals, three penalty goals, two tries), AUSTRALIA 11 (one goal, two penalty goals). Sydney Cricket Ground.

NEW ZEALAND 22 (two goals, one drop goal, one goal from mark, two tries), AUSTRALIA 9 (two penalty goals, one try). Exhibition Ground, Brisbane.

1958 NEW ZEALAND 25 (two goals, five tries), AUSTRALIA 3 (one try). Athletic Park.

AUSTRALIA 6 (one penalty goal, one try), NEW ZEALAND 3 (one try). Lancaster Park.

NEW ZEALAND 17 (one goal, four penalty goals), AUSTRALIA 8 (one goal, one penalty goal). Epsom Showgrounds, Auckland.

1962 NEW ZEALAND 20 (one goal, one penalty goal, one drop goal, three tries), AUSTRALIA 6 (two penalty goals). Exhibition Ground, Brisbane.

NEW ZEALAND 14 (one goal, two penalty goals, one try), AUSTRALIA 5 (one goal). Sydney Cricket Ground.

AUSTRALIA 9 (three penalty goals), NEW ZEALAND 9 (two penalty goals, one try). Athletic Park.

NEW ZEALAND 3 (one penalty goal), AUSTRALIA 0. Carisbrook.

NEW ZEALAND 16 (two goals, one drop goal, one try), AUSTRALIA 8 (one goal, one penalty goal). Eden Park.

1964 NEW ZEALAND 14 (one goal, two penalty goals, one drop goal), AUSTRALIA (two penalty goals, one try). Carisbrook.

NEW ZEALAND 18 (three goals, one try), AUSTRALIA 3 (one try). Lancaster Park.

AUSTRALIA 20 (one goal, three penalty goals, one drop goal, one try). NEW ZEALAND 5 (one goal). Athletic Park.

1967 NEW ZEALAND 29 (four goals, two penalty goals, one drop goal), AUSTRALIA 9 (one penalty goal, two tries). Athletic Park.

1968 NEW ZEALAND 27 (three goals, one penalty goal, three tries), AUSTRALIA 11 (one goal, two penalty goals). Sydney Cricket Ground.

NEW ZEALAND 19 (two goals, two penalty goals, one penalty try), AUSTRALIA 18 (five penalty goals, one try). Ballymore Oval, Brisbane.

1972 NEW ZEALAND 29 (three goals, one drop goal, two tries), AUSTRALIA 6 (two penalty goals). Athletic Park.

NEW ZEALAND 30 (two goals, two penalty goals, three tries), AUSTRALIA 17 (one goal, one drop goal, two tries). Lancaster Park.

NEW ZEALAND 38 (four goals, two penalty goals, two tries), AUSTRALIA 3 (one penalty goal). Eden Park.

1974 NEW ZEALAND 17 (one penalty goal, two tries), AUSTRALIA 6 (one goal). Sydney Cricket Ground.

AUSTRALIA 16 (one goal, two penalty goals, one try), NEW ZEALAND 16 (one goal, two penalty goals, one try). Ballymore Oval, Brisbane.

NEW ZEALAND 16 (two goals, one try), AUSTRALIA 6 (two penalty goals). Sydney Cricket Ground.

1976 NEW ZEALAND 13 (three penalty goals, one try), AUSTRALIA 12 (one goal, two penalty goals). Athletic Park.

NEW ZEALAND 22 (two goals, one penalty goal, one drop goal), AUSTRALIA 6 (one penalty goal, one drop goal). Lancaster Park.

AUSTRALIA 30 (two goals, one penalty goal, one drop goal, three tries), NEW ZEALAND 16, (one goal, two penalty goals, one try). Eden Park.

1979 AUSTRALIA 12 (three penalty goals, one drop goal), NEW ZEALAND 6 (one penalty goal, one drop goal). Sydney Cricket Ground.

1980 AUSTRALIA 13 (one goal, one drop goal, one try), NEW ZEALAND 9 (three penalty goals). Sydney Cricket Ground.

NEW ZEALAND 12 (one goal, two penalty goals), AUSTRALIA 9 (one goal, one penalty goal). Ballymore Oval, Brisbane.

AUSTRALIA 26 (two goals, one penalty goal, one drop goal, two tries), NEW ZEALAND 10 (two penalty goals, one try). Sydney Cricket Ground.

1982 NEW ZEALAND 23 (two goals, one penalty goal, three tries), AUSTRALIA 16 (one goal, two penalty goals, one try). Lancaster Park.

AUSTRALIA 19 (one goal, three penalty goals, one try), NEW ZEALAND 16 (one goal, two penalty goals, one try). Athletic Park.

NEW ZEALAND 33 (two goals, five penalty goals, two drop goals), AUSTRALIA 18 (one goal, three penalty goals, one drop goal). Eden Park.

1983 NEW ZEALAND 18 (one goal, four penalty goals), AUSTRALIA 8 (two tries). Sydney Cricket Ground.

1984 AUSTRALIA 16 (one goal, one penalty goal, one drop goal, one try). NEW ZEALAND 9 (two penalty goals, one drop goal). Sydney Cricket Ground.

NEW ZEALAND 19 (five penalty goals, one try), AUSTRALIA 15 (one goal, three penalty goals). Ballymore Oval, Brisbane.

NEW ZEALAND 25 (one goal, five penalty goals, one try), AUSTRALIA 24 (one goal, six penalty goals). Sydney Cricket Ground.

1985 NEW ZEALAND 10 (two penalty goals, one try), AUSTRALIA 9 (one goal, one penalty goal). Eden Park.

1986 AUSTRALIA 13 (one goal, one penalty goal, one try), NEW ZEALAND 12 (one goal, two penalty goals). Athletic Park.

NEW ZEALAND 13 (two penalty goals, one drop goal, one try), AUSTRALIA 12 (three penalty goals, one drop goal). Carisbrook.

AUSTRALIA 22 (one goal, four penalty goals, one try), NEW ZEALAND 9 (three penalty goals). Eden Park.

1987 NEW ZEALAND 30 (one goal, three penalty goals, one drop goal), AUSTRALIA 16 (three penalty goals, one drop goal, one try). Concord Oval, Sydney.

1988 NEW ZEALAND 32 (three goals, two penalty goals, two tries), AUSTRALIA 7 (one penalty goal, one try). Concord Oval, Sydney.

AUSTRALIA 19 (one goal, three penalty goals, one try), NEW ZEALAND 19 (two goals, one penalty goal, two tries). Ballymore Oval, Brisbane.

NEW ZEALAND 30 (three goals, four penalty goals), AUSTRALIA 9 (one goal, one penalty goal). Concord Oval, Sydney.

1989 NEW ZEALAND 24 (two goals, four penalty goals), AUSTRALIA 12 (one goal, two penalty goals). Eden Park.

1990 NEW ZEALAND 21 (one goal, one penalty goal, three tries), AUSTRALIA 6 (two penalty goals). Lancaster Park.

NEW ZEALAND 27 (three goals, two penalty goals, one drop goal), AUSTRALIA 17 (two penalty goals, one drop goal, two tries). Eden Park.

AUSTRALIA 21 (one goal, five penalty goals), NEW ZEALAND 9 (two penalty goals, one drop goal). Athletic Park.

Against British Isles

Matches played 29

New Zealand 22 wins, British Isles 5 wins, 2 drawn

1904 NEW ZEALAND 9 points (two tries, one penalty goal), BRITISH ISLES 3 (one penalty goal). Athletic Park.

153

1930   BRITISH ISLES 6 (two tries), NEW
       ZEALAND 3 (try). Carisbrook.
       NEW ZEALAND 13 (two goals, goal
       from mark), BRITISH ISLES 10
       (two goals). Lancaster Park.
       NEW ZEALAND 15 (one goal, one
       dropped goal, two tries), BRITISH
       ISLES 10 (two goals). Eden Park.
       NEW ZEALAND 22 (two goals, four
       tries), BRITISH ISLES 8 (one goal,
       one penalty goal). Athletic Park.

1950   BRITISH ISLES 9 (two tries, one
       penalty goal), NEW ZEALAND 9
       (one penalty goal, two tries, one
       penalty goal). Carisbrook.
       NEW ZEALAND 8 (one goal, one
       try), BRITISH ISLES 0. Lancaster
       Park.
       NEW ZEALAND 6 (one try, one
       penalty goal), BRITISH ISLES 3
       (penalty goal). Athletic Park.
       NEW ZEALAND 11 (one goal, one
       drop goal, one try), BRITISH
       ISLES 8 (one goal, one penalty
       goal). Eden Park.

1959   NEW ZEALAND 18 (six penalty
       goals), BRITISH ISLES 17 (one
       goal, one penalty goal, three
       tries). Carisbrook.
       NEW ZEALAND 11 (one goal, two
       tries), BRITISH ISLES 8 (one goal,
       one penalty goal). Athletic Park.
       NEW ZEALAND 22 (two goals, one
       penalty goal, one drop goal, two
       tries), BRITISH ISLES 8 (one goal,
       one penalty goal). Lancaster Park.
       BRITISH ISLES 9 (three tries), NEW
       ZEALAND 6 (two penalty goals).
       Eden Park.

1966   NEW ZEALAND 20 (one goal, two
       penalty goals, one drop goal),
       BRITISH ISLES 3 (penalty goal).
       Carisbrook.
       NEW ZEALAND 16 (two goals, one
       penalty goal, two tries), BRITISH
       ISLES 12 (three penalty goals, one
       drop goal). Athletic Park.
       NEW ZEALAND 19 (two goals, two
       penalty goals, one try), BRITISH
       ISLES 6 (two tries). Lancaster
       park.
       NEW ZEALAND 24 (three goals, one
       penalty, one drop goal, one try),
       BRITISH ISLES 11 (one goal, one
       penalty, one try). Eden Park.

1971   BRITISH ISLES 9 (two penalty goals,
       one try), NEW ZEALAND 3
       (penalty goal). Carisbrook.
       NEW ZEALAND 22 (two goals, one
       penalty goal, three tries including
       one penalty try), BRITISH ISLES
       12 (one penalty goal, one drop
       goal, two tries). Lancaster Park.
       BRITISH ISLES 13 (two goals, one
       drop goal), NEW ZEALAND 3 (one
       try). Athletic Park.
       BRITISH ISLES 14 (one goal, two
       penalty goals, one drop goal),
       NEW ZEALAND 14 (one goal, two
       penalty goals, one drop goal).
       Eden Park.

1977   NEW ZEALAND 16 (two goals, one
       try), BRITISH ISLES 12 (four
       penalty goals). Athletic Park.
       BRITISH ISLES 13 (three penalty
       goals, one try), NEW ZEALAND 9
       (three penalty goals). Lancaster
       Park.
       NEW ZEALAND 19 (one goal, two
       penalty goals, one drop goal, one
       try), BRITISH ISLES 7 (one penalty
       goal, one try). Carisbrook.
       NEW ZEALAND 10 (two penalty
       goals, one try), BRITISH ISLES 9
       (one goal, one penalty goal). Eden
       Park.

1983   NEW ZEALAND 16 (three penalty
       goals, one drop goal), BRITISH
       ISLES 12 (three penalty goals, one
       drop goal).
       NEW ZEALAND 9 (one goal, one
       penalty goal), BRITISH ISLES 0.
       Athletic Park.
       NEW ZEALAND 15 (one goal, three
       penalty goals), BRITISH ISLES 8
       (two tries). Carisbrook.
       NEW ZEALAND 38 (four goals, two
       penalty goals, two tries), BRITISH
       ISLES 6 (two penalty goals).

Against Anglo-Welsh

Matches played 3

New Zealand 2 wins, Anglo-Welsh 0, 1
drawn

1908   NEW ZEALAND 32 (four goals, one
       penalty goal, three tries),
       ANGLO-WELSH 5 (one goal).
       Carisbrook.

ANGLO-WELSH 3 (one try), NEW
ZEALAND 3 (one penalty goal).
Athletic Park.

NEW ZEALAND 29 (one goal, eight
tries), ANGLO-WELSH 0. Potter's
Park, Auckland.

Against South Africa

Matches played 37

New Zealand 15 wins, South Africa 20
wins, 2 drawn

1921　NEW ZEALAND 13 (two goals, one
try), SOUTH AFRICA 5 (one goal).
Carisbrook.

SOUTH AFRICA 9 (one goal, one
drop goal), NEW ZEALAND 5 (one
goal). Eden Park.

SOUTH AFRICA 0, NEW ZEALAND 0.
Athletic Park.

1928　SOUTH AFRICA 17 (two penalty
goals, two drop goals, one try),
NEW ZEALAND 0. Kingsmead,
Durban.

NEW ZEALAND 7 (penalty goal,
drop goal), SOUTH AFRICA 6
(penalty goal, goal from mark).
Ellis Park, Johannesburg.

SOUTH AFRICA 11 (one goal, two
tries), NEW ZEALAND 6 (two
tries). Crusader Ground, Port
Elizabeth.

NEW ZEALAND 13 (two penalty
goals, one drop goal, one try),
SOUTH AFRICA 5 (one goal).
Newlands, Cape Town.

1937　NEW ZEALAND 13 (two penalty
goals, one drop goal, one try,
SOUTH AFRICA 7 (one drop goal,
one try). Athletic Park.

SOUTH AFRICA 13 (two goals, one
penalty goal), NEW ZEALAND 6
(two tries). Lancaster Park.

SOUTH AFRICA 17 (one goal, four
tries), NEW ZEALAND 6 (two
penalty goals). Eden Park.

1949　SOUTH AFRICA 15 (five penalty
goals), NEW ZEALAND 11 (one
goal, one penalty goal, one drop
goal). Newlands, Cape Town.

SOUTH AFRICA 12 (one penalty goal,
one drop goal, two tries), NEW
ZEALAND 6 (one penalty goal, one
drop goal). Ellis Park.

SOUTH AFRICA 9 (three penalty
goals), NEW ZEALAND 3 (one
try). Kingsmead.

SOUTH AFRICA 11 (one goal, one
penalty goal, one drop goal), NEW
ZEALAND 8 (one goal, one try).
Crusader.

1956　NEW ZEALAND 10 (two goals),
SOUTH AFRICA 6 (one penalty
goal, one try). Carisbrook.

SOUTH AFRICA 8 (one goal, one try),
NEW ZEALAND 3 (one try).
Athletic Park.

NEW ZEALAND 17 (one goal, two
penalty goals, two tries), SOUTH
AFRICA 10 (two goals). Lancaster
Park.

NEW ZEALAND 11 (one goal, two
penalty goals), SOUTH AFRICA 5
(one goal). Eden Park.

1960　SOUTH AFRICA 13 (two goals, one
penalty goal). NEW ZEALAND 0.
Ellis Park.

NEW ZEALAND 11 (one goal, one
penalty goal, one drop goal),
SOUTH AFRICA 3 (one try).
Newlands.

NEW ZEALAND 11 (one goal, two
penalty goals), SOUTH AFRICA 11
(one goal, two penalty goals).
Free State Stadium,
Bloemfontein.

SOUTH AFRICA 8 (one goal, one
penalty goal), NEW ZEALAND 3
(one penalty goal). Boet Erasmus
Stadium, Port Elizabeth.

1965　NEW ZEALAND 6 (two tries), SOUTH
AFRICA 3 (one drop goal).
Athletic Park.

NEW ZEALAND 13 (two goals, one
try), SOUTH AFRICA 0.
Carisbrook.

SOUTH AFRICA 19 (two goals, two
penalty goals, two tries), NEW
ZEALAND 16 (two goals, one
penalty goal, one try). Lancaster
Park.

NEW ZEALAND 20 (one goal, one
drop goal, four tries), SOUTH
AFRICA 3 (one penalty goal).
Eden Park.

1970　SOUTH AFRICA 17 (one goal, two
penalty goals, one drop goal, one
try), NEW ZEALAND 6 (one

penalty goal, one try). Loftus Versfeld Stadium, Pretoria.

NEW ZEALAND 9 (one penalty goal, two tries), SOUTH AFRICA 8 (one goal, one penalty goal). Newlands.

SOUTH AFRICA 14 (one goal, two penalty goals, one try), NEW ZEALAND 3 (one penalty goal). Boet Erasmus.

SOUTH AFRICA 20 (one goal, four penalty goals, one try), NEW ZEALAND 17 (one goal, four penalty goals). Ellis Park.

1976 SOUTH AFRICA 16 (one goal, one penalty goal, one drop goal, one try), NEW ZEALAND 7 (one penalty goal, one try). Kings Park, Durban.

NEW ZEALAND 15 (one goal, two penalty goals, one drop goal), SOUTH AFRICA 9 (three penalty goals). Free State Stadium.

SOUTH AFRICA 15 (one goal, two penalty goals, one drop goal). NEW ZEALAND 10 (two penalty goals, one try). Newlands.

SOUTH AFRICA 15 (one goal, two penalty goals, one drop goal), NEW ZEALAND 14 (one penalty goal, one drop goal, two tries). Ellis Park.

1981 NEW ZEALAND 14 (one goal, two tries), SOUTH AFRICA 9 (one goal, one penalty goal). Lancaster Park.

SOUTH AFRICA 24 (one goal, five penalty goals, one drop goal), NEW ZEALAND 12 (four penalty goals). Athletic Park.

NEW ZEALAND 25 (one goal, four penalty goals, one drop goal, one try), SOUTH AFRICA 22 (two goals, two penalty goals, one try). Eden Park.

Against Scotland

Matches played 14

New Zealand 12 wins, Scotland 0, 2 drawn

1905 NEW ZEALAND 12 (four tries), SCOTLAND 7 (one drop goal, one try). Inverleith, Edinburgh.

1935 NEW ZEALAND 18 (three goals, one try), SCOTLAND 8 (one goal, one try). Murrayfield, Edinburgh.

1954 NEW ZEALAND 3 (one penalty goal), SCOTLAND 0. Murrayfield.

1964 SCOTLAND 0, NEW ZEALAND 0. Murrayfield.

1967 NEW ZEALAND 14 (one goal, two penalty goals, one try), SCOTLAND 3 (one drop goal). Murrayfield.

1972 NEW ZEALAND 14 (one goal, two tries), SCOTLAND 9 (two penalty goals, one drop goal). Murrayfield.

1975 NEW ZEALAND 24 (four goals), SCOTLAND 0. Eden Park.

1978 NEW ZEALAND 18 (two goals, two penalty goals), SCOTLAND 9 (one goal, one drop goal). Murrayfield.

1979 NEW ZEALAND 20 (two goals, two tries), SCOTLAND 6 (two penalty goals). Murrayfield.

1981 NEW ZEALAND 11 (one penalty goal, two tries), SCOTLAND 4 (one try). Carisbrook.

NEW ZEALAND 40 (six goals, one try), SCOTLAND 15 (one goal, two penalty goals, one drop goal). Eden Park.

1983 SCOTLAND 25 (five penalty goals, two drop goals, one try), NEW ZEALAND 25 (two goals, three penalty goals, one try). Murrayfield.

1990 NEW ZEALAND 31 (four goals, one penalty goal, one try), SCOTLAND 16 (two goals, one try). Carisbrook.

NEW ZEALAND 21 (one goal, five penalty goals)), SCOTLAND 18 (two goals, two penalty goals). Eden Park.

Against Ireland

Matches played 9

New Zealand 8 wins, Ireland 0, 1 drawn

1905 NEW ZEALAND 15 (three goals), IRELAND 0. Lansdowne Road, Dublin.

1924 NEW ZEALAND 6 (one penalty goal, one try), IRELAND 0. Lansdowne Road.

1935 NEW ZEALAND 17 (one goal, two penalty goals, two tries), IRELAND

9 (two penalty goals, one try). Lansdowne Road.

1954 NEW ZEALAND 14 (one goal, one penalty goal, one drop goal, one try), IRELAND 3 (one penalty goal). Lansdowne Road.

1963 NEW ZEALAND 6 (one penalty goal, one try), IRELAND 5 (one goal). Lansdowne Road.

1973 IRELAND 10 (two penalty goals, one try), NEW ZEALAND 10 (one goal, one try). Lansdowne Road.

1974 NEW ZEALAND 15 (one goal, three penalty goals), IRELAND 6 (two penalty goals). Lansdowne Road.

1976 NEW ZEALAND 11 (one penalty goal, two tries), IRELAND 3 (one penalty goal). Athletic Park.

1978 NEW ZEALAND 10 (two drop goals, one try), IRELAND 6 (two penalty goals). Lansdowne Road.

1989 NEW ZEALAND 23 (one goal, three penalty goals, two tries), IRELAND 6 (two penalty goals). Lansdowne Road.

Against England

Matches played 15

New Zealand 12 wins, England 3 wins

1905 NEW ZEALAND 15 (five tries), ENGLAND 0. Crystal Palace, London.

1925 NEW ZEALAND 17 (one goal, one penalty goal, three tries), ENGLAND 11 (one goal, one penalty goal, one try). Twickenham, London.

1936 ENGLAND 13 (one drop goal, three tries), ENGLAND 0. Twickenham.

1954 NEW ZEALAND 5 (one goal), ENGLAND 0. Twickenham.

1963 NEW ZEALAND 21 (three goals, one penalty goal, one drop goal), ENGLAND 11 (one goal, two penalty goals). Eden Park.
NEW ZEALAND 9 (one goal from mark, two tries), ENGLAND 6 (one penalty goal, one try). Lancaster Park.

1964 NEW ZEALAND 14 (one goal, two penalty goals, one try), ENGLAND 0. Twickenham.

1967 NEW ZEALAND 23 (four goals, one try), ENGLAND 11 (one goal, one penalty goal). Twickenham.

1973 NEW ZEALAND 9 (one goal, one drop goal), ENGLAND 0. Twickenham.
ENGLAND 16 (two goals, one try), NEW ZEALAND 10 (one goal, one try). Eden Park.

1978 NEW ZEALAND 16 (one goal, two penalty goals, one try), ENGLAND 6 (one penalty goal, one drop goal). Twickenham.

1979 NEW ZEALAND 10 (two penalty goals, one try), ENGLAND 9 (three penalty goals). Twickenham.

1983 ENGLAND 15 (one goal, three penalty goals), NEW ZEALAND 9 (one goal, one penalty goal). Twickenham.

1985 NEW ZEALAND 18 (six penalty goals), ENGLAND 13 (one goal, one penalty goal, one try). Lancaster Park.
NEW ZEALAND 42 (three goals, three penalty goals, one drop goal, three tries), ENGLAND 15 (two goals, one drop goal). Athletic Park.

Against Wales

Matches played 14

New Zealand 11 wins, Wales 3 wins

1905 WALES (one try), NEW ZEALAND 0. Cardiff Arms Park.

1924 NEW ZEALAND 19 (two goals, one penalty goal, two tries), WALES 0. St Helen's, Swansea.

1935 WALES 13 (two goals, one try), NEW ZEALAND 12 (one goal, one drop goal, one try). Cardiff Arms Park.

1953 WALES 13 (two goals, one penalty goal), NEW ZEALAND 8 (one goal, one penalty goal!). Cardiff Arms Park.

1963 NEW ZEALAND 6 (one penalty goal, one drop goal), WALES 0. Cardiff Arms Park.

1967 NEW ZEALAND 13 (two goals, one penalty goal), WALES 6 (one penalty goal, one drop goal). Cardiff Arms Park.

1969 NEW ZEALAND 19 (two goals, one penalty goal, two tries), WALES 0. Lancaster Park.

NEW ZEALAND 33 (three goals, five penalty goals, one drop goal), WALES 12 (two penalty goals, two tries). Eden Park.

1972 NEW ZEALAND 19 (five penalty goals, one try), WALES 16 (four penalty goals, one try). Cardiff Arms Park.

1978 NEW ZEALAND 13 (three penalty goals, one try), WALES 12 (four penalty goals). Cardiff Arms Park.

1980 NEW ZEALAND 23 (two goals, one penalty goal, two tries), WALES 3 (one penalty goal). Cardiff Arms Park.

1988 NEW ZEALAND 52 (six goals, four tries), WALES 3 (one penalty goal). Lancaster Park.

NEW ZEALAND 54 (eight goals, two penalty goals), WALES 9 (one goal, one penalty goal). Eden Park.

1989 NEW ZEALAND 34 (three goals, four penalty goals, one try), WALES 9 (three penalty goals). National Stadium, Cardiff.

Against France

Matches played 27

New Zealand 22 wins, France 5 wins

1908 NEW ZEALAND 38 (four goals, six tries), FRANCE 8 (one goal, one try). Parc des Princes, Paris.

1925 NEW ZEALAND 30 (three goals, five tries), FRANCE 6 (two tries). Stade des Ponts Jumeaux, Toulouse.

1954 FRANCE 3 (one try), NEW ZEALAND 0. Colombes Stadium, Paris.

1961 NEW ZEALAND 13 (two goals, one drop goal), FRANCE 6 (two drop goals). Eden Park.

NEW ZEALAND 5 (one goal), FRANCE 3 (one try). Athletic Park.

NEW ZEALAND 32 (four goals, three penalty goals, one try), FRANCE 3 (one try). Lancaster Park.

1964 NEW ZEALAND 12 (one penalty goal, one drop goal, two tries),

FRANCE 3 (one penalty goal). Colombes Stadium.

NEW ZEALAND 21 (three goals, one penalty goal, one try), FRANCE 15 (three penalty goals, one drop goal, one try). Colombes Stadium.

1968 NEW ZEALAND 12 (three penalty goals, one try), FRANCE 9 (two penalty goals, one drop goal). Lancaster Park.

NEW ZEALAND 9 (three penalty goals), FRANCE 3 (one penalty goal). Athletic Park.

NEW ZEALAND 19 (two goals, two penalty goals, one drop goal), FRANCE 12 (one drop goal, three tries). Eden Park.

1973 FRANCE 13 (one goal, one penalty goal, one try), NEW ZEALAND 6 (two penalty goals). Parc des Princes.

1977 FRANCE 18 (one goal, three penalty goals, one drop goal, one try), NEW ZEALAND 13 (two penalty goals, one drop goal, one try). Stadium de Toulouse.

NEW ZEALAND 15 (one goal, two penalty goals, one drop goal), FRANCE 3 (one penalty goal). Parc des Princes.

1979 NEW ZEALAND 23 (one goal, three penalty goals, two tries), FRANCE 9 (one goal, one drop goal). Lancaster Park.

FRANCE 24 (one goal, one penalty goal, one drop goal, three tries), NEW ZEALAND 19 (one goal, three penalty goals, one try). Eden Park.

1981 NEW ZEALAND 13 (two penalty goals, one drop goal, one try), FRANCE 9 (two penalty goals, one drop goal). Toulouse Stadium.

NEW ZEALAND 18 (two goals, including one for a penalty try, two penalty goals), FRANCE 6 (two penalty goals). Parc des Princes.

1984 NEW ZEALAND 10 (two penalty goals, one try), FRANCE 9 (one goal, one drop goal, one try). Lancaster Park.

NEW ZEALAND 31 (two goals, five penalty goals, one try), FRANCE

18 (two penalty goals, three tries). Eden Park.

1986　NEW ZEALAND 18 (one goal, one penalty goal, three drop goals), FRANCE 9 (three drop goals). Lancaster Park.

NEW ZEALAND 19 (three penalty goals, two drop goals, one try), FRANCE 7 (one penalty goal, one try). Municipal Stadium, Toulouse.

FRANCE 16 (one goal, two penalty goals, one try), NEW ZEALAND 3 (one penalty goal). La Beaujoire Stadium, Nantes.

1989　NEW ZEALAND 25 (two goals, three penalty goals, one try), FRANCE 17 (one goal, one penalty goal, two tries). Lancaster Park.

NEW ZEALAND 34 (three goals, four penalty goals, one try), FRANCE 20 (four penalty goals, two tries). Eden Park.

1990　NEW ZEALAND 24 (two goals, three penalty goals, one drop goal), FRANCE 3 (one penalty goal). La Beaujoire Stadium, Nantes.

NEW ZEALAND 30 (two goals, six penalty goals), FRANCE 12 (three penalty goals, one drop goal). Parc des Princes.

Against United States

Matches played 1

New Zealand 1 win, United States 0

1913　NEW ZEALAND 51 (six goals, seven tries), ALL-AMERICA 3 (one penalty goal). Berkeley, California.

Against Romania

Matches played 1

New Zealand 1 win, Romania 0

1981　NEW ZEALAND 14 (one penalty goal, one drop goal, two tries), ROMANIA 6 (one penalty goal, one drop goal). Bucharest.

Against Argentina

Matches played 4

New Zealand 3 wins, Argentina 0, 1 drawn

1985　NEW ZEALAND 33 (one goal, four penalty goals, one drop goal, three tries), ARGENTINA 20 (three penalty goals, one drop goal, two tries). Ferrocarrill Stadium, Buenos Aires.

ARGENTINA 21 (four penalty goals, three drop goals), NEW ZEALAND 21 (one goal, one penalty goal, three tries). Ferrocarrill Stadium.

1989　NEW ZEALAND 60 (seven goals, two penalty goals, three tries, including one penalty try), ARGENTINA 9 (one goal, one penalty goal). Carisbrook.

NEW ZEALAND 49 (six goals, three penalty goals, one try), ARGENTINA 12 (one goal, two penalty goals). Athletic Park.

INDEX

For All Black internationals, please refer to the alphabetical list on pp. 139–49 as well as to this index. For countries that took part in the 1987 World Cup, please refer to the list on p. 150 as well as to this index.

The History of the Royal Warwickshire Regiment

Front Cover Illustration: 6th Foot Shako Plate (Authors own collection) Postcard
of the Royal Warwickshire Regiment at Rest c. 1914 (Authors own collection)

Rear Cover Illustration: The Royal First Warwickshire Regiment Cap Badge
(Authors own collection)

Also Available from the Author:

Where Peacocks Pace – A Natural Historians Guide to Warwick

Dedication

This book is dedicated to all the servicemen and women of the British Army and in particular those that served and died in the 6th Regiment of Foot and the Royal Warwickshire Regiment.

Acknowledgements

I would like to thank the staff of Warwick Library and County Record Office for their help in finding research material. I would also like to thank the curators of the Royal Regiment of Fusiliers Museum at St John's Museum in Warwick for their advice and help. I would like to credit Mr Callaghan for inspiring a love of history in me and for Mrs Lee who guided me on my first study of the regiment during my A-levels. Lastly big thanks must go to my supportive family.

CONTENTS

LIST OF FIGURES

INTRODUCTION

It is a simple truth that for as long as mankind has existed they have been in conflict with one another. From the early struggles of Neolithic man through the charging knights of the middle-ages to the mud soaked fields of the First World War man as a species has fought. The driving factors of war breakdown to just one root cause, territory. From territory flows resources, power and control. As society and civilisation developed so too did the way in which we waged war. The simplistic one on one struggle for survival became replaced by organised units and the evolution of professional warriors and by extension the first soldiers and armies.

It could be said that it was the development of farming that created the first armies. Prior to farming the majority of a person's time was spent hunting and gathering food. Wider concerns regarding resources boiled down to who controlled the best areas for these activities and clashes tended to be on the small scale, family versus family or tribe versus tribe. With the discovery of farming it was now possible to produce more food than one family could use. Communities could store extra food for hard times improving health and lifespan considerably. Less time was needed to provide for the family and they could spend this extra time in other pursuits such as arts, crafts, society and of course warfare. Bodies of men could now train exclusively to defend a population and be used to extend control over other resources.

For much of Britain's history the country lacked a single army. Early Britain was a fragmented collection of first tribes and then provincial kingdoms. The Roman invasions of 55 BC and 43 AD showed how effective an organised well trained army could be in seizing and subjugating a population. This model of an efficient army was, however, not replicated in Britain following Romes departure from 419 AD. This period was known as the Dark Ages and in this time Britain was invaded by Saxons, Vikings, Jutes and Angles to name but a few. These invaders inter-mixed with the native Britons and the Romanised locals to create the foundation of our modern country and culture.

For Warwickshire the most prominent government of this era was the Kingdom of Mercia, one of the seven Anglo-Saxon kingdoms that emerged following Roman rule. Covering much of the Midlands and indeed the East the kingdom was led most famously by King Offa. Mercian armies comprised of three classes of warrior, aristocratic Housecarls, the common levy called the Fyrd and lastly the noble leadership of Thegns. Standard warfare for the Anglo-Saxon was the static shield wall. In which two lines of shield bearing spearmen would push, shove and stab against one another.

When Alfred the Great united the kingdoms to form the basis of what would become England Mercia became an Earldom with its Earl marrying Alfred's daughter Ethelfleda. Mercia had a responsibility to supply 'spears', men, to the king in times of need; and times of need there were as the Vikings began their invasions.

In 1066 with the rise of the Norman kings the structure of the armies in England changed. The French and Normans had a feudal approach to land management and her armies. Feudalism gave landholders, mostly aristocratic Knights and most of them French or Norman, the right to muster a household of men at arms and the ability to raise a levy force from the locals to support the crown as required. This was an effective strategy; Henry II could call upon some 5000 knights in times of need and the forces were distributed across the country to be used wherever needed. Feudalism also led to problems, rich nobles could sometimes muster more men and in better equipment than the king and created a situation in which an individual Earl's personal power could be used to broker power at a national level and influence the decisions of kings themselves.

By 1415, the time of Henry V's famous victory at Agincourt, a professional body of soldiery under the command of the crown was starting to supersede the feudal system. This professional body was however small and kings still needed the support of individual Earls. Richard Neville, the Earl of Warwick, created much upheaval during the Wars of the Roses and placed not one but two Kings on the throne. The actions of Richard Neville made Warwick and the growing county a powerful force in Britain and despite his demise it continued to have great influence at court.

The first truly national English army can be attributed to Oliver Cromwell and his New Model Army. The Parliamentary forces of the English Civil war were dissatisfied with the disorganised nature of local militias and in 1645 established a professional army that boasted 20,000 well trained and drilled men, mostly cavalry, supported by Foot Artillery. This army proved superior to the Royalists and to the Irish armies Cromwell subsequently set it against.

In 1660 when King Charles II was restored to the English throne he was left with two armies, Parliaments New Model Army and the survivors of Charles's own Royalist supporters. He disbanded the New Model Army but began to adopt the structure it had created. These disbanded troops he formed into nine Regiments of Foot.

During the Anglo-Dutch Wars between 1695 and 1674 the number of these regiments fluctuated reaching a peak of 41 and numbered 20,000 men in total. The Royal Warwickshire Regiment was born in this period. Regiments at this time were named after their Colonel-in-Chief. This tradition continued until 1747 when the regiment was named the 6th Regiment of Foot, it being the sixth most senior regiment in the army. The Act of Union in 1707 created the Kingdom of Great Britain and made the regiment truly part of the British army. In 1782 as part of army reforms the regiment was assigned a region, this region was Warwickshire. It kept the registration of the 6th Foot until 1881 when the regiment became simply the Royal Warwickshire Regiment.

All these changes in name do little to explain the actions of the regiment and the men it contained. This book therefore follows all these changes exploring the path the regiment took from its earliest days to the present explaining the battles they took part in and the context in which they were fought. Inevitably there is a greater wealth of information available for the regiment in the 20th century but where possible details of individual officers will be recounted throughout the regiment's long history.

CHAPTER 1 - THE DUTCH GUARDS

The Royal Warwickshire Regiment was formed from the 6th Regiment of Foot whose origins dated from Dutch service in 1665. Europe was a very different place in the 17th Century, kingdoms vied endlessly for supremacy and Spain and France were still bitter enemies of England. England herself had established links with Holland during the later Tudor period when the Low Countries were part of Spanish territories. This link resulted in the English Crown loaning armed forces to the Dutch Army in their fight with the French. Constantly under pressure from France, Holland gained independence after what amounted to an 80 year struggle.

The resulting Dutch nation was a stronger more independent country that developed into a republic and became wealthy enough through the establishment of the Dutch East India Company to create a small empire. Such trading strengths inevitably brought it into conflict with England whose own East India Company was a key trading rival. Imposition of navigation acts hurt Dutch interests heavily and resulted in a series of Anglo-Dutch Wars. These wars were essentially a series of intensive but ultimately inconclusive naval wars over trade rights.

When Charles II gained the English throne during the English restoration he took special interest in the Low Countries or the United Provinces as it was often known. He hoped to establish his nephew and ward William II of

Orange as Stadtholder (ruler) of Holland. This power brokering was opposed by the Dutch and resulted in a second Anglo-Dutch War. At this time several English regiments were still in Holland in Dutch service. One such regiment was Sir Walter Vane's Regiment who, when the Second Anglo-Dutch War broke out in 1665, returned to England quickly.

Vane had been in Dutch Service since 1649 and a staunch royalist unlike his father who had switched sides to the Parliamentarians during the English Civil War. Back in England Sir Walter was made a Captain of Foot serving in the regiment that would later become the Grenadier Guards. In 1668 he was made a colonel of one of the regiments that had returned from Holland. This regiment would become the Royal Warwickshire Regiment.

In 1672 William III of Orange, son of William II succeeded in becoming Stadtholder of the Netherlands. His appointment however was prevented by strong opposition. To ensure his place on the throne England entered into a brief alliance with France and so started the Third Anglo-Dutch War. William III himself became a Captain-General of one of the armies aged only 22 little knowing he would later become King of England. In 1674 peace negotiations ended Holland's conflict with England and once more allowed them to recruit from England. Allegiances could be fickle things and sides shifted regularly.

With the close of the Third Anglo-Dutch War Vane was charged with raising an Anglo-Dutch Brigade to assist the Dutch against the French who now hoped to take advantage of a weakened Netherlands. The French had invaded the Netherlands in 1672 and had conquered five of the seven provinces in just six weeks.

Vanes new brigade was comprised of three English and three Scottish Regiments and in the summer of 1674 the brigade sailed to the United Provinces. On his arrival Vane was granted the rank of Major-General in the Dutch Army and quickly sent to join the main armies. Each regiment consisted of ten companies of soldiers but whilst being organised Vane was killed at the Battle of Seneffe in which a Dutch-German-Spanish force under William III of Orange attempted an invasion of northern France. Alliances at this time were a fluid and complicated affair. At some points King Charles II of England had regiments fighting both in the French Army and in the Dutch Army.

A series of brigade commanders followed Vane on his death until the brigade was reformed in 1765. One of the English Regiment's commanded by Luke Lillingston would later form the 6th Foot. There is some confusion as to whether Luke Lillingston himself or his father Henry was in command. The Regimental history describes Luke as the Colonel but Dutch sources indicated that Henry was given command when the regiment passed from Walter Vane's control and that Luke served as a junior officer in the regiment before taking command himself later.

Lillingston's Foot took part took part in its first military action at the Siege of Grave in October 1674. When England had signed the peace agreement with the United Provinces they began to aid them once more against the French. At this time only the cities of Grave and Maastricht remained in French hands but William was determined to eject the French from Dutch soil and resolved to liberate both cities swiftly.

The siege of Grave was commanded by Lieutenant-General Karl Rabenhaupt. With 16,000 men, he approached on a narrow front to find the city adequately provisioned and armed against him. Rabenhaupt relied on the siege engineer Baron van Menno Coehoorn, a Swedish born Dutch military engineer who played a key role in the Franco-Dutch War. The Baron invented the Coehoorn Mortar that became a key instrument in many sieges during this campaign. Lillingston's Regiment were assigned firstly to siege work duty which involved the digging of zigzagging trenches that led up to the city walls. Then led by Captain Savage the regiment was part of an attack on the scarp. This attack was repulsed easily and was not sanctioned by Rabenhaupt. Captain Savage was arrested for disobeying orders. Despite heavy losses the city was eventually liberated on the 28th October.

THE SIEGE OF MAASTRICHT

From Grave the next major engagement was at Maastricht. In 1673 the city had been a key point in King Louis XIV plan of attack in the Netherlands. He had laid siege to the city using new techniques developed by Sebastien de Vauban, the master of siege works. Sebastien Le Pestre, Marquis de Vauban had an aptitude for military engineering. He had gained experience during the War of Devolution at the sieges of Graudines and Ypres. He came to Louis XIV's notice when French forces with Vauban took the towns of Douai, Tornai and Lille. As part of the French forces army invasion of the United Provinces Vauban took part in a total of six sieges and took only 13 days to take Maastricht. The town fell on the 24th June to an assault by Captain-lieutenant Charles de Batz de Castlemore, Comte d'Artagnan. Several attempts were made by Spanish auxiliaries and James Scott, Duke of Monmouth to hold out but despite a brief recapture the Anglo-Dutch forces were forced to surrender the city. Vauban was declared a hero in France with a popular saying stating, "City besieged by Vauban, city taken; City defended by Vauban, city untakeable".

So it was in 1676 following the success at Grave a renewed attempt at the liberation of Maastricht was made. The assault force included Lillingston's Regiment now under the command of Colonel Thomas Ashley. This new siege was led personally by William III of Orange who granted the regiment its own quarter of the siege and allowed them to take part in the assault that made the first breach. Unfortunately the arrival of a French relief force led by Marshal de Schomberg forestalled victory and William was forced to retreat leaving Maastricht still in French hands. Frustrated William petitioned King Charles to stop supplying troops to the French. Charles agreed and withdrew his mercenary forces in the employ of the French crown freeing up more men who could be deployed to support William in his defence of the Netherlands.

The regiment remained in Dutch Service for the next few years with a new colonel, Sir Henry Belayses, taking command in 1678. French forces continued to press into Dutch territory advancing through Ghent and Ypres to lay siege to Mons, forestalling any counter attack William planned.

The Prince of Orange, William, rallied his forces and attacked the French at Mons on the 14th of August 1678. The English and Scottish regiments in the army were under the command of the Earl of Ossory and held the right flank, the remaining Dutch Army was led by Count Waldeck. They attacked the French with heavy losses at the Abbey of Saint Denis. Six officers in, Lillingston's Regiment now called Belasyse's Regiment, were killed and Major Philip Babington of the grenadier company was injured and taken prisoner. The battle was inconclusive and pointless as three days before; the Treaty of Nimeguen was signed ending the war between the United Provinces and France.

Despite the new peace the English and Scottish regiments remained in Dutch service for several years with the English troops getting special praise for their work. The fact that the regiment had fought almost exclusively in the protestant United Provinces and recruited from there would prove to be a key factor in the future role of the regiment.

In 1685 King Charles II of England died and his brother James was crowned. James however was an unpopular choice as he was a Roman Catholic. Four years earlier James Scott, the Duke of Monmouth, an illegitimate son of Charles attempted to have James excluded from the succession, his failure led to his self exile to Holland where he served with some distinction. When James II was crowned Monmouth decided to seize the throne by force. He landed in south west England and began to raise an army. Concerned about wider rebellion King James II recalled all English and Scottish forces from Holland to protect his crown from the Duke of Monmouth, however, by the time they arrived Monmouth had been defeated by the Earl of Feversham at the Battle of Sedgemoor. James Scott was executed on Tower Hill in July.

King James in the wake of the rebellion reorganised the army and formalised them under his rule. No longer would regiments change names with each commanding colonel now regiments would be numbered. Sir Henry Belayse's Regiment of Foot became the 6th Regiment of Foot with Sir Henry as its Colonel in Chief. The regiment was returned to service in Holland in 1685 where it was to play a key role in the growing disquiet of the protestant community in England.

King James II's victory over Monmouth emboldened him and he began a series of sweeping measures to consolidate his power moving catholic supporters into key posts throughout the kingdom and increasing the size of the standing army. When the Archbishop of Canterbury asked him to reconsider his religious position, in effect become a protestant he had the Archbishop and his other bishops imprisoned for sedition and libel.

In 1688 his wife, Mary gave birth to a son creating a catholic line of succession. This was too much for many of the protestant gentry to bear. Initially unwilling to support Monmouth during his rebellion these lords and members of parliament conspired to undo the King and replace him with someone they viewed as more suitable. The conspirators knew that for any kind of legitimacy they needed to find someone with a direct line to the throne and someone who shared their religious views. King James's niece, King Charles II's daughter, Mary, had married William III of Orange. William was a protestant and had proved himself a competent commander in the wars on the continent and looked to be a good choice.

By June 1688 a group of seven protestant nobles had made the decision to remove King James and invited William to come to England to assume the throne. Many of the English officers in Dutch service were protestant including Philip Babington now Colonel of the 6th regiment after Belasyse was promoted to overall command of the Anglo-Dutch brigade. In November William of Orange sailed from Holland. He arrived in Torbay on the 5th November having lost only one ship. This lost ship was captured by HMS *Swallow* and included four companies of Babington's soldiers. Despite this small set back William still had 4000 men under the command of Major-General Hugh MacKay.

William's arrival heralded a swift change in fortunes for King James. Many once loyal nobles such as John Churchill, Duke of Marlborough, allied themselves with William and James II was quickly both outnumbered and out maneuvered especially when much of his army refused to fight. Unable to defend his throne James was allowed to flee to France. When Parliament met they declared that James' desertion of the country was equivalent to abdication and assented to William's coronation to England's throne with his wife Mary. The pair ruled jointly establishing a new line of protestant succession. The four companies captured by James were released and Babington's regiment who were in fact mostly Dutch themselves became known as the 'Dutch Guards' and were a favourite of Williams, no doubt a reminder of his homeland of the United Provinces and his time along-side the Anglo-Dutch Brigade at Grave and Maastricht.

THE BATTLE OF THE BOYNE

In 1689 James II made a bid to reclaim his throne. He landed in Kinsale, Ireland with the support of a French army and sought to ally with the catholic Jacobites. Richard Talbot, 1st Earl of Tyrconnell appointed as Lord Deputy of Ireland by James in his reign had already made preparations to support him and had begun to fortify Ireland and raise a Jacobite army. James began by marching on the only remaining protestant garrison in Derry.

William, alerted to the danger moved quickly to oppose James and sent a fleet to relieve the siege. William landed an army under the command of Marshal Schomberg who over the year of 1689 prosecuted the war for King William engaging Tyrconnell's forces wherever possible, capturing Carrickfergus and marching into Dundalk before both sides settled in for the winter.

At the start of 1690 Babington's regiment recruited heavily ensuring each of the regiments 12 companies was a hundred men strong. In April they left England and sailed to Carrickfergus. Their first engagement was at Charlemont in the same month. Whilst the town was well defended its garrison, under the command of Teague O'Reagan was ill fed and under equipped. The defences included a strong fort at Dungannon. Despite reinforcements and attempts to sally out it wasn't long before the English forces won through and three companies were left to garrison the fortress the rest joining King William's army at Armagh.

William was now with the army himself which was some 36,000 strong and a truly international force comprising English, Dutch, German, Danish and French Huguenot troops. The Jacobite and French army numbered 25,000 and moved to meet William at Drogheda. In July William forded the river Boyne to meet James in battle.

The 6th Foot were brigaded with Hanmer's Regiment and deployed to the centre of Williams' line. To the right was Belayse's Brigade, a brigade of Huguenots and the Dutch Guards. To the left were Danish infantry who with Hanmer's Brigade formed a division under the command of the Count of Nassau. Much of this army was

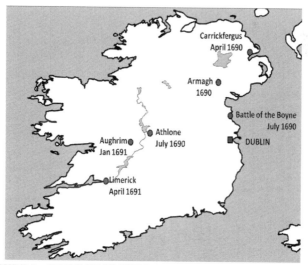

FIGURE 1 - BATTLES IN THE WILLIAMITE WAR IN IRELAND

professional in nature and armed with flintlock muskets, the Jacobites however were more poorly armed and organised. Some only carried scythes or pitchforks whilst those with guns had the older style matchlock muskets. James was forced to rely on his 6,000 French soldiers and his Irish Cavalry.

The Battle of the Boyne despite the significance it held in Irish history was in fact are rather indecisive affair. 1500 Jacobites and only 500 Williamites were actually killed although Babington's regiment suffered heavy casualties with only half their number being fit at the end of it. The battle was won by William through the steady advancement of his more experienced troops. James was able to withdraw his troops in good order and mount a retreat to Duncannon but his nerve was broken and he abandoned the Jacobite cause and fled to France once more.

The Battle of the Boyne could have ended the conflict in Ireland especially as during the following day William was able to march unopposed into Dublin, however William sought to punish the Jacobites and imposed harsh peace terms on them. So harsh were the terms that many felt it better to fight on rather than surrender. Following Boyne Babington's regiment took part in Lieutenant-General Douglas's failed siege against Athlone. Athlone's main defence was Moyelly Castle. The castles commander, Colonel Richard Grace when asked to surrender declared defiantly that we would 'defend Athlone until I eat my boots'. Grace would not be so deprived as to eat his boots. The artillery train was late and upon being dug in was unable to make a suitable breach in the walls before the ammunition began to run out. Douglas acknowledged failure and raised the siege. More worryingly were the reports of his men's ill discipline especially concerning the locals.

In January 1691 Babington died and was replaced as Colonel by Prince George of Hesse who would go on to command Austrian forces in the War of Spanish Succession. The regiment became part of a force led by the Dutch General Godart de Ginkel that marched again on Athlone. Athlone was in essence two towns split by the river Shannon, an English town on one side and an Irish one on the other. The river was crossed by a bridge guarded by a castle on the Irish side. This time the regiment was better prepared having received 300 new recruits.

The Jacobites were led by the Marquis de St Ruth who vigorously held the bridge against the English force. To stop further advancement the Marquis destroyed the bridge but de Ginkel found another crossing upriver. From there he took the Jacobites in the rear whilst 200 men of the 6th Foot under the command of Lieutenant-Colonel Columbine held the castles attention. A storming party on the 20th June failed but on the 30th June a forlorn hope was mounted to ford the river backed by 3000 men under the command of Major-General MacKay. General St Ruth's men were quickly over powered and the town seized, however both the Prince of Hesse and Lieutenant-Colonel Columbine were injured. The Jacobites retreated to Augury pursued by Ginkel.

The taking of Athlone was key to Williams advance. The Jacobites had been relying on the defences along the

Shannon to hold up William and allow French troops from Louis XIV to arrive by sea. Ginkel had broken the line and allowed Williams forces to meet the Jacobites at Augury. St. Ruth positioned his 18,000 men on a ridge called Kicommadan Hill. The left flank was protected by a bog and the village of Aughrim so on his right he placed his strongest units.

Ginkel opened the attack by challenging the strong right flank whilst William moved up in the centre. William tried three assaults on the ridge but each time he was beaten back and finally routed losing some of his guns in the process. Ginkel's advance was likewise inconclusive and he withdrew. Ginkel mounted a second attack, this time down the left flank along a causeway through the bog. This assault should have been turned aside easily but the Jacobites were running low on ammunition. William reinforced the attack with a charge of Anglo-Dutch cavalry who managed to seize the village. Here the Prince of Hesse was again wounded. A counter attack by the Jacobites failed to materialise but nevertheless the Jacobites were still in a strong position.

The Jacobites may even have succeeded in defeating William's army at this point. Buoyed by the sight of William's centre crumbling and the king himself retreating General St Ruth had tried to rally his own cavalry to counter attack and pursue them. Unfortunately St Ruth was decapitated by a cannonball at the critical moment and without his leadership the Jacobite line began to collapse. Their cavalry retreated leaving an opening on the flank for William to advance through. With both flanks now failing the Jacobites on the ridge began to find themselves encircled and they were quickly slaughtered by William's own cavalry who chased them down as they abandoned their positions.

What was nearly a stinging defeat for William was turned into a crushing defeat for the Jacobites with an estimated 7000-8000 killed, wounded or captured. Of Hesse's regiment both he and Major Columbine were injured with 10 killed and 50 wounded. The victory at Aughrim caused much of the Irish army to lose heart and within ten days Galway had surrendered to de Ginkel. Survivors of the Jacobites retreat fled to Limerick and this city became the last bastion of resistance.

Limerick had already been besieged once in the Williamite War by William himself a year earlier and this time de Ginkel had far fewer men at his disposal. Since the previous siege French engineers had also improved the defences and it seemed unlikely the English could take the city by storm. De Ginkel easily swept aside the outlying infantry defences all of whom offered little resistance retreating instead inside the walls.

The 6th Foot were sent as part of a force led by the Prince of Hesse with the 27th Foot, St John's Regiment, 700 dragoons and horse and 5 cannons to destroy the fort at Castleconnell, 4 miles upriver of Limerick. With the surrounding countryside secure Ginkel brought up his artillery to lay siege to the city. The artillery were directed to various points throughout August and September until in mid-September de Ginkel changed his tactics and looked to blockade the city from the River Shannon. When de Ginkel moved more troops across the River the Irish sallied and tried to stop the advance but were beaten back and although the walls had yet to be breached surrendered the town on 23rd September.

Hesse and his men played little part in Limerick and after the action at Castleconnell they were ordered to return to Dublin where they sat out the remainder of the war. The fall of Limerick essentially ended the Jacobite uprising and a treaty was signed on 3rd October 1691 offering the Jacobites generous terms as long as they gave their oath of loyalty to William. Unfortunately the terms laid out by de Ginkel and his Irish counterpart, Patrick Sarsfield were not upheld by the protestant dominated Irish Parliament. This betrayal formed a corner piece to the troubles in Ireland up until the Good Friday agreement of 1998.

The engagements were among the first of the regiments land battles that were not sieges. Warfare at this time saw the emergence of linear tactics. Regiments used smaller battalions set in supporting lines from the Dutch model, salvo fire from the Swedish model and lighter muskets and thinner ranks to bring more guns to bear. During the English Civil War pikemen had been as important as musketeers but now the balance was shifting to a 1 to 1 ratio, with the pikemen's role to protect the battalions from cavalry during reloading. Most battalions now contained an elite company of the tallest and strongest men, these men sometimes carried axes for breaking in doors and grenades, they became known as Grenadiers.

A standard fusilier would carry a flintlock musket that was more advanced than the matchlocks used by the New Model Army and came with a bayonet as standard from 1680. To start with these bayonets plugged into the barrel but this severely limited the firepower available. In 1697 the British and Germans developed the socket bayonet that allowed a bayonet to be fitted without obstructing the barrel and further rendered the pike redundant.

CHAPTER 2 - WAR IN EUROPE

Following their tour of duty in Ireland the 6th Foot returned to England for a brief period of recruiting. With Ireland pacified William III could once more turn his attention to events in Europe. The Jacobite uprising was but one aspect of a large conflict, the Nine Years War.

Also known as the War of the Grand Alliance, the Nine Years War had its roots back in the Franco-Dutch War in which the regiment had originally fought alongside their King. King Louis XIV of France had come out of the Franco-Dutch was in a very strong position and his influence dominated Europe. He supported the exiled James and the Jacobite cause in Ireland hoping to place a sympathetic king on the throne of England. Louis was an aggressive ruler and prosecuted a series of wars against different European powers and led a merciless persecution of Huguenots in France itself.

In 1688 Louis XIV led an army across the river Rhine to increase his influence in German Rhineland and pre-empt any possible German attack. The Germans mustered some resistance and gathered their allies to them. William III was still Stadtholder of the Netherlands as well as King of England and so took great interest in events in Europe especially those that threatened his homeland. He drew together an alliance of nations including the Holy Roman Emperor Leopold I, Charles II of Spain and Victor Amadeus of Savoy to oppose Louis XIV. Relieved of the problems in

Ireland William III could now dispatch troops to the main arena in the heart of Europe.

The 6th Foot, restored to full strength was one of many English regiments that was despatched to Flanders to form the backbone of this allied army. The regiment was inspected by King William III himself at Genappe in June 1688 before they entered the war proper.

THE BATTLE OF STEENKERK

Whilst the English Army had been in Ireland France was pretty much winning the war in the Netherlands and Belgium. He hoped to bring the Dutch to heel quickly allowing for a swift invasion of England to once more attempt to install James as King.

The French forces in the Netherlands were led by François-Henri de Montmorency, Duc de Luxembourg. Luxembourg had fought in the Franco-Dutch War and had led Louis XIV French forces to victory at Fleurus and Leuze before seizing Namur before William III's new army could relieve it. In August 1692 the Duc de Luxembourg met William III at Steenkerk, a small town 13 kilometres south-west of Brussels.

The two armies were evenly matched with approximately 80,000 combatants on each side. Whilst Luxembourg's force was all French Williams was again an international mix of English, Scottish, Dutch and Danish soldiers.

The battle started well for William with him being able to bring up his artillery so silently that he nearly surprised

Luxembourg completely. Once roused, the French were quick to organize and Luxembourg commanded his own artillery to return fire on Williams.

Once the artillery duel abated William ordered a general advance which at first swept the French aside. The French managed to hold their ground however and by deploying greater numbers at the advance point quickly outnumbered the attackers causing the advance to falter. Dutch support for the advance led by Count Solms was slow in coming and soon William's whole line was wavering with breaks beginning to appear. Luxembourg reacted decisively and ordered the remaining French Infantry and Swiss Guard into the breaches. There was little the Alliance forces could do to counter what was fast becoming a rout and William was forced to sound the retreat.

The failure of Count Solms to bring up his Dutch Infantry quickly enough led to much disgust and distrust amongst the allies with tensions growing within the multi-national assembly daily. Five of the English regiments at Steenkerk were nearly completely destroyed and the 6th Foot suffered heavy loses including Lieutenant-Colonel Foxon and four other officers. So depleted were their ranks that the regiment was instantly withdrawn to Malines from where they left for England in the autumn to recover and recruit once more. In actual fact the total losses in the Battle of Steenkerk were relatively even with Allied losses of 10,000 to the French's 8,000. Nevertheless this was a tactical French victory to challenge William's strength in the Netherlands and only went to cement the Louis XIV the 'Sun Kings' dominance in Europe.

The 6th Foot was not returned to action for a full year and did so under a new commanding officer, the Prince George of Hesse-Darmstadt. The Prince however was a Catholic and found working within the Protestant dominated Allied forces very difficult. William wanted to reward the Prince for his loyal service but was unable by law to promote a catholic so instead he arranged in February 1694 for the Prince to be given a position in the Spanish Army. The Prince was replaced by the Dutch noble, Henry, Marquis de Rada. De Rada was Colonel of the regiment for only a short period dying of a fever in the summer of 1695. Under De Rada's short command the 6th Foot were returned to full fighting strength and left England in August for the Low Countries once more.

They arrived back on the continent at a time when the French and Allied armies had broken for the winter. Most armies had difficulty with supplies lines and cold weather and so campaigning in the winter was avoided at all cost. Both sides tended to withdraw to the territories they controlled to sit the bad weather out before resuming the conflict in the spring. The 6th Foot spent the following months garrisoned in Bruges before in May 1695 they were assembled in Arseele where they were placed in a brigade under the command of Brigadier-General Sir David Collier with Lieutenant-Colonel Ventris Columbine promoted from within the regiment to lead the 6th Foot itself.

The French throughout 1693 had made impressive gains in both the Low Countries and Italy but this had pushed their finances and manpower to their absolute limit. They now began to prosecute a defensive war in the hope of forcing a stalemate and securing a treaty to give diplomatic ownership of some of their gains.

The Grand Alliance now stronger itself began its counter offensive. Anglo-Dutch fleets sailed up and down the channel bombarding French towns whilst William attempted to retake the city of Namur lost in 1692.

THE SIEGE OF NAMUR

The town of Namur sits on the confluence of the rivers Meuse and Sambre. It contained a well protected citadel and had already seen much action. In 1692 the renowned siege engineer Vauban had assisted King Louis XIV in storming the castle within a single month.

Command of Namur at this time had been this generations other siege expert, Baron von Coehoorn. He was unable to hold the citadels and relief was not possible due to the Duc de Luxembourg holding an army to cover the siege. Coehoorn was forced to surrender and was allowed to leave the city in peace. Coehoorn therefore returned to Namur with William's army intent on taking revenge on his rival Vauban who had made some improvements to the defences in the intervening years.

The 6th Foot now under the temporary command of Lieutenant-Colonel Ventris Columbine were initially assigned to support the Prince of Vaudemont's covering army but on 8th July they were reassigned to join 12 other English and Scottish regiments to take the citadel.

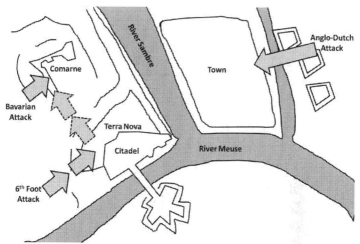

FIGURE 2 – THE REGIMENT ATTACKING NAMUR

Progress against the citadel was slow. Vauban's defences made Namur nearly impregnable and much of the regiment's time was spent in trenches. The trenches allowed the soldiers to slowly approach outlying defences protected from the guns of the main citadel.

On 27th July English Grenadiers include those of the 6th Foot were able to seize and hold the counterscarp by the St Nicholas Gate of the town. The assault resulted in the death of Captain Young and the injury of 2 more officers from the 6th Foot. This toehold was sufficient to maintain the momentum however, and over the next few days the grenadiers advanced more and more in to the town until on the 6th August the town surrendered.

The towns fall gave the 6th foot a moment of respite and they were withdrawn to rest but by the 30th August they were back in the thick of the fighting as the army attempted take the Citadel.

The Citadel at Namur was situated on a promontory where the two rivers met. It was protected by two other defensive positions the Terra Nova and Comarne (Cohorne). The storming of these two fortifications was to be led by Baron John Cutts. Cutts was renowned for his calm manner on the battlefield and was nicknamed 'The Salamander' for the way in which he used to ignore heavy fire. Cutts was a staunch supporter of William III and had served with him in Ireland for which he was awarded the peerage of 1st Baron of Gowran.

Cutts had been wounded early in the siege with a gunshot to the head but he was deemed fit enough to command the troops assigned to take the citadel. The attack took the form of a two pronged strike. English troops would storm the Terra Nova and Bavarian soldiers the Comarne. The English assault faltered due to lack of support and was forced to retreat, but Cutts realised the Bavarians would be having the same trouble and so threw the English into support them. Despite heavy losses including two more officers of the 6th Foot the Comarne was taken.

Marshal Louis Francois, Duc de Boufflers the commander of the citadels garrison was a proud man and despite the odds had refused to yield until the main fortifications had been assaulted. With the outer works taken the citadels position was now untenable and there was little hope for relief. Boufflers had lost nearly 8000 of his 13,000 men and so on 1st September he surrendered. William III accepted and 5 days later the garrison marched out leaving Namur fully in the control of the allies.

The Siege of Namur was the regiment's first battle honour although the title was not bestowed on them until the 1800's. The siege was also the last action of the 6th Foot in the Nine Years War. They were retired to Bruges and in early 1696 they returned to England in the light of another possible Jacobite uprising.

It was the 6th's action in the earlier Jacobite Rebellion and its Dutch history that probably saved them from army reforms that ended some regiments of foot at this time. The 6th remained where others had been disbanded. The Nine Years War would last until 1697 when the Treaty of Ryswick brokered by the Swedish was reluctantly accepted by all combatants. It redrew the borders depending on gains and losses made in the war and allowed William III to secure his position in both Ireland and Scotland.

The 6th Foot remained in England until the summer of 1697 when they briefly travelled to Brussels where they were part of an inspection by King William III. After returning home they were sent to Ireland.

The Treaty of Ryswick unfortunately avoided one major European issue. Who would succeed King Charles II as King of Spain? The problem of Spanish succession ultimately led to war.

Charles II of Spain was unable to bear children and so the question of who was to succeed him was something that was obvious to all. Spain at this time was a great power with territories in Italy and the New World. Gold flowed from these new South American colonies compensating Spain's natural lack of natural resources and making it a very desirable acquisition. All the monarchs of Europe vied for a link to the Spanish Empire with two claims being the stronger than the others.

The French supported the Bourbon line, King Louis XIV of France's own son Louis 'Le Grand' Dauphin. The Dauphin a nephew of the King of Spain and staked his claim through this birthright. King Louis XIV pushed for his sons claim vehemently, hoping to create a vast empire by tying the succession of France with Spain. This idea caused much concern amongst the English and the western European powers.

The Germans and Austrians supported the Austrian Habsburg line whose head was Leopold I, Holy Roman Emperor. Leopold was both Charles' brother in law and first cousin. To complicate matters Leopold's grandson Electoral Prince Joseph Ferdinand of Bavaria also laid claim to the Spanish throne.

Charles himself bequeathed in his will the title of King of Spain to Philip Duc d'Anjou the Dauphins second son. He was however aware of the risk of war if Spain and France became tied and so made a provision that if Philip were to inherit the French throne, that Spain instead would go to the third brother Charles Duc d'Berry or Archduke Charles of Austria thereby keeping France and Spain as two separate countries. This line of succession was reluctantly accepted by all parties by treaty in 1700.

On the 1st November 1700 Charles II of Spain died and 23 days later King Louis XIV of France proclaimed his grandson Philip, Duc d'Anjou King of Spain and its territories. This was not exactly as was agreed. Philip was only to have inherited Spain and not all its territories and this gave many of the great nations pause for thought. War at this stage was averted however; William III was not in a position to go to war with France and so reluctantly recognised Philip as King of Spain. This may well have been an end to the matter but Louis XIV was eager to use France's new power to its maximum and began to impose trade embargos on England and the United Provinces in the Netherlands. By stifling trade he hoped to reduce England's strength and thought that the combined power of France and Spain would hold them in check.

William was not about to let this challenge go unmet and so negotiated the Treaty of Den Haag with the Netherlands and Austria. The treaty recognised King Philip V as the rightful King of Spain but gave the Spanish territories in Italy to Austria and secured commercial trade rights between Spain, England and the Netherlands. This should have stopped a renewed continental war but days after the signing of the treaty James II whom William III had ousted from the English throne and crushed in Ireland died in exile in France. Louis despite acknowledging William as king of England suddenly changed his mind and recognised James II's son, James Francis Edward Stuart as the rightful King of England and the Netherlands. This single act was the straw that broke the camel's back and William declared war on France thus beginning the War of Spanish Succession.

The Holy Roman Empire of Austria's claim on the Spanish throne was supported by England, Scotland, the Netherlands, Prussia and the Kingdom of Portugal whilst the Electorate of Bavaria and the Hungarians allied with France and Spain.

Whilst the alliance was instigated by William III he died before the 6th Foot even went into action. A broken shoulder from a fall from his horse led to pneumonia and he died on 8th March 1702 so ending the line of the House of Orange. He and Mary, who had died 8 years earlier, had no children and so the English throne passed to Anne, Mary's sister whilst the position of Stadtholder of the United Provinces was more complicated and the position became defunct with each region having its own leader.

Whilst diplomats ran from royal court to royal court across Europe and treaties were made and broken the 6th Foot were garrisoned in Ireland. In the lull between the wars King William had been prudent enough to strengthen his armed services. The 6th were raised now to be 12 companies of in size with total battalion strength of some 840 men.

The senior company were grenadiers. Grenadiers were elite troops, usually large and stronger men than the regular soldiers. They were named for the grenades with which they were equipped. Each man wore a mitre like cap rather than the tricorn hats worn by regular troops which enabled them to throw the grenades with greater ease without an arm catching on the brim of a hat. A belt tube contained a glowing fuse that would be used to light the grenades before throwing. The Grenadier Company was led by two Lieutenants, three Sergeants with two drummers, whilst the regulars had two Sergeants, three Corporals and only one drummer. Each company had about 40 privates.

By the time war was formerly declared the 6th Foots effective fighting strength was 40 officers and 684 of other ranks. Lieutenant-Colonel Ventris Columbine was still commanding officer and beneath him were Lieutenant-Colonel James Rivers and Major William Southwell future commanding officers. The regiment was due to form part of an expedition to Cadiz on the Spanish coast. This force was led by the Duke of Ormonde with Sir George Rooke as commander of the fleet. With the landing force were two former commanding officers of the 6th Foot, Prince George of Hesse-Darmstadt and Sir Henry Belasyse both now in important positions in the army. The taskforce left Torbay on 6th August 1702.

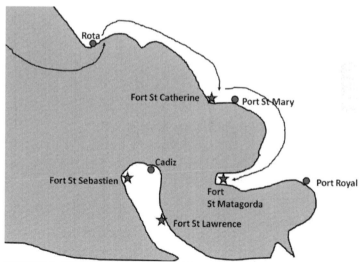

FIGURE 3- THE ATTACK ON CADIZ

Admiral Rooke and the Duke of Ormonde were instructed to seize Cadiz quickly and if that was not possible to ensure that a victory was had at either the ports of Vigo or Corunna thereby maintaining the pressure on the Spanish army and its fleet. The task force was composed of 30 English Warships, 20 Dutch Warships and 110 transports that carried the 14,000 English and Dutch soldiers and 4,000 Marines. The expedition to Cadiz was if anything too cautious. Admiral Rooke was unhappy about French counter attacks from Brest and intelligence seemed to suggest that Cadiz was heavily garrisoned. He began to suspect that the port could not be taken.

The fleet anchored itself north of the Cadiz peninsular in the Bay of Bulls where Rooke, Ormonde and his officers held a 3 day council of war. Originally Ormonde had wanted a direct assault on the walls of Cadiz but his enthusiasm was tempered by Rooke who urged a more cautious approach. They agreed to begin by securing the fortresses of Santa Catalina (Catherine) and Port St. Mary on the approaches to the peninsula.

On the 26th August the first landings were made near the town of Rota. These were hampered by both the enemy and the elements. 25 of the landing craft were lost in strong winds with 20 men drowning and their arrival was met by fire from a Spanish battery and a charge of light cavalry. Once ashore the army formed up and marched on Rota. They found the town practically deserted and it surrendered immediately to Allied forces.

On the 31st August the army left Rota and headed for Port St Mary. Like Rota they found the town undefended. The allies fell upon Port St. Mary raiding the unguarded warehouses and looting the whole city. Prince George of Hesse was appalled by the allies' behaviour believing that such actions would only serve to alienate the Spanish populous who needed to be won over to the allies.

With Rota and Port St. Mary in allied possession a strong beachhead had been established upon which to run a campaign. The garrison at the fort of Santa Catalina capitulated on the 2nd September giving Ormonde complete control of the northern end of the bay. Next he marched upon the fort of St. Matagorda. Ormonde hoped to secure the fort quickly which would allow Rooke's fleet to travel through the narrow water into the anchorage where the Spanish and French fleet were holed up near Port Royal. With a force of 2,200 English and Dutch troops and a battery of guns Baron Sparr was instructed to secure the narrow sand spit which led to the Fort and then to storm the fortress. This time the Spanish garrison held its ground. Close to the enemy fleet the allied attacking force were now within range of the Franco-Spanish fleets guns which they turned on the soldiers to devastating effect. 65 casualties were inflicted including Captain Devenish of the 6th Foot before Sparr was ordered to withdraw to safety.

THE BATTLE OF VIGO BAY

The failure to seize St. Matagorda did not seem to concern Rooke as he doubted he could have got his ships past the forts partner on the other side of the channel, Fort St.

Lawrence, he was more concerned with matters at their rear.

The Marquis Villadarias had led a Spanish force around their lines of communication and retaken Rota whilst their attention had been on St. Matagorda. The allies' position suddenly seemed untenable. No Spanish nobles had risen to support them locally and they still didn't hold Cadiz. It was briefly suggested that the town should be shelled from the sea but poor weather scuppered that plan, so with much chagrin it was decided to abandon the whole expedition. The troops re-embarked and the fleet headed for home.

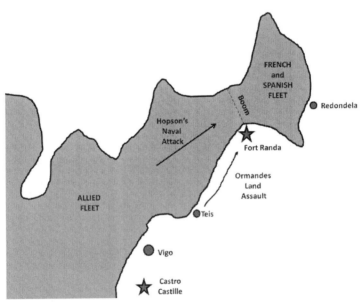

FIGURE 4 – THE BATTLE OF VIGO BAY

It was now late September and approaching the time when armies would usually put an end to fighting for the winter but Ormonde was determined to fulfill his orders if only to save some face for the failure at Cadiz. Rooke and Sir Henry Belayse opposed any further action but Ormonde was able to persuade them to attempt an attack on Vigo a town on Spain's west coast and on the way home to England.

News reaching Admiral Rooke on 23rd September 1702 that a Spanish treasure fleet from the Americas had arrived at Vigo no doubt helped make up his mind. The prospect of being able to seize so much silver galvanised Ormandes doubters and Rooke led the Anglo-Dutch fleet to Vigo arriving on the 22nd October.

Much of the silver from the fleet had already been unloaded and was on its way to Lugo by the time the allies arrived but the main fleet of 22 Spanish Galleons and 34 French ships remained anchored in the bay. The fleet was protected by a timber and chain boom stretched across the bay and gun batteries on the shore at Fort Randa. Whilst French troops were in the majority of the defenders the Governor of Galicia raised a levy of local Spaniards to supplement the defence of Vigo.

With the enemy fleet bottled up in the bay the Anglo-Dutch Fleet controlled the coast but the tight entrance to the bay meant that traditional fleet tactics could not be used and they would be required to break the boom under the fire from Fort Randa's 30 guns. Rooke and Ormande developed a strategy involving a two pronged attack.

Vice Admiral Hopsonn on the *Torbay* led a squadron of ships to break the boom whilst Ormonde landed 2,000 men at Teis a few miles south of Fort Randa. With grenadiers in the lead Ormonde's men including members of the 6th Foot stormed the Fort and quickly silenced the seaward facing guns. Whilst Ormonde secured their position in the fort the *Torbay* smashed through the boom. A change in wind left her temporarily on her own amongst the Franco-Spanish ships and she succumbed to a Spanish fireship. The rest of the squadron eventually entered the bay and dealt a devastating blow to the Spanish and French. None of the French vessels escaped with six being captured, the Spanish fared no better. This decisive victory completely ended Spain's power at sea and dealt the French a significant setback in the war.

Rooke took his time to thoroughly plunder the trade ships seizing tons of pepper, cocoa, snuff, hides and of course silver. Captain Browne of the 6th took a large silver dish and Major Southwell a ring. Some £1,000,000 of booty was taken and it took some great effort to ensure that everything taken was logged and not kept by the troops; nevertheless the average soldier was not hard done by. When the spoil was eventually divided up the 6th Foot got £565.

Although Vigo Bay made up for the disaster at Cadiz and encouraged the King of Portugal, Peter II to switch his allegiance from France and Spain to the Grand Alliance the officers involved were still persecuted. Both Ormonde and Belayse were court-martialled and whilst Ormonde was eventually pardoned Belayse was cashiered from the army for allowing his troops to pillage Port St. Mary.

The 6th Foot returned to Britain with Admiral Rooke's fleet but barely had they arrived in Portsmouth than they were tasked with a new mission and one that would prove to be a disaster.

THE AMERICAS

Whilst the War of Spanish Succession was mostly centered on Europe (Spain and Western France in particular), the global nature of the Kingdoms colonies and trade necessitated that military action often be taken far from English shores. Lieutenant-Colonel Columbine was promoted to Brigadier and given orders to sail to the West Indies and place himself under the command of the Governor, Colonel Codrington. The plan was to attack French interests in the West Indies and then to capture Placentia in Newfoundland. Such a strike would hit French trade and debilitate their supply chain.

Poor preparation by Admiral Graydon and too little wind delayed the expedition's departure by three months and by the time they arrived in the West Indies Colonel Codrington had already taken Guadeloupe the first of their assigned targets. After delays in Jamaica, whilst the fleet was put in order, the regiment eventually reached Newfoundland in August 1703.

Placentia, Newfoundland, was a fortified town and so required guns to take it, dense fog reduced visibility and so no assault was possible for a further month. By then the expedition was in no state to fight. Winter was drawing on and the expedition was ill equipped to handle a Canadian winter. The fleet was in disrepair and the troops were

49

depleted by sickness, in fact Brigadier Columbine himself died whilst still at sea. It was decided no sensible attack could be made and so the fleet returned home further hampered by storms. Admiral Graydon was cashiered from the navy for his poor planning and the overall failure of the expedition.

The 6th Foot sorely depleted and now leaderless were garrisoned in Deal where on 2nd November 1703 Lieutenant-Colonel James Rivers assumed command. Rivers like Columbine he was a veteran of their service in the Netherlands and benefitted from the patronage of Queen Anne. They spent until March recovering and recruiting before they were sent to garrison Plymouth and the Isle of Wight. Rivers was ordered to get the regiment back to a fighting strength of 743 men but by the time the regiment was returned to active service he was still 40 men short. In April 1705 the regiment was placed under the command of Sir Charles Mordaunt the Earl of Peterborough and Admiral Sir Cloudesley Shovell for a new expedition to Spain.

THE SIEGE OF BARCELONA

Whilst the 6th Foot had been crossing the Atlantic from Canada the war in Europe had continued apace. Eugene of Savoy challenged the French in Italy winning key battles at Carpi, Chiari, Luzarra and Turin; whilst the famous Duke of Marlborough, John Churchill led English, Dutch and German troops against the French in the Low Countries and along the Rhine. Marlborough and Eugene met the French and Bavarian Army together at Blenheim decisively defeating them and knocking Bavaria out of the

50

war. With success in the west greater focus was placed on King Philip V in Spain. The Earl of Peterborough and Admiral Shovell's plan was to first seize the city Barcelona on the Spanish East coast and from their take the war to the heart of Spain.

Prince George of Hesse had been a well liked Governor of Catalonia under Charles II a position he had taken up once he had left the 6th Foot. It was hoped that reinstalling him would rally the Catalonians to their cause. Prince George was currently in Gibraltar having captured it from the Spanish in 1704. The English fleet stopped at Lisbon in Portugal to join up their forces before making an unopposed landing on 22nd August 1705 north-east of Barcelona.

Barcelona was protected by a number of strategic forts the principal of which was the Montjuic situated to the south west of the city upon a hillside. It was defended by Don Francis de Velasco and 5000 men. Peterborough knew that the forts had to be carried before the city would ever fall and so directed Prince George of Hesse to assault the Montjuic. Prince George was a good choice to lead the attack he represented Archduke Charles of Austria's claim to the Spanish throne and had defended Barcelona in 1697. Prince George took a force of 400 grenadiers led by Lieutenant-Colonel William Southwell of the 6th Foot and 600 musketeers to try and take the fort by stealth.

The plan was to sneak up to the walls during the night of the 13th September and scale the walls before the Spanish knew what was happening however the small force was unable to get into position before dawn broke and the element of surprise was lost. Despite now being clearly in the view of the fortress the advance was sounded. The attack went well at first and they managed to carry the outer works and ditch. Southwell led the regiment up steep rocks and managed to reach a covered archway and another ditch. Under fire they they reached the Escarp Wall but it was then that they found that the ladders were too short, unable to progress further the attack was aborted. During the retreat they were set upon from all sides and on several occasions Lieutenant-Colonel Southwell himself was surrounded by enemies. Each time he managed to fight his way free but not without being wounded.

Having failed to take Montjuic in the first strike Prince George turned his attention to the smaller Fort St. Bertran, surely that would be easier than the main fort. Again disaster struck when Prince George was mortally wounded. With their leader dead the attack began to falter and several units began to flee. Luckily Peterborough saw the attack in disarray and sent in reserves to shore up the assault this worked and by the end of the day the Fort was stormed. Prince George was a great loss to the army. He was popular with the locals. His body was embalmed and buried in Esglesia del Josepets in Barcelona. His heart was returned to his homeland where it was interred in the Stadtkirche in Darmstadt.

With St. Bertran in allied hands the army now had a more secure position from which to assault Montjuic Fort Rather than risk another quick attack a traditional siege was now laid with trench works and artillery bombardment. On 17ᵗʰ September Lieutenant-Colonel Southwell was in command of the trenches when he noticed that one of the mortars was firing too far to the left. Ever a man to lead from the front rather than leave the matter to the Gunners he repositioned the mortar himself and fired a shell into the defences. The shell flew true and struck a chapel behind the walls. This single shot should not have caused much damage but unbeknownst to Southwell the French had been using the chapel as a powder magazine. The resulting explosion blew a huge hole in the wall. Quickly Southwell exploited the breach and launched an assault with those around him under his command. Taken by surprise the Fort fell and soon after Barcelona itself.

With the fortifications at St. Bertran and Montjuic gone Barcelona had no hope of resisting and surrendered on 3rd October. This emboldened the locals and started a general uprising by the native Catalans in support of the allies. For his heroic actions during the battle Lieutenant-Colonel William Southwell was rewarded with the title of Governor of Montjuic as well as command of the regiment when Rivers died over the winter.

After Barcelona another popular uprising for the Archduke in Valencia gave the allies a chance to further press their advantage in Spain. The 6th Foot returned to the Earl of Peterborough's army. The army marched south to Valencia unopposed and on the 24th January 1706 entered the city. The regiment remained in Valencia for much of the next year whilst the Spanish and French tried to retake Barcelona.

King Philip of France gathered 20,000 reinforcements by stripping soldiers from his armies on the frontiers of Portugal, Italy, Provence, Flanders and the Rhine. This new army would be sent to liberate Barcelona and then Valencia. Elsewhere The Earl of Galway entered Spain with his own allied army.

Peterborough's, Galway's and the Archdukes forces joined up at Guadalajara in central Spain where Galway's army had already successfully sacked the city. Here the momentum that had been gained in the past few months was lost as the three commanders disagreed on their next target. Peterborough was intent on seizing Madrid but the others preferred to attack the French reinforcements. They spent so long deliberating that eventually Peterborough was recalled to London to explain the delay. In his absence the command of the English forces including the 6th Foot was passed to the Earl of Galway.

By time any decision was made matters were already out of their hands. The Duke of Berwick led the French reinforcements towards the allies and maneuvered to block their access to Madrid and so Galway retreated back to the safety of Valenica. The Duke of Berwick was a Jacobite in service to the French crown. He was the illegitimate son of James II and Arabella Churchill. He was therefore also the nephew of John Churchill who was fighting in the Netherlands. Berwick was a competent commander and would prove to be a thorn in the alliances side in Spain.

In September 1706 the regiment was detached from the main army to successfully besiege the towns of Requena and Cuenza under the command of Major-General Wyndham. They rejoined the main army at Veles and remained in Murcia for the duration of the winter.

The following spring saw Galway renew his attempt on Madrid and he led several attacks on outlying towns in an attempt to pave the way. The Duke of Berwick, leading the French however was confident of success knowing that he had some 10,000 more men than Galway and he knew that the Duke of Orlean's was marching to his aid with a second French army.

On 25th April 1707 Berwick placed his forces, which were a mix of French, Spanish and Irish troops, at Almanaza in a strong position from which his artillery commanded a flat open plain before the town.

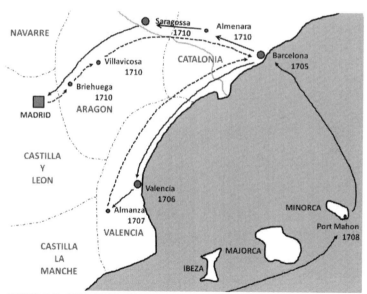

FIGURE 5- THE WAR IN EASTERN SPAIN

The Earl of Galway marched out from Valencia to meet Berwick. The 6th Foot were part of this army and were positioned with Wade's Brigade on the left wing between two brigades of cavalry. Berwick opened the battle with a cannonade from his artillery which was returned by the allies own artillery.

When the artillery duel abated Spanish Cavalry descended upon the English Cavalry driving them back. The cavalry could have run rampant but a well directed volley from the infantry dissuaded them from any further attack. The 6th Foot were brigaded with the 33rd Foot and the 17th Foot. These three regiments advanced with support of a unit of Dragoons and opened fire on the French cavalry and Spanish Lifeguards putting both of them to flight. Rallied English Dragoons continued the pursuit of these troops annihilating the enemy before being counter-attacked by French and Spanish cavalry themselves.

Advancing in the centre, English and Dutch infantry made huge gains and succeeded in pushing Berwick's own centre so far back that they were nearly left with their backs to walls of Almanza itself. Such an advance whilst normally a battle winning action left the allied centre horribly exposed and when the Portuguese failed to come up in support the tide of the battle turned.

On the left flank Wade's Brigade along with some English Cavalry successfully held their ground but when the Earl of Galway was wounded and with so many other officers either dead or injured even this part of the line began to crumble. Berwick seized the advantage and ordered nine battalions in to action supported by cavalry. The 6th and 33rd regiments came under attack first and they quickly found themselves overwhelmed. They pulled back to link up with the 9th Foot, 17th Foot and Lord Montjoy's Regiment but they were still unsupported. Engaged by seven of the battalions the remaining French units slipped around and attacked in the flank. Wade's Brigade was unable to stand and fled. In the centre the fight had become a close quarter's affair and with the left wing gone it now found itself almost completely surrounded. A hurried retreat to Onteniente was prepared, covered by Harvey's Dragoons, but this just prolonged the inevitable. The small force was soon surrounded and forced to surrender.

Of the 22,000 allies that had taken to the field at Almanza only 5,000 staggered safely into Tortosa. In total some 4,000 were killed or wounded and the rest taken prisoner. The army lost 88 officers of which 9 were from the 6th Foot. This was a major defeat for the allies and the Earl of Galway was forced to retire from the field taking the remains of his army back to Barcelona to lick their wounds.

THE CAPTURE OF MINORCA

Although Almanza had been a crushing defeat for the allies the Earl of Galway was able to rally an army of 15,000 men in just five months. He used this new force in October to attempt to relieve Lerida which was under siege by the French unfortunately they were unsuccessful. Galway still suffering from injuries sustained at the Battle of Almanza was given leave to return to England and he was replaced as overall allied commander by Count Staremberg.

Six days after the defeat at Almanza the Act of Union was passed unifying the English and Scottish thrones as the United Kingdom of Great Britain the 6th Foot was no longer an English regiment but a British one. Individual command of the British forces was given to James Stanhope. Stanhope was a soldier and a politician; he had served with the Earl of Peterborough and was the British Minister for Spain.

There were changes for the 6th Foot as well; Lieutenant-Colonel Southwell left the regiment later becoming a Colonel of the Battle Axe Guards in Ireland and a member of Irish Parliament before his death in 1719. He was replaced as the regiment's commanding officer by Thomas Harrison who bought his commission for 5,000 guineas. Buying a commission was a common method of gaining rank in the army at this time. All officers were generally from good families and generals and colonels usually from the nobility. It was more common for a commissioned officer to pay for a promotion once a slot was available than to be awarded the position on merit. This was the accepted class order but caused tactical problems for the army, the right person was not always in the right place at the right time.

The Duke of Marlborough, John Churchill, who had spent his time fighting to great effect in Flanders and Germany advised that the small Spanish island of Minorca should be taken to act as a British Naval outpost to help control the Mediterranean Sea. The British parliament agreed and on the 2nd September 1707 James Stanhope took a small force to Minorca including 600 men from the 6th foot led by Lieutenant-Colonel Abraham Hunt, 150 dismounted dragoons, 760 marines, 750 Portuguese, 700 Neopolitans, 300 Spaniards and a train of English artillery.

The taskforce landed on the 13th September near Port Mahon, the islands capital, which surrendered swiftly. The citadel protecting the town however did not. It was unlikely the citadel would prove much of a problem and so Stanhope began a siege and bombardment of the Citadel whilst he seized the towns of Cittadella and Fornelle.

The bombardment of the citadel lasted until the 28th September when two breaches were made and the castle was stormed. The forlorn hope, those that led the attack, were the grenadiers of the 6th Foot. The attack was a success and the Governor quickly capitulated. When he marched his men out under the watchful eye of the allied troops he registered dismay and shame that he had surrendered to such a small force, had he known the true size of the force he would probably have kept fighting. While Stanhope returned to Barcelona the 6th Foot remained to garrison the island.

BATTLE OF ALMENARA

In August 1709 plans were afoot for a renewed attempt to take Cadiz. The regiment was tasked with taking part and so were collected by a fleet under the command of Sir George Byng. They sailed first for Gibraltar where they were due to rendezvous with fresh troops from England. These forces were delayed however and so the thrust of the new offensive was changed to take place in Catalonia.

Whilst the regiment had been on Minorca General Staremberg had consolidated his position in Catalonia and by July 1710 he had been reinforced by a large force of Germans that were accompanied by Archduke Charles himself. These reinforcements were sorely needed as in the spring the French and Spanish had opened the campaign season by massing an army led by King Philip to enter Catalonia from Aragorn. The scene was set for a clash between two of the leading men competing for the throne.

Of the 25,000 men gathered by General Staremberg less than a fifth was English. James Stanhope, recently returned from London, commanded the British contingent and personally led a significant number of cavalry units. The 6th Foot joined this British element of the army.

General Staremberg had assembled his forces at Agramont and wanted to take the battle to the enemy and not allow them to enter Catalonia unopposed. He ordered Stanhope to advance offensively with twelve squadrons of Dragoons and twenty companies of grenadiers. This advance force marched north and seized the Pass of Alfaraz on the other side of the River Noguera. The rest of the army with Staremberg followed behind taking up position on the Heights of Almenara thereby denying King Philip the use of the road.

The following day, 27th July 1710, the battle began. The Spanish force was led by Francisco de Villadarias who had previously successfully defended Cadiz during Rooke's failed assault on the city and had led the invasion of Portugal. At Almenara he began by unleashing his cavalry in a direct charge. The attack was successful but the flaw in many cavalrymen throughout history was their impetuosity and as the allied forces began to break the Spanish horsemen allowed themselves to be distracted by the fleeing soldiers. Stanhope recognised a potential advantage opportunity when he saw one and quickly urged a counter attack with his own cavalry. General Staremberg agreed with the move and the British cavalry plunged in, supported on the left wing by British infantry. The disciplined attack broke the Spanish frontline and drove them back into their second line of defence. On the right flank Austrian forces attacked and had similar success.

Hard pressed at two points the Spanish Bourbon Army imploded. King Philip fought viciously but was forced to flee narrowly escaping capture by the allies. The Spanish Army straggled back through Catalonia only reforming once back in Aragon.

THE BATTLES OF SARGOSSA

The Spanish main base of operations in Aragon was the town of Sargossa it was here that King Philip rallied his forces using a screen of cavalry to delay the pursuing Staremberg. After Francisco de Villadarias' failure at Almenara King Philip had him replaced by the Marquis de Bay who had fought in Dutch service. Even with a new commander the Spanish were still out numbered with 20,000 men to oppose the allies near 30,000.

General Staremberg was eager to maintain the pressure but cautiously halted his forces a mile from the town's walls taking up positions with the river Ebro on his left and the Torrero Heights on his right. His army now contained a Catalan and Aragonese element alongside the Dutch, British, German and Austrian men already in the army. The Catalans and Dutch were given the left under the command of Count Atalya. Staremberg held the centre himself with the bulk of the German infantry whilst Stanhope had command of the British and Austrian contingent on the right. The 6th Foot were brigaded here under the command of Major-General Wade.

At 8 am on 20th of August 1710 artillery batteries on both sides began a fearful duel that lasted until mid day, when in a replay of the events of Almenara the Spanish Cavalry charged forward. Staremberg countered this by ordering a general advance along the whole line that broke the Spanish centre. Attempts to steady their line were disrupted by Stanhope who attacked from the flank.

By 2 pm the slow retreat of Spanish forces became first a trickle and then a rout. Nearly 10,000 Spaniards were either killed or wounded and up to 5,000 were captured. King Philip was forced to flee again. This time it was not so easy and he only escaped by disguising himself as a common soldier and relying on the help of locals to reach Madrid.

So successful was the battle of Sargossa that Lieutenant-Colonel Harrison was sent back to England to present Queen Anne with the 30 banners and standards captured from the Spanish Army. It is from here that it is suggested that the image of the Antelope was adopted by the Regiment and added to its own colours to be used as the regimental emblem for the next two hundred and fifty years.

It is believed that one of the banners was taken by the 6th Foot during the battle from the Spanish was Moorish in origin and depicted an antelope of some kind. When presented to the Queen they were permitted to keep it as a mark of their valour in the battle.

The Battle of Sargossa was a decisive point in the war as a whole. Archduke Charles marched unopposed into the town and from this point threatened Madrid itself. King Philip knew his forces were stretched too thin and by 9th September had abandoned the city completely. The allied vanguard lead by Stanhope entered Madrid on 21st September.

Finding the city hostile to their new masters, Madrid was not held for long. In November Marshal Vendome brought in French reinforcements for their Spanish allies. Vendome was a true Bourbon, a son of Louis II de Bourbon-Vendome. He was a career soldier having served in the Netherlands and distinguishing himself during the Nine Years War. Earlier in the War of Spanish Succession Vendome had been successfully countering Prince Eugene of Savoy on the French/Italian border but had failed to oppose Oudenarde in Flanders.

Gathering a superior force about him Vendome marched to Madrid. Seeing the size of the force and already depleted from the battles fought Madrid was abandoned by the allies. Archduke Charles at the head of the cavalry raced back to Barcelona leaving Staremberg and the infantry to follow slowly behind, hampered by their supplies and wounded. Stanhope was given command of the rear guard containing the bulk of the British forces including the 6th Foot.

With no more than eight squadrons of cavalry and eight battalions of infantry Stanhope's rear guard force numbered less than 4,000 men and was incredibly vulnerable. The role of the rear guard was to stop the pursuing French from catching up with the main body of the army. Believing Vendome to be still some distance from them Stanhope paused to rest at the town of Brieuhega on the 6th December 1710.

Marshal Vendome was much closer than Stanhope had anticipated and a fast march had the French-Spanish Army arriving at the towns meagre walls just two days later. Stanhope was hopelessly isolated. He had no option but to make hasty defences and send out riders to Staremberg's main column to plead for help. The following day Vendome's artillery arrived and a bombardment began.

The simple walls of Brieuhega stood no chance against the French guns and were soon breached. Vendome's forces numbered 12,000 and so outnumbered Stanhopes 3 to 1, odds that led him to believe that it would be easy to take the town quickly and easily and move on to attack the main army in the rear. This was not to be the case.

The English soldiers, the 6th Foot among them, fought viciously. They managed to repulse wave after wave of attackers. When their powder ran dry they met the French soldiers in the streets with bayonets in close hand to hand combat. As the hours went by without any sign of relief Stanhope was forced to surrender the town to the French and plead terms, stating that 'I thought myself in conscience obliged to try and save so many brave men who had done good service to the Queen...if after this misfortune, I should ever be entrusted with troops, I never desire to serve with better men.' These bold words reflected the fact that 1,500 French had died to capture the town whilst the British only suffered 500 casualties. Of the 6th Foot only those not with Stanhope's force remained either alive or at liberty. They joined the 3500 prisoners taken by the French and would play no further part in the war.

General Staremberg turned too late to save Brihuega but he was able to prepare an adequate defence against the advancing Marshal Vendome. He met the Frenchman at Villavicosa where an inconclusive battle was fought. Both sides claimed victory but as it was the allied force that withdrew it was tactical victory for the Bourbons. Vendome harried Staremberg all the way back to Barcelona in doing so he undid all of the gains made by the allies during the war to this date.

In Flanders the allies led by the Duke of Marlborough continued to do well with success at the Battle of Bouchain whilst in Italy Prince Eugene was beaten by French forces at Denain. Changes in opinion at home and the resurgence of the Spanish and French armies led England to push for a peaceful solution. In 1711 Archduke Charles had become Emperor of the Holy Roman Empire after the death of his brother and so his claim to the Spanish throne seemed less important and he began to relinquish his claim to the Spanish throne. The Duke of Argyll, Stanhope's replacement as commander in chief, withdrew all British troops to Gibraltar and Minorca whilst diplomats entered into negotiations. In August 1712 a conference at Utrecht ended the war completely.

Barcelona remained the only part of Spain to support Archduke Charles and held on until 1714 but eventually a large Bourbon force surrounded the city under the command of the Duke of Berwick. The city was bombarded and overwhelmed finally falling on 11th September 1714.

The War of Spanish Succession had cost many nations dearly and was pejoratively a victory for the French backed Spanish. Philip V was acknowledged as King of Spain and denounced his claim to the French throne.

The war changed the map of Europe. Austria gained the Spanish Netherlands, Milan, Naples, and Sardinia and Sicily went to Savoy. The treaty also benefited Britain, besides the granting of Minorca and Gibraltar, France acknowledged Queen Anne as the rightful monarch of Britain and agreed to cease their support for the Stuart claim on the throne. Ironically in the long run it was Spain that came off the worse. Despite allied with France she had lost much of her overseas territories and would forever be beholden to foreign powers such as France for support.

CHAPTER 3 - CONTROLLING AN EMPIRE

The resolution of the war of Spanish succession did little to end the various disputes throughout Europe. Spain, having lost a lot of her overseas territory was soon looking to expand where ever she could and started to challenge Britain for trade supremacy. In Eastern Europe wars would be fought over the thrones of Austria and Poland whilst Russia and Scandinavia fought in a series of Northern Wars.

It was against this backdrop of instability that the 6th Foot was required to rearm itself. Most of the regiment had been taken prisoner at Brieuhega and for all intents and purposes the regiment was no more. As diplomats struggled to reach an agreement over the cessation of hostilities concessions were made on all sides including the release of prisoners of war. On the 25th July 1715 the soldiers of the Sixth Foot and their commanding officer Lieutenant-Colonel John Ramsey were released. These 15 sergeants, 12 corporals, 3 drummers and 80 privates arrived in Ireland to rejoin their surviving compatriots.

A great effort was made to revitalise the regiment and her numbers were swelled when the Regiments of Gore, Manden and Dalzell were disbanded and their men transefered to the 6th Foot. In 1715 Lieutenant-Colonel Harrison was promoted to Brigadier-General. He sold his colonelcy of the regiment to Robert Dormer who took command in 1716. His first action was to begin a thorough campaign to recruit volunteers to the regiment.

The regiment had been assigned to Ireland in a peace keeping role. The Jacobites were still a threat to Queen Anne's throne and Ireland, like Scotland were hot bed of Jacobite supporters. In 1715 Lord Mar led a short-lived uprising in Scotland and the regiment was distributed across Ireland at towns like Londonderry, Coleraine and Calmore to ensure that Ireland didn't also rise up against the crown. Life in Ireland was considerably easier than on campaign but there were still dangers. Major Harrison was killed in a duel with Captain Agnew of the 1st Foot whilst Lieutenant Jolly was killed by Robert Martin, a well known Jacobite, in Galway during a bar fight partly instigated by the men of the 6th Foot.

THE WAR OF THE QUADRUPLE ALLIANCE

By 1718 Spain was really starting to chafe at the restrictions placed on them by the Treaty of Utrecht at the close of the war of Spanish succession. King Philip V of Spain, was advised by Giulio Alberoni, Archbishop of Plasencia and the Prime Minister to make a move for the French throne.

In 1715 Louis XIV of France had died leaving the infant Louis XV, his great grandson as heir. Philip V as a grandson of Louis XIV believed he had a stronger claim and in taking the throne thought he could revitalise Spain's falling position and wealth. The other signatories of the Treaty of Utrecht, opposed this claim and so began the War of the

Quadruple Alliance which was in essence a war of French succession. The war lasted just two years and found Britain on the same side as France who needed the aid of the British navy to keep the Spanish at bay.

Like the French, Philip saw the Jacobite cause as a way to destabilise the United Kingdom. Queen Anne had died in 1714 and so now the Jacobites were working on ousting George I. The Spanish supported them by launching a daring attack and landing 300 marines at Eilean Donan in Scotland in the hope of inciting a popular uprising. This action roused the British government who now decided to increase their involvement in the war.

The expedition planed to capture the Spanish port of Corunna and then cross the Atlantic Ocean to challenge the Spanish colonies in Peru. The Sixth Foot was assigned to this expedition and were placed under the overall command of Viscount Cobham. 4000 troops embarked in September 1719 but their destination was changed at the last minute to focus on attacking the port of Vigo, something the 6Th foot had help achieve 17 years earlier.

On the 1st October the force approached the bay of Vigo to find the towns of Vigo itself and St Sebastian abandoned. Unopposed General Honeywood led the British soldiers ashore and headed for the town. They discovered that 9000 Spanish soldiers had holed themselves up in the nearby citadel. Honeywood put the castle to siege which eventually surrendered after the loss of only 300 British soldiers. The 6th Foot themselves were tasked with securing the surrounding area and were part of a force that headed in land to take the town of Pontevedra. The fact that the British had managed to penetrate so deeply into Spain worried King Philip deeply and he started to feel insecure in the wars progress. In December he dismissed Alberoni and by February 1720 had made peace with the allies by signing the Treaty of The Hague. The terms he accepted included returning captured territory and relinquishing his claim to the French throne and any claims in Italy.

At the close of the war the 6th Foot returned to their duties in Ireland. In the same year Robert Dormer died and the colonelcy of the regiment was passed to his brother James. James Dormer had a distinguished career having fought at Blenhiem, Saragossa and Brihuega during the War of Spanish Succession but he himself was replaced in 1731 by John Guise an experienced officer who had served 30 years in the Guards. Guise inherited a regiment comprised of 10 companies each of 43 men. The regiment was quickly increased when in 1739 the regiment were returned to England and then stationed in Aberdeen.

THE WAR OF JENKINS EAR

Although Britain as a major world power was involved in many of the conflicts on the continent the 6th Foot didn't see action again until the War of Jenkins Ear in 1739. This unusual war was primarily a maritime affair between Britain and Spain and eventually became considered part of the wider War of Austrian Succession.

In the Caribbean, Spanish coastguards had started to resist some of the treaties they had signed at Utrecht and The Hague and used every opportunity available to them to resist. In 1731 the British brig *Rebecca* captained by

Robert Jenkins was boarded by the Spanish. An altercation ensued that resulted in Jenkins' ear being cut off. Nothing would have come of the incident but in 1738 Jenkins addressed the House of Commons displaying his ear that had been cut off. Britain was already concerned that Spain was reneging on their agreements and seized upon this as an opportunity to reassert their authority and declared war. Much of the war was conducted in the Caribbean with the wars greatest action being the capture of Portobello by Admiral Edward Vernon in 1739 even though it was only held for a mere three weeks.

In 1741 Lieutenant-Colonel Haldane was ordered to join the 6th Foot in an expedition to Cuba. Lieutenant-Colonel Guise was already with the army in the Caribbean but as the 6th Foot left Cork the main British attack on Cartagena failed. Led by Admiral Vernon, in-fighting between the Navy and the ground commanders, the tropical climate combined with a sound defence by the Spanish commander Blas de Lezo ultimately doomed the invasion. Later Vernon would blame the failure on the Navy and the British Prime Minister Walpole. It was hoped that the 6th Foot and the other fresh forces being sent would reinforce their efforts. The fleet arrived in fairly good time but 16 men had died on the voyage and a further 87 were sick. In the tropics disease, mainly yellow fever, and poor health killed more soldiers than enemy action. Tobias Smollett an assistant surgeon wrote that 'patients had not room to sit upright in their beds. Their wounds... being neglected, contracted filth and putrefaction, and millions of maggots were hatched amidst the corruption of their sores'. It was therefore decided to abandon the Cuba expedition completely. On the 6th January 1742 the army put to shore at St Christopher in Jamaica. The men of the Sixth were unaccustomed to the tropical climate and fever continued to run rampant through the regiment. A further 67 men died whilst waiting for new orders.

By March a decision to make another attempt to take and hold Portobello was made. On the 28th March the force numbering some 2000 men anchored off the isthmus but poor weather and more sickness meant that any attack was doomed to failure, the 6th Foot had lost a further 98 men just on the journey. They returned to Jamaica but whilst there ill health continued to take its toll with only 188 of the 770 who had sailed from Cork now being fit for duty. A hundred soldiers were sent to Georgia to assist settlers against Indians but the rest returned to Britain landing at Plymouth in early 1743 calling to a close one of the most disappointing chapters in the regiment's history.

THE JACOBITE RISING OF 1745

When William III ascended to the throne in 1688 he did so at the expense of King James II of England and VII of Scotland who had been removed from the throne during the Glorious Revolution. James' attempt to retake the throne through Ireland in 1690 was a failure and he went into exile in France. His time in France was essentially one of quiet reflection as various powers on the continent tried to use him as leverage against the British throne. There was some move by King Louis XIV to get him elected as King of Poland but James was focused on returning to England.

When William died in 1702 James son, James Francis Edward Stuart, was acknowledged as the rightful King of England and Scotland by France, however in England the throne was passed to Anne, James II daughter and sister in law to William. James was furious and determined to gain the throne, He decided to rely on Jacobite support in Scotland attempting invasions and uprisings in 1708 and 1715, both of which failed. The failure of the 1715 rising resulted in a change in James' fortune. His patron, Louis, had died and the security of France was no longer offered to him by the new King, Louis XV, instead he was offered sanctuary in Rome by the Pope.

James married a polish noble called Marie Clementina Sobieska and they had two children. Harry the youngest, entered the church becoming a Cardinal whilst the eldest, Charles became intent on regaining the crown for his father. Charles or Bonnie Prince Charlie, the Young Pretender as he became known got the closest either his father or grandfather had ever come to restoring the family throne in Scotland and England.

Charles, like his grandfather, gained the support of the French who both wouldn't mind a catholic king on England's throne but also saw the merit of causing its age old enemy, Britain, as much difficulty as possible. In 1740 the death of Charles VI of Austria led to another Europe wide conflict of succession over whether Charles VI's daughter Marie Theresa could succeed him to the throne. Battle lines were drawn with, France, Spain and Prussia lining up against Austria, Britain and Hanover with other minor countries taking up alliances where they could. The war of Austrian Succession was another global affair with battles around the globe and with every European power except for Poland-Lithuania and the Ottoman Empire taking part.

Much of the opening salvos of the war were directed in central Europe. George II King of the United Kingdom led his forces personally on the continent. King Louis XV saw in Bonnie Prince Charles an opportunity to distract England from the war on the continent by supporting an invasion of Scotland by Charles. If all went well James could be installed as King of Scotland and later England following a rising of English Jacobites, creating a secure northern front for France. Bad weather however delayed the initial invasion plans and Frances attentions were drawn more towards the battles in Silesia.

The plans however had given Charles a sliver of hope and he became determined to seize the opportunity and get his father back on the throne with or without Frances help. Charles believed that he could secure Scotland with relative ease using only his own supporters and that he didn't need French assistance.

In 1744 he put out feelers among his supporters in Scotland and found that many Clan chiefs were ready to support him. Charles gathered about him 700 volunteers of the Irish Brigade and in July 1745 landed in Scotland. His welcome was not quite what he expected. The clan chiefs expected a larger force and on the voyage Charles had lost his only supply vessel with arms and gunpowder. At first only Donald Cameron of Lochiel XIX and ten of his men joined the army. Charles continued undaunted, and in August went to Moidart raising his standard at Glenfinnan.

Four clans answered this call and rallied immediately giving Charles a total force of 3000 men.

Scotland was not entirely undefended. The 6th Foot were among several units garrisoned in the country. On returning from the Caribbean the regiment had been recruiting hard to bring themselves up to full strength. At one recruiting drive in Coventry a young man named

FIGURE 6 - HANNAH SNELL

James Grey joined the regiment and placed in Captain Millers Company. James Grey was a most unusual soldier, James was actually Hannah Snell.

In 1740 when Hannah was just 17 she moved to Wapping where she fell in love with and married a Dutch sailor called James Summs. At the end of the year he returned to his ship and disappeared. Heartbroken Hannah was convinced that James had been drafted into the army or navy and was unable to return to her. Hannah decided to try and find her husband and aware of the dangers of a young woman travelling alone disguised herself as a man by binding her breasts and borrowing her brother-in-laws clothes. When she heard of war brewing in Scotland she decided that if Summs had been drafted into the army he could well be on his way north. She decided to head north herself and when she stopped at Coventry where she encountered a recruiting band of the 6th Foot. She reasoned that being a soldier herself might make it easier to find another soldier and so joined the regiment. It was a shrewd move; whilst she searched the army would feed her, house her and pay her a wage.

She went with the regiment to Carlisle where she found herself in trouble. Sergeant Davis tried to co-opt Hannah in the rape of a young girl, horrified Hannah warned the girl who managed to escape. Sergeant Davis was furious and conspired to bring charges against Hannah for neglect of duty. This offence carried a heavy penalty, 600 lashes. Hannah was tied to the barracks gate and the back of her jacket torn open. She bore 500 lashes with barely a sound so impressing the senior staff that they commuted the final 100 lashes. Whilst her identity was still uncovered the event must have unsettled Hannah as she deserted. She fled to Portsmouth. Here she joined Frazer's Regiment of Marines bound for the East Indies. She fought at Pondicherry killing several Frenchman and even taking a bullet wound. She operated on herself to avoid discovery but was declared unfit for duty. When she learned that James Sums had been executed for murder in Genoa she returned home to live with her sister. Her story now came out and she gained much notoriety and took to the stage before becoming the land lady of a tavern. She died in 1792 after a remarkable life.

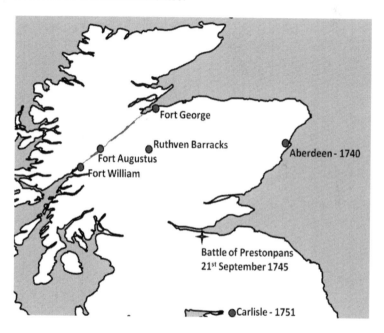

FIGURE 7 - THE POSITIONS OF THE REGIMENT IN THE RISING OF THE '45

From Carlisle the regiment entered Scotland and was posted to a number of forts that ran from Loch Lochy to Loch Ness garrisoning Fort George, Fort Augustus, Fort William and providing troops to the government army. The government army in Scotland however was not strong enough to oppose Charles army on the field of battle whilst maintaining order in the rest of the country. Concerned by this strong Jacobite uprising at home 4000 soldiers were quickly withdrawn from Flanders and Germany and under Sir John Cope landed at Inverness.

Charles had not been idle whilst the British army readied itself. The Jacobite army captured Perth and Coatbridge with little effort and whilst marching to Edinburgh routed two regiments of English Dragoons. The officials in Edinburgh panicked and were unable to mount a defence with the gates being opened to Charles from the inside. Upon marching in to the city Charles proclaimed his father as King James VIII of Scotland.

Cope's government army resupplied in Inverness and then sailed from Aberdeen to Dunbar in a hope to catch and stop Charles. The army caught up with Charles on the 20th September at Prestonpans. Sir John Cope's force was composed mostly of inexperienced troops and they drew up in line with a marshy ditch to their front and the park walls of Preston House on their right. Charles' army whilst not appreciably larger (the Jacobites had only 200 more men) relied on local knowledge and the ferocity of the clansmen to give them an edge.

At dawn using discrete paths 1,400 highlanders sneaked across the marsh and out of the mists attacked the government army from behind. Sir John Cope tried to move up his artillery to support his troops including companies of the 6th Foot but the charge continued. A flanking maneuver by highland troops routed Cope's Dragoons thereby sandwiching the Royal Foot who took heavy losses. Cope attempted to rally his men but only managed to lead only 170 men to safety. The Battle of Prestonpans lasted only ten minutes but in that time 300 government soldiers were killed, 500 wounded and 1510 more captured. Charles lost only 30 men with 70 wounded. The 6th Foot lost an entire 2 companies with both Captains Holwell and Pointz being killed.

Following this stunning victory the Jacobite army went on to advance out of Scotland and into England reaching Derby by December. Misinformation led Charles to believe that a large government army was en route to intercept him. Deciding it was easier to hold Scotland the Jacobites retreated back north, hoping to consolidate the gains they had made.

FIGURE 8- THE BARRACKS AT RUTHVEN
(BY NIFANION, 2009)

In this phase of the rebellion much of the fighting focused on the forts still held by the government in the highlands. In 1745 a detachment of the 6th Foot had been sent to Ruthven to work on the roads. They based themselves in barracks that contained a few buildings and a perimeter wall set on a low rise.

In August 1745 a Jacobite force tried to seize Fort Ruthven. The work party and fort was defended by 12 men led by Sergeant Molloy. The Jacobites numbering some 300 men offered terms to Molloy he replied saying 'I [am] too old a soldier to surrender a garrison of such strength without bloody noses'. The parley party retreated and the Jacobites began their assault at mid-day. Deploying half their strength they focused on breaching the main gate and the sally port. Determined defence however repelled the assault. Again the Jacobites came forward to demand surrender and again Molloy refused allowing them to freely collect their dead and wounded from beneath the walls. By now the Jacobites were needed elsewhere and withdrew from Ruthven.

Molloy had managed to successfully manage a defence against a superior force with the loss of only one man, who had been shot in the head after an ill timed look over the parapet. Sergeant Molloy was rewarded by being granted a commission and promotion to the rank of Lieutenant. It was unusual for a man to be 'raised from the ranks' and reflected the degree to which this defence was viewed by Lieutenant-Colonel Guise. For most men only those of money attained rank. Commissions' could be purchased with a Colonels rank available for over £1000 and ensigns for £200. In this way many officers in the army were not there on merit but on the basis of loot taken or familial wealth.

Molloy was still in command at Ruthven on the 12 February 1746 when a much larger force of Jacobites led by Gordon of Glenbucket approached the fort this time with artillery support. Molloy decided on this occasion that discretion was the better part of valour and so surrendered the fort. The garrison was permitted to leave unmolested and was given safe passage back to Perth. Despite the final outcome this act must stand alongside many of the British army's most famous stubborn defences alongside the likes of Rorke's Drift and the Siege of Khartoum.

Four days after the surrender of Ruthven on the 16th February 1746 the newly constructed Fort George near Inverness was put to siege. Lieutenant-Colonel Innes led two companies of the 6th Foot and two companies of independent Highlanders in its defence. The battle went badly and soon the defenders were wavering. Lieutenant Graham tried to rally the troops but was ordered to hold a ceasefire by the Governor, Major Grant and on the 20th February the fort surrendered.

On the 22nd February the Jacobites laid siege to Fort Augustus the second of the forts the 6th Foot garrisoned. Here the defenders were supported by a highlander engineer who posted a battery of four 4-pounders to provide covering fire. Despite this assistance the fort held out for only 2 days before being stormed and forced to surrender.

Things appeared to be going badly for the 6th Foot and their defence of the highland forts. On the 20th March Fort William had its turn to be besieged. The fort was commanded by Captain Scott and defended by two companies of the 6th Foot and members of Clan Campbell and Clan Scott. They were opposed by Major-General Cameron with 1500 Jacobites with 200 French Artillery. Cameron assumed the siege would be quick but the Jacobites were unable to stop the fort being resupplied by the Royal Navy via Loch Linnhe. On the 22nd March Cameron demanded the forts surrender but it was defiantly refused. Time was off the essence for Cameron, the Duke of Cumberland was leading a new government army to end the uprising. He had retaken Edinburgh in January 1746 and was moving north swiftly, therefore to ensure a quick victory Cameron ordered his artillery to bombard the fort into submission. Fort William remained resolute even under such heavy fire; holding out for two more weeks with various sallies out of the fort to destroy some of the canon and mortars opposing them. A final sally on the 31st March resulted in the destruction of the last of the Jacobites artillery and so on the 3rd April Cameron abandoned the siege.

Two weeks later on 16th April 1746 the rebellion of the '45 was finally crushed at the Battle of Culloden. Bonnie Prince Charlie ignored the advice of his most experienced officer, Lord George Murray and met the Duke of Cumberland on flat open ground where the Jacobite forces were torn apart by the English artillery. The Jacobites fought tenaciously in the face of grapeshot and even succeeded in breaking the English line at one point but were unable to break the second line. Murray managed to rally some troops and tried to regroup at Ruthven but Charles believed he was being deserted and so fled. Embarrassingly Charles only affected an escape from Scotland by dressing as Betty Burke, Flora MacDonald's Irish hand maid. He boarded the French Frigate *L'Heureux* and returned to France where he spent the rest of his life in exile.

With Scotland once more in government hands and the Jacobite threat ended the 6th Foot remained in Scotland until 1751 where they were posted to garrisons along the border and in northern England. In the same year the regiment was given a warrant by King George II to change their uniforms to deep yellow facings and awarded two colours. One bearing the Antelope and the other with three rose and crowns, additionally the grenadiers were given the motto 'Nec aspara terrent' meaning 'difficulties be damned'.

REBELLION IN THE AMERICAS

In the 1750's the regiment were garrisoned in England and spent several years on quiet routine garrison duties across the country. During the Seven Years War (1754-1763) they were garrisoned in Gibraltar. In 1765 the 6th Foot were transferred to Scottish command. Its full strength now included 25 officers, 25 Sergeants, 18 Drummers and 432 soldiers.

The West Indies were the heart of the tea, tobacco and sugar industries and so were valuable assets to the various powers of Europe. Many of the islands in the Caribbean changed hands many times over the years. The tiny island of St Vincent was one such island. It was claimed by Britain in 1627 but actually colonised by the French in 1700. It was these French settlers that established coffee, tobacco, indigo, corn and sugar plantations on the island worked by African slaves. The native populations of the West Indies were pretty much exterminated by the colonial powers and replaced with African slave workers. Pockets of these native Caribs, as they were called, did remain on Dominica and St Vincent.

On Dominica the Carib's struggled with both French and British colonial forces. This resistance intensified in 1759 after the island was seized by British forces and it was they who brought the situation under control. In 1763 at the close of the Seven Years War the Treaty of Paris ceded St Vincent, Dominica, Grenadines, Tobago and Grenada to Britain from France.

In 1769 the native Carib's rose up in rebellion along with many black slaves. In the autumn of that year the 6th Foot, 412 men in all, were assigned to an expedition led by Major-General William Dalrymple to quell the insurrection by any means possible. The 6th Foot were deployed to the island of St Vincent.

The fighting consisted mostly of skirmishes in thickly wooded areas with no pitched battles at all. The expedition was a great success and the Carib uprising was ended by February 1774 with very few losses and the Caribs acknowledging British sovereignty with new boundaries drawn up for British and Carib territories. For the Sixth Foot only one sergeant and four men were killed and 14 were wounded. By far the greatest concern was the spectre of disease, something that beset most European armies in the West Indies. At the close of the conflict 90 men of the 6th were on sick roll and this only got worse. In this short period the regiment went through a succession of Colonels. They arrived in St Vincent under the command of Lieutenant-Colonel Rufane who died in February 1773. He was replaced by Lieutenant-Colonel Gore who himself died in the November with Major-General Sir William Boothby from the 63rd Foot taking over from him.

In 1776 the thirteen colonies of America themselves rose up in revolution declaring independence from the crown. In Britain the general consensus was that the revolution was a hindrance and not an important affair however poor leadership in several actions and the intervention of the French on the side of the Americans ensured that Britain eventually took more notice.

Being so close to America it was inevitable that the 6th Foot would be called into action on the mainland and they were ordered to New York to join the army however by the time they had mustered illness had reduced their ranks to only 158 men. Instead of joining the armies in America they were instead returned home to recruit. For the duration of the American War of Independence the regiment remained in England garrisoned once at strength in Warwickshire.

In 1782 the army was reorganised with the battalion becoming the tactical unit of choice. Each regiment became composed of one or two battalions. Every battalion was to be commanded by a Lieutenant-Colonel and the Regiment itself led by another Lieutenant-Colonel. In the case of the 1st Battalion, 6th Foot the men were led by Lieutenant-Colonel Charles Home whilst the Colonel of the Regiment was Major-General Prince William of Frederick of Gloucester. Another part of the reorganisation was to assign each regiment in the army a territory which it would be attached to and recruit from. Given their time spent in Warwickshire during the late 1770's the 6th Foot became the 1st Warwickshire's, their full title becoming The Sixth Regiment of Foot (1st Warwickshire's). In 1785 they gained new colours and mustered 392 men in eight companies in one battalion. The Warwickshire Regiment had been born.

The reformed regiment spent much of the following years garrisoning towns in England, Jersey and Nova Scotia. By 1791 they were in New Brunswick, Canada but were soon called upon to take action again in the Caribbean. In 1789 the traditional make up of Europe was thrown into disarray by the French Revolution.

Monarchies across Europe watched in horror as the people rose up and over threw King Louis XVI. The execution of nobles and the persecution of the aristocracy unsettled all of Frances neighbours deeply. If one nation could over throw their monarch, especially one like France then it could happen anywhere. Prussia acted first, working with French nobles to try and restore order in France. The new French Government, termed the Directory, however got ahead of the game, declaring war on Austria and invaded the Austrian Netherlands. In January 1793 the Revolutionaries executed King Louis XVI and declared war on Britain and the United Provinces whilst entering into an alliance with Spain and Portugal.

With each of these powers having colonial interests in the West Indies it was inevitable that the conflict would be played out on that stage as well as in Europe. Through much of what would become known as the Napoleonic Wars Britain was loathed to become too militarily involved, instead it funded European allies to fight by proxy and used its navy to control the trade routes.

The British Prime Minister, William Pitt and Sir Henry Dundas decided that it was important to destabilise France by striking at her colonies. In 1793 Sir Charles Grey a former lieutenant of the 6th Foot who had also served with General Wolfe the champion of Quebec in the Seven Years War was charged with capturing the island of Martinique. Originally a French colony Martinique had been established as a base from which to seize slaves and was briefly under British control before it was returned to France by the Treaty of Paris that had ended the Seven Years War.

Grey's expedition was due to consist of 17,000 men including 340 men of the 6th Foot. They assembled in Barbados but by the time they were ready to depart disease had halved the armies fighting force. Grey's expedition was ferried to Martinique by a fleet commanded by Captain John Jervis. Jervis was a respected sailor having served in the War of Independence as a Captain and his actions in the West Indies resulted in his promotion to Admiral on his return to Britain.

The fleet arrived in the February of 1794 and quickly managed to secure much of the island. The capital, Fort-de-France however was strongly protected by a line of four forts built in 1769 by the engineer Le Boeuf on designs first laid down by Vauban. Completed in 1780 the forts had a 300m subterranean gallery that linked the lunette (arch) to the main body of the fort.

Fort Saint Louis was initially attacked by sea. Jervis sent the *Asia* and the *Zebra* to attack but only the *Zebra*, a sloop, could get close enough under the walls to effectively challenge the fort. Once out of the reach of the guns Commander Faulkner, the ship's captain, used the sloops boats to land the ship's company of marines and soldiers to take the fort. By the 20th March only two of the forts remained in enemy hands, Fort Desaix (renamed to Fort de la Republique by the Revolutionary's) and Fort Royal. These both fell to concerted attacks by British forces in the following four days.

The army in Martinique was arranged so that all grenadier companies and light companies were taken to form specialised grenadier and light infantry battalions, the centre companies remaining with their parent regiments. The 6th Foot were placed in Colonel Sir George Gordon's 3rd Brigade. The 6th Foots actions on Martinique earned them a second battle honour. Throughout the fighting they only lost one man and had another wounded. Rather than hold Martinique themselves control of the island was handed over to French Royalist Bourbons with the proviso that they swore allegiance to the British king. From Martinique the fleet and army went on to seize St Lucia, Guadeloupe, Port au Prince and Saint-Dominique. These actions didn't involve the 6th Foot much with them being kept aboard ship as reserves during the attack on Guadeloupe although detachments of the regiment were used in the capture of St Lucia. Colonel Whyte of the 6th was temporarily commander of the West Indies force when General Bruce fell ill.

Conditions both on land but in particular on ship were dire. Disease was prevalent and accounted for more casualties in the regiment than actual fighting. By the end of 1794 over 200 men had died from various ailments leaving the 6th foot unable to muster a suitable fighting force again. Some of the survivors were drafted to bulk up the 9th Foot the rest were sent home. The regiment arrived back in August with only 58 men.

THE 1798 IRISH REBELLION

The ideals of self rule stirred up by the French Revolution found much support in Ireland causing many secessionists in particular the United Irishmen to believe that now would be the time to slip out from under England's rule.

The United Irishmen had considerable support from France who, at war with much of Europe, again saw an uprising in Ireland as a perfect opportunity to deal a blow against Britain. Their first attempt had been made in 1796 when a 20,000 strong army named the Expedition d'Irelande. Led by General Lazare Hoche the army tried tried to land in Bantry Bay in December but bad weather completely thwarted their attempts and Hoche was swiftly reassigned to the German front.

The British government were all too aware of the risky nature of their Irish possessions and between 1796 and 1798 introduced a series of draconian measures such as martial law and the suppression of the Northern Star newspaper as well as increasing the number of troops across the whole country.

The 6th Foot were already in Ireland for recruiting purposes when trouble started to break out and were ordered to join a government column that was hastily prepared to advance to Bantry Bay and stop the invasion but when this failed to appear the regiment was posted to Kilkenny in 1796 and later to Loughlinstown near Dublin in 1797.

In March 1798 unrest began to spread across Ireland and built up into action. Government forces were quick to act and tried to nip it all in the bud. They swept up many of the United Irishmen leadership and put down a small uprising in Cahir. The main uprising was planned by Theobald Wolfe Tone for the 23rd of May. Much of the action centered on Dublin's surrounding districts with fighting in Leinster and County Kildare. Such was the strength of the uprising that the British were withdrawn to Naas but it didn't take long for government forces to respond and they stamped down brutally on the rebellion.

They defeated the Irishmen at Carlow, Hill of Tara and County Meath, ending any resistance in those places. The 6th Foot and the Light Battalion took part in these suppression operations and in County Wicklow the rebels were massacred at Dunlavin. In June, Presbyterian rebels rose up but were quashed in County Antirim, and battles at New Ross, Arlow and Bunclody halted any further risings in County Wexford. Despite the government successes the spread of the uprising concerned Prime Minister Pitt and he was determined not to let the French intervene again. He ordered the Royal Navy to patrol the

Irish Coast and assigned the American War of Independence veteran General Cornwallis as Lord Lieutenant of Ireland despite the protestations of many of the landed gentry. Cornwallis started strongly defeating an army of United Irishmen at the Battle of Vinegar Hill.

On the 22nd August 1798 a 1000 strong French invasion force led by General Humbert was able to slip past the Royal Navy and wade ashore at Sligo to assist the rebels. Humbert was a career soldier who had been part of the French Revolution. He left 200 men in Killala to cover his rear and marched to join with a force of United Irishmen at Castlebar in County Mayo.

Government forces in excess of 6000 men including the 6th Foot were deployed to meet Humbert's force of 2000 on the Ballina Road. This deployment was ruined however when locals revealed to Humbert an alternative route to Castlebar along the west side of Lough Conn. Quickly General Lake repositioned his British forces to meet Humbert head on.

The Franco/Irish force arrived at 6 a.m. and was greeted by a bombardment by British Artillery causing heavy casualties. Trying to avoid the overwhelming fire Humbert's men found a defile that offered them some cover from the artillery and from there launched a ferocious bayonet charge. These were not poorly disciplined rebels but trained French soldiers and the aggressive charge unnerved the local militia units in the British line causing them to panic and then flee. This panic soon began to spread to others and a unit of Dragoons and several British regulars turned tail and ran. The 120 men of the 6th foot among others attempted to hold the line and

91

despite Major MacBean's efforts and distinguished action by Sergeant Archibald Reith and his 12 yr old Drummer Boy son James, they were overwhelmed resulting in a humiliating defeat. Lake lost 80 men with more than 250 men wounded, captured or missing. Lakes own baggage and a great deal of equipment was abandoned. The government forces continued to flee and only rallied at Athlone when General Cornwallis arrived.

The defeat had wide repercussions. General Humbert declared Connaught an independent republic causing widespread panic to break out across Ireland. The victory at Castlebar and the declaration of a republic swelled Humbert's ranks with Irish rebels from across Ireland and in September he successfully defeated a second smaller government force in Sligo at the Battle of Collooney. Word of rebellions in Wexford and Longford shifted Humbert's focus and he moved his forces to Cloone where he received word that these uprisings had been defeated and that Cornwallis had a large blocking force en route with a second army led by General Lake on the way. Humbert retreated immediately to Ballinamuck where he chose to make a stand against Lake whose army now outnumbered his own two to one.

After a brief artillery duel and some small amount of fighting it was clear that this was a fight Humbert couldn't hope to win and so he offered his surrender. Humbert's surrender may not have been an end the rebellion but 3000 French reinforcements led by Wolfe Tone were intercepted by the Royal Navy attempting to land near Lough Swilly in County Donegal. Without fresh French support and the loss of Humbert's army the rebellion crumbled. The French soldiers involved in the 1798 rebellion were eventually repatriated to France but the Irish ringleaders were all hanged doing nothing to ease the tensions between the British and the Irish.

With the greatest threat of the rebellion crushed and the French removed from the fight the government hoped that the insurrection was at an end, but pockets of resistance continued for several years often acted upon with great discrimination by government forces. The rising ended Irelands small fraction of autonomous rule held by the Protestant Ascendancy and its governance was incorporated into direct British control from London's parliament in the Act of Union in August 1800. Instead of granting them freedom the rebellion had removed what little self rule they had once had.

CHAPTER 4 - OPPOSING NAPOLEON

The Napoleonic Wars were in fact a series of wars that began with the French Revolution. The risk the revolution in France posed to neighbouring monarchies made France many enemies. Prussia, Britain, Russia and Austria all feared popular peasant uprisings in their own countries. France did little to assuage these fears declaring pre-emptive wars against Spain, Austria and Great Britain and supporting the rebellions in Ireland. This may on one hand have seemed overly aggressive but it was highly likely that Prussia and Austria would have invaded sooner or later to restore King Louis to the French throne; this was a calculated pre-emptive strike to ensure the revolution succeeded.

The Revolutionary War as the French called it was fought on many fronts and really stretched the French army. There was still an enormous amount of turmoil on their home soil with Royalists fighting Republicans and even Republicans fighting Republicans. The government changed several times between 1789 and 1802 all the while fighting Prussia and Austria. This stage of the war was considered to have ended with the Treaty of Amiens in 1802 but in fact this pact merely delayed a much larger conflict.

The fate of much of Europe came to rest on the career of a Corsican artillery officer in the French Army. Napoleon Bonaparte became both the scourge of Europe and one of the world's greatest military minds. Bonaparte's tactical brilliance led to his rapid rise up the ranks. In 1796 his career was given the focus it needed when he was appointed as commander of the Army of Italy. This period was known as the 1st Coalition in which Austria, Sardinia, Naples, Prussia, Spain and Great Britain attempted to restore Bourbon rule. These allegiances would alter and change as the war progressed.

Success in Italy led to Napoleon becoming the most popular of the members of the Directory, Frances ruling government, and he used his influence in an ill fated invasion of Egypt. The first coalition eventually collapsed as Spain declared war on Britain following a deal with France and peace between France and Austria was signed at Campio Formio in October 1797.

Napoleon's initial successes in Egypt, defeating the Mamelukes at the Battle of the Pyramids, lead to a 2nd Coalition being formed with Russia, Portugal, the Ottoman Empire and the Papal States joining the remaining allies to oppose the seemingly unstoppable French armies that now controlled much of southern Europe. The decisive Battle of the Nile, commanded by Admiral Nelson, resulted in Napoleon's Egyptian forces being left without a viable supply chain and he returned hastily to France whereupon he overthrew the Directorate governing France and created a Consulate with him as First Consul a position he declared his for life in 1802.

When Napoleon abolished the consulate and declared himself Emperor in 1804 a third coalition was launched against France and her ally Spain. This stage of the conflict threatened Great Britain with invasion until Nelson destroyed the joint French/Spanish fleet at Trafalgar in 1805. The third coalition collapsed when Austria was defeated at Ulm and a joint Austrian/Russian army was crushed at Austerlitz. It was beginning to look as if the war would continue in stalemate until the following year when Prussia, Russia, Saxony, Sweden and Great Britain created a 4th coalition. This coalition lasted barely a year with Napoleon consolidating gains in Saxony and Bavaria. Two decisive victories against Prussia at Jena and Auerstadt on the 14th October 1806 knocked Prussia out of the war.

Turning on Russia Napoleon fought them to a standstill at Eylau and then defeated them at Friedland forcing a peace at Tilsit in July 1807. Fearful that French advances might secure a Danish Fleet in Copenhagen and therefore be free to invade Great Britain the British Army attacked and destroyed the fleet inevitably drawing the Danes into an alliance with France. This was the first major engagement of land forces by the British in all of the coalitions thus far but this was about to change dramatically.

It was becoming apparent that Great Britain could not win the war by just financing the allies and engaging France at sea with her Navy. Years of essentially fruitless proxy coalition warfare and Napoleons attempt to strangle Britain's economy with a continental system meant that definitive action on the ground was needed. Napoleon had skillfully engineered the removal of the Spanish throne from Charles IV, and had installed his brother Joseph in his place. The British Government reasoned that this was a good place to challenge Napoleon who up until now had been focused on the threats of Austria, Prussia and Russia in the east. It was decided to make a stand on the Iberian

FIGURE 9- THE REGIMENT IN SPAIN

Peninsula and stretch Napoleons forces as much as possible, protecting Portugal and liberating Spain.

The British army had evolved considerably since the last major European conflict. Regiments generally had one battalion made up of 10 companies of 120 men each, giving a total field strength of 1200 men. One company was designated a grenadier company but they no longer carried grenades. A second company was designated as a light company. Their role was to act as light infantry and to be able to operate in skirmish order. So successful were the light infantry that the 95th Regiment became exclusively a skirmishing unit, adopted a green uniform and were issued with Baker rifles.

Privates were issued with 'Brown Bess' muskets. Brown Bess muskets had been the workhorse of the British army since they were developed in 1722 and were only replaced in 1838. They were flintlock muskets using paper cartridge ammunition. The British soldier became highly trained in its use and a well drilled battalion could fire 3-4 shots per minute as opposed to the standard 1-2. British tactics also differed from the French in that they deployed in thin lines to present as many muskets at the enemy as possible. The French preferred to advance in column. Columns maneuvered slightly better and had the advantage of looking intimidating bringing a lot of men to bear in one area; they however only presented a small number of guns to the enemy. These two styles would challenge each other throughout the Napoleonic Wars.

THE BATTLE OF ROLICA

The Portuguese royal family and government had fled to Brazil in January 1808 to avoid the French occupation that was commanded by one of Napoleons most trusted generals, Marshal Junot. Whilst Junot secured Portugal, Napoleons brother-in-Law General Murat secured Spain. In August 1808 a plan developed by Sir Arthur Wellesley (Later the Duke of Wellington) to land in Portugal was agreed. Wellesley was a respected officer at this time having led British troops to great success across India however he had yet to face a European army on European soil, this perceived lack of experience gave Horse Guards (British Military Command) pause for thought and the command of the expedition was given not to Wellesley but to three other Generals. Wellesley was granted interim

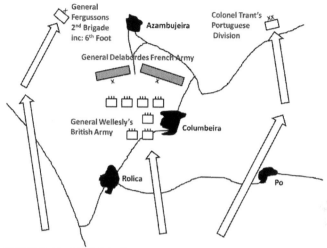

FIGURE 10- THE BATTLE OF ROLICA

command until theses Generals could arrive however.

The 6th Foot were currently in Gibraltar, a tenuous but strategic location for the British and a territorial gain from the War of Spanish Succession. In 1804 as part of further army reforms a 2nd battalion was added to the regiment. These 2nd battalions often remained in Britain and acted as a constant point from which to recruit and train new soldiers that could then be transferred to the 1st battalion on active service.

From Gibraltar the 6th Foot were swiftly moved to Cadiz on the *Amphian* where General Brent Spencer assembled a corps of infantry that moved to the banks of the Mondego River. The regiment was joined to the 32nd Foot as part of the 4th Brigade under the command of Brigadier-General Foord Bowes. The regiment was now at maximum strength fielding some 1,063 men with Sir George Nugent as Colonel in Chief of the regiment. Spencer's corps joined the main army at Leira in western Portugal and moved south through Obidos and Torres Vedras.

General Junot in command of the French army was not idle. Whilst the British moved her armies Junot marshaled his own forces in Lisbon and prepared to expel the British quickly. The 1st Division of the Army of Portugal led by General de Brigade Delaborde stood in the path of Wellesley's mixed British and Portuguese force. Delaborde waited at Obidos for General Loison with a further 9,000 men but Wellesley realised the danger of allowing the French to concentrate their superior forces and so advanced swiftly to defeat them in detail. Delaborde instead of meeting the British retreated into a more secure position in the mountains and waited for Loison.

The two forces met finally in battle at Rolica on 17th August 1808. Wellesley fielded 4,000 men against General Delaborde's 3,000. Wellesley advanced his force in three columns. Bowes Brigade containing the Sixth was on the left with General Fergusson's Brigade and six guns. Delaborde, aware that Wellesley threatened to catch him in a pincer opened up with his artillery in a hope that the fire would break up the advance. He was met by return fire from the British artillery. The pincer maneuver failed as Delaborde withdrew once more, taking up position in a stronger location on the steep hills south of Rolica. Trant's Portuguese Brigade and Fergusson's 2nd Brigade pressed Delaborde's flanks whilst artillery fire continued to be poured upon the French lines.

A mistake by Colonel Lake of the 29th Foot nearly spelled doom for the British advance when four companies were led up a gully into the French centre. Originally intended as a diversion, Lake pushed hard into a Swiss regiment. They took heavy losses including Lake himself who had galloped to the front to steady the line. Reinforcements by the 9th Foot quelled a rout but steady French fire kept them pinned down and slowed the whole British centre. It was only Fergusson's move around the hill threatening Delaborde's flank that caused the French to retreat and that liberated these trapped troops.

Rolica was a significant affair. It proved firstly that Wellesley could command an army in a European theatre of war, that British and Portuguese troops could work together and that the French could be beaten. A defeat here would have unsettled Horse Guards and may have resulted in a withdrawal from Portugal. Instead Wellesley was able to push the French back, bring up his own forces and meet Marshal Junot's full army four days later at Vimeiro.

By now Sir Harry Burrard had been made commanding officer of the expedition supported by Generals Moore and Dalrymple, both of whom were senior to Wellesley. Stuck however on the coast Wellesley commanded the forces at the Battle of Vimeiro. The Sixth were not heavily engaged in the fighting and took only light casualties at Rolica (only 3 men wounded) and were placed in support again at Vimeiro. This battle saw Wellesley defeat Junot in bitter house to house fighting and a costly cavalry charge. Eager to pursue and truly break the French army Wellelsley was forced to cede command to Burrard and Dalyrmplye who arrived as the battle came to a close. Burrard was a cautious commander and was happy to sit with the victory and didn't force a pursuit. Burrard and Dalrymple were best known for their next action, the Convention of Cintra.

The Convention of Cintra was enabled to accept the complete capitulation of Junot and his Army of Portugal. Whilst an obvious success a mistake was made in allowing the French army to march out of Lisbon fully armed with their plunder and even assigning the Royal Navy to ferry them back to France. Instead of robbing Napoleon of an army Burrard and Dalrymple had merely allowed it to escape. Outrage back in Britain led to all three commanders, Burrard, Dalrymple and Wellesley being recalled to a board of enquiry. All three were ultimately cleared but both Burrard and Dalrymple were forced into retirement. Wellesley who had opposed the convention however was returned to active duty.

THE ESCAPE FROM CORUNNA

With winter approaching General Sir John Moore, the only remaining senior General after the disciplining of Burrard and Dalrymple, consolidated his forces. At first the Sixth Foot were garrisoned in Almeida before being brigaded under the command of General Beresford in Fraser's Division. It was at this time that they failed to impress Moore who commented that they were in a disgraceful state!

Moore was caught in a dilemma between pressing the advantage and not over exposing himself. Spain was originally an ally of France but Napoleon had been able to manoeuvre the removal of the King of Spain in June, replacing him with his brother Joseph Bonaparte. This

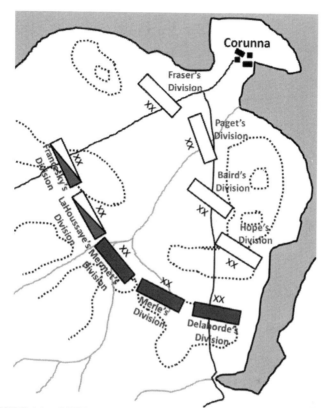

FIGURE 11 – DEFENDING THE RETREAT FROM CORUNNA

action caused many Spanish nobles to rise up against France and indeed some Spanish troops in French service left their posts to return to Spain. One such unit was the Marques of La Romana whose division left Denmark on Royal Navy vessels returning to Santander.

The Spanish uprising forced Joseph to abandon Madrid but reinforcement by Marshal Soult's army moved to reinstate him. This state of affairs suggested to Moore that Spain could be taken and held. La Romana's Spanish division

103

landed on the 23rd October and were perhaps the only soldiers of any quality still remaining in the Spanish army. Sir John Moore contemplated moving north to Corunna and sending General Hope south back to Portugal but was reassured by La Romana rallying more Spanish troops every day that an attempt must be made to defend Madrid.

During November Moore moved his forces into Spain to Salamanca and it began to look like Soult really was vulnerable and a small cavalry victory at Sahagun was encouraging, however a number of Spanish failures and the fall of Madrid soon reversed this. Joseph was reinstalled on the Spanish throne and Soult now reinforced by other armies including Junot's now fielded 80,000 men to Moore's just 25,000. Fearing being cut off from Portugal Moore began a retreat, deciding to lead his men north to the port of Corunna for evacuation.

The Sixth Foot as part of Fraser's Division moved up through Maygora, Benevente, and Astorga before arriving at Corunna in good order. Many of the regiment along with the heavy cavalry were evacuated immediately arriving back in Kent some 491 men strong. The rest of the army fared less well. Moore fought a holding action at Monte Mero to give the evacuation time in the face of Soult's advance. On the 16th January the French attacked the British line en masse supported by heavy artillery fire. Struggling to hold the line Moore brought in his reserves.

At the height of the battle Moore was struck in the chest by a cannon ball and mortally wounded, command was passed to General Baird but he too was wounded and so finally General Hope took over. By now the battle had become just an artillery duel. Soult's army pulled back slightly to reform giving the British time to board their ships and escape. Moore lived just long enough to see this success before succumbing to his wounds. So impressed was Soult with Sir John Moore that he ordered a monument built on the spot where he died to commemorate him.

Not all of the Sixth Foot made it safely back to England. Three officers and 94 men were left in Portugal and 343 were stranded in Spain, some of these were split up and distributed to other regiments one even fought at the famous Battle of Talavera where an Eagle was taken.

EXPEDITION TO WALCHEREN

Whilst the British Army licked its wounds from its push from Spain it was already planning its next front. Britain was always reluctant to engage its ground forces preferring to support the war financially with her allies and by using her navy. A way she could keep up the pressure was through a series of expeditions to stretch and press the French. This tactic had worked well in South Africa and Jakarta but less well in Buenos Ares.

Walcheren was to be the next such expedition. Led by Lord Chatham the plan was to land on a series of islands on the Dutch coast with an aim to distracting troops away from an Austrian advance on the continent along the Danube and to seize a French fleet suspected to be at anchor at Flushing.

The whole expedition was a disaster from start to finish. By the time the 39,000 men landed on the 31st July 1809 not only had Austria been defeated by Napoleon at the Battle of Wagram and forced in to a peace treaty but the French fleet had been moved to Antwerp. The Sixth Foot led by Colonel Murray were brigaded with General William Dyott in the Marquis of Huntley's 2nd Division. The 2nd Division along with the Light Division and the Reserve Division were landed on South Beveland Island.

The disaster apart from the poor timing was not a result of pressing enemy action in fact only 106 men died in combat during the whole expedition; in this case, like the Sixths earlier missions in the West Indies, it came in the form of disease. What became known as Walcheren fever struck the troops with a brutal ferocity. Private Benjamin Harris of the 95th Regiment commented that '...strong and fine young men who had been but a short time in the service seemed suddenly reduced in strength to infants, unable to stand upright!'. Walcheren Fever was probably a mixture of diseases including typhoid, typhus, malaria and dysentery. 4,000 men died in the four months up until the eventual withdrawal in December. The Sixth had arrived in Walcheren with 967 soldiers but left on the *Prosperity* with only 93 fit for duty. Disease followed the army back to England and there continued to spread infecting over 11,000 men weakening them substantially, in fact Wellington now back in Portugal and Spain requested that no unit from Walcheren be sent to him for fear that the disease would spread to his own forces.

THE BATTLE OF VITORIA

The Sixth Foot spent the next two years on relatively light duties as they recruited troops to bring them back to full strength. With Lieutenant-Colonel Murray ill Major Carnie took command in Ireland before in 1812 Lieutenant-Colonel Archibald Campbell arrived and led the regiment back to Spain via the site of their escape at Corunna arriving on the 28th October 1812.

On arrival the regiment, now 1169 men strong, was assigned to Lieutenant-General Dalhousie's 7th Division and brigaded with the 2nd Battalion of the 24th Foot (the 2nd Warwickshire's), 2nd Battalion of the 58th Foot and a battalion of Brunswick Oels (German soldiers). The brigade was commanded by Major-General Barnes a soldier Wellesley regarded well and who went on to become the governor of Ceylon. The 7th Division moved swiftly through Spain from Villasexmir to Apricano in just a few weeks.

Wellesley's forces had done well in Spain, he had pushed the French back at Salamanca and forced the French to evacuate Madrid. Initially in this position of strength Wellesley under estimated the French forces and so began to pull back to Salamanca and then Ciudad de Rodrigo. He spent the winter reorganising his army forming a force of 53,000 British, 39,000 Spanish and 27,000 Portuguese soldiers. They managed to outflank Marshal Jourdan and pursued them to Burgos. Wellesley pushed hard to cut the French off from the road to France. King Joseph I and Marshal Jourdan found themselves in constant retreat and decided to make a stand at Vitoria.

Vitoria was a village on the Zadorra River. Marshal Jourdan planned to use the river as part of his defence and was relying on the arrival of 15,000 men led by Marshal Clausel to bolster his 57,000 man strength and 80 guns.

Illness however on the day before battle restricted their final disposition.

Wellesley approached the town with some caution camping nearby before launching an attack on the 21st June 1813. He formed his men in to three columns. General Hill led the right column along the south bank of the river to force them back whilst Generals Cole and Picton led the centre column to move along the north bank of the Zadorra to outflank the French right. General Graham's left column was sent around the Monte Arrato to cut off the French retreat. Dalhousie with the 7th Division including the Sixth Foot was tasked with crossing the Monte Arrato and to strike east linking with Wellesley.

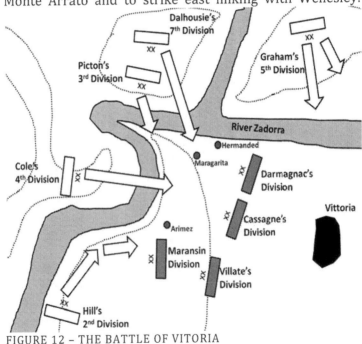

FIGURE 12 – THE BATTLE OF VITORIA

Under heavy rain the 6th Foot left their camp on the River Baya and took up their positions. The battle started well, with Hill taking the south of the valley by 8.30 am and at 10.30 am Graham's troops were well into the fighting on the north bank. Kempt's Brigade of the Light Division with Picton's 3rd Division crossed the south side of the river and forced the Comte D'Erlon, the commander of the Army of the Centre to retreat. The 6th Foot as part of the rearguard advanced behind Picton's division and were engaged at the villages of Maragarita and Hermanded held by elements of Darmagnac's and Cassagne's divisions.

By 5 pm the French line looked as if it was on the brink of collapse nearly across the whole battlefield. To make matters worse Clausel's reinforcements' were cut off. Cole's 4th Division advanced on Major-General Gazan of the Army of the South, and as they were pushed back, a gap began to appear. Gazan refused to close up to D'Erlon and seal the gap, instead he moved for a complete withdrawal. Safely at the rear Joseph Bonaparte, King of Spain realised with growing alarm that things were lost and he ordered a full retreat. Instead of a careful strategic withdrawal this retreat became a rout.

Over 150 guns and the French baggage train were captured, only a timely intervention rear guard action by General Reille's Army of Portugal saved the entire French army from disaster. Even so the allies captured precious artworks, silverware and valuables from the baggage train along with 400 wagons containing ammunition. This baggage train was pillaged by the common soldiery appalling Wellington by the lack of discipline, he was quoted as saying 'We have in the service the scum of the earth of common soldiers'. He would later, however, praises these 'scum' as being the reason he was able to beat the French and enjoyed a close relationship with many of them. The 6ᵗʰ Foot themselves received praise, Lieutenant-Colonel Archibald Campbell was awarded a gold medal and the regiment were given the right to place the battle honour of Vitoria on their colours.

This victory at Vitoria turned the tide of the war in the Peninsular from now on France would be on the back foot and on a constant retreat back to the French border. Success in Spain was not just due to Wellesley and the allied forces. Much of Napoleons focus was still on recovering from the disastrous fiasco in the invasion of Russia the previous year. Now defeated on his western border as well as in the east Napoleon found himself in a precarious position.

BATTLE OF THE PYRENEES

The war in the peninsular was slowly drawing to a close. Portugal was safe, Madrid liberated and the French thrown back to their own borders. Marshal Soult was not however prepared to given in just yet. He gathered his army and prepared a defence and counter attack from defensive positions in the Pyrenees Mountains.

Wellesley aware that only a final push was needed realised he needed a supply port to support any further actions so far from his bases in Portugal. He moved north to secure the port town of San Sebastian. Here a cautious siege by Lieutenant-General Thomas Graham with elements with the 1ˢᵗ and 5ᵗʰ Divisions failed to breach the

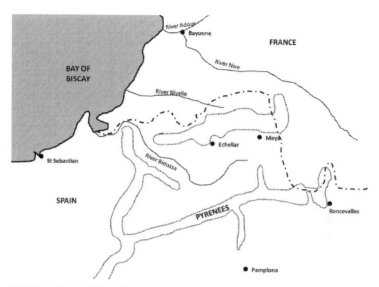

FIGURE 13- SITES OF THE BATTLE OF THE PYRENEES

walls defended by Brigadier-General Louis Rey. Even a personal assault led by Wellesley on the 25th July failed to budge the defenders and Wellesley withdrew the siege allowing Marshal Soult to reinforce the town. Success eventually came in Pamplona where the Spanish Army of the Reserve of Andalusia breached the walls and secured the only surviving French garrison on the Spanish side of the mountains.

With Marshal Soult preparing a counter attack Wellesley arranged his army into a series of defensive positions. The defence was made more difficult by the fact that the front ran for 50 miles in very hilly difficult terrain. Soult faced Wellesley directly whilst Marshal Suchet led a second French army from the south east. Wellesley expected Soult to try and relieve the siege at San Sebastian in the west; instead Soult pressed his attack in the east focusing on two key passes through the mountains at Maya and Roncesvalles.

Lord Dalhousie's 7th Division were given the Heights of Echalar in the mountains to hold in the centre of the line. On 25th July the French began their attack. D'Erlon broke through the 2nd Division holding the Maya Pass and began to move behind British lines. By 3 pm the British were on the verge of disaster after attempts to retake the pass failed. Major-General Edward Barnes leading the 6th Foot, a company of Brunswick Oels and one battery of Portuguese Foot Artillery came down from the Heights to steady the defence. They hit General Maransin's Division on D'Erlon's flank hard. The action slowed the Frenchmen who, no doubt aware of more of the 7th Division on the hill, opted to become more cautious in their attack. In this action Major Henry Gomm of the 6th Foot was killed along with 2 other men and 19 men were wounded. Their losses did not go unnoticed, Wellington on receiving news that Major-General Barnes had held the heights of Echelar wrote 'Major-General Barnes' brigade... [advanced] with a regularity and gallantry which I have seldom seen equaled, and actually drove two divisions of the enemy, notwithstanding the resistance opposed to them, from those formidable heights'.

Elsewhere along the line Cole's Division of 13,000 men held Roncesvalles pass against 40,000 French led by Generals Reille and Clausel. As the day drew to a close despite being reinforced by General Picton Cole decided to retreat to a better position at Saracen just north of Pamplona.

Wellesley having initially held the line realised that he couldn't continue to hold with Cole's hole in the defence and joined him at Sorauen. Wellesley positioned his 20,000 men on a steep ridge south east of the village with Soult setting up on the opposite ridge with 35,000 men. Here the 7th Division were positioned on the far left with the 6th Foot brigaded with the 2nd/24th and the 2nd/58th.

The defensive line took time to form and a storm on the 27th July delayed General Pack's 6th Division's arrival until the following day. As Pack arrived the battle was just starting and he began to engage the enemy right away. General Soult threw five divisions against General Cole on the ridge but concerted musket fire managed to hold them back.

As eluded to before British tactics varied greatly from the French. The French with larger battalions preferred to march at the enemy as a block of troops in column. Whilst very imposing it gave only a very narrow front from which to fire, the British on the other hand deployed in a thin line up to 3 ranks deep. This allowed them to bring many more muskets to bear. With rolling fire and good discipline a British battalion could hold off forces many times its number. This tactic saved British forces on many occasions and again that day.

In the east a Spanish Army led by General Morillo was driven back but the French brigades advance was halted by the 1st Battalion of the 40th Foot. The pace of battle began to stall and soon became an artillery duel with minor skirmishes, skirmishes that on the 30th July were to wound 6 men of the 6th Foot.

Doubtful that he would be able to break through and without support from D'Erlon from Maya Marshal Soult fell back. This retreat became very disorganised.

Meanwhile in the north Wellesley reinstated the siege of San Sebastian and on the 8th August Wellesley finally achieved success. A Portuguese brigade was beaten back along the river but a breach was made in the walls. Rey retreated from the town to the fortress and watched as allied troops ransacked the town below. Unable to hold out indefinitely Rey surrendered on the 8th September.

This series of engagements became collectively as the Battle of the Pyrenees and was yet another battle honour awarded the regiment. The engagement at Echalar had proved costly for the 6th Foot. Captain Brownlow, Major Campbell and Lieutenants Everest, Tarleton and Addison were all killed along with 12 other men and 118 were wounded of which 28 died later of their wounds.

These losses however prompted a reorganisation in the regiment Lieutenant-Colonel Campbell had been sent home ill and Major Gomm and been made Brevet Lieutenant-Colonel. When he also died the brevet command passed to Major Campbell and finally to Major Scott. A new interim commanding officer was appointed in the form of Lieutenant-Colonel Gardiner. The division also gained a new commanding officer, General Carlos Le Cor. Le Cor was a distinguished Portuguese soldier who when Portugal was invaded refused to serve in Napoleons armies and fled to Plymouth. He became a brigade commander in Wellesley's Anglo-Portuguese 7th Division. His position as Divisional commander was an acting position before being appointed commander of the

Portuguese Division. At the end of the war Le Cor became the Military Governor of Alentjo and later commanded Portuguese forces in wars in Brazil and Uruguay.

IN TO FRANCE

Spain was now fully liberated and Wellesley was able to prepare for an invasion of France itself. He moved his forces over the Pyrenees towards Bayonne and Marshal Soult's main supply depot. A series of rivers gave Soult a key strategic defensive line. As the British army advanced a number of small engagements took place as local garrisons and the stragglers of Soult's army were caught and dealt with. On the 7th October Wellesley surprised the French by crossing the river Bidossa and closing in on the River Nivelle. The French had strong defences along a long stretch of this river from Finodetta to Fort Soca.

On the 10th November 1813 Wellesley mounted his artillery on Mount Atchubia in the east supported by Generals Hill and Beresford's commands. General Alten's Light Division advanced to take the French forward defences on Greater Rhune including the Moviz plateau. Under the cover of the artillery and with the high ground at Rhune under his control Wellesley ordered all divisions to advance. General Colvilles 3rd Division smashed through the French defences to take the bridge at Amotz thereby securing a crossing point at the heart of Clausel's Division's line of defence and splitting the French army in two.

The 7th division and the 6th Foot were focused on a bridge at St Pe north of the 3rd Division. Like the 3rd Division they were able to storm the redoubts and secure the bridge with little trouble. The regiment crossed the stream and pushed the French column from the ground surrounding the village with only 1 man killed and 6 wounded. Soult's army was now definitively split in two and he had little option but to retreat to the River Nive just outside the city of Bayonne and try and hold there. The 7th Division were held in reserve in this action with the 6th Foot being stationed at Ustaritz and Urcuray receiving welcome reinforcements to bring their strength back to 1080 men.

The battle of Nive would prove to be a stiffer affair than those previously fought as Wellesley now found himself with a much smaller army. During the siege of San Sebastian and the travel through France the Spanish troops in Wellington's army had pillaged widely. Wellesley needed to keep the French citizenry undisturbed and abhorred the common soldier's propensity to rape and plunder after a battle. Whilst he felt could control his own troops he could not rely on his Spanish allies who were eager to wreak revenge on their former French overlords. He sent all but General Morillo's troops back to Spain.

Marshal Soult sensed an opportunity here to defeat Wellesley in detail. He advanced Marshal D'Erlon's division quietly and quickly; and managed to re-take the villages of Anglet and Barouillet. General Hope's Light division was attacked heavily at Arcangues and managed to withstand four attacks by taking up defensive positions inside a church. D'Erlon's attack continued to do well and Wellesley was forced to commit Generals Beresford's and Hill's commands in to the fight. Hill met D'Erlon at the village of St Pierre where a bloody battle ensued. Finely balanced the tide of battle ebbed and flowed often at the point of a bayonet. Luckily repairs to a pontoon bridge at Villefranque allowed the 3rd and 4th British divisions to cross the river and engage the French. Combined with the advance of General Pack's 6th Division from Ustaritz the French were finally broken and Marshal Soult was left with no alternative but to retreat from Bayonne leaving General Thouvenot with 10,000 men to hold the town for as long as possible.

The year 1814 began quietly with little happening over the winter months. In February the 7th Division now under the command of Major-General George T Walker was quartered in Gambourg and was used to drive out French forces at Hastingues before crossing the River Gave to join Wellesley's Army at Orthez.

The battle of Orthez took place on the 27th February 1814 and was the start of a new campaign which would eventually see Wellesley defeating the French at Toulouse in April a defeat that ultimately resulted in total French defeat and the surrender of Napoleon. Taking several days to cross the River Gave Wellesley deployed his forces on hills to the north west of Orthez opposite Marshal Soult's own. Colonel Ross's Brigade of General Cole's 4th Division began the attack by pushing the French out of the village of St Boes, but a counter attack by General Taupuin stopped any further gains. General Picton's 3rd Division attack on Soult's centre held by Marshal Reille was delayed by enemy artillery and quickly the battle became bitter and bloody. The counter attack at St Boes became a vicious house to house fight.

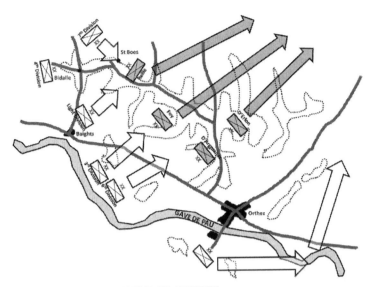

FIGURE 14 – THE BATTLE OF ORTHEZ

Wellesley ordered a general advance along the whole line, keeping the Light Division in reserve. The 7th Division was positioned on the extreme north west of the line, when the 4th division was retired from St Boes they were sent in to replace them. The 7th Division came under heavy fire and during the fight Lieutenant-Colonel Gardiner had his horse shot from under him. They fell badly and Gardiner became trapped beneath the horse. A sergeant of the Sixth and a private ran over to rescue him but musket fire killed the private and hit the sergeant, a musket ball passing through both his hands. Without direct command the regiment could have foundered but Wellesley suddenly came past, he reined in his horse and ordered them 'Sixth, incline to your right'. The regiment complied and when reinforcements in the form of the 52nd Foot arrived they were able to push the enemy from St Boes. The 52nd then took Taupin in the flank causing then to withdraw in panic. This panic spread to a full scale withdrawal of Soult's men to Toulouse. Despite the victory the regiment suffered heavy casualties, the 6th Foot lost 2 officers (Lieutenants Patullo and Scott) and 27 men with a further 10 officers and 114 men being wounded. Again Wellesley was struck by the character of the 6th Foot during the battle he took a silver snuff box engraved with 'Seek Glory' that had been with the regiment since 1785 and scratched on to it the lines 'Huzza for the 6th Regiment Now Keep Glory'.

At the close of the Battle of Orthez the 7th Division were drawn up and held a line from Bazas to Libourn. A returned Lord Dalhousie resumed command of the 7th Division from a wounded Walker. Minor skirmishes during March when they were on detached duties cost the 6th Foot 1 killed, 1 missing and 1 captured. On the 5th April the regiment were part of forces taking the towns of Garonne and Dordogne whilst they remained there Wellesley marched and defeated the French at Toulouse. Lieutenant-Colonel Campbell returned to the regiment from leave around the 10th April and ordered Major J.T Robertson to march the regiment to Bordeaux.

The defeat at Toulouse was the hammer blow to Napoleon and he was forced to surrender and abdicate. Sent into exile on the Isle of Elba many believed the threat to be over but Napoleon would return in 1815 to terrorise the continent once more in what became known as the Hundred Days Campaign. The Sixth Foot had acquitted themselves well in the peninsular proving to Wellesley himself their worth on several occasions. They picked up battle honours for Rolica, Vimerio, Corunna, Vitoria, Pyrenees, Nivelle, Orthez and Peninsula.

CHAPTER 5 - COLONIAL DUTIES

Having left Bordeaux on the 15th May 1814 the 6th foot arrived in Canada at York (later Toronto) in August with an effective strength of 650 men to take part in the War of 1812. The War of 1812 was in many ways an extension of the Napoleonic Wars and in some ways a second round of the War of Independence.

During the Napoleonic conflicts in Europe the United States were essentially neutral preferring to remain outside of the distant conflict, they did however resent the power the British still held in the Americas. Britain retained colonies in Canada and across the Caribbean and dominated trade across the Atlantic.

In 1807 the first spark of war was lit. Searching for deserters along the coast of Virginia the HMS *Leopard* approached the USS *Chesapeake* and demanded she stand to and be inspected. Commodore James Barron, captain of the *Chesapeake* refused; she was in US waters and did not recognise British authority. Angered and assured of their dominance at sea Captain Salusbury Pryce Humprheys ordered the *Leopard* to open fire, killing 21 men aboard the US vessel. The *Chesapeake* quickly surrendered after firing a face saving shot at the *Leopard*. When boarded the crew of the *Leopard* found four Royal Navy deserters. Of these deserters one was British and was hanged, the other three were American. They were given 500 lashes which were commuted and offered repatriation to America. The seizure of a US ship in US waters by what they Americans saw as an arrogant Royal Navy pursuing American seaman angered the Senate and nearly started the war there and then.

Over the next few years' tensions ratcheted up as annoyance over trade and sailor's rights continued to build. Many in the US government wanted to assert America's strength and stop suspected aid being given to natives such as Shawnee Chief Tecumseh by the British. President Madison wanted to remove trade competition and looked hungrily at British territories in Upper Canada.

In June 1812 war was declared and an invasion of Upper Canada was mounted. It was an opportune time, Britain was mostly distracted by the war in Spain and Napoleons advance through Eastern Europe. British garrisons were mostly in Montreal and Quebec and Major-General Issac Brook had only 1,600 regular British soldiers under his command.

Much of the fighting took place at sea, on the lakes and in the Niagara River region. A lot of maneuvering by the British soldiers and Canadian militia quickly showed that America would not be able to seize Canada as easily as they had first thought, instead in 1814 they changed their tactics and decided to push as hard as they could to give themselves a favourable position for the inevitable peace negotiations. This push was focused on Lake Erie.

FIGURE 15- THE NIAGARA CAMPAIGN

THE NIAGARA CAMPAIGN

In early July two armies crossed the border from America in to Canada. One crossed the Niagara River from Buffalo whilst the other sailed north from Detroit to retake MacKinac. On 3rd July Major-General Jacob Brown led 5,000 men and 600 Indian warriors against the British Fort Erie garrisoned by just 170 men who surrendered quickly. Major-General Phineas Riall commander of the British army heard of the new offensive and moved his own forces to Chippewa. Here on the 4th July a brigade of Brown's army encountered them. Outnumbered they pulled back and awaited Brown to reinforce them. So on the next day General Browns 3,500 men fell upon Rialls 2,500 who were mostly composed of Light Infantry and

123

native allies. In a classic line battle common to European battlefields Riall was defeated with 600 killed or wounded.

Despite a significant victory Brown was cautious and felt he didn't have the troops necessary to press forward much more and instead he fell back to south Chippewa whilst Riall fell back to Forts George and Niagara and the still under construction Fort Mississauga.

Reinforced General Riall marched his men out to meet Brown once again. At dusk on the 24th July the British set up their lines at Lundy's Lane near Niagara Falls. The battle the following day ended in stalemate with 2,800 US soldiers opposing 3,500 British soldiers and native allies, although Riall himself was captured. On the 26th July both sides pulled back with Brown leading the US troops back to Fort Erie where he strengthen the defences and set up entrenchments.

Following these tit for tat battles Lieutenant-General Drummond assumed command of the British army on the Niagara Peninsular and marched directly on Fort Erie and blockaded it. On the 14th August Drummond attempted a surprise attack on the fort that failed spectacularly. This defeat combined with poor supply routes and sickness prompted Drummond to abandon the siege briefly to wait on reinforcements. These reinforcements took the form of a reserve brigade comprised of the 6th Foot and 82nd Foot, both now veteran units. Their arrival did much to bolster the forces at the siege. Arriving on the 24th August the 6th Foot were immediately set to piquet duty. Day to day running of the siege had now passed to Major-General Louis de Watteville, a Swiss national in the British army. A chance shot on the 29th August wounded the commander of the fort – General Gaise forcing Brigadier-General Ripley to take over.

On the 31st August Watteville was preparing for a daylight assault and that night the 6th Foot volunteered to set up a fourth battery to support any attacks. On the 4th September Porter's Brigade of New York Volunteers and Pennsylvania militia attacked Battery number 2. These sorties and small attacks served to keep the British off balance and exasperate their supply problems. To respond to these sorties the British pushed back at the American piquet's. First the 6th Foot under the command of Captain R. Pattison set up a strong piquet and then on the 7th September a company of the 6th Foot with the Glengarry Light infantry successfully surprised an American piquet on the Bank's road.

Finally on the 17th September a decisive action took place. With Drummond preparing to abandon the siege the Americans led a strong sortie from the fort. Porter's Brigade managed to surprise Watteville's own regiment. A regiment composed of mostly Swiss, German and other nationals it had been set up by Watteville himself but had a low reputation, with a high desertion rate. At the same time Brigadier-General Miller led several US detachments to attack the British centre and MacArthur with 1500 men raided along the banks of Lake Erie with the intention of destroying supplies that the British and their native allies may have needed. The attack went well with six siege guns being spiked. Drummond launched a counter attack with the 82nd Foot led by Major Proctor with three companies 6th Foot under command of Major Taylor to recapture Battery 2. This action went well with Lieutenant-General

Drummond expressing his '...admiration, and [to] entitle those troops to his particular thanks'. Even though three of the four batteries were successfully recaptured 600 men were killed or wounded including Captain R. Pattison and 17 men of the 6th, a further 14 would die of their wounds. Drummond continued with his retreat. The 6th Foot and the field artillery were withdrawn to Chippewa eventually holding a position at the bridge on the 8th October.

On the 21st October the US advanced once more on the British heading for the fortifications and troops established at Chippewa. Drummond decided to meet force with force and advanced his whole army with the 6th Foot brigaded with Watteville. The advance paused however on the 23rd when seeing the strength opposing them the Americans had withdrawn. Having failed against British detachments at Cook's Mill and news reaching them of the loss of naval superiority on Lake Erie meant that to continue in the Niagara region was too risky for the American forces to consider. This was to be the last action of the 6th Foot in the War of 1812. The Americans blew up the fort in November and returned to Buffalo. Peace came with the Treaty of Ghent in December with the regiment remaining in Chippewa until May 1815.

GUARD DUTY

May 1815 was an important time for Europe. In February Napoleon had escaped from his exile on the Island of Elba and landed back in France rallying his armies to him. Many of Britain's regiments were abroad and her allies in Austria and Prussia caught unprepared. In what became known as the Hundred Days Napoleon pulled together his forces and moved north to challenge Wellesley's Army (now the Duke of Wellington) and the approaching Prussian Army led by Blucher. He hoped to destroy each in turn stopping them from combining to face him. The 6th Foot in Canada were quickly embarked on ships and returned to Europe. On the 18th June 1815 Napoleon was defeated by Wellington and Blucher at Waterloo. The 6th Foot arrived in Ostend on the 1st July at a time when the remains of Napoleons troops were being finally mopped up. They joined Wellingtons Army who by now was advancing on Paris. On the 15th July Napoleon surrendered to the *Bellerophon*. Wellington and his allies secured Paris with the 6th Foot being stationed in the northern suburbs of St Denis and Ecouen where they remained until February 1816 when they moved to the Pas-de-Calais. In October 1818 they returned to Britain with their companies assigned to various garrisons in Stirling, Aberdeen, Berwick, Leeds and Halifax with headquarters in Edinburgh.

OUT TO THE FRONTIERS

Having missed Napoleons defeat at Waterloo it looked as if the 6th Foot may have been able to see the great General when they were assigned to guard duty on Napoleon's prison island of St Helena in the Atlantic west of Africa. Unfortunately on the 5th May 1821 Napoleon Bonaparte died and so the regiment were re-routed to the Cape.

The Cape, originally a Dutch colony seized by the French had become British territory as a part of settlements made at the conclusion of the Napoleonic Wars in 1814. South

Africa was fast becoming the fiercest frontier of the British Empire and the 6th Foot were entering an area of long term disquiet. Since 1779 the Dutch and following colonialists had been engaged in a boundary dispute with the Xhosa, a local tribe living to the north and north east of the Cape. This had broken out in four wars before even the British took over control. A fifth war where the British intervened in a dispute between the colonists and the Xhosa over cattle thefts had ended only in 1819 with the Xhosa having their borders pushed back to the Keiskanna River.

It was against this backdrop that the 582 men of the 6th Foot arrived in Africa. Two companies were immediately despatched to garrison the frontier at Fort Wilshire and Fort Beaufort. In 1823 Lieutenant-Colonel Mark Napier arrived as the regiment's new commanding officer. Over the next few years the regiment maintained companies right across the colony and was inspected by General Lord Charles Somerset the Governor-General of the Colony in 1825.

In March 1825 the regiment were transferred to Britain's other great colonial interest, India. Britain's interest in this vast country had begun a hundred years earlier. Throughout the European wars of the 18th century India had been fought over by the Dutch, French and British. Britain's interest in the continent was provided by the East India Company, a trading conglomerate that managed their own armed forces to secure trade. Initially the Company traded with local kings known as Raj's and set up a network of alliances. As other empires began to vie for control and some rulers resisted the ideas of the

Company peaceful trade gave way to armed aggression. A series of wars and clever actions in which one Princely State was played off against another resulted in the British establishing a wide range of protectorates and allied states across the country. The Company often acted unilaterally with the British Government having to step in to assist or smooth the way. The British saw themselves as bringing a kind of enlightenment to India and in some ways respected the religious freedoms of its peoples. In most cases the British preferred to allow native rulers to rule where possible as long as they were loyal to the crown, something the long and proud history of the Princely States didn't always allow.

The 6ᵗʰ Foot arrived in Kutch one of the Princely States that had become a British protectorate in 1815 and were stationed in the capital Bhooj. In 1826 they transferred to Bombay and the barracks in Colaba before in 1830 they were sent to Akkalkot where an uprising was taking place.

Akkalkot was a part of the Satara Raj that had been brought into the Bombay Presidency after the Third Anglo-Maratha War, a war that had brought the huge Maratha Confederacy under British dominion. A dispute over the governance of Satara prompted an uprising by the local watanadar's and inamdar's (landowners) who seized the town and fort of Akkalkot.

The 6ᵗʰ Foot were brigaded with the 21ˢᵗ Regiment of Siphees, a local regiment of Hindustani Sepoys and the Bombay European Regiment (a regiment of the East India Company). Command of the brigade was given to the colonel of the 6ᵗʰ Foot, Lieutenant-Colonel Scott with Major Algeo taking his role in the regiment. The brigade took part in the storming of Akkalkot in which Lieutenant Crofton and Sergeant-Major Sowrey were praised for their bravery. Whilst losses in action were minimal losses from disease were high. In the first six months one officer and sixty-nine men died and a further forty-one were invalided out. In 1828 during the monsoons an outbreak of cholera killed 2 officers and 121 men with a further 62 invalided out. In the following year the regiment moved to a more healthy location in Poona. In 1832 King William IV conferred on the regiment the title of the 6th Foot, Royal First Warwickshire Regiment and changed their uniform from yellow facings to blue.

The 6th Foot remained in India until 1841 performing many garrison duties across western India and working closely with the native sepoy regiments. In 1841 the regiment now under the command of Lieutenant-Colonel Gascoyne were briefly despatched to Aden. Aden had been ceded to the East India Company in 1838 by Sultan Muhsin bin Fadl and was occupied by the 102nd Foot (Bombay Fusiliers) and a battalion of Bombay natives. Local Arab tribes however disapproved of this hand over and massed several times outside the city. The 6th Foot were used to disperse them. The following year the regiment returned to Britain but in later years it would return to both India and Aden.

THE 7TH XHOSA WAR

Much of the 6th Foots deployment in the first half of the 19th Century seemed to be concerned with quelling uprisings and maintaining garrisons. After 2 years garrisoning Fort Garrey, now Winnipeg in Canada the first battalion was deployed back to Africa. They arrived during the 6th Xhosa War (War of the Axe). The war was sparked between two local tribes the Xhosa and the Khoi Khoi. It began when a Khoi Khoi transporting a Xhosa accused of stealing an axe to Grahamstown was killed by a Xhosa rescue party. Sandile one of the chiefs of the Xhosa refused to surrender the murderers and General Somerset led an expedition over the Kei River including the 6th Foot. The war was short-lived with Somerset successfully defeating the Xhosa on the banks of the Gwangu near Fort Peddie. The result however was the annexation of more Xhosa land from the Keiskamma to the Upper Kei river. Sir Harry Smith proclaimed the region as British Kaffraia Colony and established a capital named after the king called King's William's Town.

It was in King's William's Town in 1850 that the Sixth foot led by Captain J.E Robertson was part of a force under the command of Colonel MacKinnon that was despatched from Fort Cox to arrest Chief Sandile. The column however was ambushed in the Boombah Pass, Lieutenant Catty was wounded and 10 men were killed. The column managed to fight its way through to Keiskamma Hoek where 68 men of the 6th led by Captain Manseragh were ordered to hold Fort White.

In early 1851 the Xhosa were beginning to show signs of unrest and mutinies in both the Kaffir Police and the Cape Mounted Police added to the general instability of the region. Sir Harry Smith, the governor of the colony had only four regiments and the local police to cover an area twice the size of Britain. Many homesteaders evacuated the area between Grahamstown and the Orange River aware that it was unlikely that the army could protect them. A series of attacks on British columns and Forts, including an attack on the 6th Foot in Fort White, ratcheted up the tension with up to 20,000 well armed Xhosa holing themselves up in the Amatola Mountains to the north.

Through March and well into May Harry Smith assembled 9,000 troops of which only 3,000 were regular soldiers and split them into 4 columns to harass the Xhosa in relentless skirmishes. This action suited the Xhosa who were able to mount a series of actions against the colonial forces and then melt back into the mountains.

During May a detachment of the Sixth led by Captain Crowder garrisoned Fort White. In July Smith began a series of attacks in the Waterkloof region in the north of the colony. These skirmishes did little to resolve the affair failing to force the Xhosa into a pitched battle where greater military discipline could crush them. Day by day the Xhosa became more and more daring and aggressive raiding along the length of the Kroome mountains spread to Blinkwater, Waterkloof and between the Great Fish and Keiskamma Rivers.

By October Smith had now organised a more effective force of 6,000 regular soldiers which included 9 regiments of foot, the 12th Lancers, Cape Rifles and detachments of the Royal Engineers and Artillery. Led by Captain Manseragh the Sixth Foot were brigaded with Colonel Michael's brigade. The plan was to use the infantry to herd the Xhosa into the path of the artillery that could then destroy them en masse. The plan worked quite well with the Xhosa being cleared from Waterkloof by November although Lieutenant Norris from the Sixth was one of those killed by the Xhosa. Fighting in Africa was remarkably tough, the heat and dust proved as much of a danger as the Xhosa and fever affected the British columns heavily. Thick scrub and jungle slowed any advances to a slow crawl and eventually the forces were returned to the garrisons with the Sixth Foot being sent to Fort Beaufort.

The British and the Xhosa now took part in burning of crops and kraals to deny each other the use of food and supplies. The Sixth Foot took part in attacks in Waterkloof and Blinkwater during which Lieutenant Armitage was killed. On the 10th March 1852 the Xhosa were finally turned back. Holed up again in the Waterkloof Smith attacked the Xhosa using three columns of troops from three different directions. Once pinned the artillery was brought up to shell them. The Xhosa however were both strong and fast and entrenched themselves in a natural rock citadel requiring an infantry attack to dislodge them.

Once rooted out of the rocks they were hunted down by the 12th Lancers and the Cape Rifles. Success here was followed up by a march in to the Amatola Mountains where four days of scouring drove the Xhosa back to the north. Chief Sandile surrendered and the war was effectively over. Harry Smith was replaced in April by Sir Geary Cathcart but he had little left to do except mop up the stragglers. In all the Xhosa lost 6,000 men, 80 chiefs and 80,000 cattle. For the British the biggest loss of life came from the sinking of the *Birkenhead.*

FIGURE 16 – BIRKENHEAD MEMORIAL IN SOUTH AFRICA
(BY DE WET CC-BY-SA-2.5)

The *Birkenhead* was one of the first iron hulled steam ships in the Royal Navy. In 1852 she was used as a troop transport to bring soldiers from Britain and Ireland to South Africa to take part in the Frontier Wars. Leaving Portsmouth in January 1852 carrying troops from over 10 different regiments including the 6th Foot she made good time to South Africa arriving at Simonstown on the 23rd February. Here they disembarked some civilians and the sick before progressing to Cape Town. Early in the morning of the 26th February the *Birkenhead* hit an uncharted rock off the aptly named Danger Point. Captain

Salmond quickly came on deck and ordered the anchor to be dropped to steady the ship and for the engines to reverse and pull the ship free. Unfortunately the ship was too badly holed and water flooded in. One hundred soldiers drowned in their beds before they could be mustered on deck for evacuation. On deck Lieutenant-Colonel Seton of the 74th Foot took charge. He assigned sixty men to the pumps to slow the sinking and a further sixty to run out and man the lifeboats. The tide pushed the ship back onto the rocks and now the ship began to split in two.

Captain Salmond ordered an immediate evacuation letting the 20 women and children aboard the first life rafts. He cut the horses loose and ordered anyone who was able to swim for it. Many of those who did try and swim for it succumbed to exposure or were attacked by sharks only a handful made it the 2 miles to shore. Of the 643 aboard only 193 survived. 46 of those killed were of the 6th Foot although Sergeant Teile and 7 men were rescued. Both Seton and Salmond perished. Corporal O'Neil commented later that 'Major Wright threatened to shoot any man who stepped towards the boats, but no-one thought of doing it...discipline was maintained until the last...but the women and children were got off safely'.

The *Birkenhead's* legacy was the establishment of the 'Women and children first protocol' known as the 'Birkenhead Drill' a protocol that became most famous during the sinking of the *Titanic*. It is an important marker to the fact that like the diseases rife in the Caribbean and Walcheren that a soldiers life was just as likely to end in other gruesome ways than at the hands of an enemy.

The Sixth Foot remained in South Africa until 1857 garrisoning Grahamstown, Fort Beaufort, Fort Peddie and patrolling the Amatola Mountains. In 1857 a revolt broke out in India. It is now known as the Indian Mutiny. As the regiment had seen during their earlier time in India the mutiny was a time bomb just waiting to go off. India was an amazing patchwork of British ruled Presidency's and independent states just as mixed was its religious make up. Sikhs, Muslims and Hindus made up the main ethnic groups. This religious mixture was what prompted the stirrings of the mutiny.

The mutiny was not really a popular civilian uprising; in fact it was the mutiny of Indian troops (sepoys) in the British army. One of the sparks came when a new musket was introduced with new cartridges. Rumours by those wanting the British out of India spread the idea that the cartridges were coated with animal grease including pork fat and cow fat. This angered the Muslim and Hindu sepoys who would become tainted by touching the fats, it played into a general feeling that the British were trying to eradicate all religion in India and replace it with Christianity. In fact it had already been decided to change the grease used so that the sepoys could use them safely but trust was stretched thin and in February 1857 sepoys in Barrackpore in the Bengal Presidency voiced their fears and refused to work. Minor fights broke out which culminated on the 10th May in a full mutiny at Meerut, the following day Europeans were slaughtered in Delhi.

Aware that they may not be able to trust their own troops the British began disarming sepoys in Lahore and Peshawar but by the end of the month garrisons in Muttra, Lucknow, Rohikland and Bhurtpore had all mutinied. Horrific crimes were committed by the mutineers on any Europeans they found, women and children alike. Soon the British found themselves trapped within their own compounds at places like Lucknow and Cawnpore. Not all the sepoys mutinied and in fact more than half of India remained loyal or neutral. Slowly with the addition of European troops the British were able to start regaining control, their retaliation however was harsh and swift.

It was towards the tail end of the mutiny that the Sixth Foot arrived in January 1858. With 750 men under the command of Major Stratton they formed part of Colonel Cornfield's column that was tasked with mopping up the remaining rebels. They were first engaged at Jagdespur before moving to Juttowra. Here an example of how the army was working in India could be seen. The Sixth Foot were brigaded with an Indian Naval Brigade and a detachment of Sikh troops and ordered to investigate shootings in the village of Juttowra. They began by entering the area in skirmish order forcing the rebels before them. They followed in pursuit burning the villages and crops as they went and then withdrawing at sunset. This tactic of slash and burn had been used in Africa and was an established military tactic designed to deny a large army's access to resources, the difference here was that these weren't large forces and did little to endear the local civilians to British rule. Casualties during the mutiny were light in the Juttowra engagement 2 men were wounded whilst 6 died of sunstroke. In May the mutiny was over and the Sixth Foot returned to barracks in Sasseram having lost 50 men including their colonel, Lieutenant-Colonel Barnes to disease.

The mutiny was undoubtedly a dark page in British history but it resulted in the abolishment of the East India Company. The British government realised that they could no longer afford to have an organisation acting on their behalf but solely focused on the aims of their own shareholders. Colonisation still continued across the globe but was now tempered by parliament who took a keener interest in how they ruled their native populaces.

THE SIKKIM EXPEDITION

In 1861 the regiment moved to Barrackpore and took part in one more significant action. Sikkim was an independent nation allied to Britain that bordered northern India and Nepal. It was an important country for Britain who wanted a link to Tibet and the wealth the Silk Road brought. Sikkim and Britain had been allies since 1814 when the Sikkim had fought the Nepalese. The Sikkim were a deeply private people and tensions with colonists often sparked tensions. In 1849 two doctors (Campbell and Hoolar) entered Sikkim without authorisation from the King. They were instantly detained but as they represented the British Crown the government sent in an expedition to have them released.

A second expedition was mounted on the 1st February 1861 leaving from Darjeeling and led by Lieutenant-Colonel John Gawler. Gawlers column was comprised of the 6th Foot and Indian Sepoys with 4 artillery pieces. The expedition met little resistance as they advanced in to Sikkim and only 1 man of the Sixth was killed. The biggest obstacles faced were the long distances and bad roads. Inevitably the King of Sikkim surrendered swiftly and agreed to an Anglo-Sikkim agreement that maintained the Kingdoms independence with Britain as an overseer. On returning to Darjeeling the regiment left India returning to Gosport in 1862.

THE JAMAICAN REBELLION

In 1857 a second battalion of the Sixth Foot was again added to the regiment to increase the size of the British army. They were raised to 1,000 men strong in Preston. To start with they remained in the United Kingdom with garrison duties in Gibraltar and Corfu until in 1864 they travelled to the West Indies.

The West Indies and Jamaica in particular rested on a knifes edge. For centuries rich colonist planters used slave labour from Africa to run their sugar and tobacco plantations, these 'Negro' slaves were often very badly treated and revolts against their masters were common. There had been a significant uprising known as the Baptist Rebellion in Jamaica in 1831, this uprising was instigated and controlled via the church on the island. It was swiftly put down but had a lasting impact. Internationally it provided more evidence and support for the Abolitionists. Britain had already begun to clamp down on the slave trade in 1807 with the West African Squadron of the Royal Navy having standing orders to stop slave trading vessels but this was still a far cry from outlawing slavery completely. In 1823 the Anti-Slavery Society was founded which included the Member of Parliament William Wilberforce. When the Baptist Rebellion ended two independent inquires were held to look at the reasons behind it. From this came the Slavery Abolition Act 1833 that emancipated all slaves except those under East India Company control. What should have eased tensions actually increased them. The planters were not happy with the £19 per slave compensation they recieved and felt vulnerable to further revolts. Falling sugar prices also meant that they were starting to lose money and they believed the free workers were to blame for this by being lazy.

The freed slaves however did not feel as liberated as they might, they were still in the same jobs and still worked hard for very little pay, for them not much seemed to have changed other than that they were no longer owned.

Matters started to come to a head when in 1864 William Gordon, the son of a white plantation owner and a black slave, berated the new governor of the colony Edward John Eyre for allowing slaves to be paid so little especially when immigrants that came from India were getting paid more. Gordon first tried to petition the British Government but their response was less than helpful. They suggested they maintain the status quo, keep their heads down and work hard and hopefully it would blow over. Many of the black workers had great respect for Queen Victoria and the government and could not believe that they would have responded like that. They began to suspect that Eyre had forged the government's response and militias began to form.

On the 7th October 1865 matters bubbled to the surface. A man called Miller had refused to pay rent and was due to be tried at the courthouse in Morant Bay. Paul Bogle a prominent 'black' agitator had gathered a mob to protest the case. They arrived too late to see Millers case and instead they saw the case of a Caribbean boy who had been convicted of assaulting a woman. He was tried by the court and fined 2 shillings and ordered to pay 12 shillings and six pence in legal costs. This was obviously too much for the boy to pay and Bogle believed the fine was exorbitant. A violent response was quick in coming and 20 officials both black and white were killed and 35 were wounded.

Three days later the police arrived to arrest Bogle at his home. The police were ambushed by 300 armed men who either took prisoners or persuaded them to join the growing revolt. On the 11th October an armed mob stormed a police station seizing weapons and prompting a wider uprising. Many white planters were killed and several black officials were killed as collaborators or sympathisers. Now 2,000 men strong Bogle tried to recruit the Maroons to his cause. The maroons were descendents of escaped slaves in the 1650's who had inter-married with the native Taino and Arawak tribes in the islands interior. Previous uprisings of their own had led to many being relocated to Nova Scotia and Sierra Leone. The remaining maroons however refused to become involved and in fact later in the conflict sided with the government forces.

Whilst Bogle tried to recruit the maroons and other freed slaves Governor Eyre contacted Major-General O'Connor in Kingston requesting military aid as it was obvious that the local police forces could no longer cope with what was happening. He sent the West India Regiment to reinforce the governor and a party of the 6th Foot was moved to Morant Bay from Newcastle. These troops began to put down the rebellion with excessive brutality.

The 6th Foot were led by Lieutenant-Colonel Hobbs and they left a tide of violence in their wake. On the 17th October an infirm man was shot trying to stop a company from burning his house. In the village of Fonthill on 20th October some of the men of the regiment slept in the cottage of a black man called Cherrington. He had treated them well by offering them dinner but in the morning they killed him and only the local constables stopped them from burning the house down as well. At Garbrand Hall men were murdered and the house put to the torch, in Monklands two men were shot and in Mount Libanus two soldiers of the 6th tried to steal a woman's wedding ring resulting in her father-in-law being shot dead. This catalogue of violent reprisals did put an end to the rebellion but at the terrible cost of 439 deaths and the burning of thousands of homes. Colonel Hobbs was responsible for shooting rebels without trial and of 28 men killed he admitted later to not even knowing the names of 18 of them. He maintained his orders given to him by Colonel Elkington D.A.C gave him the right to come down hard on the rebels and civilians.

Back in Kingston Governor Eyre had William Gordon arrested, believing him to be a key instigator despite being miles away at the time. Initially Eyre pushed for a military trial but was persuaded to allow a civil court to try the case. They found Gordon guilty of insurrection but sentenced him to imprisonment instead of death. Eyre over turned this ruling and had him hanged. Paul Bogle himself was caught and hanged on the 23rd October.

The loss of both Gordon and Bogle began the end of the rebellion but not the end of the atrocities. On the 10th November 1865 Colonel Hobbs stated a desire to test the long range power of the new Enfield rifle. In executing a rebel named Arthur Wellington Captain Spencer Field was ordered to command a fire party. Captain Field had Wellington tied to a tree some 400 yards away and then fired 10 shots into him using the new rifle. Questions were soon asked. At first Edward Cardwell, Secretary of State for the Colonies was pleased with Governor Eyre's decisive actions in putting down the rebellion but slowly reports of the actions of the 6th Foot and the other troops began to arrive and by the 23rd November Cardwell was furious. He immediately set up a commission of inquiry focusing on the trial of Gordon. After 51 days in session the commission merely thanked Eyre for his prompt action. The government disapproved with of this weak response and the Jamaica Committee charged Eyre with murder several times but each time the case was thrown out. Unable to prosecute him the government replaced him as Governor by Sir Henry Storks. Eyre escaped punishment completely in the end dying in 1901 aged 86.

Colonel Hobbs was recalled to Horse Guards to account for his actions but failed to attend straight away due to failing mental health and was deemed unfit for duty. On 21st April 1865 he boarded the steamer 'Talisman' for Southampton. He was accompanied by another officer and two soldiers

143

to watch over him. The following day whilst at sea, Hobbs knocked out his guard and committed suicide by leaping overboard. Ironically also travelling on the 'Talisman' was William Gordon's widow who had been asked to address the Anti-Slavery Society and the Jamaica Committee in Britain. The final result of the uprising was to get rid of the domination of the planters and former slave owners. There was a clampdown on corruption and Jamaica was made a crown colony giving it greater governance with its capital in Kingston no further rebellions occurred in the future. Following the shame of their actions the 2nd Battalion returned to Britain in 1867 and did not venture abroad again until 1878 where they were posted to the North-West Frontier.

Whilst the 2nd Battalion were in the West Indies the 1st Battalion were in the original Indies on the North-West Frontier. They had spent much of the year in Bombay before moving up in to Karachi in modern day Pakistan. Led by Lieutenant-Colonel Greagh Osborne they joined a force of 12,500 mostly Indian troops under the command of Major-General A.T Wilde for an expedition into the Black Mountains on the Hazara border. The expedition was in response to an attack on a police post in Oghi in the Agror Valley by three local tribes. The regiment saw little action in what was essentially a policing action.

After the expedition they returned to Cherat where they were issued with the new khaki uniform that was replacing the distinctive scarlet red. They remained at various posts in India being reviewed by the Prince of Wales and providing an escort to the Viceroy in 1867 during Victoria's proclamation as Empress of India. They left India in 1880 where they joined the 2nd Battalion in England and Ireland.

CHAPTER 6 - NORTH AFRICA TO SOUTH AFRICA

For Britain Africa was not only one of its most valuable assets but also one of the most difficult to control. Whilst India and the West Indies were heavily under the influence of the East India Company Africa was under the influence of ambitious men such as Cecil Rhodes and General Gordon.

In 1869 whilst the battalions of the 6[Th] Foot were in India and South Wales the Suez Canal was opened. This considerably shortened the route to India and became a strategic asset for the empire. Originally against the building of the canal because it had used slave labour to build it the British government were forced to take more notice when in 1875 Isma'il Pasha, Khedive of Egypt ran into money problems. Britain eagerly agreed to buy his shares in the canal to avoid control passing to an enemy power like Russia. Since the Crimea War Russia was now Britain's most powerful enemy. Russia had vast resources and had begun to exhibit her own imperial and colonial interests, many of the wars and interventions in the middle-east, India and China were part of a struggle for dominance between the rise of the Russian Empire and the already established British Empire.

In 1879 the Urabi Revolt in Egypt prompted Khedive Tefwiq to request help from both Britain and France in maintaining order in Egypt. The British succeeded in defeating the Egyptian rebels at the Battle of Tel El-Kebir and stabilised the Khedives rule. In return the Khedive accepted British protection as a protectorate of the empire, this suited the Khedive well who had been trying to modernise his armed forces. During the 1860's until financial problems occurred they had used American advisors but in 1882 Major-General Sir Henry Evelyn Wood was appointed the commander in chief of the Egyptian Army and he set about creating a modern army of Egyptians led by European officers.

The Khedive controlled the two kingdoms of Egypt and Sudan. Between 1877 and 1880 Sudan was governed by Colonel Charles G. Gordon. He worked hard to improve conditions and clamped down on slavery, however in 1881 the Madhi led an uprising of Dervishes that besieged Khartoum, the capital of Sudan and attempted to set up a fundamentalist Islamic state to be called Mahidya. Dervishes were the followers of the Madhi. Their name was a derivation of the Persian word darawish for beggar. The Dervish army was a mixture of local tribesmen including the Baggara from the north of Sudan and the Beja from the east. The Beja were often called 'fuzzy-wuzzies' by the British after the way they styled their hair with fat and butter so that they resembled mops. Despite appearances they were disciplined capable soldiers that obtained modern arms after each engagement. In fact in 1884 they were able to break a British square at the battle of Tamai something the military thought could only be achieved by a modern European army.

A British relief column led by Sir Garnet Wolseley one of Britain's foremost generals was unable to reach Khartoum in time to save Gordon or its population and withdrew, leaving Sudan in the hands of the Madhi. The Madhi himself died only 6 months later from Typhus. He was succeeded by one of his Khalifa's, Abdullah ibn Mohammed. Formerly from Darfur the Khalifa was handpicked by the Mahdi to rule Sudan, he pursued the Madhi's goal of ruling Egypt but was defeated by the British at the Battle of Ginnis in 1885. Life in the Mahidya was harsh and there were some uprisings that occupied the Khalifa before he could continue his goal of spreading Islamic law across the world. In 1887 he attempted to invade Abyssinia and in 1888 attempted to invade the rest of Sudan. In 1889 the Khalifa once again attacked Egypt and was defeated by an Egyptian Army at the battle of Toski. Further attacks into Belgian and Italian held territories were also repulsed. It seemed that for now the Madiya State was restricted to the land it had originally seized.

BATTLE OF ATBARA

In January 1898 the 6th Foot now more commonly referred to as the Royal Warwickshire's were assigned to Lord Kitchener's forces for the re-conquest of Sudan. Originally content to stand by and allow the Mahdists to maintain their limited zone of control the risk that the anti-British Emperor of Abyssinia might ally with the Khalifa began to grow. Such an alliance could threaten the Suez Canal, Britain's link to India, and meant that more direct military action was inevitable. Kitchener had already recaptured

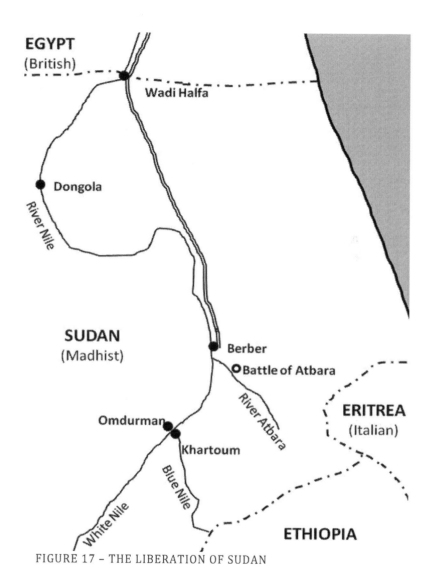

EGYPT
(British)

Wadi Halfa

Dongola

River Nile

SUDAN
(Madhist)

Berber

O Battle of Atbara

River Atbara

Omdurman

Khartoum

ERITREA
(Italian)

Blue Nile

White Nile

ETHIOPIA

FIGURE 17 – THE LIBERATION OF SUDAN

149

the province of Dongola in 1896 and seized Wadi Halfa and Abu Hamed during 1897 now in 1898 Kitchener moved to 'liberate' the whole of Sudan. Under the command of Lieutenant- Colonel Quayle Jones 856 men of the 1st Battalion of the Royal Warwickshire Regiment left Cario by rail for Wadi Halfa where 2 companies led by Major Etheridge were left to garrison Korti. The battalion was brigaded with the Lincolnshire's, Cameron Highlanders and Seaforth Highlanders under the command of Major-General Gatacre, a general who had made his name on the North-West Frontier and was known by the nickname, 'Back-acher'.

The regiment was now fully dressed in the Khaki field uniform and armed with the new Lee-Metford Rifle. This rifle had a magazine of 10 rounds and had twice the firing rate of the Martini-Henry. The brigade advanced to where the river Nile met the river Atbara, here they built a fort whilst Major-General Kitchener concentrated his Egyptian troops around Berber from where he feared an attack might be mounted. In fact Khalifa Emir Mahmund at Metemneh with 20,000 men had been allowed to attack Berber and was beginning to move his forces north to link up with Osman Digna at Shendi. By the 15th February Kitchener had learned of the impending attack and on the 13th March gunboats on the Nile sighted the Dervish Horde moving towards them.

Unsure whether to defend or attack Kitchener focused his forces on Atbara beginning a game of cat and mouse between the two forces. Mahmud changed course towards Atbara. Kitchener responded by taking 14,000 men up river to Hudi where he could threaten the enemy and shield Berber. By the 21st March Kitchener was just 20 miles from the Dervish Army who had dug in behind a zariba (thorn fence). Reconnaissance forces found the army on the 30th March and a council of war was formed. General Gatacre suggested attacking the zariba immediately whilst General Hunter advised caution and delay. Undecided Kitchener requested advice from London, before this advice arrived however Hunter changed his mind siding with Gatacre and the army was readied for the attack. As it happened the government agreed with General Hunter and suggested caution.

On the 4th April the British army crept 4 miles closer to the enemy. At first the zariba appeared to have been abandoned when suddenly Baggara horsemen appeared on both flanks and Dervish guns opened fire. The British cavalry quickly countered the Baggara horsemen and secured a point in which to deploy. By sun up on the 8th April Major-General Gatacre's brigade were lined up on the left beside Egyptian Cavalry. The centre was held by General MacDonald's brigade and on the right was General Maxwell's. Across the line a front was made with battalions in line supported by battalions in column. The Warwickshire's were placed in column on the left behind the Cameron's. Those regiments in line presented the greatest number of rifles to the enemy whilst those reserves in column were more flexible in movement and able to reinforce units or plug gaps in the line.

At 6.20 am the Egyptian Artillery opened fire with all four batteries. The Baggara Horsemen once again threatened the left flank but concentrated Maxim machine gun fire and the Egyptian Cavalry stopped them from becoming a problem. After over an hour's bombardment the Dervishes remained entrenched and so the entire army advanced along a 1500 yard front. When within 300 yards they opened fire and reached the dry camel thorn hedge forming the zariba. The heaviest casualties were received by the 11th Sudanese regiment but even so they, along with the 10th Sudanese, were able to storm Mahmud's inner redoubt.

The Warwickshire's route took them along the east side in enfilade whilst Maxwell's brigade hemmed the dervishes in on the far flank. The dervishes soon collapsed. The Baggara horse and Osman Digna were able to escape but Mahmud was captured. The dervish army suffered 2000 fatalities whilst the Anglo-Egyptian Army only 8 with 479 wounded.. With the threat relieved the army returned to both Berber and Atbara. Here the regiment was reunited with the garrison from Korti and Lieutenant-Colonel W.E.G Forbes assumed command from Quayle.

The men's time when not soldiering was hardly idle as the railway was extended and reinforcements were brought in. By mid-August Kitchener fielded a force of 25,800 men and he felt comfortable enough now to advance on the Dervish capital at Omdurman near Khartoum. As the army approached the city the Khalifa fortified it as much he could and withdrew with his 2,000 strong Taaisha bodyguard behind a 14 foot stone wall.

Now commanded by Major-General Wachope the 1st British brigade containing the Warwickshire's was joined by a second British brigade to form a British Division led by now Brigadier-General Gatacre. An Egyptian Division was led by Major-General Hunter. The Khalifa commanded a total of 52,000 men assembled on the plains between the White and Blue Niles. On the 1st September the cavalry sighted the Dervish Army moving south of Jebel Surgham. Kitchener brought his brigades up in an arc near the village of El Egeiga to receive them. Whilst the armies prepared to face each other gunboats travelled up the Nile and began to bombard Omdurman.

At 6 am on the 2nd September 1898 Osman Azrak began the attack throwing 8,000 men forward supported by a further 4000 on his right. Two other Dervish forces under the green flag Abd Allah Abu Siwar and Osman Sheikh-Ed-Din advanced to the north but were stopped by Egyptian Cavalry. By 6.25 am the Warwickshire's and the 1st Brigade were facing some 20,000 dervishes, careful disciplined fire however made short work of the enemy and few reached closer than 800 yards. This courage by the Mahdists under such withering fire impressed the regiment one of whom commented 'those black chaps knew how to fight and die.' Within 40 minutes the first phase of the battle was over. As Kitchener reviewed the essentially destroyed Dervish infantry the 21st Lancers advanced and stumbled upon the forces of Osman Digna. They charged the 2,000 battle hardened Dervishes in a dry watercourse and found themselves in a trap. In a swift melee and retreat 21 men were killed, 71 wounded and a further 199 became lost.

On speaking of the battle of Omdurman the reporter Winston Churchill commented, 'bright flags appeared as if by magic, and I saw arriving from nowhere Emirs on horseback and around them the mass of the enemy. The Dervishes appeared to be ten or twelve deep at the thickest, a great grey mass gleaming with steel'. Under such overwhelming numbers and fervor it was up to British infantry tactics to win the day.

As the infantry advanced a certain amount of disorganisation appeared. Maxwell wheeled right over the summit of Jebel Surgham with Lyttleton on the left and Lewis on the right. A gap formed between Lewis and MacDonald and so Wauchope quickly moved the 1st Brigade up to fill the growing space. The Camel corps brought up the right rear. Heroic charges by Yakub's Black Flag reserve met stiff fire from MacDonald's brigades and the remaining Green Flags were met by Wauchope. By 11.30 am both these Dervish forces had been shattered and the Khalifa fled the city. It was estimated over 10,000 dervishes were killed in the battle and 16,000 wounded. The Anglo-Egyptian army lost only 48 men of which only 28 were British, with 434 wounded. The Royal Warwickshire's themselves lost Captain Caldecott and Lieutenant Etches and 3 men were wounded. Kitchener marched into Omdurman attributing victory as much to luck as tactics. By the 14th September the regiment were back in Alexandria bound for India where they were to remain until 1912.

Whilst the war in the Sudan was an example of British firepower and excellence the next war in the Africa's was to prove very different. In South Africa the British Army would meet its stiffest challenge and be humiliated on more than one occasion.

In 1899 a second war broke out with the Boers in South Africa. The Boers were local farmers named for the people of Dutch descent that had left the Cape Colony and moved north between 1836 and 1846 to create their own republics. They established the Orange Free State and the Transvaal in doing so they had fought and defeated both the Zulu and Matebele tribes. Initially eager to seek British recognition when Natal was designated a British Colony a series of skirmishes soon broke out between the Boers and British forces over land. These clashes continued through the 1840's as the Boers expressed distaste for the expansion of Britain. Eventually the Sand River Convention in 1852 and the Bloemfontein Convention in 1854 recognised the Boer States including the South African Republic (Formerly the Transvaal). When large diamond fields were found in South Africa and Britain annexed Basutoland tensions with the Boer exploded.

During the Zulu War of 1879 the Boers assisted the British, the Zulus were after all a common enemy, but by 1880, they were becoming more militant opposing Britain's assertion that the Transvaal could only be independent as part of a wider South African Confederation. This led to the First Boer War which lasted only 1 year. The Boers soundly beat the British forces

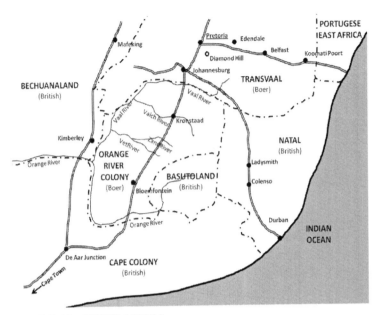

FIGURE 18- SOUTH AFRICA

resulting in Britain granting the Transvaal independence but maintaining suzerainty.

The Second Boer War was mostly as a result of the actions of Cecil Rhodes the governor of Cape Colony. There was much dispute over the rights of foreigners in the Transvaal where immigrants could not be granted citizen status. In 1895 and 1896 Rhodes supported an unsuccessful raid by Leander Starr Jameson to over throw the Transvaal government. This ultimately escalated already high tensions until on 11th October 1899 the Boer states declared war on Britain.

The Boers hoped to make a swift decisive attack on the British Colonies and at first they did well. Commando units of Boers attacked across the border hoping to seize territory before the British could bring in more troops from overseas. Under the command of Commandant-General De la Rey the Boers won a skirmish at Kraaipan whilst other forces laid siege to garrisons in Mafeking, Ladysmith and Kimberley. British forces were also defeated at Nicholson's Nek and Lombard's Kop.

In October 1899 General Sir Redvers Buller was designated commander in chief of South African forces and he began to assemble an army to reinforce the colonies. He divided this army into three elements; one, led by Lieutenant-General Methuen, was to relieve Kimberley whilst Lieutenant-General Gatacre was to stem the Boer advance in the north east of the colonies. Buller himself would relieve Ladysmith. Things didn't begin well with defeats at Stormberg, Magerfontein and Colenso all occurring in one week in December. Such failure resulted in Buller being replaced by Field Marshal Roberts. Buller remained in South Africa commanding troops at a disastrous defeat at Spion Kop in January in which 322 men were killed, 585 wounded and 300 captured.

As the 1st Battalion was only just back from action in Sudan the 2nd Battalion was mobilised to join the 9th Brigade of the 5th Division. Lieutenant-Colonel Quayle Jones sailed with 1000 men on the 'Gaul' arriving in Cape Town in December 1899. They arrived too late to join the division that had already departed to join Buller in Natal, instead they were assigned to guard the lines of communication in Britstown and De Ar district.

In January the battalion was reassigned to the 6th Division in Major-General T.E. Stephenson's 18th Brigade with the 1st Welch, 1st York's and the 1st Essex Regiments. They continued to provide defence to the railways and telegraph lines with 3 companies under Major Morrice forming a HQ unit whilst the rest moved up to Bloemfontein. Here Lieutenant-Colonel Jones had his foot crushed and he was replaced as commanding officer by Major London. Protecting the railway lines was important; one of the Boers key strategies was to mount commando raids around major British columns to strike at key junctions and disrupt supplies. The Boers were tenacious fighters as had been illustrated in the first Boer war. They operated in smaller more mobile units and tried to avoid open plain engagements that favoured the British military machine with infantry tactics and artillery support.

The 2nd Battalion after their questionable behaviour in Jamaica had spent the following years in Britain and on the North-West Frontier. It had been present in Britain whilst the Regiment was reorganised to include a 3rd and 4th Battalion from volunteer militia units and a 5th and 6th Battalion from territorial units. These extra units became vitally important as it appeared the Boer war would need large numbers of men to protect the huge African continent. On 5th March the 2nd battalion was joined by the 1st militia battalion that formed an extra company in the battalion. Some of the men of the 1st battalion and the 3rd and 4th battalions were used to form Mounted Infantry units. These units saw action at Paardeburg in February and were used as a mobile force to combat the swift guerrilla style attacks of the Boers. The 5th and 6th Territorial battalions were assigned to guard prisoners of war in Simonstown, Hopetown and Bloemfontein. General Kitchener the local commander used the militias and the brigade to quell localised uprisings in Britstown, Carnarvon and Prieska districts.

In April the 18th brigade including the 2nd battalion was moved to the 11th Division under the command of General Pole-Carew and finally given orders to advance. General Roberts' plan was to focus on heading directly north and seizing the Boer capital at Pretoria believing this would force a Boer capitulation. The regiment saw their first action at the Koornspruit near Bloemfontein. On the 30th March a column of British troops was ambushed by General Christian De Wet. The British convoy of 92 wagons and 2 batteries of horse artillery under the command Brigadier-General Broadwood were retreating from Thaba Nchu and camped near Koornspruit Drift. The 1,700 British Colonials were attacked at dawn by 400 Boers who with artillery and sharp shooting inflicted over 500 casualties on the British. The brigade pushed up on the Boers following this defeat clearing the way north. The Boers harassed the army at every opportunity but refused to engage them in direct combat preferring to oppose them at river crossings such as the rivers Vet and Zand.

As the army crept closer to Boer territory the Boers resolve began to stiffen. Their strike and fade tactics started to give way to more static conventional combat. Up until now results against the Boers had been limited. The Boers used smokeless rifles and relied on small mobile commandos whilst generals like Kitchener relied on old fashioned military tactics that at Paardeberg had cost the British 1270 casualties.

From the Warwickshire Regiment Captain Charles Beatty was on the staff of General Alderson in the Mounted

Infantry. On the 17th February 1901 whilst operating in the Transvaal Captain Beatty had been with Major Howard, an orderly and a native scout of a Canadian unit when they were ambushed by Boers. The four men became pinned down behind a wagon. Attempts to reach help were hindered by the intense fire but Beatty was able to reach his horse and gallop off. The horse took three bullets in the escape but Beatty was able to reach Howard's men who quickly came up in support. Unfortunately, despite Beatty's efforts they arrived too late to rescue the other men. One other Mounted Infantry officer of note was Lieutenant John Costeker who was awarded the Distinguished Service Order for the capture of Commandant Kolde in November 1901. He remained in South Africa for the duration of the war and was eventually killed during the First World War.

BATTLE OF DIAMOND HILL

Throughout May the army was under fire from Boer artillery but determined effort by the Mounted Infantry kept the Boers moving back. General Roberts supported this pace hoping to deny them the chance to dig in. On the 31st May Johannesburg surrendered without a fight and the Boers fell back on Pretoria. In early June the Boers stopped and a fight was in the brewing. On the 4th June the battalion crossed Six Mile Spruit under fire and took Zwart Top losing 1 man with 12 wounded. The following day the army entered Pretoria. General Robert's was happy that the capital had fallen but still remained cautious. The Boers had not surrendered and they still remained close by in significant numbers. He rallied his army and decided to drive them away from the city.

The Boers under the command of General Botha withdrew 15 miles to the east to Diamond Hill. They dug themselves into a series of steep hills along a 16 mile front. Roberts faced them in the valley arriving on the 11th June with 14,000 British, Australian and Canadian forces to face Botha's 4,000. Pole-Carew and General Hamilton with 4 divisions held the centre whilst the Mounted Infantry held the left flank and the Guards cavalry the right.

So entrenched were the Boers that it seemed impossible to outflank and envelope them. Holding the high ground as they did meant that the cavalry were essentially useless. A direct assault under the cover of artillery was made up the slopes of the hill. Artillery began by scouring the Boer positions before Hamilton's men advanced. They managed to secure an advanced position as night approached. The following morning (12th June) the British lines were met by bombardment from the Boer guns. Hamilton once again led his brigade up the hill side rooting out the Boers from between the boulders and other defenses. The Royal Warwickshire's with Pole-Carew advanced in support with the Guards Brigade. As night fell again both sides bivouacked but in the morning it was found that the Boers had abandoned their positions for new defences in the East. The Warwickshire's followed and by the 23rd were dug in around Edendale just 3000 yards from the Boer lines. Here they held off occasional Boer counter-attacks whilst also suffering from an outbreak of enteric fever. The army maintained its pressure of the Boers advancing on the 23rd July to Elands River Station before digging in again on the 27th July at Balmorral.

In the dust and heat an infantry man's life was a poor one. Long marches and the constant threat of ambush made for a difficult journey and when actually engaged it was often quite difficult to identify the near invisible Boer sharpshooters hidden in rocks. Lieutenant David Millar summed up the prevailing attitude at this time, stating '...very nasty- very tiring- very greasy- very hungry- very thirsty- everything very beastly. No glitter- no excitement-no nothing, just bullets and dirt'. This was a different warfare from earlier wars and a prelude to the changing face of warfare that would come to dominate the next century.

BATTLE OF BELFAST

The brigade reached Belfast on the 24th August. This was the last major town before Komati Poort and the border of Portuguese East Africa. Now pushed as far as they could go the Boers dug in well. The Warwickshire's were stationed between the railway and the town. By the following day it was clear that the action would take place on Monument Hill and the British artillery opened up on the Boer positions whilst in the cold wind the regiment advanced to the crest and dug trenches.

The main battle took place the following day. Artillery from both sides opened up the battle. General French's cavalry attacked the Boers on the North-west whilst General Buller engaged on the South-east. Pole-Carew and the Warwickshire's under the cover of their guns assisted the assault in the centre. The 18th Brigade containing the Warwickshire's held the ridge whilst the 4th Mounted Infantry and the Guards Brigade moved north. In their holding position the regiment saw little action and received few casualties only 1 killed and 3 wounded. The Guards fared worse taking the brunt of the attack and the casualties.

By the 27th August the British were in the Boer trenches who were by now retreating to Lydenburg and Komati Poort. Buller pressed on to Lydenburg whilst the regiment joined up with French's Cavalry and the Mounted Infantry and marched to Zwartkopje's where they were used for advance and flank duties. During September the regiment was split up with the 2nd Battalion garrisoning Waterval Boven and the Volunteer Company, Waterval Onder. Here on outpost duty it was noted that they saw more 'Baboons than Boers'. For the 2nd Battalion and the Volunteer Militia the war was essentially over. Pole-Carew led the Guards Brigade to take Komati Poort and by the 10th October the regiment had orders to withdraw and for the Volunteers to return home.

In November General Roberts returned to England leaving General Kitchener in charge but he was quickly replaced by Field Marshall Wolsely. The standard pitched battle part of the war was over and until the wars close in May 1902 most actions were a result of guerrilla actions by the Boers. One such action was the Siege of O'Okeip on the 4th April 1902 just 1 month before the treaty of Vereeniging ended the war. The Boers laid siege to the town of O'Okiep in the west of Cape Colony. The town was defended by Lieutenant-Colonel W.A.D Shelton with the 3rd Battalion

Queens Royal Regiment, 5th Battalion Royal Warwickshire Regiment, Town Guard, Namaqualand Border Scouts and Cape Garrison Artillery. They were besieged by forces led by Jan Smut's; this was a final roll of the dice for Smuts who realised that the war was reaching a close. Fortunately for the British the town managed to hold out until the 15th May when a relief column arrived. Smut's abandoned the siege and came to the negotiating table who with Kitchener drew up the treaty that ended the war. Jan Smuts would later become the 4th President of South Africa.

Whilst the war was a win for the British, 21,942 men had been killed and over 440,000 imperial and colonial soldiers had to be deployed to combat just 87,000 Boers of whom approximately 7,000 died. These casualties however are nothing compared to the deaths in the concentration camps set up by the British to detain Boer civilians during the war. It is estimated between 18,000 and 25,000 perished there of poor hygiene and starvation. Many male Boers captured were sent abroad to prisons around the globe. The British victory resulted in the annexation of the Orange Free State and the Transvaal which in 1910 would become incorporated into the self-governing Union of South Africa.

CHAPTER 7 – THE GREAT WAR

The Boer War was but a minor conflict compared to the Great War that loomed on the horizon. The 2nd Battalion on leaving South Africa spent 1901 in Bermuda guarding Boer prisoners before returning to England in 1902 and then departing for Malta in 1912. The volunteer companies and the 3rd and 4th Battalions were all reorganised. First in 1907 the 3rd and 4th Battalions were disbanded and then in 1908 under the Haldane Reforms reconstituted along with the whole regiment. The 1st and 2nd battalions remained untouched, and the 3rd and 4th were re-established as a Special Reserve. The 1st Volunteer Companies were merged with the Territorial 5th and 6th Battalions; the 2nd Volunteer Companies were expanded to create the 7th and 8th Territorial battalions. Each battalion now consisted of four companies labelled A, B, C and D.

THE NORTH-WEST FRONTIER

Whilst most of the regiment had been involved in the Boer War in some form the majority of the 1st Battalion left Egypt and returned to what was becoming their second home in India. They spent 3 years in Bombay and Madras before in 1901 they moved to the edge of the North-West Frontier to Quetta and Belagun. They stayed here until 1908 when they were assigned to an expedition led by Major-General James Willcocks. The north-west frontier was a very dangerous and unpredictable place it was

FIGURE 19 – THE REGIMENT ON PARADE IN BERMUDA IN 1901

however an important bulwark against Russia's interest in India. The rugged terrain was home to a range of tribes that constantly warred with each other and the British. Willcock's was tasked with punishing the Zakka Khels, a tribe of Afridis. They left Peshawar on the 14th February with the Seaforth Highlanders, 37th Lancers and battalions of the British Indian Army. They travelled through Jamrud and up the Khyber Pass before heading into the Bazar valley. The Warwickshire's formed a rear guard whilst the rest pressed on to attack the village of Halwai. Even though not directly engaged they still had one man wounded by a sniper. The expedition ended successfully on the 1st March causing it to be termed 'Willcock's Weekend War'.

The battalion remained in the area and was garrisoned at Chara. In April four companies joined Brevet-Major Spearman's Mohmand Field Force. Again their role was to

166

punish local tribesman this time the 25,000 strong Mohmand people of the Kabul River. They went first to Matta to stop raiders and then onto Garhi Sadar where they encountered stiff resistance with one man killed and another wounded. Forced back they regrouped and then managed to re-occupy Garhi Sadar an action for which Lieutenant Martin was commended. Following these two police actions three companies under Colonel Bourne were assigned to Shabkadar Fort, two to piquet's whilst another under the command of Major Westmorland was involved in a reinforcement of Matta.

THE WAR BEGINS

On the 1st August the German Empire declared war on Russia and two days later on France. Neither of these events in themselves would have caused Britain to enter the war but on the 4th August the German Empire invaded Belgium. Britain was a guarantor of Belgian independence and so declared war on Germany and prepared an expeditionary force. This is a very simplistic analysis of the start of the First World War. It was in essence a coming together of two spheres of influences in Europe. France and Britain had entered a new alliance called the entente cordiale and were close to the Russians whilst the German Empire, Austro-Hungarian Empire and initially Italy formed the Triple Alliance. These two power blocs were forced to respond to a series of Balkan wars that ended Ottoman interests in south-eastern Europe. As various powers vied for influence and control the assassination of Archduke Franz Ferdinand, heir of Austria by the Serbian Gavrilo Princep lit the touch paper that prompted Germany to attack Russia.

The British Expeditionary Force was assembled under the command of General Sir John French. The force including the Royal Warwickshire's assembled in northern France ready to meet the advancing German army. The 1st Battalion were assigned to the 10th Brigade in the 4th Division of Major-General Pulteney's 3rd Corps and arrived in France via Boulogne. The 2nd Battalion arrived via Zeebrugge and joined the 22nd Brigade in the 7th Division in Lieutenant-General Rawlinson's 4th Corps.

The British Expeditionary Force was deployed to the northern end of the French line on the edge of Belgium. Their first role was an advance to Mons and Le Cateau to provide a holding force that would allow the French to retreat and regroup. The force consisted of seven corps including a Cavalry Corps and the Indian Corps. With the Germans held back and the French forming new defensive lines John French, essentially a cavalry officer, petitioned for the BEF to withdraw and leave France this idea was over-ruled by the Minister for War, Lord Kitchener. Whilst the French had managed to form a defensive line it was feared that the past may repeat itself, in the Franco-Prussian War in 1870, German forces had quickly defeated the French armies and even successfully besieged Paris. Kitchener believed that every man was required to hold the French defences and stop another fall of Paris. In September an allied counter-attack along the River Marne pushed the Germans back west of Paris and slowed the German war machine. Up until this point the Regiment had seen little real action this however was to change in October as they took up positions around Ypres.

THE FIRST BATTLE OF YPRES

The Battle of Ypres was in fact a series of battles throughout October and November 1914 and effectively ended the regular British Army. Ypres was planned as a decisive attack on German lines and ended more as a stalemate.

It began on 12th October when the 3rd Corps arrived at the Ypres-Armentieres Road between Wytschaete and Le Bizet. In concert with the 2nd Corps the plan was to oppose the German 4th Cavalry Corps along the banks of the Meterenbecque. The 4th Division including the 1st Battalion Royal Warwickshire's were placed on the left of the line with the 6th Division on the right. They were given orders to go forward and clear the enemy from in front of them.

Transport was always a problem in the war and Major-General Pulteney organised the transport himself from St Omer, even so it took 12 hours to reach their battle positions. As the action began the 6th Division were halted by the Germans but the 7th were more fortunate. Led by the under-strength 10th brigade with the 1st Battalion they pushed forward to Fletre near Mont des Cats. At noon the Warwickshire's were sent forward and were successful until the enemy began an artillery bombardment. Brigadier-General Haldane in command of the brigade ordered a return of artillery fire. The 1st Battalion continued their advance clearing Jaegers (German skirmishers) from Meterenbecque with the leading

169

FIGURE 20 - THE ALLIED COMMANDERS. FROM LEFT TO RIGHT
MARSHAL JOFFRE, PRESIDENT POINCARE, KING GEORGE VI, MARSHAL FOCH AND
GENERAL HAIG.

elements reaching Meteren itself. Up until now the
battalion had lost only 11 men but indecision by General
Snow commander of the Division led to this number rising
significantly. Just as the battalion reached Meteren Snow
dithered and ordered their withdrawal despite the fact
that the Germans were organising their own evacuation.
The withdrawal cost the battalion 246 casualties and after
regrouping they advanced again to reoccupy the ground
they had already taken once. In the afternoon the rest of
the corps attacked, and Meteren and Fontain Houch were
fully occupied. The German 3rd Cavalry and Infantry were
put in to full retreat. Further north the 4th Corps arrived
and cavalry began to reach Ypres. The 7th Division
containing the 2nd Battalion were deployed ready to
assault Menin, Courtrai and Roulers.

On the 14th October the 3rd Corps advanced on Bailleul with the 4th Division. They encountered the German 1st Cavalry division at Neuve Eglise Spur. The 2nd Corps held its line but most of the day was essentially taken up by the German withdrawal from Armentieres whereupon they re-equipped and reformed. They may have pulled back but they certainly weren't out of the fight.

The following day a new assault was planned to capitalise on the German withdrawal. The 2nd Corps was to capture La Bassee and advance on Lille, the 3rd Corps were to occupy Armentieres and then move east. The Cavalry Corps were to cover the left flank and the 4th Corps were tasked with advancing on Menin, Courtrai and Roulers. The enemy opposing them were two corps at Lille and two cavalry corps east of Armentieres and the 3rd reserve corps somewhere behind. The 4th division itself captured two of four assigned bridges at Pont de Nieppe and Erquinghem, these bridges were inspected by Pulteney on the 16th October. On the 17th October Armentieres fell to the 3rd Corps but the capture of some German stragglers surprised the British leadership. Many of the prisoners were from the German 6th Army that were not known to be in the area, perhaps German numbers were greater than expected. The advance split the 2nd and 3rd corps with the gap being plugged by General Conneau's French Cavalry.

The following day was relatively quiet with movements of the 4th and 6th divisions pushing through some well armed opposition. The advance at this point was slow. Generals Smith-Dorrien, Rawlinson and Pulteney were cautious perhaps made more so by the appearance of the 6th

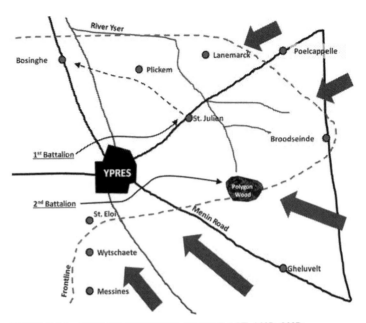

FIGURE 21 - THE MOVEMENTS OF THE 1ST AND 2ND
BATTALIONS AT YPRES

German Army. They had little enthusiasm for General
French's grand offensive and luckily this wariness saved
the BEF from stumbling into a trap. On the 19th October
the 2nd corps started to meet resistance near La Bassee
and the 3rd corps advance was slowed. The 1st Corps
arrived from Aisne and assembled at Hazebrouck.

The German army led by General Erich von Falkenhayn
was reinforced and he believed that he could easily defeat
the BEF in a short time. Ostend was already in German
hands and he launched an attack along the line from Arras
to the sea. The general British and French advance became
slowed by heavier and heavier German resistance. The
retreat of French troops left the division exposed and 200

men were lost. General French did not see the German reinforcements and counter-attack as a problem and told Haig's 1st Corps to advance to Bruges and for the 2nd and 3rd Corps to continue the offensive capturing Le Pilly on Aubers Ridge.

On the 20th October the Germans attacked along the entire line with five and a half corps. Problems with the supply of ammunition started to create real issues for the frontline troops. The Royal Irish suffered the brunt of the attack, 257 were killed, 240 taken prisoner and 50 wounded. Such was the ferocity of the attack that the Germans were able to retake La Vallee and Ennetieres. General Pulteney ordered an immediate withdrawal.

The 7th Division containing the 2nd Battalion were ordered to hold Ypres at all costs with support from the 3rd Cavalry Division. They faced an attack by the 23rd German Reserve Corps but despite heavy attacks and only 186 casualties they managed to hold. The following day Sir John French was melancholic, the BEF were on the brink of a major reversal from heroic victory to devastating defeat. He decided that the 2nd and 3rd Corps should contain the enemy advance and for Haig's 1st Corps to attack towards Thourout. The French commander, General Joffre diverted the 9th French Corps from the defensive line in the south to support the BEF in Flanders but even so Sir John French suggested a withdrawal and entrenching at Bologne, Joffre point blank refused this. The line was holding, just, and General Joffre didn't want to risk giving ground to the Germans in his own country. By the end of the day the rest of the 1st Corps slowly engaged and by the end of the day the German advance was halted completely.

By the 23rd October the 7th Division was positioned south of Zonnebech and poised for some very heavy fighting. Heavily bombarded by German artillery the line cracked on the 24th. Major-General Capper got news that the Germans were breaking through to the north at Polygon Wood. He assembled an ad hoc blocking force made from his own staff officers, cooks and auxiliaries some not even armed to advance and counter the break.

The 2nd Battalion of the Warwick's held a part of the line with the Northumberland Hussars and managed to check every attack on them losing 300 men and their commanding officer in the process. General Haig sent up the 5th Brigade as reinforcements along with the French 6th Cavalry but the Germans were content to sit in the newly taken Polygon Wood. By this time the whole division was starting to tire, in total the day had seen the loss of 120 officers and 2700 men. The 2nd Wiltshire's were nearly gone, the Scots Guard, Royal Welch and South Staffordshire's all lost 500 men a piece. The Grenadiers, Queens and the Warwick's had lost 300 men each. Overall 45% of the officers and 37% of the men were gone.

In the south the 2nd Corps were attacked by 11 battalions of German infantry but managed to hold, the 3rd division however had to abandon ground and pull back a mile with the loss of 1079 officers and men. The rest of the 3rd Corps held a 12 mile front against numerous attacks although infiltration and enfilade forced them back. Further north Allenby's cavalry division defended Messines ridge but fell back to St Eloi leaving a hole in the line. The 7th division remained in position under bombardment from Paschendale ridge all day and into the night. Further retreats and miscommunications created more holes that were plugged as quickly as possible. The 2nd battalion as part of Lawford's 22nd brigade were eventually given permission to withdraw at dusk to link with the 1st Corps.

Over the 25th and 26th October the 7th division were driven from Kruiseeche during heavy rain and enemy bombardment. Elsewhere along the line there was less action as the German advance began to stall. Sir French in constant contact with Kitchener at home began to report that the shortages of ammunition were becoming a major problem. Kitchener either didn't get them or was confused by the fact that French continued to report successful engagements, whatever the facts Kitchener refused the BEF more supplies and told them to economise more.

It was during October that Bernard Law Montgomery got his first taste of war. Later known as Field Marshall Montgomery and the regiment's future Colonel-in-Chief, Bernard Montgomery joined the Royal Warwickshire Regiment in 1908 as a Second Lieutenant. During the battle of Ypres he was shot through the chest by a sniper. The bullet punctured his lung and left him incapacitated in no man's land. One of his platoon ran out to rescue him but he was shot in the head and caused the snipers to fire at the bodies. Montgomery was shot again in the leg. With the soldier collapsed over him he feigned death until nightfall when a stretcher team found and rescued him.

In the lull in fighting between the 27th and 31st of October General Falkenhayn reviewed his forces and tried to examine why his 4th and 6th Armies had failed to break the BEF despite outnumbering them significantly, its only success so far had been to draw French troops away from other key battlegrounds in the south. He decided to attack at Gheluvelt between the 1st and 7th divisions of the BEF in an effort to force a breach in the lines. The attack was swift and vicious. Many units such as the 1st Scots and Black Watch were forced to fight hand to hand and bore the bulk of the fighting. By the start of November the 1st Loyal North Lancaster's had been reduced to just 1 officer and 35 men.

Successful German attacks occurred along the line but were repulsed at Gheluvelt. Haig, now in command of this section after Rawlinson had been recalled to Britain ordered a counter-attack but needed assistance from General Dubois' French infantry. They failed to retake the village of Zandvoorde but the German advance was halted. The Germans had taken heavy losses and they had only pushed the British back 3 kilometers. Gheluvelt was finally taken by the Germans on the 31st October when the 16th Bavarians and 246th Infantry managed to overrun the depleted British battalions.

The fall of Gheluvelt was an indication to General Haig that the line was on the point of collapse but knew he had to hold as long as possible. The battered 7th division with remnants of the 1st division held the line on the right nearly collapsing under the weight of three attacks. General Bulfin of the 1st Division realised that defence was impossible and chose instead the wild plan of attack. He launched a counter attack on the Germans retaking just 800 meters at the cost of 1090 men. At Holkebeke and Zandvoorde the BEF's assault met the German attack head on with allied bombing delaying and depleting the

Germans. The ridge at Messines was lost and regained several times as the battle ebbed and flowed.

On the 5th November the 7th Division were finally relieved on the frontlines and the Battle of Ypres slowly ground to a halt, the last actions took place on the 11th November when a last push by Falkenhayn proved too feeble. At Nonneboschen the German 1st Foot lost so many officers and were so demoralised that they fled before the 1st Division effectively ending the battle.

Between the 7th October and the 5th November the 7th Division of which the 2nd Battalion of the Royal Warwickshire Regiment was a part lost 10,000 of its 12,000 men. Total losses for the whole battle amounted to 581,155 killed, wounded or missing. The regular British army was effectively destroyed in a battle in which both sides expected a swift and easy victory but had deteriorated into a bitter stalemate.

The losses at Ypres indicated to many that the war would go on a lot longer than Christmas as had been promised at the start of the war. Peace movements began to crop up across Europe but all of them were turned down by the governments however an informal unofficial truce was held over Christmas in the trenches. Some 100,000 British and German troops ceased fire on Christmas Eve. The two sides shouted greetings to each other across no man's land, some even left the trenches to meet the enemy to talk and play football. The Warwickshire's met the soldiers of the 134th Saxon Regiment on Boxing day in Plogsteert Wood, they chatted with the German soldiers and exchanged gifts such as buttons. Although condemned by senior officers the informal truce held until New Year whereupon the war resumed.

With the loss of experienced soldiers and the severe depletion of the BEF recruiting and conscription was made a priority. Throughout the spring of 1915 fifteen new army divisions, six Territorial Army divisions and the 2nd Canadian division were all assigned to the BEF and moved to the frontlines. These units took a larger section of the frontline including La Bassee Canal, Lens and 15 miles along the river Somme. Conscription was not hard as many young men felt it their duty to fight for the country and gladly took the kings shilling to join up.

The 5th, 6th, 7th and 8th Battalions of the Royal Warwickshire's, all territorial units, arrived in France in March 1915. They were brigaded in the 143rd brigade of the 48th Division and began their war with training at Bailleut before being moved up to the trenches. The 1st and 2nd Battalions so depleted by the Battle of Ypres were reinforced. They received some experienced men from surviving regiments but the majority were novices. General Haig was recorded as saying 'I have not got an army in France really, but a collection of divisions untrained in the field. The actual fighting army will be evolved from them'.

A second action at Ypres saw the 1st and 2nd battalions engaged once more in a battle that revealed more horrors of the Great War to the average soldier. The 2nd Battle of Ypres can be divided in to two actions, that of Festubert and that of Loos. They were part of a major offensive by the Germans and saw the first use of chlorine gas in warfare. The German plan was to use the 23rd and 26th Reserve Corps to seize Langemarck, Pilckem Ridge and Ypres Canal. They faced the French 45th (Algerians) and the 87th Territorial Division of the BEF.

The attack began at 5 pm on the 22nd April 1915 with a short bombardment in which chlorine gas was released from 5,730 cylinders. Completely unequipped the French divisions immediately retreated in panic opening up a 5 mile gap to the left of the 1st Canadian division however, the Germans were too cautious to take advantage of this and the allies were able to form a new defensive line. At St Julien the 1st Battalion Royal Warwickshire's were heavily engaged with Lieutenant Jowett being killed along with a whole platoon save a single survivor. Throughout the day the battalion suffered 7 officers being killed, 9 wounded and 500 other men being either killed or wounded. Attacks continued at Shell Trap farm where Lance Corporal W. Milner won a Distinguished Combat Medal for storming an enemy machine gun post.

On the 24th April a second gas attack was made, this time on St Julien. Canadian troops survived by soaking cloth in urine or water and holding it against their mouths and noses to filter out the effects of the gas. Marshal Foch, the French general in charge of co-coordinating the defence of France ordered the local French forces to launch a counter-attack against the Germans but they felt it too risky and sat tight. Instead the BEF conducted a series of assaults between the 23rd and the 26th April with inadequate artillery cover and no French support. General

French became concerned that General Smith-Dorrien was becoming too eager to withdraw from combat and had him replaced by General Plummer to command the 5th Corps. It was a common perception that the British army at this time was one of 'lions led by donkeys' and much can be said to agree with this viewpoint. The Generals were unprepared and untrained for this type of all out confrontational battle. Most were veterans of the colonial wars in which battles were either simple affairs at one location or they were up against armies with inferior weapons and tactics. In World War I the Germans were equal in weaponry and tactics and instead of one on one battles at key locations the battlefield became strung out over long distances with multiple assaults, bombardments and counter-attacks existing along its length at any one time.

During May the Germans launched four more gas attacks and seized both the Bellewarde and Frezenberg ridges. At Festubert on the 15th May the BEF using mostly Indian troops attempted a counter attack including the first use by the British of a night attack. It began with a 60 hour bombardment before the advance of six allied divisions against only three German ones. The 2nd Battalion took part suffering 200 casualties with two officers killed and four wounded. In total the allies suffered 16,000 casualties for the gain of only 1300 yards. By the 25th May the Ypres salient had been reduced to a depth of only three miles but the German advance had been halted.

In June the 1st Battalion saw action at Lancashire Farm and Bosinghe losing 2 officers and 12 men with 54 wounded. Captain Stevens was awarded the Military Cross for an attack at Pillem. By the 22nd July the 1st Battalion was at Mailly with losses to date totaling 20 officers and 324 men killed and 1,500 other casualties. This total figure of 1,844 exceeds by over three quarters the battalions operating strength.

The other part of the 2nd Battle of Ypres occurred between the 25th September and 14th October 1915 at Loos. The action here was part of Marshal Joffre's campaign in the Champagne region. It was to be a British attack on German lines. It was preceded by four days of bombardment designed to wear down the Germans before the infantry assault. At 5.50 am on the morning of the 25th September 140 tonnes of chlorine gas were released against the Germans however changing wind patterns actually blew some of the gas onto British lines stalling some elements of the attack. At 6.45 am with a 7 to 1 advantage over the enemy the British attacked.

The 2nd Battalion in the 22nd Brigade now under the command of Brigadier-General Steele took part in the 7th Divisions attack. They captured some quarries and managed to reach the 2nd German line before stiff resistance began to hold them. Private Arthur Vickers won both the Victoria Cross and the Medalle Militaire for his efforts in cutting the wire defending the German lines. This advance however was very costly. Lieutenant-Colonel LeFroy and 2 other officers were killed, 7 officers were wounded and 1 taken prisoner. This left the surviving 140 men without any senior command. 64 of their comrades had been killed, 171 wounded and 273 were missing. Lieutenant William Freeman was forced to take command.

Elsewhere in the battle the 9th Scottish Division took the Hoenzollen Redoubt whilst the 15th Scottish Division took Loos itself. The 10th French Army took Sochez but the Germans retained control of Vimy Ridge. With such an advantage over the enemy it was expected that the attack would take more ground. This failure was laid squarely at General French's door for being too slow to bring up the reserves to support the general advance; he was replaced as commander of the BEF by General Haig.

THE DISASTER OF GALLIPOLI

In November 1914 the Ottoman Empire had joined the Austro-German Alliance. Their control of the Middle East was seen to be pivotal to the British. Their involvement threatened links with India and it had opened up another front to threaten the Balkans and Greece. With dead lock on the Western Front both the Allies and the Germans saw Turkey and the Middle-East as a theatre of war in which the war could be pressed forward.

Originally the Ottoman Empire although allied with the Germans against the Russians were not required to provide military aid this however changed in late 1914 when British Naval advisors were replaced by German ones. They closed the Dardanelles, Russia's only access to the Mediterranean, to shipping and bombarded Russian installations on the Black Sea. With shipping threatened the French and British offered an ultimatum to the Turkish authorities which when unanswered led to war. Allied intervention in to this theatre of operations was designed to decisively reopen the Dardanelles Strait and relieve trade and support the Russians who needed their Black

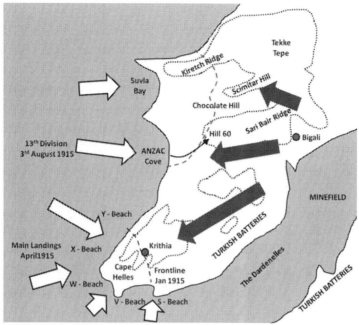

FIGURE 22 - THE LANDING BEACHES OF GALLIPOLI

Sea ports to help them in their struggle against the German advances in the west.

The attack was directed on the Aegean side of the Dardanelles at Gallipoli. An amphibious landing would take out the Turkish batteries allowing the British and French navies to safely clear the Dardanelles of enemy ships and mines whilst Russian forces attacked overland through the Caucasus mountains.

Command of the attack on Gallipoli was given to Sir Ian Hamilton. Hamilton was the commander of the Mediterranean Expeditionary Force (MEF) with a good service career. With so many British troops tied up in the trenches of the Western Front much of the troops for the

183

MEF came from the colonies. The Australian and New Zealand Army Corps (ANZACs) formed the bulk of the forces with some French. The first landings occurred on the 25th April 1915 after a short naval action. The landings took place on the southern tip of Gallipoli across six beaches. Mistakes in navigation led to many of the ANZACs landing in a difficult position named Anzac Cove and losses were heavy. A beach head was established and the Turkish defenders were forced to retreat north towards Krithia a series of battles were fought and the allied advance was halted. The terrain and the under estimation of the quality of the Turkish soldiers ended all hope of a quick decisive strike by the allies.

By the middle of 1915 reinforcements were badly needed and Hamilton was allocated five new divisions including the 13th Division that contained the 9th Battalion of the Royal Warwickshire Regiment. Hamilton asked for an experienced commander to lead this new corps. He wished for someone like Byng or Rawlinson but as both were junior to the commander of the 10th division he was sent Lieutenant-General Stopford instead. Stopford was an elderly officer who had never commanded a large formation and was unprepared for the horrors found in Gallipoli.

Supplies for both sides were short and for the British nearly all water had to be shipped in from Egypt as the Turkish held the majority of the freshwater springs. Nearly all the soldiers had dysentery and there were so many corpses, often left unburied in no man's land that clouds of flies covered the skies. This was the battlefield that the 120,000 reinforcements arrived in. The main landing was designed to be made at Suvla Bay in the north with an aim of allowing an outbreak of the ANZACs and outflanking the Turkish positions.

On the 3rd August the 13th Division and 29th Indian Brigade were landed at Anzac Cove secretly at night. They came ashore and were led into secretly constructed trenches and caves. These reinforcements were placed under the command of the ANZAC commander, Lieutenant-General Birdwood. The plan was to use attacks in the south at Helles and at Anzac Cove as a diversion to allow the main landings at Suvla Bay to take place. On the 6th August 1915 the 9th Battalion took part in the ANZAC diversion joining troops in an assault on Lone Pine in a line from Russell's Top to the Sea. The assault was across a narrow front with much hand to hand fighting. At Russell's Top three Light Horse Brigades made repeated charges but insufficient numbers led to a massacre, with 75% of the cavalrymen falling within 15 minutes.

On the 7th August, Mustafa Kemal commander of the 19th Turkish Division and later known as Attaturk, the future leader of Turkey, realised that a major offensive was beginning and moved to occupy the ridge of Sari Bair halting the current advance. Two columns were created to advance on Chunuk Bair and take Hill Q and Cheman Tepe. At Suvla things did not go well, only Major Willmers Anafarta Detachment defended the area against the 25,000 allied troops but the landings were delayed and confused orders created many problems. Hamilton's orders to get all the men ashore and then advance were taken literally no soldiers left the landing zone until they were all ashore. The beaches soon became crowded as transport after transport delivered their troops in the same space. Turkish reinforcements arrived swiftly and the tactical advantage was lost, a general attack was ordered on the 9th August at the same time as a Turkish attack was mounted which retook Chunuk Bair at a cost of 5,000 casualties. Like on the Western front a stalemate was developing.

Between the 27th and 28th August the 9th Battalion saw action in which waves of under strength soldiers suffering from dysentery unsuccessfully attempted to seize Hill 60. The 13th Division in the campaign lost 6,000 out of the 10,500 engaged and the 9th Battalion lost all of its officers. One of the wounded was Second Lieutenant William Slim. Slim would later lead troops in Burma during the Second World War as a Field Marshal. Slim was so badly wounded at Gallipoli that he was invalided out of the army for awhile. He rejoined the battalion in Mesopotamia in October. He served only a short time before being wounded again and transferring to the Indian Army.

The disaster at Gallipoli cost the lives of 25,000 British, 10,000 French, 7,300 Australians, 2,400 New Zealanders and 1,700 Indians. In October Hamilton was relieved of command and replaced by General Monro. He decided it was better to focus on the Western Front and in November Kitchener allowed an evacuation to be ordered. The 9th Battalion were evacuated from Suvla Bay and returned to Helles where they rested for a few weeks. The evacuation from Helles began on the 19th December and lasted until the 9th January. The winter in Gallipoli was particularly hard as Second Lieutenant Philip Gething recounted; 'I found six men had crawled back and were huddled together on a step frozen to death. We then found about twenty men lying by a hedge with ground sheets over them more or less frozen stiff' The battalion had only to endure this for a short while before they left Gallipoli and arrived at Port Said in Egypt from where they were posted to the defence of the Suez Canal for much of the rest of the war.

AWAY FROM THE ACTION

Whilst many of the battalions of the regiment were engaged across Europe there were inevitably periods of down time. The British Army tried to rotate its forces away from the frontline trenches when they could, giving them rest periods to avoid battle stress. This was not always possible, for example the 2nd Battalion was nearly engaged for the whole of the war. In contrast the 1st Battalion had a significant time spent manning the trenches, this was not as peaceful as may be expected; they were still on the front lines even if they weren't taking part in active attacks on the enemy.

Following the second battle of Ypres the 1st Battalion were sent to man the trenches at a location named Lancashire Farm here intermittent shelling and sniper fire accounted for 4 fatalities and 40 casualties, being away from offensive action did not guarantee safety. Throughout 1915 and up to July 1916 when they would take part in the Battle of the Somme the 1st Battalion moved from trench line to trench line. July was spent in Canal Bank Trenches near Ypres where heavy shelling caused a constant stream of casualties before at the end of the month they moved to Mailley-Maillet. They remained here until July 1916. Every few weeks they would be rotated from the trenches to rest or form Royal Engineer work parties at places such as Acheux, Forceville or Varennes. They spent much of their time maintaining the defensive line and repairing and cleaning trenches.

THE BATTLE OF THE SOMME

The BEF had already struggled to hold Ypres on the French-Belgium Border whilst the French were engaged in vicious combat at Verdun, between these two battlegrounds lay the River Somme. Marshall Joffre decided that this section of the line was vulnerable. He believed that an attack here might not necessarily make ground but was likely to kill more Germans than they could replace this was to be a battle of annihilation by attrition.

With French forces tied up in Verdun planning fell to Sir Henry Rawlinson the commander of the BEF's 4th Army to organise what was planned to be the decisive action of the war. Originally looking at Ypres again he eventually turned his attention south to the interface of the BEF and the French Army on the Somme. Haig argued for a broad frontal assault with deep penetration whilst Rawlinson preferred a more cautious step by step advance securing ground as they went. He advocated that the infantry should only have to advance no more than 3,000 yards in each attack. This was a sensible plan; the German defences in the Somme were based on 2 lines between 2,000 and 4,000 yards apart fixed around fortified villages with strong points. Each line had three or more trenches protected by copious amounts of barbed fire. Additionally

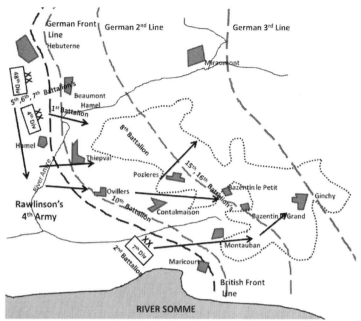

FIGURE 23 - THE POSITIONS OF THE REGIMENT AT THE
BATTLE OF THE SOMME

German standard operating orders required immediate counter-attack when assaulted. Whilst this brought more enemy under British guns it denied them the ability to advance too quickly. General Haig disapproved of this overly cautious plan and a compromise was sought. He was particularly keen on an element of surprise. Rawlinson provided this by suggesting Allenby's 3rd Corps perform a diversionary attack against German forces in Gommecourt.

Sixteen British divisions and five French divisions were assigned to attack the German trenches. There would have been more French but significant attacks on their lines at Verdun had pulled many of them south to defend this key

189

point. The British plan, now led by General Haig, was a steady advance along a 14 mile front from Serre in the north to Maricourt in the south. Lastly Rawlinson's 4th Army had two cavalry divisions which would be used to exploit any gaps or advances. The true element of surprise was lost when the divisions raised observation balloons alerting the Germans to massing forces and a vicious bombardment was used that indicated an imminent attack.

The bombardment began on the 29th June. 1,400 British Guns fired over 1.6 million shells at the German lines. This was designed to soften the enemy's lines. Next came 1 million shrapnel shells that were hoped to tear apart the wire in the no man's land so that the infantry could advance in good order. Finally 283 howitzers joined the bombardment and counter battery fire aimed to take out the Germans own artillery began. The bombardment was only partially successful with some areas completely cleared of wire and enemy artillery and others left completely unscathed. The bombardment continued up until the attack and even then proceeded using a creeping barrage in which the gunners altered their aim so that the barrage crept ahead of the advancing infantry. On the 1st July at 7.28 am 17 mines that had been dug under the German lines were detonated giving the signal to attack. Along the line pressed by their officers 60,000 soldiers left their trenches and advanced across the wastes of no man's land to attack the German trenches.

The Royal Warwickshire Regiment were heavily engaged right along the line. The 1st Battalion were at Serre and Beaumont Hamel. This section of the line was well defended by the Germans with the topography in their favour. The Germans had a mine field to defend them and the British lacked a suitable observation point. Once the 8th Corps had closed on the German lines their commander, Lieutenant-General Hunter-Weston pressed the attack on Serre, Redan Ridge and Beaumont Hamel simultaneously, much of this was led by the 31st Division. The Warwickshire's own division, the 4th, was to the right of the 31st division and suffered 61 casualties as they advanced on a narrow front near Heidenkopf and up the slope of Redan Ridge. Although damaged by the bombardment the Germans were able to put up stiff resistance. In places the line crumpled and pockets of German infantry became outflanked. Casualties increased when as the Germans withdrew their own artillery came into play. Due to rotations the 1st Battalion left the front returning to the trenches on the 7th July before moving back up to Ypres.

The 2nd Battalion, part of the 7th Division attacked Mametz where their brigade formed the left flank of the assault. Progress was slow. They did manage to secure the first line of trenches but were unable to advance further. Two companies of the battalion including Captain Hodgkinson, a sergeant and 4 men were able however to capture 200 German prisoners. By 4 pm the village of Mametz was clear and a new front established.

The 7th Battalion secured the trenches behind the advancing infantry. They, like the 5th battalion, suffered light casualties. The 6th and 8th Battalions however were nearly annihilated in front of Beaumont Hamel where they acted in support of the main attack. The 6th battalion had

191

10 officers killed and 10 wounded with 436 others killed, wounded or missing. The 8th battalion had its commanding officer – Lieutenant-Colonel Innes killed with 7 other officers and 14 more wounded. 569 soldiers were either killed, wounded or went missing. They did however manage to reach the third German line. Private Sidney Willamson of the Royal Warwickshire's described the Somme as; 'the battlefield was nothing but shell holes and barbed wire, but now I noticed many dead and dying, and the line of soldiers was not to be seen. With no officers or NCO near I felt alone and still went forward from shell hole to shell hole'.

The day's action was somewhat of a mixed bag of successes and failures. In the north few gains were made and attacks by the 8th, 10th and 3rd Divisions all failed. Between La Boisette and Fricourt the BEF managed to penetrate half a mile into the enemy lines. The south fared better with the 13th Corps and the French divisions taking all their objectives. In terms of the Royal Warwickshire Regiment, they could have been proud to have been involved in actions that proved successful but instead of collapsing the German line had held and Haig's plans of pushing through were looking more unlikely. Rawlinson's fixation on step by step advance and secure meant he missed an opportunity to throw in the reserves to overwhelm the German defences. Ironically his cautious approach probably cost more lives in the long run as the battle would now last for days longer. At the close of the 1st Day of the Somme the British had advanced 1 mile along a 4 mile front at the cost 19,240 killed and 35,493 wounded, it had been the bloodiest battle in the history of the British army.

The following day little happened; there were no real plans at the command level for anything other than the initial push so convinced were they that the Germans would be in full retreat. So it was left to individual Corps to push forward on their own initiative. General Falkenhayn although content that his lines had held was prudent enough to realise that there was a real risk of a breakthrough. He reinforced his immediate counter-attack orders and added a no surrender policy to it. This galvanised the line but sapped away at materiel and would lay more men beneath the British guns during any attack. Back at Headquarters General Rawlinson organised the 4th Army in to a series of assaults that took the village of Contalmaison and the woods of Mametz and Trones.

With a stalemate starting to develop General Gough's Reserve Army took over control of the northern zone of the BEF lines to free up more men for future attacks. On the 14th July Sir Henry Rawlinson ordered elements of Horne's XV Corps to attack up Caterpillar Valley using night as cover. During the initial stages of the action the 7th Battalion attacked near Ovillers and the 11th Battalion reached Pozieres.

The 15th July 1916 saw a landmark in warfare. The deployment of the first tanks in combat by the BEF. Thirty five of the new and sometimes unreliable machines took part near Trones Wood. Again the 2nd Battalion as part of the XV corps advanced to Fleurs and took Courcelette. Nine tanks led this attack with a further nine mopping up behind them. During this action the 5th Battalion distinguished themselves by taking Ovillers between the 16th and 18th July. The 7th Battalion took heavy casualties here with Lieutenants Knox and Fowle being killed along with 140 other casualties.

The 7th Division including the 7th Battalion supported by the 2nd Battalion advanced on the left flank of the attack with the 21st Division. The attack here focused on the woodlands on top of the ridge line. The attack was successful and the woods of Bazentin were taken whilst on the right a 6 day struggle took place over Delville Wood. The 7th Battalion had 1 officer and 41 men killed and 200 other casualties. The 7th battalion went on to perform brilliantly during an attack at Pozieres in which Captain Hoskings and Lieutenant Carey were highly praised for their performance during this attack.

Between the 22nd and 27th July the 14th and 15th Battalions saw action at Montauban on the right of the line. The 14th Battalion were hit hard and lost 4 officers with 10 more wounded or missing, of the other ranks 470 were made casualties. The 15th battalion fared little better with heavy losses taken whilst moving through High Wood. The attack continued from Montauban on to Longueval and Delville Wood. Here officer losses were so great that Company Sergeant Major Baker was left in charge of 2 platoons.

Whilst the 14th, 15th and 16th Battalions struggled up through Montauban the 10th battalion were at the trenches at Becourt Wood where heavy shelling killed the commanding officer, Lieutenant-Colonel Henderson. Lieutenant-Colonel Dakeyne took command of the battalion and renewed the attack taking only 154 casualties in return. At the close of July the 14th, 15th and 16th the battalions finally secured a front from Delville Wood to High Wood. The 15th battalion relieved the 14th whilst the 16th supported this attack. It was during this action that Lieutenants Dell and Sander of the 16th battalion distinguished themselves by carrying back wounded under fire.

Since the opening of the battle and the horrific losses of the first day the British and French continued to make some, if a little slow, progress. Throughout July Marshal Joffre insisted that the BEF attacked the centre of the line but Haig resolutely refused preferring to push harder in the south closer to his French allies. With Montauban and the wooded ridges east of it secured Haig now felt safe enough to assault the centre and began an attack between Thiepval and Pozieres. The attack, launched on the 5th August, was initially led by ANZAC (Australian and New Zealand Army Corps) troops who focused on Mouquet Farm.

On the 18th August the 5th and 6th battalions joined the attack pushing 1,000 yards into enemy lines taking a fortified outpost and capturing 6 officers and 594 German soldiers. Captain Crockford of the 6th battalion won a Military Cross for crack shooting by disabling one machine gun post whilst Corporal Haseler won a Distinguished Conduct Medal for distracting another. Between the two battalions they lost 8 officers and 292 men. Elsewhere along the line the 11th Battalion had attacked Martinpuich but were forced to retire with 152 casualties. The 8th battalion renewed this attack but 'D' company were wiped out and 'C' company found the resistance too strong to succeed. Still the German centre refused to yield.

The 2nd Battalion were by this time in trenches near Bosigny. The Battalion was led by Lieutenant-Colonel John

Elkington, son of the Lieutenant-Colonel Elkington who had commanded the battalion in Jamaica. The battalion was part of an undermanned brigade that were given orders to withdraw from their positions. Elkington led his men through the trenches. In the dark of night his battalion mixed with those of Colonel Mainwarings and together they arrived at the village of St. Quentin. Here Elkington hoped to get the men some rest and food. They were met by the village's mayor, the mayor believed the presence of soldiers in the village would endanger them. Elkington agreed to occupy the railway station outside the village to avoid bringing any Germans down on St. Quentin.

Later Colonel Mainwaring went into the town to get food and signed an agreement in exchange for food. Although Mainwaring and Elkington successfully removed their troops from the area the agreement note reached allied command who interpreted it as an agreement to surrender to the Germans to save the town. Elkington and Mainwaring were charged with cowardice and conspiring to surrender, a treasonous charge. The court martial cleared both men of cowardice but convicted them of surrendering to the enemy. Mainwaring accepted the dishonourable discharge but Elkington was from a family of soldiers and wanted to fight and regain his honour. On leaving the British army he enlisted in the French Foreign Legion. He served with distinction, being severely wounded when storming a German redoubt and winning both the Medaille Militaire and the Croix de Guerre.

Another push came on the 3rd September this time along the River Ancre that ran just north of Thiepval. During this action the 2nd, 14th, 15th and 16th battalions were all involved, consolidating gains made earlier in the battle. The 2nd battalion went into action alongside the Manchester Regiment and the Welch Fusiliers managing to gain a footing in the village of Ginchy. Here they dug in as best they could in fact Lieutenant Harrowy managed to maintain a post in Ginchy for 5 days before German counter-attacks forced the battalions to withdraw. Three officers were killed, 8 were wounded or missing and 320 others were taken casualty.

The 14th battalion attacked Falfremont Farm and Wedge Wood during which Captain Brooke and 2nd Lieutenant Barrow of 'C' company captured several gun pits. 'A' and 'B' companies both managed to advance well but were soon withdrawn. The 15th Battalion made a second attack on the Farm but were driven back by machine gun fire. A third attempt was made by the 16th battalion from a reserve position in the evening but this too was unsuccessful. The following day the 16th battalion supported the Royal Norfolk's dug in as close as practical to the German lines. The farm was finally captured and the 15th battalion cleared Leuze Wood. These New Army battalions were fast becoming seasoned combat troops.

On the 25th September the 16th battalion returned to a reserve position to hold gains made by the Cheshire Regiment. The advance began at 12 pm and within an hour and a quarter had made good ground. The 15th battalion advanced 2 miles attacking and gaining ground north of Morval. The following day Thiepval fell and the BEF was now in possession of the crest of the Thiepval-Pozieres-High Wood Ridge.

During October further attacks on the lines were made by both sides. On the 12th October the 1st Battalion under the cover of a creeping barrage left their trenches at Les Boeufs and took part in 4 waves of unsuccessful attacks before being withdrawn, they had 5 officers killed and 260 other casualties. By the 22nd October they were back in the trenches where they provided support to the Royal Dublin Fusiliers.

The battle lurched on into November with the last major action of the Somme occuring on the 13th November. Bad weather delayed this attack aimed north of the river Ancre at Beaumont Hamel. Beaumont Hamel was secured successfully and 7,000 prisoners were taken however Serre remained in German hands, slowly the battle of the Somme petered out. Only the 10th Battalion of the Royal Warwickshire's took part in the final attack that occurred on the 18th November at Beaucourt sur Ancre. The attack was hampered by snow but Sergeant Kimberley and two platoons were able to establish a bombing post near Grandcourt which they held well into the evening.

Winter even in modern warfare was a difficult affair and the Battle of the Somme intended to be a lightening attack was inevitably slowed and prolonged into the approaching bad weather. The 2nd Battalion remained in trenches at Ploegsteert Wood. The 10th and 11th Battalions manned trenches at Neuve Chapelle whilst the 5th, 6th, 7th and 8th Battalions occupied trenches around le Sars and Butte de Warlincourt. The 182nd brigade containing the second units of the 5th to 8th Battalions finally completed training and joined the rest of the troops at Fauguissant. These battalions remained in France in to 1917.

The 1st Battalion spent the rest of the war in trenches across the front but took part in no more major engagements. The 2nd Battalion were back in Beaumont Hamel in December 1916. During January they ran communications through the trenches and in March they were part of a successful occupation of Courcelles. They spent time at the front at St Leger until their redeployment to Italy. The 5th battalion held the trenches at Peronne. The 6th Battalion were attacked by a German raid on the 4th February, the attack was repulsed but one officer and 37 men were killed. Corporal Bardell was awarded a bar to his Military Medal in this action. The 8th Battalion crossed the Somme and entered Halle and began patrols into St Radegarde, Mont St Quentin and Peronne. The 10th battalion moved to the Hebuterne Sector whilst the 11th, 14th, 15th and 16th Battalions remained near Bailleul.

WAR IN THE MIDDLE EAST

While the majority of the regiment had been run through the grinder of the Somme the 9th Battalion that had served in Gallipoli were moved to the Middle East. When the Ottomans had entered the war on the Germans side they threatened much of Britain's lucrative and important links to India and the oil fields in Mesopotamia. With the increased mechanisation of the army and the world as a whole, oil was fast becoming a vital commodity. Whilst the landings at Gallipoli were designed to be a key strike against this new enemy it was decided that interests in the Middle East needed to be protected more than a new front be attempted through the Dardenelles.

In August of 1914 Force D a weak division of the British army in the Persian Gulf were called into action. The force was landed from India at the port of Abadan at an Anglo-Persian Oil refinery. Led by General John Nixon this force advanced up the Shatt el-Arab waterway to Basra. In Egypt a second force looked to the defence of the Suez Canal.

In April of 1915 steamers and barges were used to forge their way up the rivers Tigris and Euphrates in to what we know today of as Iraq. This advance was opposed by the Turkish armies but despite this the British Army was able to seize Ctesiphon and Kut-al-amara with some ease. Major-General Townshend's 6th division was able to attack Baghdad itself on the 22nd November 1915. A vicious counter-attack led by General Colmar von der Goltz evicted the British on the 25th November and they fell back on Kut-al-amara where they were put to siege.

It was at this point that the 9th Battalion as part of the 13th Division arrived in Mesopotamia. They were hastily assembled into a relief force for Kut-al-amara leaving their positions in the south in February 1916. Led by Lieutenant-General Aylmer the force consisted of mostly Indian troops that had seen action at the Battle of Loos. The 9th Battalion were sent to join this relief column that was mustering at Sheikh Sa'ad. Here the advance column under the command of Major-General Younghusband encountered heavy Turkish defences and was slowed to a crawl. Two further attempts were made to relieve Kut-al-amara both unsuccessful. Soon the garrison were in dire straits; morale was low and supplies even more so. By April they had to butcher horses for food but due to their religious beliefs the Indian troops in the army were unable to do this. On the 29th April General Townshend surrendered the town. The 13,000 strong garrison was taken prisoner and marched across the desert to Turkey. Malnutrition and disease killed 4,000 British soldiers on this journey. This was a big embarrassment for the British army and General Nixon was swiftly replaced as commander in the region by General Frederick Maude.

General Maude planned a new offensive in Mesopotamia beginning in December 1916 with the retaking of Kut-al-amara. During January the 9th battalion were in the frontline trenches where they became caught up in a Turkish counter-attack. The Turks managed to push the battalion out of their trenches. Colonel Henderson the commander of the 9th battalion rallied the troops and tried to retake the position but in doing so he was severely wounded. Lieutenant Philips on attachment from the 13th battalion braved heavy fire to rescue Henderson and brought him back into the trenches. Unfortunately Henderson did not survive his wounds but Philips was awarded a Victoria Cross for his actions. He went on to become a Captain and survived the war.

In February 1917 the 13th division began to take part in the new offensive. This new Mesopotamian Expeditionary Force outnumbered the Turkish army two to one. Maude was a more cautious leader than General Nixon and carefully moved his troops forward. The 13th Division was targeted on the Turkish defensive line along the river Hai. Between the 25th January and 5th February this line was taken and the division moved on to a second Turkish strongpoint at Dahra Bend that was taken on the 16th February.

Between the 7th and 10th March the division became part of 'Marshall's Column', a flying column lead by Lieutenant-General William Marshall. The column crossed the river Diyala and pursued the fleeing Ottoman army back to Baghdad. General Maude's army entered Baghdad on the 11th March 1917 thereby taking control of the Ottoman province. The next few months were spent securing the area around the city. Elsewhere the Russians that had advanced through Turkey and Persia were pushing the Ottomans back towards Baghdad from the north. Ali Ishan Bey led 15,000 Turks of the Second Division to join Khalil after the Russian forces became destabilised by the start of the Russian Revolution. Moving through Delli Abbas and Duqma Maude focused on securing the Euphrates and Diyala rivers.

The rivers surrounding Baghdad were all heavily defended and despite superior numbers the British forces advanced with caution. A major push was set for the 11th April but Turkish forces were seen heading to Jebel Hamrin, a series of barren hills. Nervous of being overwhelmed by Ali Ishan's 2nd Division an evacuation was scheduled to withdraw the British troops. Luckily the 39th Brigade marched overnight to reinforce their positions. On the 18th April the division reached the Adhaim. This was an embankment along which the Turks had created defensive structures and trenches over some 3.5 miles. Crossing the Adhaim was disrupted by the almost biblical troubles including the flooding of the river Tigris and a plague of locusts they did however successfully dislodge the Turkish infantry taking 1,250 prisoners as they did so.

On the 30th April whilst an action was fought at Jebel Hamrin the division launched a simultaneous attack on the Shatt al'Adhaim during a sandstorm. The Battle of Jebel Hamrin did not go well for the British after expected Russian assistance from General Baratoff failed to materialise. They took heavy losses and failed to dislodge the Turkish from their positions. Ali Ishan took this opportunity to cross the Diyala River and join up with the Turkish 6th Army allowing the British to secure the hills.

The summer of 1917 was exceptionally hot with temperatures reaching 123 degrees Fahrenheit and both sides took the opportunity to rearm and prepare for the next campaign. In the Ottoman Empire it was decided to try and retake Baghdad whilst the British opted to hold the ground it had and try to push the Turks from Mesopotamia completely. In October further fighting took place at Jebel Hamrin and then on the 18th November the British commander, General Maude died of cholera. Command of the Expeditionary Force was passed to General Marshall who pressed on with a third action at Jebel Hamrin in December.

In February 1918 an advance on the Turkish Headquarters in Mosul was prepared and launched however the 9th Battalion remained in Baghdad. March was a major turning point in the war when the new Russian government that had emerged from the abdication of Tsar Nicholas signed an armistice with the axis powers. This in stroke removed a whole theatre of war from the German front. Troops that had once been committed to opposing the Russians could now be redeployed. In May the battalion moved to Dawalib before the 39th brigade as a whole was detached from the 13th Division and reassigned to General Lionel Dunstervilles North Persia Force. This force, nicknamed Dunsterforce, was aimed at supporting Armenia and attacking the Turks through the Caucasus via Persia.

During July there was fighting throughout Azerbaijan when they encountered Russian Red Army pressure. Unable to defend themselves Azerbaijan asked the Ottoman empire for help threatening Dunsterforce and the Russians. An Army of Islam marched on Baku to liberate it from Russian control and so Dunsterville quickly despatched troops to help them. In August the Armenian commander Colonel Stepanov prepared a force of 600 to attack north of Baku. The 9th Battalion of the Royal Warwickshire's and the North Staffordshire's were sent to assist. Later that month Turkish troops shelled the city and the British troops were pushed back to the hills surrounding the city. Initially advocating retreat the government persuaded Dunsterville to stay and after 600 Russian reinforcements arrived the force remained in place. The full Turkish assault began in early September. Heavy fighting and counter attacks continued for several days but on the 14th September the Baku Army and the British Dunsterforce evacuated the city and withdrew to Anzali. British losses totaled some 200 men whilst the Turks lost 8,000. Over 8,000 Armenians were killed and an equal number of Azeri's as well as over 20,000 Armenians being deported or killed. Within Baku between March and September sectarian violence accounted for terrible massacres by Armenians and Bolsheviks.

During October, Mosul's Oilfields were secured and finally the Ottoman defence collapsed. The armistice of Mudros was signed between Rauf Bey and Admiral Gough-Calthorpe on HMS *Agamemnon* in Mudros Harbour. The armistice ended Ottoman involvement in the war and a general demobilisation. British forces began a withdrawal and the 9th Battalion left Mesopotamia from Kirkuk on the 31st December.

THE BATTLE OF ARRAS

In 1917 the nature of the war began to change. On the home fronts new leaders in the form of David Lloyd George in Britain and Aristrade Briand in France prompted a reappraisal of the losses incurred at the Somme and in Gallipoli, more and more troops were seemingly being sucked into the battlefields across Europe and little progress seemed to be made on the Western Front. Essentially reduced to a static war of two opposing forces sitting in trenches opposite each other the war in France and Belgium were punctuated by sporadic offensives and counter-offensives. Some glimmer of hope came on the 6th April 1917 when the United States declare war on Germany although troops would not see action on the front for some time afterwards.

In France a plan was developed for a spring offensive, a failure of Russian troops on the eastern front meant that a planned pincer attack was abandoned and a new plan involving an attack in the Arras sector of the lines was developed. Involving Horne's 1st Army Allenby's 3rd Army and Gough's 5th Army the offensive was scheduled to begin on the 9th April.

205

FIGURE 24 - FRENCH POSTCARD OF THE RUINS OF ARRAS

Allenby's 3rd Army attacked on the right flank with a strong attack on the fortified village of Neuville Vitasse and managed to reach the edges of the Hindenburg Lines front trenches. Success continued along the river Scarpe where the 12th and 15th Divisions seized 67 field guns and advanced 3 miles. The 1st Battalion took part in this action.

Having marched from Camblan Chatelaur on the 7th April the battalion moved to the mustering area at X camp south of Ecoivres before 'D' Company were detached to the 11th Field Ambulance Unit to act as stretcher carriers. At 9.50 am on the 9th April the battalion with the rest of the 10th Brigade formed up at the assembly area and then advanced up to the Blue line that had already been secured. Here they formed work parties and despite snow fall worked on the lines. The following day the attack continued. 'A' and 'C' companies supported an advance by the Royal Irish Fusiliers with 'B' Company acting as a reserve. As they approached they found the Royal Irish pinned by machine gun fire from a chemical works and a railway embankment.

The battalion dug in along Huddle Trench unable to advance any further. The failure of the attack was due to the open ground allowing the Germans to observe all the activity prior to and during the attack. The battalion remained in Huddle Trench with the Royal Irish and Seaforth Highlanders until the 13th April when they returned to the trenches at Fampoux. They garrisoned these trenches and suffered several artillery barrages in the extreme cold and snow, finally on the 21st the battalion was withdrawn from the area for a rest before returning to regular trench duties.

On the left General Gough's attack was also less than successful. Gambling on attacks by tanks and with some false starts they failed to make much ground. In the centre General Horne led a mainly Canadian contingent towards Vimy Ridge. The 14th, 15th and 16th Battalions of the regiment were part of the 5th Division that had remained near Bailleul after the events on the Somme at the end of 1916, they now found themselves alongside the Canadian Corps led by Sir Julian Byng assaulting Vimy Ridge.

The Canadians led the attack advancing in the wake of an artillery barrage to secure the villages of Thelus and Farbus by the end of the 10th April. The 3rd Canadian division took the central position of La Folie Farm whilst on the left the 4th Canadian division were unable to secure their target hill until the evening. The 13th brigade of which the Warwickshire's were part was moved up on the 10th April as part of a reserve element to support the 1st and 2nd Canadians next advance. The Brigade along with a number of tanks assisted the 2nd Canadian Division as they secured Thelus. They were then redirected to support and consolidate the gains made.

The storming of the ridge was counted among the greatest actions of the war costing nearly 11,500 casualties. By the end of the day of the 12th April the Canadians had complete control of the ridge and had humiliated the German army. Supreme Commander Field Marshall Hindenburg demanded an enquiry that concluded that General Falkenhausen in command of the 6th Army had not reacted flexibly enough and had remained too static allowing the Canadian artillery to inflict too many casualties.

After Vimy Ridge the brigade was part of an attack in La Coulotte and a third engagement on the River Scarpe. Both of these actions occurred between the 23rd and 24th April 1917 after a period of rest and recovery both sides rearmed and consolidated their positions. Food, reinforcements and ammunitions were brought in and the battlefield could be cleared.

At the Scarpe a British push against Vis-an-Artois encountered stiff resistance and the British command were unwilling to press on and so a third attempt was made on the 3rd May using land secured around Achleux as a staging ground. Coinciding with an Australian attack the assault met resistance and failed to make much head way, heavy casualties resulted in the attack being called off. The Battle of Arras resulted in a total of 158,000 allied casualties and an estimated 120,000 German casualties.

After the Battle of Arras the 14ᵗʰ, 15ᵗʰ and 16ᵗʰ battalions of the Royal Warwickshire's found themselves part of a renewed campaign at Ypres. This battle is often referred to as the battle of Paschendaele and was made up of a series of battles. Very like the campaign on the Somme the over ambitious plan for the first day was well prepared with little thought of what came after. The campaign included 2,936 guns, the British 2ⁿᵈ Army, 9 divisions of Gough's 5ᵗʰ Army and the 1ˢᵗ French Army. The attack began at 3.50 am on the 31ˢᵗ July 1917. On the left two French divisions struck between the villages of Steenstraat and Bosinghe. On the right the 2ⁿᵈ Army attacked Pilckem Ridge to advance on the Gheluvelt plateau. Early successes were stalled by bad weather and multiple German counter attacks and the action began to be dragged out into a series of battles across the length of the battlefield.

On the 26ᵗʰ September the 14ᵗʰ, 15ᵗʰ and 16ᵗʰ Battalions provided support to ANZAC forces in Polygon Wood and on the 4ᵗʰ October they took part in the Battle of Broodseinde. This action was delayed by heavy rain which was quickly turning the Ypres area into a wasteland of mud. The attack was part of General Plummer's cautious 'bite and hold approach' to taking ground. Seizing Broodseinde would secure the Gheluvelt plateau.

Despite worsening weather the 5ᵗʰ division containing the Warwickshire's attacked the Reutelbeek Valley at the same time the Germans prepared to attack the same target. British artillery slowed the Germans and the division were able to advance and secure key objectives only one of which was lost by subsequent German counterattacks.

Italy began the war as an independent nation bargaining with both sides. Being close to the Austro-Hungarian border placed them in a delicate position but after negotiations failed with the central powers Italy joined the entente powers by declaring war on Austro-Hungary on the 23rd May 1915 and eventually Germany in August 1916. Italy was in the war for really only one goal and that was territory, ideology meant a lot less than retrieving land lost to the Austrians over the centuries. Much of the fighting therefore was on the Austrian border in the foothills of the Alps in the regions known as Trentino and Isonso.

Neither the Austrians nor the Italians were very well equipped and for the first time recorded in history avalanches were used as deliberate weapons of war. The Italian general, Cadorna led several successful attacks through Trentino in June 1916 and again at Goriza in August 1916 but a strong counter-attack on the 24th October 1917 in the Caporetta sector on the Isonso front soon turned the tide back to the central powers. The Austro-Hungarians with six German divisions in support defeated the Second Italian Army forcing them to retreat to a defensive line along the Piave River. It seemed likely that the Italians could be knocked out of the war thereby enabling the Germans to focus on the Western Front it was therefore deemed necessary to aid the Italians and keep this vital front open.

In November 1917 General Herbert Charles Onslow took 11 divisions of Anglo-French troops with a regiment of Australians from the western front to help the Italian forces. This force included the 2nd Battalion in the 7th Division, the 5th, 6th, 7th and 8th Battalions in the 48th Division and for a short while the 14th, 15th and 16th Battalions in the 5th Division.

The allied force was deployed in April 1918 on the frontline north of Mont Grapa in time for a June offensive by Austrian troops. Four waves of attack were eventually successful at Asiago before flooding slowed the Austrian advance. By the 15th and 16th June the 7th and 48th Divisions were posted to the Asiago Plateau. The 5th battalion took up a key defensive position at Cesunna where in heavy fighting 'D' Company were completely over run and taken prisoner. The 7th Battalion maintained a line between Mont Lemele and Cesunna.

In October the British 14th Corps led by General Cavan were attached to the 10th Italian Army to take part in the battle of Vittorio Veneto on the 24th October. This offensive by the Italians easily defeated the enemy troops and forced the Austrians to begin a withdrawal. Between the 23rd October and 4th November the 4th division pursued crossing the Piave and then attacking in the Monte Grappa sector to draw in Austrian reserves. The division captured Grave di Papadopoli, an island in the Piave in an exercise in which the British forces were dressed in Italian uniforms so as to disguise their movements. The 7th division attacked from the north whilst the 33rd Italians did so from the south.

On the 28th October at the same time as the Czechoslovakians declared independence from the Austro-Hungarian Empire the Austrians issued a general retreat resulting in a general push by the Italian army. 51 Italian, 3 British, 2 French, 1 Czech and 1 American divisions pursued the retreating Austrians, crossing the Tagliamento on their way to Trieste. The 48th Division remained on the Asiago Plateau, with General Sladen formally of the 5th Battalion being commended for his work. By the 4th November the 7th Division had reached Udine and an Armistice begun on the 29th October was finally ratified. In the Italian Campaign Austro-Hungary lost 30,000 men with a further 300-500,000 taken prisoner whilst the Italians suffered 37,461 casualties including 145 French and only 374 British.

THE FINAL YEAR

At the start of 1918 it looked to many as if the war could roll on forever. Young men across the country had been drafted to feed the military machine with no appreciable gains on either side. Successes in Italy and the collapse of the Ottoman Empire did however indicate a glimmer of hope for success. The battalions of the Royal Warwickshire Regiment were by 1918 spread across the various of theatres of war. The 2nd battalion were still in Italy, the 5th, 6th and 8th battalions were in Austria and the 9th Battalion were in Persia. The remaining units of the regiment were all stationed at various points on the Western Front in France and Belgium.

The 1st battalion spent the remainder of the war in a series of trenches east of Arras in the northern section of the western front. Their daily life became one of mud, disease and shelling. The boring chore of maintaining this defensive line was punctuated by raids both against the enemy and by them and the ever present threat of shelling.

On the 21st March 1918 Erich Ludendorff executed Operation Michael known in Germany as the Kaiserschlacht (Kaisers Battle). The operation was a series of five offensives launched on the western front between March and July. Operation Michael was to be the German High Commands hammer blow that would crush the exhausted British forces.

The attack was very successful and the German army pushed both the French and British army from their frontline trenches only in the north on the edge of the assault did the line hold. Here the 1st battalion sat in their trenches and desperately tried to maintain their position. Slightly further south the 10th battalion were stationed between Velu and Beaumetz. They found themselves in the path of attacks towards Amiens which was attempting to push north to surround Arras and force the BEF to surrender.

The 10th battalion as part of the 19th division had seen little action in the war up until this point operating as a service battalion. The 19th division formed part of General Byng's Third Army that tried to stem this German assault. Supported by Gough's 5th Army the division fought at St Quentin, Bapaume, Rosieres and Arras. It was during these actions that Captain Gribble of the 10th won a Victoria

Cross. At just 21 years old Gribble was a temporary Captain in command of a body of men in Beaumetz. On the 23rd March 1918 he was in command of the right most company of the battalion when he received the dreaded orders to 'hold on to the last'. They quickly found themselves exposed and isolated but still Gribble refused to order a retreat. Eventually the company was surrounded and over run with the Captain himself seen fighting to the last moment. The company's last stand bought time for the remainder of the brigade and three batteries of artillery to withdraw safely. Captain Gribble was not killed in the battle but was captured. He died of pneumonia on the 24th November 1918.

By the end of the German Spring offensive 75,000 British soldiers had been captured and they had lost substantial ground including the hard fought over Somme region. At the widest part of the line the German army had advanced up to 40 miles. Despite these successes it had failed to achieve its aims. The German army had thrown in all of her specialist shock troops and still the allies stood firm. They had been pushed back yes but not defeated.

Such an offensive could not be left unopposed and so in August the allies drew up a counter offensive that became known as the Hundred Days offensive. It began on the 8th August 1918 at Amiens and eventually reached and breached the Hindenburg line. The attack was made possible by the addition of reinforcements from Italy and Palestine. One of these reinforcement units was the 8th battalion that arrived in France from Italy on the 11th September 1918. The battalion was placed in the 75th brigade in the 25th division. The brigade was a new one, the old one having been renumbered the 236th and sent to northern Russia. This new brigade was composed of three infantry battalions and a trench mortar battery.

The brigade was part of one of the final actions of the war on the River Sambre. Right along the western front the allied armies were overturning the losses they had taken in the previous month. Operation Michael had ironically been too successful for the German army who had advanced over an area larger than they could reasonably defend and faster than their supply chains could keep up with. On the 3rd November the Austro-Hungarian Empire beaten in Italy surrendered, the next day British and French divisions supported by 37 tanks advanced towards the Sambre and the flooded ground around it. They faced heavy fire from a series of German strong points and it was difficult to erect the temporary bridges. The 8th battalion took part in the attack on the village of Landrecies with orders to secure a lock on the canal section of the Sambre.

The attack like all those on the Sambre was hampered by machine gun posts and strong points. Lance-Corporal William Amey won a Victoria Cross for his actions this day. The day of the attack was clouded by fog and several enemy installations were missed during the advance. Amey led his section against one of these missed strong points, a machine gun nest. His section performed well under fire and they drove the garrison away from their position and into a nearby farm. The section pursued and captured 50 Germans and several machine-guns. Later as the battle wore on Amey attacked a machine-gun post in a farmhouse on his own. He killed two of the men garrisoning the house and forced the rest into the cellar whom he imprisoned until more help arrived. Lastly he rushed a third strong point and captured 20 more prisoners. Amey's actions and those of the battalion enabled the capture of Fauborg Sayer and their objective. Amey survived the war and was presented the Victoria Cross by the king himself and lived until he was 59.

The victory at Sambre opened up a bridgehead some 50 miles long and up to 3 miles deep. Added to the successes at Serre, Lys, Valenciennes and Thierache the German army seemed to be in complete collapse. In the south General Pershing had reached the German border. General Haig and the BEF had crossed the Belgian border and General Albert in the north had pushed Rupprecht's army to the other side of Ghent.

Things were looking dire for Germany and the Kaiser and his chiefs of staff were abundantly aware that the war was pretty much over. On the 7th November Marshall Foch met Field Marshal Hindenburg to discuss terms. On the 9th November a revolution in Germany by republicans forced Kaiser Wilhelm II to abdicate and flee to the neutral state of the Netherlands. The revolutionaries declared an end of the Empire and pronounced Germany a republic from the Reichstag. This unrest at home effectively secured the treaty and an armistice was drawn up by Marshall Foch in a railway carriage in a siding in the forest of Compiegne. Once signed it came into effect at 11 am on the 11th November 1918, the Great War, the war to end all wars was over.

In total Britain suffered 1 million casualties, France 1.5 million, Russia 1.7 million, Germany 1.9 million, Austro-

Hungary 1 million and the Ottoman Empire 325,000; a total death toll of over 7.5 million soldiers.

CHAPTER 8 – THE LULL BETWEEN STORMS

At the end of the First World War the many battalions of the regiment were scattered across the globe. In November 1918 the 1st, 8th, 2/6th, 2/7th, Battalions and the 10th, 14th and 16th Service Battalions were in France, the 2nd, 5th, 6th and 7th Battalions were in North Italy and the 9th Service battalion was in Turkestan. The war had effectively eradicated the regular army with most trained soldiers being lost in the first year of the war. All that was left were Territorial soldiers and conscripts, although after all they had gone through in the years after the first battle of Ypres many of these could be now be considered regular units.

At the close of the war the army was completely reorganised. Demobilisation sent those that had survived home and regiments were returned to a more recognisable structure. For the Royal Warwickshire Regiment the 1st and 2nd battalions were maintained as the regular battalions whilst the 5th, 6th, 7th and 8th battalions remained as Territorial units associated with Birmingham and Coventry. All the Service Battalions were disbanded. Although pretty much all of the British army returned to barracks a small unit of the 1st Battalion remained on the continent in Belgium under the command of Lieutenant-Colonel Sir George Lacon.

War had devastated much of central Europe and prompted the collapse of both the Ottoman and Austro-Hungarian Empires. In 1919 the need to repair the damage to Europe still weighed heavily on all the government's minds. One of the British government's ideas was to raise some new units for specific roles. Three new battalions (51st, 52nd and 53rd) were raised to occupy the Rhineland. They were stationed near Cologne and remained there until February 1920. Their role was one of humanitarian support as well as the general occupation of Germany which struggled reconstitute itself as the Weimar Republic. Major WC Dibben led 100 men of the 2nd Battalion to escort food convoys to Vienna in Austria.

Whilst the war was over in France the Russian Revolution that had removed the Russians from the war was still raging. The western powers were cautious about the rise of the Bolsheviks and Britain especially was disturbed by the murder of the Tsar and his whole family. The allies therefore decided to support the remaining royalist forces, known as 'white Russians' and try to stabilise the country. A single company of the 2nd Battalion were deployed to the North Russian Relief Force. This relief force included troops from Britain, France, Canada, Italy, Serbia, Finland and America, they struck in northern Russia through the Barents Sea and into the White Sea. Simultaneously a second force attacked through the Black Sea. The company of the 2nd Battalion was led by Captain Peck. They were assigned a sector in Arkhangelsk that they held against the Bolsheviks for six months. Ultimately the Russian civil war ended in a full Bolshevik victory and in mid-1919 the British withdrew.

During the summer of 1919 the 1st and 2nd regular battalions were properly reformed drawing officers and men from other battalions and regiments. The 1st Battalion also gained a new commander, Lieutenant-Colonel P.J Foster. With all major theatres of war now ended and the thought of another conflict of that scale seemingly impossible Britain turned her gaze once more to looking after her imperial interests. At home the 1st Battalion were called out to guard the Leeds-Hull railway line during a strike in September 1919 before re-entering action in December 1920 when they were deployed to Ireland at a time when Irish independence was only around the corner in 1922. In 1920 violence was erupting across Ireland as Sin Fein stirred up resistance to British rule. It had declared Ireland an Irish Free State in 1919 and was now working to get this status recognised.

The battalion was posted to Devon Castle in Newcastle West and around Limerick. Here they maintained a policing action searching for Feiners and repairing broken bridges. They continued police actions into 1922 during which Lieutenant R.A Hendry, two other officers and one private were killed by terrorists. In August an Anglo-Irish Treaty was signed and the Irish Free State was officially created. The 1st Battalion returned to Chatham in March 1923 where they joined the 12th Infantry Brigade, moving to the 10th Brigade in February 1925 at Shorncliffe. They remained at various British postings for the next few years. In 1928 like much of the British Army the battalion was reorganised. 'D' company was disbanded and reformed as a Rifle Company and a Machine Gun company was added to the HQ.

In 1931 the battalion boarded HMT *Neuralia* for Palestine under the command of Lieutenant-Colonel Bernard Montgomery, the regiment's most famous member. The HQ and machine gun companies were garrisoned in the Talavera Barracks in Jerusalem whilst 'A' company was stationed in Hebron and 'B' company in Tel Aviv. Sadly in the summer Bobby the regimental mascot, an antelope, died of pneumonia. They remained in various parts of Palestine until December of 1932 when they travelled down the Gulf of Suez to Bombay where now under the command of Lieutenant-Colonel J.P Duke they spent the next several years between Poona, Lucknow and Meerut.

The 2nd battalion themselves had already arrived in India. They had travelled on the *Himalaya* in July 1919 and garrisoned Poona and Kirklee. In October they moved to the north-west frontier to the head of the Khyber Pass. In 1922 they took part in a military containment on the Rajputana plains 600 miles north-east of Bombay. In 1927 they were called on to put down a riot in the old city of Bombay and again in 1929 when the battalion were forced to actually open fire on the rioters.

Their tenure in India ended in March 1930 when they left aboard the *City of Marseilles*. They arrived back at Woking in 1930, being assigned to the 6th Experimental Brigade at

Aldershot. Like the 1st Battalion they were reorganised in 1934. It too lost its 'D' company becoming a Machine Gun company. The HQ Company received a Mortar and Anti-tank platoon.

CHAPTER 9 –
OPPOSING HITLER

It may have seemed during the 1920's that life was going back to what could be considered normal for the British army but things were about to change. Most countries felt that the chance of another global war were slim. At the end of the Great War the major nations formed the precursor of the United Nations called the League of Nations. It was hoped that this global talking shop could help stop wars before they broke out and mediate ones that did. Unfortunately this did not go as planned. During the 1930's many nations began to slip away from democracy towards nationalism. In Spain a civil war erupted in 1936 between Nationalists and Republicans and in Italy Mussolini tore up the democratic government replacing it with a fascist one.

In central Europe the fall of the Habsburg Austro-Hungarian Empire created a vacuum into which the Balkans were formed in to Yugoslavia and Hungary became an independent country. Austria, Hungary, Romania, Bulgaria and Greece all became nationalist states either under royal dictatorship, single-party rule or military control.

Germany had suffered heavily from the Treaty of Versailles that ended the First World War. As a country she was economically crippled by war reparations which was made worse by the Great Depression. Germany was also restricted in the size of its standing army and they began to feel vulnerable when it became obvious that their old enemy, the French now had the largest standing army in Europe.

The country became increasingly communist but in 1933 elected the Fascist Nazi party led by Adolf Hitler. Hitler was committed to returning Germany to strength and believed that this could only be done by avoiding the restrictions of the Versailles treaty. In 1935 with little international opposition Hitler began a programme of rearming. Not being challenged emboldened Hitler who began to focus on enlarging the territories of Germany and retaking some of her lost possessions. This started in March 1938 when Austria was occupied and incorporated into Greater Germany. In May he began to plan for the invasion of Czechoslovakia. He was stopped from acting by the infamous Munich Agreement. The agreement was made by the British Prime Minister Neville Chamberlain who hoped to avoid conflict by appeasing some of Germany's plans. The agreement allowed Germany to incorporate Sudentenland, the German speaking part of Czechoslovakia.

In 1939 Hitler accelerated his programme of expanding Greater Germany. In March Germany occupied Bohemia and Moravia and made Slovakia into a puppet state. Hitler went on to force Lithuania to return Memel on the Baltic coast and demanded the return of the free city of Danzig. In August 1939 Hitler organised a non-aggression pact with Josef Stalin, leader of the USSR with a deal concerning the partition of Poland between them. On the 1st September 1939 the German and Slovakian armies invaded Poland. This was the last straw for Britain and France who declared war on Germany two days later.

At the outbreak of war the Regiment was very different from the vast size it had become in the First World War. The 1st Battalion under the command of Lieutenant-Colonel Dibben were on colonial duties in Meerut, India. The 3rd and 4th battalions were special reserves. The 5th and 6th battalions had been reorganised in to a searchlight and Anti-Aircraft unit. This left the 2nd, 7th and 8th Battalions as the only operational forces available for deployment to aid France and Belgium. From barracks in Aldershot the 2nd Battalion moved in September 1939 to France and moved to Saarfront near Lille where the British Expeditionary Force were forming.

In January they were placed in the 144th brigade of the 48th Division and joined by the 7th and 8th Battalion from Swindon via Le Havre who were part of 143rd brigade. The division advanced towards the frontlines passing along the French defences of the Maginot Line. The Maginot Line was Frances master defence, a line of fortifications along the French/German border and believed to be impregnable.

From the declaration of war until spring 1940 nothing happened militarily between Britain and Germany this period became known as the 'phoney war'. This changed in May 1940 when Hitler launched a devastating blitzkrieg attack around the Maginot line, through the Ardennes to attack Belgium and the Netherlands. The speed of the attack was like nothing that had been seen before, whereas the First World War had only introduced the tank the second war fully embraced mechanisation, with tanks, aircraft and armoured transports changing conflict from static trench lines to a fluid dynamic affair. The British Expeditionary Force quickly moved up from Lille through Tournai, Ath, Enghien and Hal to Waterloo just south of Brussels. They were too late to support the Belgians and were just in time to join a French withdrawal to a rear ward line of defence along the river Dendre.

THE RETREAT FROM BELGIUM

The Royal Warwickshire Regiment were posted to the Escaut Canal on the 19th May 1940 essentially to cover the withdrawal of French and Belgian troops south of Tournai. Seven divisions of British infantry with little RAF cover were assigned a 30 mile stretch of the river to defend.

The enemy were sighted the following day when the mortar fire being received by the British increased considerably. German patrols and advance parties began to probe the forward defences and shelling continued to increase as more artillery was brought up. Communications began to be disrupted as German patrols began to cut wires and the pressure of the situation began to take its toll on some of the men. They knew a superior German army had just walked over the Belgians and was now coming towards them. For some it became too much, Captain Glover of 'B' Company was shot by his own corporal who either from shell shock or fear had lost his mind.

On the 21st May 1940 the German attack began in earnest and soon the first platoons of the regiment were starting to be over run despite their best efforts. Major Morley was killed attempting to grenade a machine gun post whilst Lieutenant-Colonel Baker's reconnaissance car was badly shot up.

Elsewhere, command of the 2nd battalion fell to Major Hicks when Lieutenant-Colonel Dunn collapsed from a burst gastric ulcer. The following day the Germans cut off the Canal de Nord. As their tanks began to appear it was clear the line couldn't hold. The 2nd battalion withdrew to the village of Hollain where they were able to hold firm.

The 7th battalion originally north of Calonne withdrew to La Glanerie and the 8th battalion in Calonne after heavy pressure and shelling withdrew to Le Preau. Now began a series of rapid withdrawals as more lines of communications were cut. The 2nd moved to Wez-Velain, the 7th to Bois des-moines and the 8th to Warnaffles. The general German advance was halted but the armour was quickly moving to occupy Amiens, Abbeville, Doullens and Le Boiselle effectively beginning to encircle the BEF. The BEF formed what became termed the Gort line after its commander General Gort and the battalions withdrew to it forming a frontier around Rumegies, Aix and La Glanaire.

On the 23rd May the battalions attempted to regroup and reform. The 8th battalion now mustered only 366 men and 11 officers, but before they could be put back into action the order to retreat came again. Calais and Boulogne were already under siege and there was heavy fighting at Arras. The 1st French Army was attempting an assault along a line from Conde to Valenciennes and Douai. Gort decided to reduce his line and withdraw via Dunkirk. The 48th division were placed into reserve around Orchies. They remained in this area until the 26th May when they were assigned to the Ypres-Comines Canal.

The Ypres-Comines Canal was a dry disused canal running between the two towns of Ypres and Comines. To any veterans of the First World War it would be a very familiar location. It was hoped this obstacle would prove useful in slowing the advancing tanks and artillery. On the 26th May the 7th Battalion led by Lieutenant-Colonel Mole were assigned a front line position towards Houthem. The 8th battalion led by Major Kendall had been reduced to only 50-60 men per company and were assigned a shorter 1,500 yard front nearby. Further north the 2nd battalion held Wormhoudt with the Royal Worcester's but more of them later.

Probing attacks towards Houthem began quickly with the 7th Battalion finding themselves alone on the line. Fearing a massive breakthrough the 2nd Cameroonian Regiment withdrew from their position on the left flank of the regiment. 'A' and 'B' companies were encircled but 'C' Company were able to escape intact. The battalion reformed at dusk.

The real attack came on the 27th May. Three German divisions tried to break through the 5th division's 143rd brigade. 'B' Company of the 8th Battalion found themselves beating back over 100 Germans at Korentje. Pressure was placed on the whole line with some British success, in fact the 7th battalion were able to take so many German prisoners that they outnumbered the staff at the battalion headquarters this was compensated however when 'A' company were over run and captured themselves. Soon communications were failing and 'B' Company became surrounded.

'C' Company fared little better on the left, being overrun in short order. Captain Lewthwaite with 4 men and a Bren gun were however able to hold on for most of the morning before being captured. Major Kendall decided a second line was required and so he gathered any stragglers together under the command of Captain Waugh and went to join with what was left of 'B' Company. A second group was assembled from the remains of 'D' Company to be led by Lieutenant Gibbs. These two new units took up new positions and started to fend off persistent German attacks.

Lieutenant Gibbs' unit found a 3-inch mortar that they used to good effect and were assisted by a machine gun section from the 4th Gordon Highlanders that helped plug a gap between Gibbs' and Waugh's units. In the afternoon artillery came into play allowing Gibbs to withdraw. That evening two British counter attacks were launched by the 4th division intended to push the Germans back over the canal but little progress was made when heavy enemy shelling slowed any momentum. Having assisted the counter attacks Waugh and Gibbs pulled back to join Major Kendall. He had reorganised what forces he still had and deployed what remained of his battalion along a new line on the river Kortekeer.

The 7th Battalion were likewise under pressure. 2nd Lieutenant Stapleton mustered cooks and auxiliary staff to counter attack a German attack including storming a machine gun post in a house. 'C' and 'D' companies formed a new line and by midnight despite heavy casualties they had managed to stabilise the front. Unfortunately this was not the case elsewhere. Belgium forces in the north had crumbled and the 3rd division was sent up to hold this now exposed flank.

News of Belgium's surrender reached General Gort at midnight and it became clear that a full evacuation from Dunkirk was inevitable so far only 8000 men had been evacuated and it didn't look like there was much time to evacuate the rest. Gort now held a line from East Ypres south to St Eloi and to Comines. He needed that line to hold as long as possible to give time for the bulk of the BEF to reach Dunkirk and escape. This was almost an exact replay of the holding action that General John Moore made at Corunna during the peninsular war in 1809. The regiment would fulfill a very similar role to that which it had then.

At dawn of the 28th May the Germans renewed their attack. The 7th and 8th Battalions were now well dug in close to each other and were suffering from heavy shelling. The right flank became infiltrated and a withdrawal was ordered with both battalions being moved back to Messines before a general retreat order was given to reach Dunkirk. In this holding action the 7th Battalion had suffered 50% casualties and the 8th Battalion had been reduced to only 54 men and 4 officers.

At the same time the 2nd Battalion were still on the western flank at Wormhoudt in a defensive line with some elements of the 4th Cheshire's and the 8th Worcestershire's. They spent a relatively quiet 27th May in which they watched British and French convoys head to Dunkirk and German bombers flying over in pursuit. In the afternoon the bombers actually attacked the infantry and although only four soldiers were killed there was substantial damage to the village and many civilian deaths. That night 'C' Company was sent to Bergues to provide a guard duty for the headquarters of the 48th Division.

On the 28th May as the 7th and 8th battalion were retreating to Dunkirk the 2nd Battalion faced the brunt of the German attack. Enemy Stuka aircraft strafed 'A' company whilst Captain Tomes saw Germans approaching their defences. 'B' Company found themselves mixed in with lots of refugees who were attempting to pass through their roadblock. At 10 am German vehicles began to appear at the roadblock but were deterred by concerted fire, these vehicles regrouped and awaited infantry in the form of

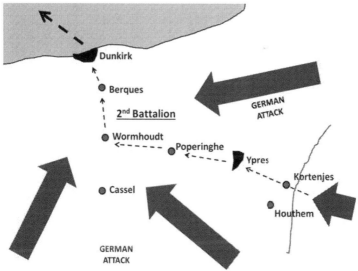

FIGURE 25- THE 2ND BATTALIONS RETREAT TO DUNKIRK

three battalions of the Waffen-SS Liebstandarte Adolf Hitler Regiment with the 20th Motorised Division led by Sepp Dietrich.

Artillery continued to fire on Wormhoudt causing several injuries whilst light tanks advanced to engage 'B' Company. Both sides began to start losing men and soon the roadblocks began to fall as the tanks became bolder. The battalion began to find itself outgunned and outmatched, Private Bert Evans commented that: 'We were entrenched, but we had hardly anything to fight with. Just one mortar and a couple of Bren guns'. Finally 'A', 'B' and 'D' companies were overrun by German infantry supported by SS troops. Some of the officers such as Major Constable and Captain Padfield fought until the end whilst many others were captured or escaped.

By late afternoon the headquarters were overrun forcing Major Hicks to give the order to disperse. A thunderstorm covered their escape and the men split up along hedgerows to avoid capture, even so many were still caught. 2nd Lieutenant Vandrey and 18 men of the HQ company managed to make it to Dunkirk along with some men of the Cheshire's and eventually Major Hicks and a few more men of the 2nd Battalion. Captain Nicholson with 'C' Company joined up with a mixture of units at Berques where along with some French troops, two light tanks and a pair of two pounder Anti-Tank guns they were able to hold out through heavy attacks and shelling. By the 29th May Captain Jerram and six men made it to Dunkirk where Major Hicks was now promoted to Lieutenant-Colonel. Whilst the survivors were organising for evacuation some of those taken prisoner fared far less well.

50 soldiers of the 2nd Battalion along with another 50 or so 4th Cheshire's, French Soldiers and Royal Artillery had been captured by the Waffen-SS. They were loaded into trucks and were taken to a remote barn near Wormhoudt. The men were taken out ordered inside. Once in the barn the SS threw in a pair of grenades. Company Sergeant Major Jennings and Sergeant Moore leapt on the grenades smothering the explosion with their own bodies. Aware that the grenades had failed to do the job the SS ordered the men to come out in groups of five. Each group were shot and soon the prisoners refused to leave the barn. To resolve this impasse the SS opened up on the barn with their machine guns riddling the structure with bullets. Luckily some of the men managed to escape this maelstrom of bullets. Captain Lynn-Allen took Private Evans and managed to get around the back of the barn without being seen. They made their escape by swimming across a stagnant pond. When they were only half way across an SS soldier spotted them and opened fire. Captain Lynn-Allen was shot dead whilst Private Evans took two ricocheted bullets to the neck and survived. Of the 100 men led into the barn 80 were killed. Those that survived were eventually picked up by a regular Wermacht German Infantry unit and given medical care before being sent to prisoner of war camps.

This undoubted war crime was never given justice. The day before the incident at Wormhoudt a similar massacre by the Waffen-SS in Le Paradis took place in which 97 men of the Royal Norfolk's were killed. Those responsible for this crime were tried and executed in 1949. However in the case of the Wormhoudt massacre insufficient evidence was able to place suffcient blame on either Sepp Dietrich the leader of the SS division or Hauptsturmfuhrer Wilhelm Mohnke the local field commander. Both denied issuing the orders and any German witnesses either died on the Eastern Front or refused to speak about it. No charges were ever filed. Wilhelm Mohnke died in 2001 having never stood trial for this war crime.

That night the remains of the battalion unaware of the deaths of their colleagues began to be evacuated. The 7th and 8th battalions were dug in along pipe works at Moeres finally being evacuated on the 31st May. The 7th battalion left with 220 men and 15 officers and the 8th with 134 men with 8 officers.

D-DAY AND THE NORMANDY LANDINGS

After the retreat from Dunkirk the British army settled in for a period of rest and rearming on the Home Front. Hitler's German army quickly secured France and the threat of invasion to Britain itself became evident. The regular army shored up defences and trained troops. The 2nd, 7th and 8th Battalions joined the 48th division forming a mobile defence force in Devon and Cornwall. The 2nd/7th and 9th battalions were posted to Londonderry; the 12th to Ulster, the 11th to Redditch, the 13th to Great Yarmouth and the 15th to Hockley Heath. New battalions such as the 50th became a holding battalion stationed near Barnstable and the 70th (Young Soldiers) entered training at Southampton.

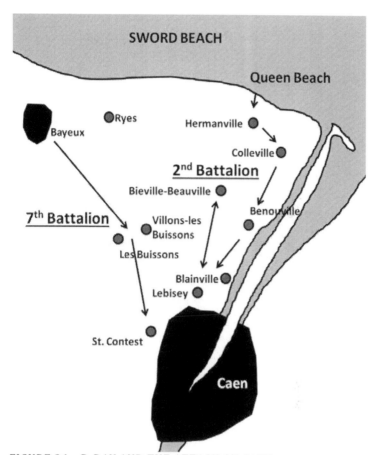

FIGURE 26 – D-DAY AND THE ATTACK ON CAEN

The war continued elsewhere in the empire but the soldiers of the Royal Warwickshire Regiment that had been evacuated from Dunkirk remained in Britain. The risk of invasion disappeared in 1940 after the Battle of Britain denied the planned German invasion air superiority. By 1942 both the Americans and the Russians had entered the war against Germany and Britain could begin to focus on taking the fight to Hitler. The 13th battalion of the Warwickshire's were reorganised as the 8th Midland Counties Parachute battalion and the 70th were disbanded completely. The rest of the regiment joined the 21st Army group and began training for invasion operations.

On the 6th June 1944 the allied invasion of France began. Codenamed Operation Overlord the attack was planned to take place on a series of five beaches in Normandy. Clever intelligence work and trickery managed to keep the German army guessing as to the true invasion site.

The 2nd Battalion were assigned to the 185th Brigade in the 3rd Division. They were tasked with landing on one of the British controlled beaches code named Sword. The attack relied on naval support and a swift advance up the beaches to secure a perimeter into which more troops could be pushed. The Germans may not have been certain where the attack was to fall but they had used the past few years installing their own defences along the length of the French coast including mines, barbed wire, pill boxes and other strong points. Normandy was by no means undefended.

The attack at Sword Beach was spearheaded by the 8th Brigade followed by 185th. The battalion were packed in to three infantry landing craft and designated to land at Queen beach in the Sword section. They advanced under heavy fire to reach the beach. The 'C' Company landing craft struck a mine and the craft containing the 'B' and 'D' companies was hit three times by shell fire it lost both landing ramps but was able to limp to the shore.

Arriving at the beach the battalion found a cluttered madhouse. Different units either assaulted the defences or attempted to form up, some regiments had become separated and the heavy fire from the top of the beach meant that there was little time to organise. Captain Illing who led 'A' Company described the attacks; 'We could see the spouts of water shoot up as enemy bombs and shells fell in the sea... ashore we stumbled, lugging our kits through the last few yards of shallow sea, up breathless and anxious on to the sandy beach'.

By 11.30 am all the battalions had arrived on the beaches and a plan was formed to secure a perimeter around the landing zone to enable further landings. 185th brigade were tasked with advancing on the key town of Caen on the far east of the invasion line. The 2nd Battalion were assigned to the right of an armoured column with the 1st Norfolk's on their left. Even during assembly for this advance the enemy kept up the pressure, snipers accounted for 12 casualties before the formation was even able to move out.

Part of the success of D-day had been the use of gliders and paratroopers to drop troops behind enemy lines to secure key points such as bridges. The 6th Airborne Division had seized some bridges across the river Orne that ran through Caen on the left flank of the advance but they were beginning to encounter resistance from a German counter attack headed by the 21st Panzer Division. Plans were quickly changed and the 2nd battalion were ordered to move south-east to support them. From there the battalion were ordered inland to Hermanville where they reassembled at mid-day with orders to secure a number of villages on the approach to Caen.

Led by 'B' Company they advanced on their targets with very little difficulty although a glider of the 6th Airborne unfortunately landed on two signalers of 'B' Company killing them. Benouville the next village objective was quickly subdued and the battalion provided support to units protecting two bridges that crossed the river Orne. By midnight the advance halted and the battalion dug in with losses of the day being only 4 killed and 35 wounded.

The morning of the 7th June presented the battalion with yet more obstacles. 'A' Company were delayed by snipers and the transports and 6-pounder ant-tank guns were judged to be unable to advance across the boggy ground in front their next objective, the village of Lebisey on the very outskirts of Caen. Lieutenant-Colonel Herdon decided that discretion was the better part of valour and postponed his attack for an hour whilst he called in an artillery bombardment from an offshore cruiser. Herdon was a well regarded officer being described by one of his men as; 'Tall, elegant and gallant, he was a charming and gifted leader whom I would have followed anywhere'. Satisfied the enemy had been softened up he ordered the general advance. Unable to reach 'B' and 'C' companies 'A' Company advanced alone through cornfields followed by the HQ company. They found the village and nearby wood defended by the 125th Panzer Grenadiers heavily dug in and they very quickly started to take heavy casualties. Lieutenant Dockerty's 'B' Company platoon made it into the wood but he was shot and his men wounded.

'A' Company managed to come up on the left of 'B' Company but found themselves also pinned down. Captain Illing and Lieutenant Adams were both wounded and Lieutenant-Colonel Herdon was killed by machine gun fire as he tried to move along the front. Command passed to Major Bundock who began to hear rumours that Lebisey had fallen. He ordered Captain Bannerman to begin an advance in the battalion's personnel carriers but these suddenly came under fire from hidden German tanks. The teams bailed out and tried to hide in a wheat field however they were captured by SS soldiers. Further members of the battalion were ambushed on the Bieville road and also taken prisoner. That evening Captain Bannerman managed to escape his SS captors during an air raid but was later recaptured.

Lebisey had not in fact fallen at all and was instead being reinforced by SS Panzers. The battalion having now suffered the loss of 10 officers and 144 other men pulled back to Beauville to reorganise and lick their wounds. They received reinforcements of five officers and 150 men and a new commanding officer in the form of Lieutenant-Colonel Gibbs from the Queens Regiment.

OPERATION CHARNWOOD

The 2nd battalion remained in position between Bieville and Beauville for the whole of June whilst the rest of the invasion force moved out west and south. On the 26th June Cherbourg surrendered to American troops and more British soldiers advanced on Caen from St Lo. Despite bad weather leading to equipment shortages a second landing was made on the Normandy beaches including the 59th division containing the 7th Battalion of the Royal Warwickshire's in the 197th brigade. With reinforcements and the west secured it was decided that it was time once more to attack Caen, the attack, code named Operation Charnwood was scheduled for the 8th July.

The 2nd battalion with the 3rd division would strike from the north whilst the 7th battalion and the 59th division would attack along the right flank. As the attack commenced Lieutenant Jarvis with 'A' Company discovered that the German troops were less aggressive than imagined and was able to advance right into Lebisey wood. In fact the 21st Panzers had been withdrawn from the defence of Caen in favour of less capable units, this was one of many questionable actions made by the German commanders in the early stages of the invasion.

On the beaches of Normandy the 7th battalion commander, Lieutenant-Colonel Walton was promoted and replaced by Lieutenant-Colonel Jerram he led the battalion south-east of Bayeux towards Caen reaching the line at Barbiere on the 3rd July. They formed up at Villons-les-Buissons and given orders to follow up an attack over 3000 yards to capture Galmanche and seize the village of St. Contest and if possible Bitot.

The advance was made under a creeping barrage which lifted 100 yards every 3 minutes. At 7.30 am 'B' and 'C' companies led the attack with 'A' Company to mop up and 'D' Company to consolidate any gains. They encountered heavy resistance towards Galmanche but were able to take some woods on the left flank. 'C' Company suffered heavily, Major Blythe and Lieutenant Dugmere were killed and Captain Bird and two platoon leaders were wounded.

'B' Company fared little better with heavy losses but they did manage to reach the western half of St. Contest. Major White won a Military Cross for bringing up 'A' Company in good order and in time to consolidate the advances made by the battalion. By 6.30 pm they had secured St. Contest but had lost 26 killed with 96 wounded and 12 missing. On the 9th July the 7th Battalion was relieved in St. Contest and moved to Bitot that they found abandoned. They remained there until the 11th July when they were withdrawn to Ryes for a rest.

North of Caen the 2nd Battalion likewise began an attack. They left base camp at 4.30 am during an artillery duel. 'C' and 'D' companies took the lead with 'A' and 'B' in support. They successfully pushed into Lebisey Wood meeting only light opposition. By 6 am they had reached the edge of the city. 'A' and 'B' companies ran into enemy mortar fire but managed to clear Lebisey of all enemy soldiers. The action resulted in the deaths of 29 men and six officers with a further 93 wounded and 25 missing. After some shelling the battalion was also withdrawn to rest.

In Mid-July the 2nd Battalion were on the east bank of the river Orne and the 7th in the village of Cristot. The noose around Caen was slowly tightening but still costing the allied army 20,000 casualties a day. The German army had defended the city with armour and lots of 88mm guns but soon supplying these with ammunition became increasingly difficult and Hitler decided that Caen couldn't be held and ordered a systematic withdrawal. By the 18th July a line from Caen in the east to Port Buil in the west was secured by the allies this was expanded to the south west by early August.

Seeing Hitler's army withdrawing gave General Montgomery the initiative and he didn't want to waste it. He planned a British push from Caen followed by an American offensive south across the Periers-St. Lo road. On 16th July a diversion was led by the 59th division whilst the 3rd division and Canadians created a diversion south and east of Caen.

The 7th battalion pushed south 3 miles to capture Noyers via the village of Landelle. This region of France is known as the Bocage. The landscape is dominated by sunken lanes, small enclosed fields and small farms. The visibility was poor and vehicles were very restricted in movement. The 197th brigade took on most of the hard work trying to seize the Landet Spur with two battalions being beaten back by heavy mortar fire, Major Banks' 'D' Company was sent to assist them.

The following day Lieutenant-Colonel Jerram brought up the rest of the 7th battalion with orders to capture the spur. The battalion was supported by Royal Artillery Field Units, a squadron of Sherman Tanks, flame-throwing Churchill's called Crocodiles, Anti-Tank units, Sappers, Machine Gun units and 17 pounder anti-tank guns. A low mist covered the attack with 'A' Company on the right, 'B' Company on the left, 'C' Company in the rear and 'D' Company in reserve. 'B' Company advanced well and took 40 prisoners and managed to reach their objective west of Bordel. 'A' Company with the flame-thrower tanks took 30 prisoners but 'C' Company were heavily mortared requiring 'D' Company to come up in support. 'B' Company beat off two Panther Tank counter attacks and by nightfall the sappers and bull dozers were able to move in to break up the Bocage thereby allowing more allied armour to move up in support. The night was difficult with 500 kilos of bombs being dropped in a series of enemy air attacks killing Captain King and 4 men and wounding 12 others.

On the 18th July the battalion took eight more prisoners and despite some mortaring were able to regroup and take stock of their situation in the safety of Cristot. In just two days of fighting they had suffered 121 casualties of which 100 were wounded leaving the battalion with 585 of actives and 20 officers. They received six more officers and 100 men from the 9th battalion as reinforcements.

By the 21st July they were back on the front line in a sector west of Vendes with its headquarters in the Chateau de Juvigney. Most of their work involved routine patrolling and probing the enemy's disposition. One such patrol proved disastrous, 2nd Lieutenant Lee led a five man patrol to investigate some houses to see if they were being used over night by German infantry. En route to the location they bumped into a German outpost north of Batte du Chene and stumbled into an S-mine minefield and numerous booby traps. Lieutenant Lee and another were killed and two more were wounded.

Whilst the 7th Battalion pushed through the Bocage the 2nd Battalion was tasked with capturing the villages of Cuillervuille and Emieville. The attack was led by the 2nd KSLI (Kings Own Light Infantry) and supported by the Staffordshire Yeomanry armour. 1,000 bombers softened up the enemy lines and severely demoralised them. Even so the Germans put up stiff resistance with the KSLI taking heavy fire. The 2nd battalion came up in support with the 1st battalion of the Norfolk's reaching Cuillervuille Wood by noon. At 9 pm the 2nd battalion took its place at the vanguard. 'A' Company led on the right with 'C' Company on the left. 'B' and 'D' were held in reserve. They advanced well for the first 100 yards before they encountered a 20 foot wall protected by heavy machine guns and a tank. They managed to punch through part of the wall taking 40 prisoners but as dusk was falling they decided to dig in for the night.

In the morning (19th July 1944) after a nights shelling the attack recommenced with the 1st Norfolks covering the left flank. The battalion headquarters was hit by a mortar shell and Major Ross was wounded in the arm. He stayed with the battalion for as long as possible before finally being evacuated two days later. During the afternoon 'B' and 'D' companies were coming under heavy sniper fire but were able to reach their primary objectives. At 6 pm an enemy counter attack containing two Tiger tanks pushed 'B' Company back and one of the tiger tanks in a nearby wood pinned down much of 'D' Company. Major Bundock, the company commander, called for an anti-tank gun, after asking how it worked he walked out of cover to a wall where he sighted and then fired on the tank. The tank suffered a direct hit and was crippled. Major Bundock was awarded the Distinguished Service Order for this act of bravery.

On the 20th July 'B' Company found themselves taking heavy fire from an emplaced machine gun at Emieville. Corporal Millard took it upon himself to remove this obstacle. He crawled towards the enemy before rushing it and spraying them with fire from his Bren gun. His attack killed two of the operators of the machine gun but Millard was mortally wounded in the process.

It became abundantly clear during the day that the Germans had withdrawn completely from the front held by the 185th brigade. The following day they entered Emieville unopposed and under heavy rain the battalion paused to rest. Despite the withdrawal shelling continued to target the British lines over the next few days, shelling that killed both the battalions Intelligence Officer, Captain Smith and the Medical Officer, Captain Lawson. In the past week 34 men had been killed in the battalion and 202 wounded.

THE 7TH BATTALION TO FALAISE

Despite all the advances the allies had made it was still less than they expected with many objectives left unsecured. The German army was more adaptable than first imagined and fought well in a defensive position without air superiority. Nevertheless the regiment had to press on.

On the 29th July the 7th battalion made a limited advance with the support of two squadrons of Churchill tanks. The advance was slowed by a lack of good lines of communication and enemy mortar fire. Several companies found themselves pinned down by enemy fire and 'D' Company found themselves surrounded by mines. Captain Bushell was killed and Major Hancock and Captain Manton were wounded. The battalion was now starting to suffer from a lack of officers. Lieutenant Hosker took command

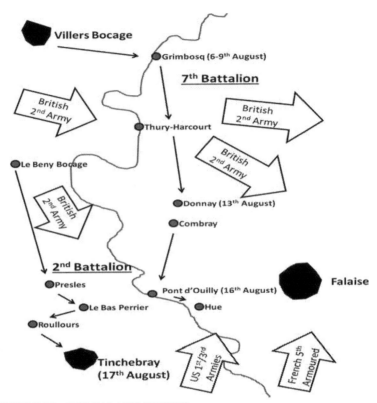

FIGURE 27 –THE FALAISE POCKET

of 'B' Company and together with 'A' Company pushed onwards. The following day Captain Purnell the commander of 'A' Company was wounded during a German counter attack that forced the rest of the company to fall back towards 'C' Company. During the day more officers were lost and command of many of the companies passed to the NCO's (non-commissioned officers). One such example of these dedicated NCO's was Sergeant Dix who despite a back wound stayed with his platoon for six days before seeking aid.

On the 1ˢᵗ August 'B' Company, now led by Captain Thompson, finally secured the objective pushing out the last of the German troopers. The battalion had little time to rest as two days later orders were received to press south despite losing 7 officers and 135 men over the past 7 days. Their objective was a position numbered Point 213 one and a half miles outside Viller Bocage. Here the 2/5ᵗʰ Lancashire Regiment was to seize the village itself with the 7ᵗʰ battalion in support. Progress through the Bocage was still slow, the lanes were narrow and the Germans had laid many mines and booby traps. Captain Thompson and CSM Deakon were killed and Major Poole seriously wounded when one of them trod on an S-mine. The level of stress on the battalion became evident on the same day when Lieutenant-Colonel Jerram awoke with a paralysed arm. The medical officer assumed he had suffered a stroke in the night as a result of the stress of the campaign. Hidden mines, shelling, wearying combat and the responsibility for the lives of his men had no doubt all contributed to Jerram's illness. He was removed from the frontline for rest and recuperation and replaced by Major Hopkins. From Viller Bocage the battalion was steered south east to join the 59ᵗʰ Division to take part in a forced crossing of the River Orne. They next saw action on 6ᵗʰ August.

Fierce fighting had broken out when attempts to cross the river had begun, the Germans may have retreated but they weren't giving up the ground easily. In the evening the battalion was sent forward to 176ᵗʰ Brigade Headquarters where a crossing was being attempted at Grimbosq. They arrived to find the North Staffordshire's under a counter attack by German infantry and tanks. These German units included the 12th Panzer Division and contained elements of the SS Adolf Hitler Regiment that had fought against the 2nd Battalion at Wormhoudt and massacred several of their comrades. It became apparent that the battalion would have to secure the bridgehead themselves and so began an attack to secure a crossroads 800 yards from the rivers far bank.

Marching swiftly up to the river, a single company were put across to act as an advance party. This was followed by some support tanks at first light on the 8th August. 'A' Company eventually crossed and pressed onto the crossroads but found themselves under heavy fire from four tanks, one of which was concealed close to the crossroads itself. The closest tank was despatched by Privates Leigh and Melhams who took a PIAT gun (Projector, Infantry, Anti-Tank) and crawled 100 yards down the lane under fire to gain a good angle on the tanks. This action not only won them the Military Medal but also enabled the battalion to secure the crossroads by 4.45 am upon which 'C' and 'D' companies were brought up. The enemy responded quickly with mortar and artillery fire followed by an attack by infantry supported by four more Tiger tanks. 'C' Company were overrun and half of the battalions supporting Churchill Tanks were knocked out. 'A' Company led by Captain Gedge fought hard to hold the crossroads and even managed to knock out another tank before they were reinforced by 'B' Company and the German attack petered out. By 4.15pm all objectives on the bridgehead were in allied hands.

With the crossing secure the order to advance came again. The Canadians and British were ordered to attack the village of Falaise itself. At just gone midnight on the 9th August 1944 'B' and 'D' companies of the 7th battalion sent patrols out into the nearby orchards where they found some remaining Germans lurking and took them prisoner. The attack on Falaise met little opposition although the Germans did attempt an ill fated flank attack in which 'D' Company took heavy fire from a wood through which the Germans were advancing but they were quickly stopped when 'A' Company reinforced the line.

It was decided there were not enough men left to continue the attack against the entrenched Germans and so the advance slowed to allow tanks to be brought up to support the regiment. At dusk the battalion were able to move up once more and began to secure high ground. There was some sporadic fighting but by midnight the bridgehead was fully secured and was now a good two miles deep. These three days of hard fighting cost the battalion 21 deaths and 57 wounded but gained the battalion much praise from the brigade commander Brigadier Fryer.

THE 2ND BATTALION TO FALAISE

At the start of the attack on Falaise the 2nd battalion were moved under the command of the 11th Division and redeployed from Cazelle to Caument. They were despatched to help the 8th Rifles and the 23rd Hussars who had been cut off some 2 miles beyond the village of Presles. Attacking on the 3rd August the battalion encountered a retreating a German army that was still attempting to hold a crumbling line. Most of the fighting was handled by 'B' and 'C' companies as 'A' and 'D' were under strength and remained with the tanks.

On the 6th August while US forces plunged through Brittany Hitler ordered a counter attack to be made across the lines with several divisions of Panzers. The 2nd Battalion encountered this resistance that same day when taking a ridge above Le Bas Perrier. Unknown to them the 9th SS Regiment were rushing to secure the ridge from the other side. The two forces met at the top. 'B' company suffered heavy losses with 30 wounded or captured and were driven back. The enemy continued to advance and several of the supporting tanks were hit, Major Bundock saw one tank catch fire and bravely ran forward to help the crews and extinguish the flames but sadly the vehicle exploded, killing him.

By 4 pm enemy artillery and mortar fire increased and more Germans could be seen reaching the ridgeline. The Battalion Headquarters responded swiftly by calling in allied artillery and a pair of tanks were brought up to support the embattled companies. Despite the struggle on the ridge the general German attack had been blunted and the following day was spent stopping flanking attacks by the Germans and although they lost more tanks the battalion held their ground. They were relieved on the 8th August and returned to Presles to rest. In the previous 6 days they had suffered 23 dead, 143 wounded and 30 missing. With the battalion depleted they reorganised themselves in to three rifle companies 'A', 'C' and 'D' with a smaller 'S' company led by Major Jerram, the brother of Lieutenant-Colonel Jerram, the commander of the 7th Battalion.

With the 7th Battalions crossing of the River Orne and the American armies advances the Allies were starting to create the 'Falaise pocket'. Fast movement by British, Canadian and American troops around the flanks were acting like a net driving local German forces in to Falaise and now threatened to seal it off completely thereby trapping a large portion of the German army in France. Now was the time to apply the pressure and this the allies did swiftly.

Whilst the 7th battalion operated around Falaise the 2nd Battalion moved up to attack Roullours and La Maslerie opposed by a strong rear guard and hundreds of mines and booby traps. On the 12th August the 2nd battalion were in the lead and took several casualties from these mines and traps. The following day a 'C' Company patrol led by Lieutenant Martin-Webb encountered the enemy confirming that the German force in front of them was from the 3rd Parachute Division. 'D' and 'C' companies swiftly moved up with a squad of tanks in support, during which Major Barratt the only surviving Company Commander from D-day was wounded. 17 men of 'D' Company were able to reach its objective and these men held on and despite casualties continued to push the enemy back. By the end of the day 10 men had been killed and 51 wounded. Already severely depleted the battalion was ordered to withdraw to await reinforcements.

By the 16th August Falaise itself had fallen and by the 19th the entire pocket containing the 7th German Army collapsed. 571 guns, 358 tanks and 5,000 other vehicles were captured. Since D-Day the allies had destroyed 15 divisions of the German army and 400,000 soldiers had either been killed or taken prisoner. The German army was now in full retreat.

Whilst the 2nd, 7th and 8th Battalions had fought in Europe the 1st battalion had been on colonial duty in India. They maintained policing actions throughout the sub-continent and encountered several difficulties with tribesmen in the North-west frontier. In November 1939 Corporal Sutton of 'D' Company won a Distinguished Conduct Medal for covering a withdrawal with his Lewis Gun despite being hit twice himself. They continued opposing the tribes throughout 1940 in Waziristan moving to Razni Camp in May 1941 where they were regularly in the sights of snipers and at risk of ambush. In June the Russian Army had joined the allies in opposing Hitler and so the British Command decided that the risk of Russian involvement in the North West frontier had reduced enough for them to pull some of the troops out however by December Japan had bombed Pearl Harbour and both America and Japan had entered the war.

Japan was a serious threat to British interests in the Indian Ocean and so in January 1942 the battalion moved to Deccan to relieve the Cameronian Regiment before moving on through Barrackpore to Calcutta to relieve the West Yorkshire Regiment. The risk of Japanese invasion began to loom large and so the regiment dug in and prepared for the worst which began as a series of air raids. The 1st Battalion were among the most experienced soldiers in the British Army and were particularly familiar with India and its people, for this reason they were assigned the role of remaining to provide security in India to avoid any unrest that might break out during the war.

During 1942 the British Army began to prepare for an invasion of Burma to drive back the advancing Japanese army. The 1st Battalion were moved to Mymensingh in Assam for jungle training but were quickly moved back to Calcutta when the civil authorities felt too vulnerable and demanded a military presence. Whilst General Slim led a major force of Indian and Commonwealth troops in the Imphal offensive the 1st Battalion could do nothing but man the defences in Calcutta. In December 1942 an air invasion was fully expected and the battalion was put on high alert however the expected invasion became only a series of bombing raids. One such raid on Christmas Eve 1942 caused 500 civilian casualties and killed Lance Corporal Kelly. During 1943 the battalion was responsible for guarding both the city jail and the docks and in 1944 received some jungle training in Bihar with the 116th Indian Infantry Brigade before returning at a strength of only 250 men to policing actions in Calcutta.

Eventually in 1945 it looked as if the battalion would at last join the main army in Burma. They boarded the HMT *Dunera* and sailed to Ramree, an island off the coast of Burma. Here they joined the 4th Indian Infantry Brigade in the 26th Indian Infantry Division of the 15th Corps. Under the command of Brigadier Forman the division began training for amphibious landings and rumours began to circulate about their final destination. During these practices Major Treasure was hospitalised after a bad sting from a ray. The plan was in fact for the division to take part in Operation Dracula.

Much of the fighting in Burma had been deep strikes from the western border into Burma, Operation Dracula was designed to open a second front by landing on the southern tip of Burma by sea and travelling up the Rangoon river to seize Rangoon and catch the retreating Japanese columns being forced out from the west. On 2nd May 1945 an infantry landing was made from the 'Persimmon' but the 1st battalion didn't debus from their landing craft until the 6th May at Elephant Point where they transferred to assault craft before heading up river and coming ashore at Rangoon without a single shot being fired. The battalion was then held in reserve whilst the rest of the army pushed north to meet the advancing 14th army and therefore join up all the allied forces in Burma.

On the 19th May whilst patrolling 'A' Company captured a lagging Japanese soldier and shot another. The following day the battalion began to prepare for a return to India but learned that a group of 50 to 100 Japanese soldiers had dug in 10 miles away. Probably eager to do something more active in the war Major Collins the current commander of the battalion asked for and was granted orders to go and root out this remaining enemy pocket. Collins received the use of divisional artillery troops and on the 23rd May he and Captain Trought led 24 soldiers through the jungle and surprised the Japanese in their camp. Using small arms and a few grenades they inflicted heavy casualties on the Japanese forcing them to withdraw from the area completely. Major Collins won a Military Cross and Lance-Corporal Brooks a Military Medal for their part in the action. On the 23rd May 1945 with some measure of honour restored and a battle under their belt the battalion boarded the HMT *Dunera* again and returned to India regrouping with the 26th division at Bangalore.

The push from the beaches of Normandy to Falaise had been the reverse of the constant retreat the regiment had suffered in the early part of the war from Ypres to Dunkirk; even so the losses had been great. Both the 7th and 2nd Battalions had seen consistent heavy fighting from the moment their boots left the landing craft. They had been moving swiftly over difficult terrain for over a month and not only were they depleted in numbers, seen friends killed and wounded but were also exhausted. These efforts had not been for nothing and alongside the various regiments of the allied forces the liberation of France had begun and already eyes were starting to turn towards Germany itself.

Towards the end of August the battalions in France had time to take stock and reorganize themselves. On the 14th August the 2nd Battalion received two officers and 97 men and were resting and training in village of Tinchebry. The 7th battalion however received the terrible news on the 18th August that the 59th Division was to be disbanded. Despite having fought at Caen and through the Bocage this battalion now found itself redundant and broken up to its constituent units. On the 21st August Lieutenant-Colonel Gibbs of the 2nd Battalion requested that as many men from the 7th as possible be moved to his battalion taking both 'B' and 'D' companies in their entirety. One other company went to their long time allies the 2nd KSLI whilst the last company were split up to join the 111th Armoured Division and the 1st Herefordshire Regiment. Lieutenant-

Colonel Jerram returned from his stroke and was given command of the Division Battle School.

OPERATION MARKET GARDEN

At the start of September 1944 the allied forces held a line along the river Seine to Paris and down to the Mediterranean. The 12th US Army now independent of General Montgomery's command covered this defensive position whilst the 6th US Army landed in the French Riveria freeing Toulon and Marseilles before heading north up the Rhone Valley.

The Royal Warwickshire's 2nd Battalion moved with the 3rd Division over the river Seine whilst the Guards Armoured Division liberated Brussels. The Battalion were billeted in Villers en Vexin and Vatimesnil and were afforded some relaxation time. By the middle of September Ghent was liberated and the 6th US Army had linked up with General Patton's 3rd US Army near Dijon. The noose was really starting to tighten on the German army and so the allied command prepared their hammer blow.

Operation Market Garden was designed to begin the final push that would drive the Germans out of Belgium and Holland and give the allies access to Germany itself. The operation took the form of the largest airbourne assault to

FIGURE 28- OPERATION MARKET GARDEN

date in the war. The plan called for a series of aerial landings to seize key bridges and stop them being destroyed by the withdrawing Germans. Three divisions took part in this initial assault on the 17th September which began well with the famous actions at Arnhem and Eindhoven. Opposition was stiff with Field Marshal Walther Model's Army Group B mustering 15,000 men and 250 tanks to defend the German line.

The 2nd Battalion itself rolled back into action on the following day (19th September) with the 3rd Division. They crossed the Belgian frontier and joined the 8th Corps. The main thrust of their advance was through northern Holland with the goal of reaching Zuider Zee where the Germans were still launching V1 and V2 rockets at British cities.

By end of the day the battalion had arrived at Peer just north of the Meuse-Escaut Canal a location they had once held in the very earliest days of the war during their retreat to Dunkirk. Whilst it seemed that Germany was on the run this was no walk in the park. German morale wasn't completely destroyed and the pace of the allied advance meant that supplies and reinforcements were hard to come by. The 8th corps had orders to broaden the corridor that the initial landings had made and the 2nd Battalion followed in its wake. During the advance they were held in reserve whilst the Bailey bridge was crossed and then took over the bridgehead created over the Bois-le-Duc canal. Much of their work was supportive in nature; mopping up enemy units and patrolling for stragglers.

On the 24th September, the last day of Operation Market Garden, the 11th Armoured Division pushed forward to Deurne and Liesel with the 2nd Battalion ordered to clear up behind them. 'D' Company under and the command of Major Bell led the attack facing retaliation by German shells and mortar fire. In the face of this fire the company began to take casualties but by night fall held the outskirts of the village of Heusden. Given the strength of opposition the company was withdrawn to allow British artillery to target the entrenched Germans. In this single action the company had 12 wounded and four killed including two officers. Despite the stiffer than expected resistance Operation Market Garden was declared a moderate success not all the bridges had been taken and some of the paratroopers became separated from the main assault and were forced to surrender, however the attack was strong enough for Model to evacuate Oosterbeek leaving behind 1485 dead and 6525 prisoners.

For the rest of September the battalion stayed in Asten where they continued to mop up German patrols. Hearing of enemy soldiers over the Deurne Canal Captain Allan and one platoon of 'B' Company were sent to investigate. They encountered a small enemy unit who they engaged. They killed two and wounded two more before driving the Germans back. That night further patrols identified that the enemy remained in strength in the area and the battalion marched to Leirop to assist US troops.

The overall plan for October was to push on across the border into Germany. This action started with a thrust into the Reichswald forest region provoking a strong counterattack from the entrenched German army. The 2nd Battalion with the 185th Brigade were placed on one flank whilst the US 82nd Airbourne Division took the lead. Heavy mortar fire killed one man and wounded five more and left 'B' Company dangerously isolated. Sniper action was particularly heavy and mortar fire continued to take lives. Fearing the Germans were massing for an attack the 2nd Battalion sent out patrols to try and determine where the enemy were massing. Corporal Mobly of 'A' Company captured three German soldiers and Lieutenant Mavins patrol penetrated so deeply in to enemy line that they were forced to lie up during the day and sneak back to British lines the next night. With resistance stronger than desired and with continuing problems on the Scheldt estuary Field Marshall Montgomery cancelled the attack on the Reichswald and redeployed his troops. The 3rd division, including the 2nd battalion, were sent to Venlo.

On 12th October the 8th, 9th and 185th Brigades were tasked with clearing a series of woods around Venraij. The going was tough and rain hampered matters considerably. The 2nd battalion suffered heavy mortar fire that killed three and wounded a further 19. The following day they still held firm but then the enemy counterattacked in strength. 'B' and 'D' companies were pushed back forcing 'A' and 'C' companies to dig in near the waterway, Molen Beek. The counter attack killed five men including Major Jerram and wounded 15 more.

Three days later the battalion were ordered to cross the Molen Beek under the cover of dark. The banks of the Beek were steep and river itself 10 meters wide, the approaches were boggy and progress was slow. Once in position recon patrols were sent out. At 3 am on the 16th October bridging equipment arrived and in silence 'B' and 'D' companies crept up the Beek and started to deploy the pontoons. Unfortunately they were spotted and started to come under heavy fire from the opposite bank. Much of this fire came from some farmhouses on the right flank. Major Bell attached to 'D' Company led an assault on this location to ease the fire. Swift hand to hand combat followed and the company took some 30 or more prisoners.

At 7 am 'A' and 'C' companies set off to join their comrades and were proud to discover that only the tank bridges set up by the 2nd Battalion remained in place. Whilst this proved the skill of the battalion it severely reduced the options for the establishment of a bridgehead across the river. 'A' Company advanced quickly over the river to the crossroads of Brabander and by mid-day all objectives had been achieved however progress elsewhere had been less successful. Failures along the line left the 2nd battalion out on a limb on a narrow salient taking heavy fire and under the threat of counter attack.

Advancing 200 yards 'C' Company under the command of Captain Gilbert were able to reach St Anna's Hospital a lunatic asylum where luckily the 8th Brigade was able to link up with them. The day's action had cost the battalion two company commanders, 3 other officers and 7 men with 50 more wounded. The following day the 2nd KSLI relived 'B' and 'D' companies in Brabander wood allowing them to advance north of Venraij where they met a stubborn German defence. 16 more men were wounded including another company commander.

On the 18th October the battalion advanced to occupy an abandoned monastery with 'B' and 'D' battalions in the lead. 'D' Company came under heavy shell fire whilst 'B' Company was pinned down by machine gun fire just 400 yards short of their target. 'A' and 'C' companies were more successful in their advance and two troops of men were sent to reinforce the other companies but these were delayed by minefields. Word reached the battalion that Venraij had fallen and was in allied hands and so the battalion dug in and brought up anti-tank weapons. The day ended with seven dead, seventeen wounded and two missing.

Over the next week the battalion suffered intermittent shelling and were mostly employed in evacuating civilians from the village that had been sheltering in their cellars. Further casualties were taken but the arrival of 100 reinforcements served to keep the battalion operational. Throughout November the battalion took part in minor clear up actions, mine laying and digging trenches. On the 16th December the battalion were returned to the front lines and were given 4000 yards to defend around Grubbenvorst. Here the territory was thickly wooded with few roads and thick with mud. Patrols however were successful in rooting out several parties of Germans. They spent Christmas in the snow on this frontline before retiring to Horst for the New Year. Not all allied troops had the luxury of rest over Christmas. To the south a large German counter offensive began near the Luxembourg border pushing nearly to Namur in Belgium. The attack was spearheaded by Panzers that raced through allied lines. The Battle of the Bulge became known as the largest land tank battle as the US 1st and 3rd Armies struggled to contain the attack. The American army did so admirably, they stemmed the tide and forced the Germans back again with the loss of 100,000 men with the Americans losing only 10,276 in return.

It was clear that despite the recent victories entering Germany would have to wait until the spring when the troops would be better rested and the weather had improved, however this delay also allowed the German army to reorganise and prepare a defence.

At the start of February 1945 allied forces were still some 20-40 miles from the river Rhine itself and the border of Germany. They faced a more prepared German army that had flooded land on the approach to key locations to slow the allied advance. Blaskowitz Army group H held the far north with Model's Army group B in the centre and Hauser's Army group G the south.

The Royal Warwickshire's 2nd Battalion had now joined the 185th Brigade in Maastricht, a city the regiment had once laid siege to at the time of its creation. From here the brigade headed east. The terrain was hard and retreating German forces had laid hundreds of mines and flooded fields. The German army itself had 700 mortars and 1000 guns facing them along a narrow front. On the 25th February the 2nd Battalion reached the battle zone which had been further reinforced by German units that had been able to move up after a US assault had been delayed.

The divisional plan was called Operation Heather and required the 8th and 9th brigades to hold ground south of the village of Goch and attack south-east. The 185th brigade was held in reserve advancing through the troops to take Kervenheim whilst the 53rd division would attack on the right flank and seize the town of Weeze. The Canadians would take Uden and Calcar whilst the 11th Armoured Division would hold the left flank.

FIGURE 29 - CHURCHILL TANKS IN ACTION

On the 27th February the operation was launched but the 2nd battalions progress was heavily hampered by thick woodland and fallen trees. The following day as planned the 185th brigade moved through 8th brigade. The 2nd battalion held the right flank with the 2nd KSLI on the left, both battalions were supported by a squadron of Churchill Tanks. 'A' and 'C' companies probed forward and took their primary targets and allowed 'B' and 'D' companies to leapfrog them to consolidate a position on the outskirts of Kervenheim. Several prisoners were taken and Major Albery of 'C' Company was wounded by a sniper, two other men were killed and two wounded.

The morning of the 1st March was wet and the battalion found itself holding a narrow salient with an exposed right flank. To make matters worse as dawn broke they came under sustained shell and mortar fire. The 75th German Paratroopers counterattacked with SP guns hitting 'B' Company hard and Lieutenant Guests platoon in particular. Under this sustained attack Private Cook won a

264

Military Medal for firing high explosives into the advancing enemy. Privates Duck and Stephenson also won the Military Medal for their sterling work as stretcher bearers taking care of the 34 wounded that accumulated during the day. The 2nd Battalion held firm and the rest of the 185th brigade were able to continue to advance all day.

This steady advance continued for the next few days with the battalion taking a role once again in the seizure of Kapellan. Here a night attack was led by Major Bell and 'B' company. They cleared the edge of the town quickly capturing 12 Germans only one of whom resisted who was shot. 'A' Company moved up in support but arrived just in time to see the enemy withdraw. This withdrawal was covered by intense artillery fire that knocked out two of the battalions supporting Churchill Tanks. This small action was replicated along the length of the assault as the British and American pincer movement met up at Gilder spreading panic through the German ranks who were frantic to withdraw across the river Rhine. Over 50,000 prisoners were taken during this mad scramble to escape the allied army.

CROSSING THE RHINE

The 2nd Battalion arrived on the river Rhine on the 12th March 1945 with a new commanding officer, Lieutenant-Colonel MacDonald having replaced Lieutenant-Colonel Gibbs. They were posted to a large flat island in the river covered in small farms. They overlooked the village of Emeriti. Movement was difficult with most bridges destroyed by the retreating German Army but surprisingly the most difficult problem was the livestock left by the civilians. A large bull gored one of the soldiers on a night patrol and so the battalion were detailed the next day with evacuating all the livestock from the frontlines. The battalion's official duty was to prepare for an amphibious assault to be led by the 51st Highland Division. They were assigned to watch a 500 yard front but it was hard to estimate the enemy strength as the Germans used smoke grenades to obscure their positions and defences.

On the 18th March 'D' Company discovered a three man German scouting party on the island. After questioning them they discovered that the scouts were due to be collected that evening by boat. Captain Dentist led a patrol to ambush this rescue party but no-one turned up. At 3 am however a German fighting patrol of around 20 men attacked 'C' Company and captured one of the Royal Warwick's and retreated across the river in an almost tit for tat retaliation. Further interrogation of the captured scouts revealed that the battalion faced the Parachute Regiment.

By the 23rd March the attack across the river was finally ready. Mortar and artillery fire ran through the afternoon up until 9 pm when the assault companies of the 51st Division successfully crossed the river and created a bridgehead. The 2nd Battalion followed up and were billeted in the ruins of Rees and Groin.

During early April the battalion were relieved by the 1st Cheshire's and they rejoined the 185th Brigade that was mopping up the straggling German forces. Travelling in cramped lorries the battalion were sent back into action on the 4th April at Legmen with orders to attack quickly on arrival. At 9am the battalion formed up and at 10.15 am they moved out with 'C' and 'D' companies in the lead. They pushed through enemy artillery whilst supported by their own artillery and managed to hit the enemy headquarters hard enough to force them to surrender. The battalion took 170 prisoners for the loss of only three dead and five wounded. They became bogged down in street fighting in Legmen itself and were relieved by the 1st Norfolk's who came up to continue the fight.

The following day saw a German counterattack and 'A' Company were sent into clear a block of houses. Their attack provoked the enemy who called in artillery cover followed by an infantry assault on 'A', 'B' and 'D' companies. They managed initially to break through the battalions lines but were slowly repelled with 37 more prisoners taken as well as four SP guns captured and a fifth one destroyed by Private Gibbon. They managed to hold their position with no deaths just 13 wounded and by the end of the day the village of Limgen was wholly in British hands.

On the 7th April 1945 the battalion was given two troop carriers to scout out German paratroopers in woods to the south of their position. One carrier had little trouble and located three sleeping troopers, quickly taking them into custody. The second carrier however had a more eventful encounter. Led by Captain Williams the carrier began to take machine gun fire when they observed a party of German soldiers heading into the village of Mundersum. Reporting their discovery to headquarters the battalion was given orders to clear the village out. Mundersum was a cluster of farmhouses and already under artillery fire. The battalion formed up, with 'B' Company held in reserve.

The other three companies with the support of flame thrower tanks and SP guns began their advance pressing the attack at 5 pm. They quickly reached the farms and began to clear them out with little opposition. Only Sergeant Graves was killed who was shot by some Germans hidden in a trench. The battalion discovered that the village was being used as an Anti-Aircraft Station and captured 5 four-barreled and 6 two-barreled 20mm guns along with 100 prisoners.

Over the next few days the battalion followed the Armoured Guards division with the rest of the 185th Brigade as the allies moved to Osnabruck. Along the way they ran patrols and continued to capture surrendering prisoners. By the 11th April the allies were just 10 miles from the German city of Bremen. Here the 52nd Lowland Division, 51st Highland Division, 43rd Division and the battalions own 3rd Division were in position around the city which continued to refuse to surrender. The battalion itself was assigned to a flat area between Kirchweghe and Brinkum.

THE SIEGE OF BREMEN

On the 13th April 1945 the 8th Brigade began to probe the German defence around Bremen towards Brinkum. Here they met stiff resistance from the 18th SS Training Battalion and so the rest of the 185th brigade was ordered up in support. Lieutenant-Colonel MacDonald decided to mount a surprise attack from the south with the 2nd KSLI holding the 2nd battalions right flank. MacDonald assembled some considerable support for the attack including 2 troops of Sherman Tanks, 17 SP guns with crew, a medium Machine-Gun platoon, a 4.2 inch mortar platoon, 3 field regiments of 22 pounder artillery and a company of the 1st Norfolk Regiment.

The 1st Norfolk's advanced first taking out a German outpost that threatened their left flank whilst a creeping artillery barrage paved the way for a general assault at mid-day. Major Illing led 'A' Company through a smokescreen to attack Leeste. 'B' Company set off in support in the south with a troop of tanks whilst 'D' Company came up to take and clear the local farms. 'C' Company pushed up the Brinkum road to clear Erichshof.

'A' Company had the hardest struggle, fighting the young SS battalion in close quarter hand to hand action from house to house. Major Illings men were able to kill 25 enemy soldiers and captured a further 160 but came under sustained attack until 'D' Company were able to reinforce them. Sadly on arrival Lieutenant Harrison of 'D' Company was shot dead. 'B' Company succeeded in taking 70 prisoners without a single casualty. By 2.30 pm in just two and a half hours Leeste was firmly in the battalions grasp. This allowed them to withdraw their tank support and send them to join 'C' Company in their attack on Erichshof. 'C' companies advance had been slowed by the number of mines they encountered but they did manage to get a 6 pounder anti-tank gun up to support them as they took a further 20 prisoners.

'A' Company continued to push forwards using the carrier platoon to clear the northern fringe of their target. Here Sergeant Frost won the Military Medal. Frost, injured down the right side by a shell burst, was still able to lead his platoon forwards and kill 12 Germans and capture 15 more. By 4.30 pm all the battalions objectives and been seized and secured but to the west the 8th Brigade continued to fight over the Brinkum crossroads.

Whilst securing their next objective 'A' Company stumbled upon a German outpost at the Railway Station north of Leeste. Using a 17 pounder gun they were able to quickly quell this enemy killing an SS officer and taking 40 prisoners with only 4 men of their own killed and 9 wounded. Major Bell and 'D' Company with a troop of tanks moved up in support and wiped out this pocket of resistance.

'B' and 'C' companies assaulted Brinkum itself at 7 pm. 'B' Company managed to advance well but 'C' Company hit some difficulties. Lieutenant Oland was seriously wounded (an injury that would cost him his leg) and the section commanding officer was killed by a machine gun post in a house. Sergeant Spindey took over command and directed one of their tanks to take out the house. As the clock struck 9 pm things were starting to calm down, however some of the German soldiers were becoming suicidal and two German NCO's blew themselves up with grenades when captured in an attempt to kill as many of the battalion as possible. As the 1st Norfolk's arrived to relieve the battalion they counted 60 dead Germans and over 200 prisoners. The battalion spent the next day resting in Leeste where a mobile bath unit and a cinema unit had been brought up. Here they were thanked personally for their efforts by Field Marshall Montgomery who was presented a Nazi standard captured by the battalion during the attack.

Right across the front the Germans were starting to collapse. The Russian army had taken Vienna and were on the outskirts of Berlin. In the south the allies had broken out of Italy and allied forces had seized the cities of Nuremberg and Leipzig, a link with the Russians was now only days away. More and more soldiers were surrendering and the civilian population seemed resigned to the fact that Germany was losing the war. In contrast to this air of despair in some German ranks others continued to fight on. For example on the 26th April over 1,000 V2 rockets hit Southern England killing 2750 people. Until a full surrender was achieved the army couldn't afford to hold back.

The battalion advanced again on the night of the 24th/25th April 1945. The 185th Brigade led a night attack to protect the right flank of the 9th Brigade as they crossed flooded land at Kattenturm. The 185th was ordered to assault the villages of Dreye and Arsten. The 2nd Battalion and 2nd KSLI set off at 11 pm up the Dreye causeway and along a railway embankment crossing the flooded land in Buffalo amphibious landing vehicles. The 1st Norfolk's advanced through Arsten to capture Habenhausen whilst the 52nd Division attacked northern Bremen. On the left the 2nd Ulster Rifles reached Katternturm at midday.

This general advance worked well using three waves to ferry all the men across the river and into their assigned positions. At 2.15 am 'D' Company crossed in six 'Buffalo' vehicles directed by Intelligence officer Lieutenant Tennant with a torch, in the next 15 minutes the rest of the battalion came across in the second wave and the tactical headquarters crossed in the 3rd wave. 'A' and 'D' companies advanced on Arsten with 'B' and 'C' in reserve. They found Arsten was clear and took 100 prisoners.

The 25th April was spent securing the ground and sending out patrols. Fire was received and the battalion's guns were taken out and 2nd Lieutenant Putsman and 3 others were wounded. It was then that news reached them that the American army had finally linked up with the Russians at Liepzig. To the general soldier this was something to celebrate but for many in government both in London and Washington they were already concerned about the next possible conflict and wary of the communist Russian state and its growing power. The race to secure Berlin began with the remaining German forces becoming almost incidental to the wider politics taking place.

Overnight whilst this news was digested the battalion prepared in an assembly area for an attack on some enemy barracks. 'B' and 'C' companies backed by a tank and two 'crocodile' flame thrower tanks advanced down quiet streets with 'A' and 'D' companies following. All seemed too quiet and the battalion was asked to push on to the railway.

On approaching the railway 'B' Company began to take fire from dug in Germans soldiers that they seemed unable to dislodge. It was in this engagement that the battalion sustained its last casualties of the war. Corporal Stacey was shot in the back during the fire fight; Private Rice ran out to rescue him but discovered the corporal was already dead. Returning to cover Private Rice was able to watch as the 'crocodiles' came up and spewed out their deadly fire forcing out some 25 Germans from their positions. The battalion halted at the railway taking 20 more prisoners unaware that this was to be their last action of the war.

On the 29th April the battalion were pulled back to Delmenhorst to protect the Canadians right flank, the following day Hitler, Goebbels and Eva Braun committed suicide and the German army was thrown into chaos finally formally surrendering on the 5th May ending the Second World War in Europe.

In all over 60 million people died during the Second World War. In terms of military losses Britain suffered 380,000 losses, America 416,000, Germany 5.5 million and the USSR a staggering 14 million.

IN THE AFTERMATH

With the end of the war all the prisoners of war were released from their incarceration and able go home or rejoin their units. Two such prisoners of war included Captain Tomes and Captain Spencer. Captain Tomes had been taken prisoner at Wormhoudt during the retreat to Dunkirk. He was lucky enough not to be with the others that the SS killed. He spent the whole of the war in a series of prisoner of war camps around Warburg. It was from here that he made his first escape; unfortunately he was quickly recaptured and sent to an Oflag near Eichstatt. On the 14th April 1945 just as the war was coming to a close he was part of a column of prisoners that were attacked by US aircraft, in the confusion he and two other prisoners slipped away from their guards and into thick woodland. They managed to stay free for nearly a week before being captured again. With swollen feet Tomes was not returned to the camp but instead to a Hospital in Eichstatt where on the 24th he was rescued when a US Recon patrol entered the town.

Captain Spencer had started POW life with a march. He and his fellow prisoners were marched by foot right across France and Germany across the river Danube to a camp at Moosburg where he joined 23,000 others and met several of his comrades from the 7th battalion. He remained here until the 29th April 1945 when the camp was liberated by a US tank.

Whilst the war in Europe was over Japan still presented a problem in the Far East. The 1st Battalion was still in India moving to Bangalore and Madras from Bombay in June 1945 where many of the men were demobbed leaving only the regular contingent. In August word reached them of the atomic attack on Hiroshima and Nagasaki and the surrender of the Japanese army fully drawing the whole war to a close. With hostilities ended men and materials needed to be redistributed and inevitably the army reorganised. December saw them in Avadi where they were presented with an Antelope mascot, Billy, by the Maharajah of Mysore. In May 1946 the battalion joined the 7th Kings Own and 1st Essex Regiments in the 72nd British Independent Brigade Group moving in October to a cooler climate near Bangalore. Here they performed police actions and training before on the 30th May 1947 they were placed on suspended animation prior to army restructure and the departure of British forces from India.

CHAPTER 10 - THE END OF EMPIRE AND THE COLD WAR

Whilst for many the end of the Second World War was a huge relief there were others who were all too aware of potential problems looming on the horizon. The changing landscape of global politics was moving away from imperial institutions towards the establishment of blocs of superpowers. Despite being vital allies during the war the USSR and China, both communist states were now becoming the enemy. The ideals of communism were diametrically opposed to those of democratic capitalism. The establishment of the Eastern Bloc from the countries liberated by Russian troops during the war staked the USSR's position clearly, we will not be vulnerable again and who can blame them out of all the nations involved in the war they took the highest casualty toll by far.

Elsewhere in the world imperial outposts began to chafe against the bit. The old colonial powers of the Netherlands, France and the United Kingdom all began to suffer from localised unrest from the indigenous populations. Many of these colonies had fought for Britain in the war but now wanted self-determination as the price for that aid. Financially crippled Britain could not afford to invest too much in retaining their loyalty or to support their populations. A growing call for liberation began to be heard within the Houses of Parliament for the independence of India, Palestine, and several African states.

A new world order was beginning to emerge. The United Nations formed from the ashes of the war would start to play a bigger part in the way armies and regiments operated and the Cold War created a whole new battlefield to fight over that had as many proxy wars as any of the old Imperial struggles of the 19th century.

The 2nd Battalion of the Royal Warwickshire Regiment had ended the war outside Bremen with the 3rd Division. The division was put on standby for service against Japan in the Far East this was forestalled by Japans surrender in August. Many of the men were demobbed and returned home. One new recruit did appear however – Bobby the Antelope from Hamburg Zoo. With the war completely over the battalion retraced its steps to Ghent in Belgium. Here they remained and allowed home leave.

EGYPT AND SUDAN

The 8th battalion at the close of the Second World War had been warned to mobilise for deployment in the Middle East but the battalion could only muster 5 officers, 1 RSM and 100 other ranks. They were reinforced by men from the now disbanded 2/7th Battalion and arrived in Port Said on 6th December 1945. They headed down into Sudan via the Suez Canal disembarking at Port Sudan. There was much unrest in the region, relations with Egypt were strained and there was violence in Palestine. Additionally there were several captured Italian territories that needed policing. During the spring of 1946 the battalions companies were spread across Asmara in Eritrea and Khartoum in Sudan and at the Sennar Dam on the Blue Nile. Here they conducted training exercises and other duties that included guard duty on an internment camp for Jews in Asmara.

In the summer there were sporadic Arab uprisings which included the Sudan Defence Force attacking a Coptic Christian community killing and wounding 100 of them. The defence force had been an indigenous regiment established in 1925 that fought the Italians in North Africa. After the war they became increasingly resistant to British rule. The battalion were rushed to the site of the attack to help maintain order and the rioting ceased. However in the spring of 1947 like the 1st Battalion the 8th was placed in suspended animation and transferred to Quassassin where their commanding officer became the commander of the 10th Ethiopian Battalion and the other officers were sent to the 2nd Battalion. The remaining soldiers all volunteered to become the nucleus of the newly formed 18th Parachute Battalion. With the 1st, 7th and 8th battalions now disbanded only the 2nd was left operational.

PALESTINE AND THE JEWISH REVOLT

In October 1945 the 2nd battalion received new operational orders, after facing some of the stiffest fighting in Europe they were now deployed to Palestine. Their journey was not an easy one. They were jammed into converted bombers that then hopped from Brussels to Castelbenito in Tripoli to Cairo and Quassassin in Egypt Here the battalion were re-equipped and became acclimatised to the climate. They then travelled by road to Jerusalem.

Jerusalem was in the grip of unrest between the Jewish Zionists and the local Arabs. Palestine was liberated from Ottoman occupation in the First World War by British forces. At the close of the war Britain retained a mandate for Palestine which was formally ratified in 1922. Throughout the Second World War Palestine, although threatened by the Italians and General Rommel's forces in North Africa, was mostly untouched by hostilities. Despite trying to control the immigration of Jews flooding into Palestine after 1939 the British Government became more focused on maintaining order. The Arab majority in Palestine were not pleased with the British Mandate and several uprisings were quelled during the 1920's. SS leader Heinrich Himmler tried to use this to Nazi advantage by recruiting Palestinian Arabs to oppose British rule. Not all Arabs were pro-German and over 6,000 joined up with nearly 30,000 Palestinian Jews to form the Palestine Regiment that fought with the British Empire.

The battalion was tasked with essentially a peace keeping role in an extremely volatile situation with elements of the Arabs and the Jewish population both attacking British rule. In December 1945 there were explosions and gun fire in the city centre. Jewish fighters had blown down the corner of a local police station killing and wounding several local police officers and Basuto soldiers. The 2nd Battalion were sent in to support them; Lieutenant Oakley won a Military Medal for his tireless efforts searching through the rubble and for pulling a wounded man free. In

278

January 1946 a battalion patrol surprised a group of Jewish terrorists about to attack a prison. The patrol managed to drive the terrorists off and only Sergeant Osborne was injured.

In April the British and Americans met to discuss the problem of Palestine. They began to draw up plans to partition the country into Jewish and Palestinian States This plan pleased neither the Zionist Jews nor the Palestinian Arabs. The battalion at this point was spending some down time in Cairo and the Suez to take part in sport and training; sadly Bobby the mascot died and was replaced by another antelope from Cairo Zoo. In August the Zionists launched a campaign against British rule including the bombing of the King David Hotel in Jerusalem.

In February 1947 the 2nd battalion was moved from the 3rd Division to the 1st Division and joined the 2nd Infantry Brigade near Hadera. They spent much of the spring and summer taking part in guard duties of Camp 87 in Pardess Hanna, internal security and routine patrols. It was at this time they were made aware that they were now the only operational battalion of the regiment and received drafts of men from the disbanding other battalions.

On the 30th November 1947 the United Nations took over the plans for the partition of Palestine giving land to both the Jews and the Arabs. The Arabs displeased by this turn of events began to destroy Jewish buildings causing the Jews to retaliate in turn. Both sides were well armed and the battalion were on constant alert often having to sally out from their bases to quell some local engagement. Throughout a bitter winter they existed in nearly siege conditions with at least one company on standby at all times. By March 1948 the battalion, like much of the army in Palestine were over stretched with companies taking on 96 hour guard duties with 24 hour rest breaks.

It was decided that the British would evacuate all forces in line with the end of the mandate in the area, leaving the UN to manage the establishment of the Palestinian and Jewish states. The Royal Warwick's left Jerusalem on 14th May the day before the handover and travelled down to the Egyptian border and on to the British bases in Quassassin.

During June 1947 the Regiment returned home to the Budbrooke Barracks outside Warwick aboard the HMS *Scythia*. Here more of the men were demobbed and the 2nd Battalion was renamed the 1st Battalion to reflect the fact that it was the only operational battalion in the regiment.

THE COLD WAR

In January 1951 the 1st Battalion was posted to Graz in the Austrian province of Styria to undertake a two year tour of duty on the Cold War's frontline. They were billeted in old SS barracks something that probably didn't sit too well with those that had tangled with the SS during the Second World War. Their role in Austria was to guard the growing border between Europe and the Eastern Bloc. They manned checkpoints along the British and Soviet demarcation line.

The Cold War was not an outright war between the West and the Communists but more a series of smaller wars and skirmishes often fought by proxy. One such war had erupted in 1950 when North Korea invaded South Korea, starting the Korean War. The United Nations at the insistence of the United States quickly threw its support behind the Southern state as a bulwark against the communist North. Britain along with many nations in the Commonwealth and the United Nations committed troops to fight alongside the South Korean Army. The war went well and it looked as if the North would be soundly beaten until in October 1951 the Chinese entered the war on the North's side. Worried about the United States influence so close to their own borders encouraged the Chinese to invest their vast manpower into assisting the North Korean army. The huge numbers that were deployed pushed the Korean War into the stagnation of a stalemate.

It was against this background in April 1953 that the 1st battalion of the Royal Warwickshire's received large drafts of men and prepared to go to war again receiving orders to proceed to Korea. However in July 1953 an armistice was signed between the two forces. Although peace was called and the country partitioned no treaty was ever signed so in effect North and South Korea remain at war to this day. In August 1953 despite the end of the war the regiment left on the long journey to Pusan in South Korea. Here the regiment was placed in the 1st Commonwealth Division in a tented camp near the river Imjin on the 38th Parallel. Its role was to build up the South Korean defences in case of further conflict. The division dug a series of bunkers and defensive features whilst also taking the time to train in mobile warfare. The regiment spent a year in Korea before being withdrawn to the Suez Canal in Egypt.

At this time, as with Palestine, Britain was preparing to withdraw its influence from Egypt. A 1936 treaty had allowed Egypt to return to full autonomous control whilst the United Kingdom were permitted to retain control of the Suez Canal, the empires vital link to colonies in the Far East. By 1954 however India had been independent for five years and Egypt under the leadership of Gamal Abdel Nasser no longer believed the Canal should be controlled by Britain and France. The government agreed and began to withdraw troops. The Royal Warwick's were stationed at a number of camps and assigned to the 1st Infantry Division conducting desert exercises. In January the battalion left the Canal Zone before being withdrawn from the country completely.

In July 1956 after the last soldiers had left President Nasser privatised the canal sparking the Suez War between Israel, France and the United Kingdom against the Egyptians. The battalion would however not return to fight in this engagement instead it was sent to Cyprus.

POLICE ACTIONS

During 1955 and 1956 the British Army went through another re-organisation in line with a general reduction in the number of soldiers in the army. The Royal Warwickshire Regiment had been grouped in the Midland Brigade with the Royal Leicestershire's, Sherwood Foresters and Royal Lincolnshire's. The re-organisation merged the Royal Lincolnshire's with the Northamptonshire's and so the smaller Midland Brigade was renamed the Forester brigade. Back in Britain the 7th Battalion Territorial Army Unit was now 1000 men strong but with an end of National Service these numbers quickly fell. The Territorial Army became entirely voluntary and the 147 Brigade of the 47th Division in which the battalion was assigned was reclassified from an Armoured Division to an Infantry one with responsibility for Home and Civil Defence.

The 1st Battalion spent six months in Normandy Camp in Nicosia, Cyprus, during a difficult period. Cyprus became a British protectorate in 1878 when the Congress of Berlin agreed that Britain would defend the Ottoman Empire from Russia in exchange for the island. The island became fully annexed in 1914 at the outbreak of the First World War when the Ottomans joined the axis powers. The island had a distinct split in population; four fifths were Greek and one fifth Turkish. In 1946 the exiled Bishop of Kyrenia, Makarios III took the archepeicospal throne becoming a national leader for the Greeks. This move concerned the Turkish nationals and friction with the Greeks grew. At the same time the Greeks grew weary of British rule. From its earliest days as a British colony Cyprus was subject to the Enosis Movement. Enosis, meaning Union in Greek was a movement to unite all Greeks under the leadership of Greece. This movement in Cyprus eventually developed a paramilitary wing called the EKOA.

The EKOA was led by Colonel Georgios Grivas formerly of the Greek Cypriot National Guard and caused many problems during 1954 and 1955 when Makarios tried unsuccessfully to get the United Nations to remove Britain. All the proposals were shelved by the UN and so demonstrations started on the streets. During 1956 the

British Governor and Markarios entered into talks to try and resolve the situation but when Makarios was deported in 1956 because of links to the EKOA Greco-Turkish Riots broke out. These riots turned in to civil war.

In 1959 independence was granted within the commonwealth and Markarios III was elected president the battle with Britain was over but a new one with the Turks erupted. Cyprus became a republic in 1960 but the civil war rumbled on. In 1964 7,000 UN peacekeepers were deployed and Cyprus became partitioned. In the six months in Cyprus the battalion suffered three deaths two of which were accidents; Sergeant Coleman shot himself whilst getting in a vehicle and Private Downing was accidentally shot on patrol at Omorphita Prison.

At the end of 1956 the battalion left Cyprus for an equally restless place, Ballykinlar in Northern Ireland to act as an aid to the civil power. This was during a time known as 'The Troubles' in Northern Ireland where sectarian violence between Catholic Republican and Protestant Loyalists held sway over the province. In the two years the battalion was stationed in Northern Ireland the Irish Republican Army (IRA) prosecuted a series of terrorist actions named the Border Campaign. Much of the action in this campaign, that saw the death of 6 policemen, 11 republicans and the internment of 400 suspected IRA members, was prosecuted by the Royal Ulster Constabulary but the battalion was present as were many other army units to provide support, garrison barracks and to render civil aid.

The battalion left Ireland in 1959 and sailed on the *Dunera* to Aden in the Middle-East. Here half of the men were stationed in Little Aden on land owned by the Shell Oil Corporation whilst the rest stayed in the desert at Nobat Dakin or on the Yemeni border at Dhala. Much of the time was spent on desert exercises although they did occasionally encounter trouble from the odd Arab sharpshooter that took pot shots at the battalion's patrols. As with Palestine, Egypt and Cyprus British control of Aden was coming to an end.

THE END OF THE REGIMENT

In 1960 the barracks at Budbrooke were closed although the Regimental Headquarters remained at St John's House in Warwick. The battalion themselves went to Hong Kong and the Fanling Camp. Here the battalion were inspected by several important dignitaries including their Colonel in Chief Field Marshal Montgomery on his way to China, John Profumo the Defence Secretary and Lord Montbatten. Whilst at Fanling the battalion undertook leadership training and developed cooperation strategies with Aircraft, Submarines and Ships. This is evidence of the general modernisation of the army. Although smaller the intensive training regime and wide deployment was developing the British Army into a well trained professional force. Some fun was to be had in Hong Kong as well. Some of the men undertook an expedition to Mount Everest whilst others assisted the locals in building jetties and adopted a Chinese Children's Home and Orphanage.

In 1961 the battalion returned Europe and joined the British Army of the Rhine in Hameln. British and American forces remained a strong presence in Germany during the

Cold War as a bulwark against Soviet pressure. Their entire time here was spent in Armoured Personnel Carriers as part of training for a possible mechanised role in the future. During the early 1960's the regiment moved between either Hameln or Minden. In November 1963 Montgomery retired as colonel in chief to be replaced by Major-General MacDonald, earlier in the year the name of the regiment was changed to the Royal Warwickshire Fusiliers and was rebadged with an Orange and Blue Hackle.

The second half of the 1960's was spent back in Britain except for a brief tour in Hong Kong and an expedition to North Borneo for Jungle Training. In 1968 another round of army reorganisation merged the Royal Warwickshire Fusiliers with the Royal Northumberland Fusiliers, Royal Fusiliers and the Lancashire Fusilier to form a larger infantry unit called the Royal Regiment of Fusiliers. This marked the end of the Regiment as an independent unit in the British Army after more than 300 years of service. The regiment inherited the red and white hackle of the Royal Northumberland Fusiliers and adopted an Indian Blackbuck Antelope called Bobby as the regimental mascot in homage to the Royal Warwickshire's. Originally each regiment formed one of the four battalions but in 2004 the regiment was downsized and merged in to two operational battalions. The Army Review 2020 launched in 2010 is due to reduce the regiment to a single battalion re-designated as an armoured infantry battalion under the 1st Armoured Brigade.

Recent battle honours won by the regiment include Wadi al Batin in the Gulf War of 1991 and Al Basra in the Iraq

War of 2003. But the regiment has also seen service in Northern Ireland, Cyprus, Kosovo and in Afghanistan. Although the name of Warwickshire has gone from the name of the regiment it still continues to give proud service to the country.

TRADITIONS OF THE REGIMENT

Nickname: The Dutch Guards
Guise's Greens
Saucy Sixth
Warwickshire Lads

Badge: White Antelope with Gold Collar and Chain

Motto: *'Honi soit qui mal y pense'*
Let him who thinks evil of it be ashamed
Also used by:

> The Coldstream Guards
> The Lancashire Regiment
> The King's Liverpool Regiment
> The Light Somerset Light Infantry
> The Royal Berkshire Regiment

Regimental Marches:

> 'The Warwickshire Lads' (Quick March)
> 'McBeans March' (Slow March)

Colours: St. Mary's Church, Warwick
Coventry Cathedral, Coventry
Regimental Musuem, St. John's, Warwick

BATTLE HONOURS OF
THE REGIMENT

War	Battle Honour
Nine Years War	Namur 1695
French Revolutionary War	Martinique 1794
Peninsular War	Rolica
	Vimiera
	Corunna
	Vitoria
	Pyrenees
	Nivelle
	Orthes
	Peninsula
War of 1812	Niagara
7th Kaffir War	South Africa 1846-7
8th Kaffir War	South Africa 1851-1853
Re-conquest of the Sudan	Atbara
	Khartoum (Omdurman)
Boer War (South African War)	South Africa 1899-1902
First World War	Le Cateau
	Retreat from Mons
	Marne 1914
	Aisne 1914,1918
	Armentieres 1914
	Ypres 1914, 1915, 1917
	Langemarck 1914, 1917
	Gheluvelt
	Neuve Chapelle
	St. Julien
	Frezenburg

First World War cont.

Bellewaarde
Aubers
Festubert 1915
Loos
Somme 1916, 1918
Albert 1916, 1918
Bazentin
Deville Wood
Pozieres
Guillemont
Fleers Courcelette
Morval
Le Transloy
Ancre Heights
Ancre 1916
Arras 1917, 1918
Vimy 1917
Scarpe 1917, 1918
Arleux
Oppy
Bullecourt
Messines 1917, 1918
Pilckem
Menin Road
Polygon Wood
Broodseinde
Poelcappelle
Passchendaele
Cambrai 1917, 1918
St. Quentin
Bapaume 1918
Rosieres
Lys
Estaires

First World War cont.	Hazebrouck
	Bailleul
	Kemmel
	Bethune
	Drocourt Queant
	Hindenburg Line
	Epehy
	Canal du Nord
	Beaurevoir
	Selle
	Valenciennes
	Sambre
	France and Flanders 1914-18
	Piave
	Vittorio Veneto
	Italy 1917-18
	Suvla
	Sari Bair
	Gallipoli 1915-16
	Tigris 1916
	Kut al Amara 1917
	Baghdad
	Mesopotamia 1916-18
	Baku
	Persia 1918
	Defence of Escaut
	Wormhoudt
	Ypres-Comines Canal
	Normandy Landing
Second World War	Caen
	Bourgebus Ridge
	Mont Pincon
	Falaise
	Rhineland

Second World War cont.   Lingen
                                Brinkum
                                Bremen
                                North-West   Europe   1940,
                                1944-5
                                Burma 1945

COLONELS OF THE REGIMENT

Name of Regiment	Colonel	Dates in Command
Vane's Regiment of Foot	Sir Walter Vane	1673 – 1674
Lillingston's Regiment of Foot	Luke Lillinston	1674 – 1675
Astley's Regiment of Foot	Thomas Astley	1675 – 1678
Belasye's Regiment of Foot	Sir Henry Belasyes	1678 – 1689
Babbington's Regiment of Foot	William Babbington	1680 – 1691
Hesse-Darmstadt's Regiment of Foot	George, Prince of Hesse-Darmstadt	1691 – 1694
De Rada's Regiment of Foot	Henry, Marquis of Rada	1694 – 1695
Columbine's Regiment of Foot	Ventris Columbine	1695 – 1703
River's Regiment of Foot	James Rivers	1703 – 1706
Southwell's Regiment of Foot	William Southwell	1706 – 1708
Harrison's Regiment of Foot	Thomas Harrison	1708 – 1716
Dormer's Regiment of Foot	Robert Dormer	1716 – 1720
	James Dormer	1720 – 1738

6th Regiment of Foot	John Guise	1738 – 1765
	William Rufane	1765 – 1773
	John Gore	1773
6th (1st Warwickshire) Regiment	Sir William Boothby	1773 – 1787
	Lancelot Baugh	1787 – 1792
	Sir Ralph Abercromby	1792 – 1795
	Prince William Frederick of Gloucester	1795 – 1806
6th Royal (1st Warwickshire) Regiment	Sir George Nugent	1806 – 1849
	Sir John Gardiner	1849 – 1851
	Henry James Riddell	1851 – 1861
	Hon. Sir Charles Gore	1861 – 1869
Royal Warwickshire Regiment	John Crofton	1869 – 1885
	Hon. Sir Francis Colbourne	1885 – 1895
	Robert Fraser	1895 – 1897
	Frederick Burroughs	1897 – 1904
	Henry Fieldon	1904 – 1921
	Sir Lancelot Edward Kigell	1921 – 1925
	Sir Robert Dundas Whigham	1925 – 1935
	Clement Thurston Tomes	1935 – 1946
	Bernard Montgomery, Viscount of Alamein	1947 – 1963
The Royal Warwickshire Fusiliers	Ronald MacDonald	1963 – 1968

COUNTRIES VISITED
BY THE REGIMENT

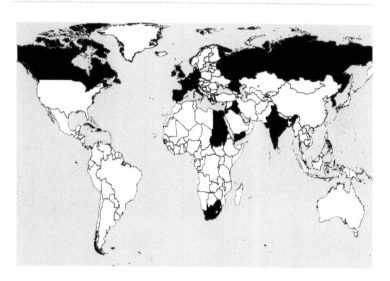

FIGURE 30 - MAP OF WHERE THE REGIMENT SERVED

List of where the Regiment served during key wars.

* indicates the regiment was involved in military action.

Conflict	Dates	Regiments Location
2nd Anglo-Dutch War	1665-67	Britain
3rd Anglo-Dutch War	1672-74	
Franco-Dutch War	1674-78	Belgium*
Nine Years War	1689-97	Ireland, Flanders*
War of Spanish Succession	1702-14	Spain*
War of Jenkins Ear	1739	Britain
War of Austrian Succession	1742-48	West Indies*, Scotland*
Seven Years War	1756-63	Gibraltar
1st Mysore War	1767-69	Scotland
American War of Independence	1775-1783	West Indies, Britain, Ireland
1st Maratha War	1778-82	Britain
2nd Mysore War	1780-84	Britain/Ireland
3rd Mysore War	1790-92	North America
French Revolutionary War	1793-1804	West Indies*, Ireland*, Canada
Napoleonic Wars	1804-15	Spain*, Flanders*, Portugal*, France*
War of 1812	1812-14	Canada*
3rd Kaffir/Xhosa War	1799-1803	West Indies*, Ireland*, Canada
1st Kandyan War	1803-04	
2nd Maratha War	1803-05	
4th Kaffir/Xhosa War	1811-12	Spain*, Flanders*, Portugal*, France*, Canada
2nd Kandyan War	1814-15	France*, Canada*

War	Date	Location
Nepalese War	1814-16	Hollan/France
3rd Maratha/Pindari War	1816-19	
3rd Kandyan War	1817-18	Britain
5th Kaffir/Xhosa War	1818-19	
1st Burma War	1824-26	Cape Town, India
6th Kaffir/Xhosa War	1834-42	India
1st Afghan War	1839-42	India, Aden, India,
1st China War	1839-42	Britain
Conquest of Sinde	1843	Britain
Gwalior Campaign	1843	
1st Sikh War	1845-46	Ireland, South Africa
7th Kaffir/Xhosa War	1846-47	South Africa*
1st Maori War	1846-47	South Africa
2nd Sikh War	1848-49	
8th Kaffir/Xhosa War	1850-53	South Africa*
Crimean War	1854-56	South Africa
Persian War	1856-57	
Indian Mutiny	1857-78	India*
3rd China War	1856-60	India
2nd Maori War	1860-61	
3rd Maori War	1863-66	Britain, West Indies
Bhutan War	1864-66	
Abyssinian Expedition	1867-68	Britain, India
Looshai Expedition	1871-72	India, Channel Islands
2nd Ashanti War	1873-74	
9th Kaffir/Xhosa War	1877-78	India, Britain
Jowakhic Campaign	1877-80	
2nd Afghan War	1878-80	Aden, Britain, India
Zulu War	1879	
1st Boer War	1880-81	India, Britain
Conquest of Egypt	1882	
Suakin of Egypt	1884-85	

Gordon Relief Expedition	1884-85	
3rd Burma War	1885-86	Ireland, India
Sikkim Expedition	1888	
Black Mountain Expedition	1888	
Manipur Expedition	1891	Britain, Ceylon
Relief of Chitral	1895	Malta, Ceylon
3rd Ashanti War	1895-1900	Egypt, India
Matebeleland/Mashonaland Rebellion	1896	
Reconquest of the Sudan	1896-98	Egypt*, Britain
Benin Expedition	1897	Egypt, Britain
North West Frontier Rising	1897-98	
South African War (Boer War)	1899-1902	India, South Africa*
Boxer Rebellion	1900	India, South Africa
Anglo-Aro War	1901-02	
World War I	1914-18	France*, Belgium*, Germany*, Italy*, Mesopotamia*
Russian Civil War	1918-20	
Turkish War of Independence	1919-23	
3rd Anglo-Afghan War	1919	
Irish War of Independence	1919-21	
Somaliland Campaign	1920	
Great Iraq Revolution	1920	
Arab revolt in Palestine	1936-39	
British-Zionist Conflict	1938-39	
World War II	1939-46	Belgium*, France*, Germany*, Burma*, India
Indonesian National	1945-49	

Rebellion		
Greek Civil War	1944-48	
1st Indochina War	1945-46	
Malayan Emergency	1948-60	
Korean War	1950-53	
Suez Emergency	1951-54	
Mau Mau Uprising	1952-60	
Cyprus Emergency	1955-60	
Suez War	1956-57	
Border Campaign	1956-62	
Indonesia-Malaysian Confrontation	1962-75	
Dhofar Rebellion	1962-75	
Aden Emergency	1963-67	
The Troubles	1968-98	

LEARNING MORE

The Royal Regiment of Fusiliers (Royal Warwickshire) Museum

Situated in St. John's House Museum in Warwick the museum covers the entire history of the regiment and the fusiliers. The museum holds a large collection of medals, uniforms and stories from the whole of the regiments history.

Admission: Free

St. John's House
Warwick
CV34 4NF

www.warwickfusiliers.co.uk

The Collegiate Church of St. Mary's

St. Mary's Church is home to the regimental chapel. It includes a memorial and the regimental colours

Admission: Donation

Old Square
Warwick
CV34 4RA

www.stmaryswarwick.org

SELECTED
BIBLIOGRAPHY

Ashby, John. (2000). *Seek glory, now keep glory. The story of the 1ˢᵗ Battalion, Royal Warwickshire Regiment 1914-18.* Helian and Company.

Bawthorp, Micheal. (2002). *Blood-red desert sand: The British Invasions of Egypt and the Sudan, 1882-1898.* Cassell. London.

Beckett, Ian. (2003). *Discovering English County Regiments.* Shire Publications Ltd. Princes Risborough.

Beckett, Ian. (2007). *Discovering British Regimental Traditions.* Shire Publications Ltd. Princes Risborough.

Benn, Carl. (2002). *The War of 1812.* Osprey Publishing Ltd. Wellingborough.

Blanning, T.C.W. (2000). *The Eighteenth Century: Europe 1688–1815.* Oxford University Press. Oxford.

Bridger, Geoff. (2009). *The Great War Handbook. A guide for Family Historians and Students of the Conflict. Pen and Sword Family History.* Barnsley.

Burnham, Robert and McQuigan, Ron. (2010). *The British Army against Napoleon. Facts, Lists and Trivia. 1805-1815.* Pen and Sword Books ltd. Barnsley.

Calvocressi, Peter. (1982). *World Politics since 1945.* 4ᵗʰ Edition. Longman Inc. New York.

Cannon, Richard. (1839). *Historical Record of the Sixth or Royal First Warwickshire Regiment of Foot.* Forgotten Books Reprint 2012.

Cunliffe, Marcus. (1956). *History of the Royal Warwickshire Regiment 1919-1955.* Willaim Clowes

Evans, Martin Marix. (1999). *The Boer War: South Africa 1899-1902.* Osprey Publishing.

Evans, Martin Marix. (2002). *Vital Guide to Battles of World War II.* Airlife Publishing Ltd. Shrewsbury.

Featherstone, Donald. (1973). *Colonial Small Wars 1837-1901.* David and Charles (Holdings) Ltd. Newton Abbot.

Fletcher, Ian. (1994). *Wellington's Regiments. The men and their battles 1808-1815.* Spellmount Limited.

Fremont-Barnes, Gregory. (2001). *The French Revolutionary Wars.* Osprey Publishing Ltd. Wellingborough.

Haythornthwaite, Philip. (1991). *Gallipoli 1915. Frontal Assault on Turkey.* Osprey Publishing Ltd. Oxford.

Hernon, Ian. (2008). *Britain's Forgotten Wars. Colonial Campaigns of the 19th Century.* The History Press. Stroud.

Hurt, Peter. (2011). *Gallipoli.* Profile Books Ltd. London

Illing, Brigadier H.C. *Royal Warwickshire Regiment 1955 to 1968.*

Jackson, Tabitha. (1999). *The Boer War.* Channel 4 Books.

James, Brigadier E.A. (1998). *British Regiments 1914-18.* Naval and Military Press Ltd.

James, Lawrence. (1999). *The Illustrated Rise and Fall of the British Empire.* Little Brown and Company. London.

Jeff, John. (1986). *The 5ᵗʰ Battalion, the Royal Warwickshire Regiment, TA and its predecessors, successors and historians.* Dulston Press.

Jeffreys, Alan. (2003). *British Infantrymen in the Far East 1941-45.* Osprey Publishing. Oxford.

Jeffreys, Alan. (2005). *The British Army in the Far East 1941-45.* Oxford Publishing. Oxford.

Kingsford, Charles Lethbridge. (1921). *The Story of the Royal Warwickshire Regiment.* George Newes. London.

Lewis-Stempel, John. (2007). *The Autobiography of the British Soldier – from Agincourt to Basra in his own words.* Headline Publishing Group. London.

Lynn, John. (2002). *The French Wars 1667-1714. The Sun King at War.* Osprey Publishing Ltd. Wellingborough.

Marshall, P.J (ed). (2001). *The Oxford History of the British Empire Vol. II. The Eighteenth Century.* Oxford University Press. Oxford.

McNab, Chris. (ed). (2009). *Armies of the Napoleonic Wars.* Osprey Publishing Ltd. Westminster.

Pitta, Robert. (1994). *UN Forces 1948-94.* Osprey Publishing. Oxford.

Sutherland, Jonathon. (2005). *Vital Guide Napoleonic Battles*. Crowood Press Ltd.

Roberts, Andrew. (ed). (2011). *Great Commanders of the Modern World. 1866 – Present Day*. Quercus. London

Robertshaw, Andrew. (2006). *Somme 1st July 1916. Tragedy and Triumph*. Osprey Publishing. Oxford.

Sutherland, Graham. (2013). *Bloody British History – Warwick*. The History Press. Stroud

The National Archives. *WO/95/1484 10 INFANTRY BRIGADE: 1 Battalion Royal Warwickshire Regiment 1914 Aug. - 1919 June.*

Tracey, Fred. C. (2005). *Not such a bad time. Diaries of Territorial Force camps in 1908 and 1909. 8th Battalion Royal Warwickshire Regiment*. Plott Green.

IMAGE CREDITS

INDEX

Printed in Great
Britain
by Amazon

31905951R00181